THE SEVEN DEADLY SINS

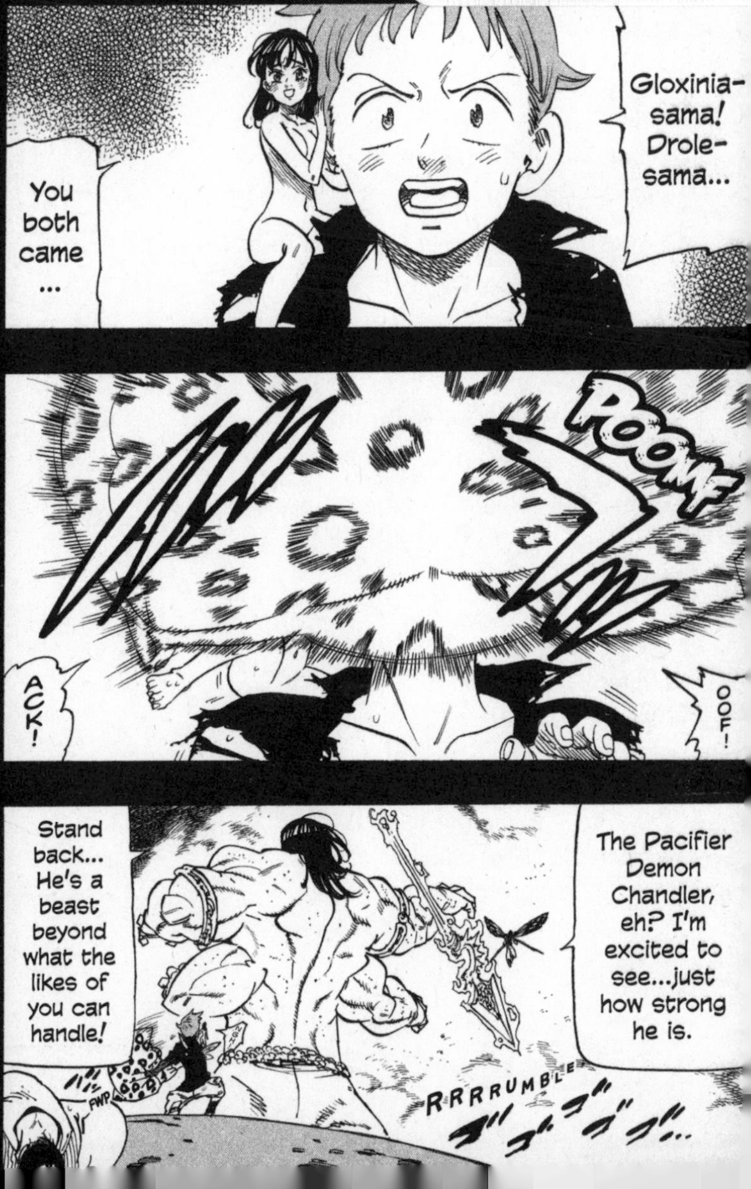
Gloxinia-sama! Drole-sama...
You both came ...
OOF!
POOOMF
ACK!
The Pacifier Demon Chandler, eh? I'm excited to see...just how strong he is.
Stand back... He's a beast beyond what the likes of you can handle!
RRRRUMBLE
FWP

CONTENTS

BOAR HAT
The Seven Deadly Sins

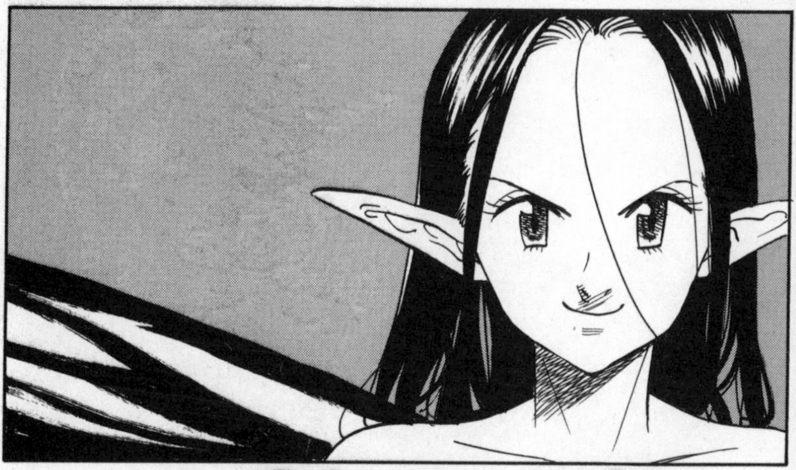

THE SEVEN DEADLY SINS

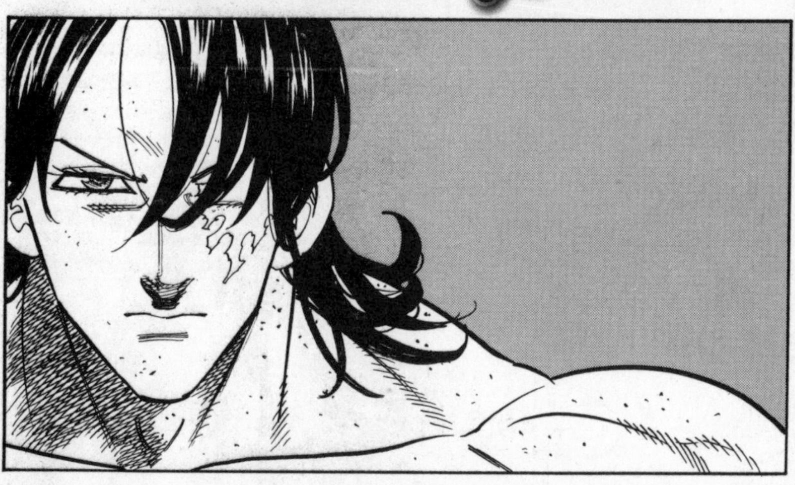

Chapter 241 - Inherited Spirit

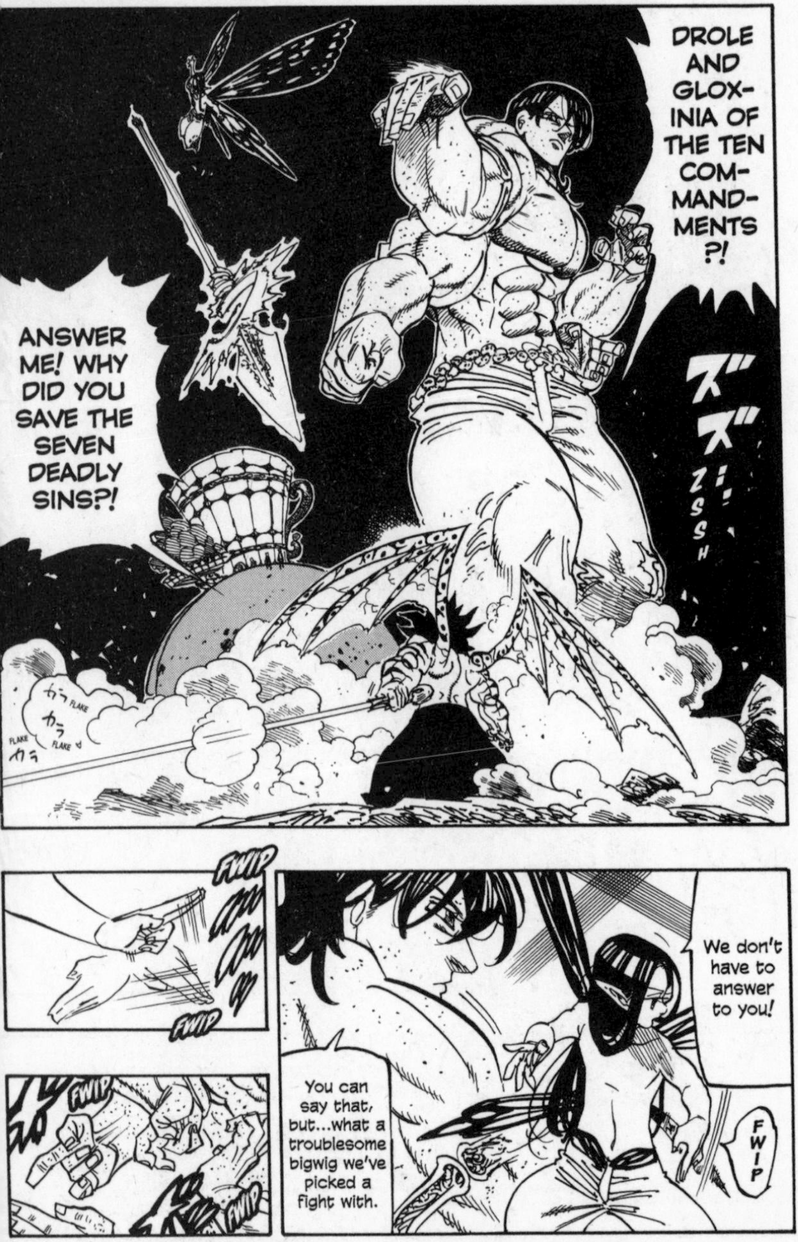
DROLE AND GLOX-INIA OF THE TEN COM-MAND-MENTS?!
ZSSH
ANSWER ME! WHY DID YOU SAVE THE SEVEN DEADLY SINS?!
FLAKE
FLAKE
FLAKE
We don't have to answer to you!
FWIP
You can say that, but...what a troublesome bigwig we've picked a fight with.
FWIP
FWIP
FWIP
FWIP

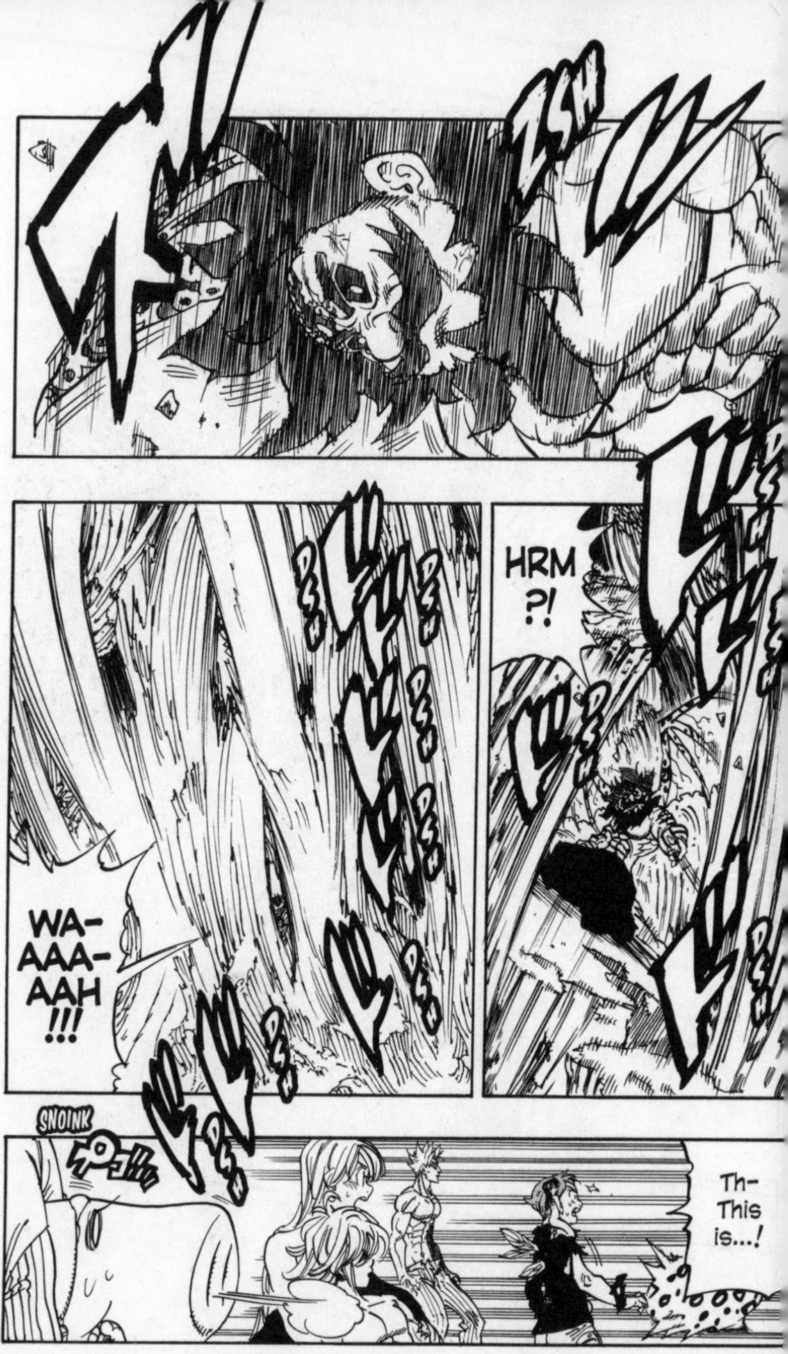
ZSH
HRM ?!
DSH
DSH
DSH
WA-AAA-AAH !!!
DSH
DSH
DSH
Th- This is...!
SNOINK

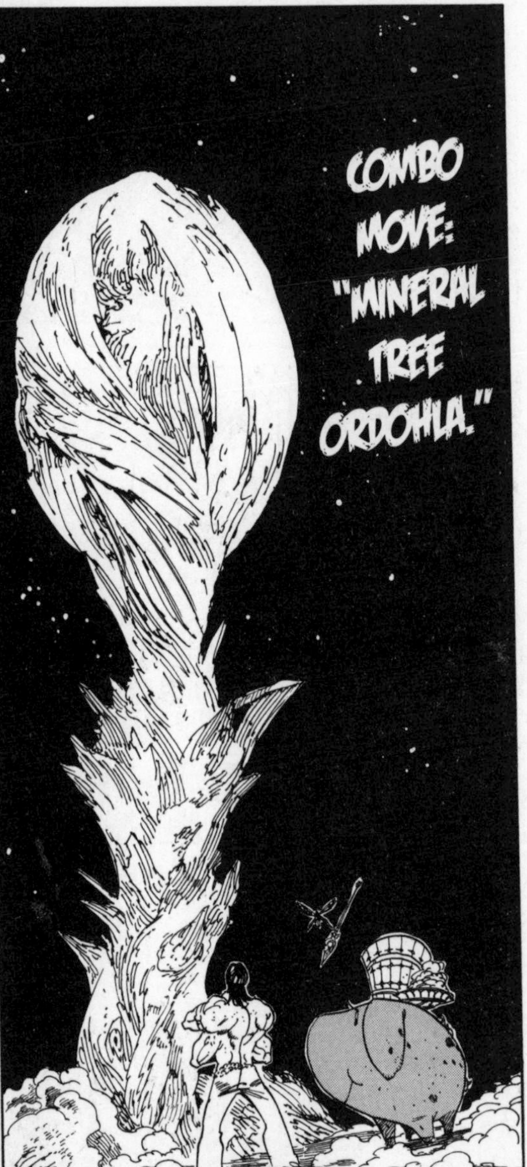
COMBO MOVE: "MINERAL TREE ORDOHLA."

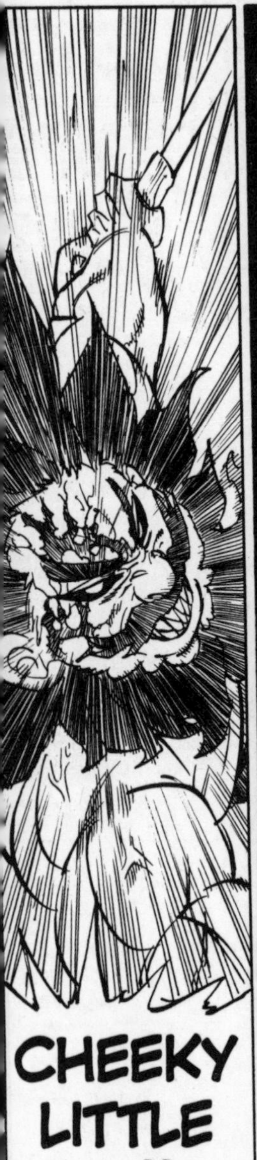
CHEEKY LITTLE ...!!

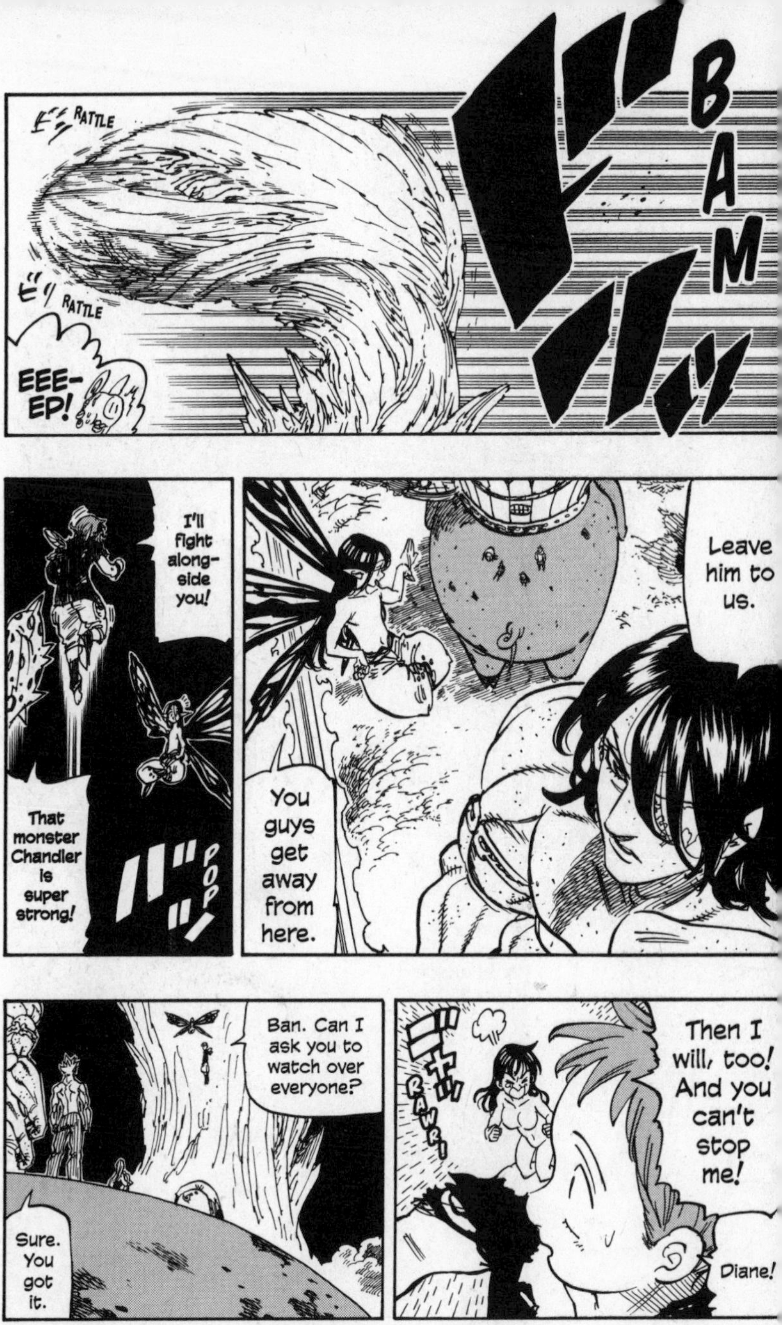
BAM
RATTLE
RATTLE
EEE-EP!
Leave him to us.
You guys get away from here.
I'll fight along-side you!
POP!
That monster Chandler is super strong!
Then I will, too! And you can't stop me!
RAWR!
Diane!
Ban. Can I ask you to watch over everyone?
Sure. You got it.

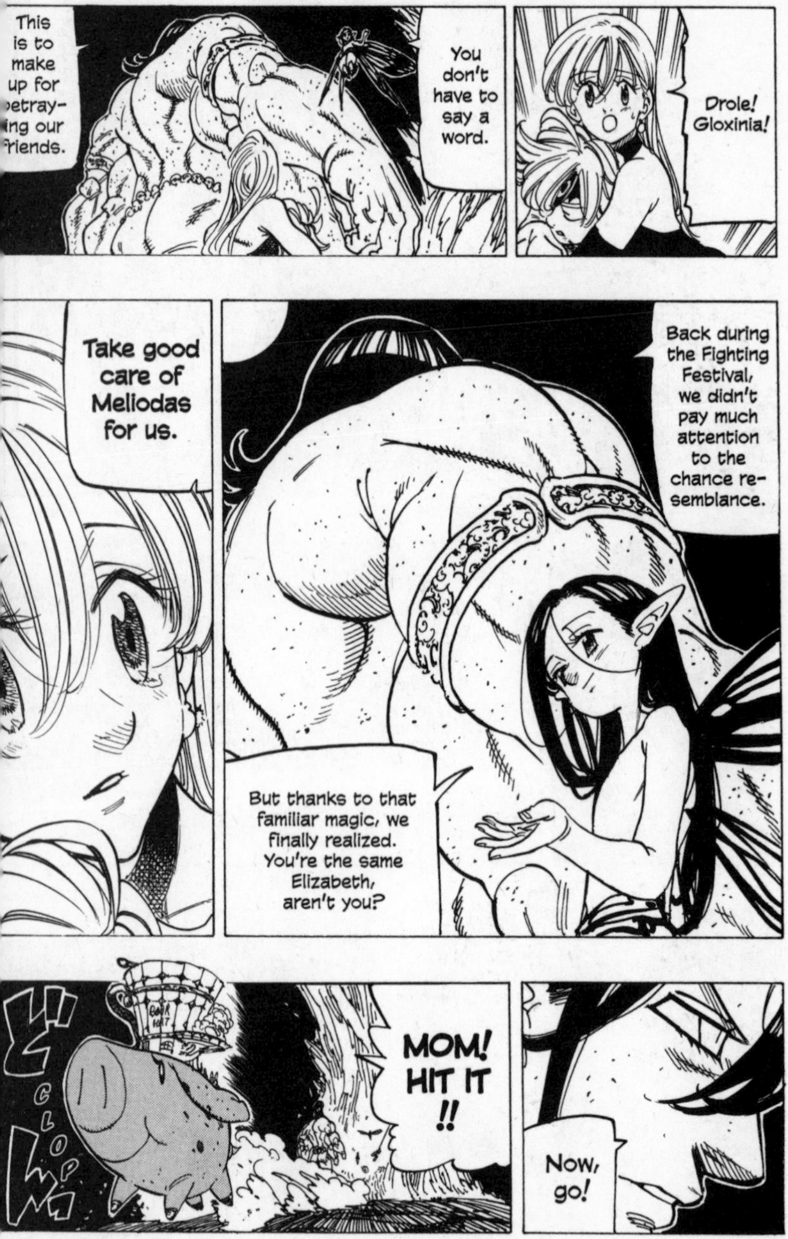
Drole! Gloxinia!
You don't have to say a word.
This is to make up for etray-ing our riends.
Back during the Fighting Festival, we didn't pay much attention to the chance re-semblance.
But thanks to that familiar magic, we finally realized. You're the same Elizabeth, aren't you?
Take good care of Meliodas for us.
Now, go!
MOM! HIT IT!!
CLOP

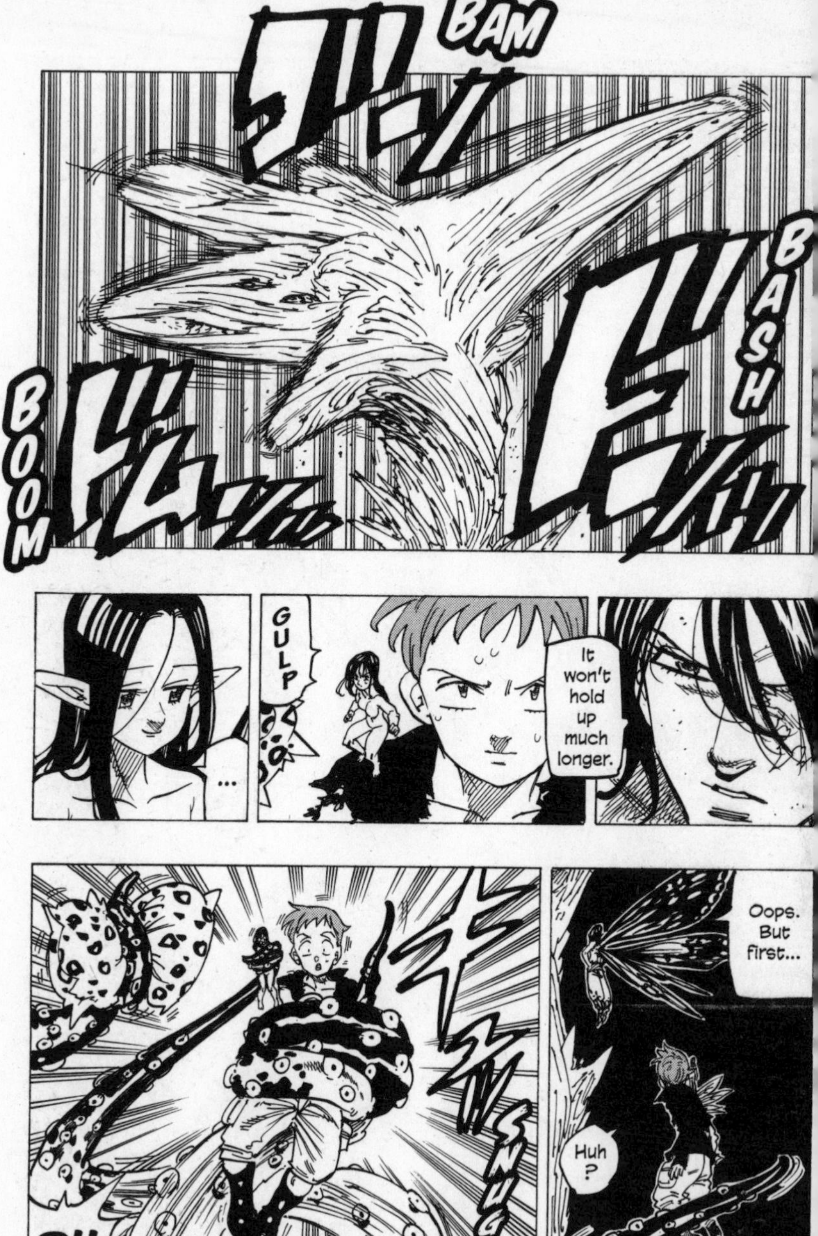
BAM
BASH
BOOM
It won't hold up much longer.
GULP
...
Oops. But first...
Huh?
SNUG
?!!

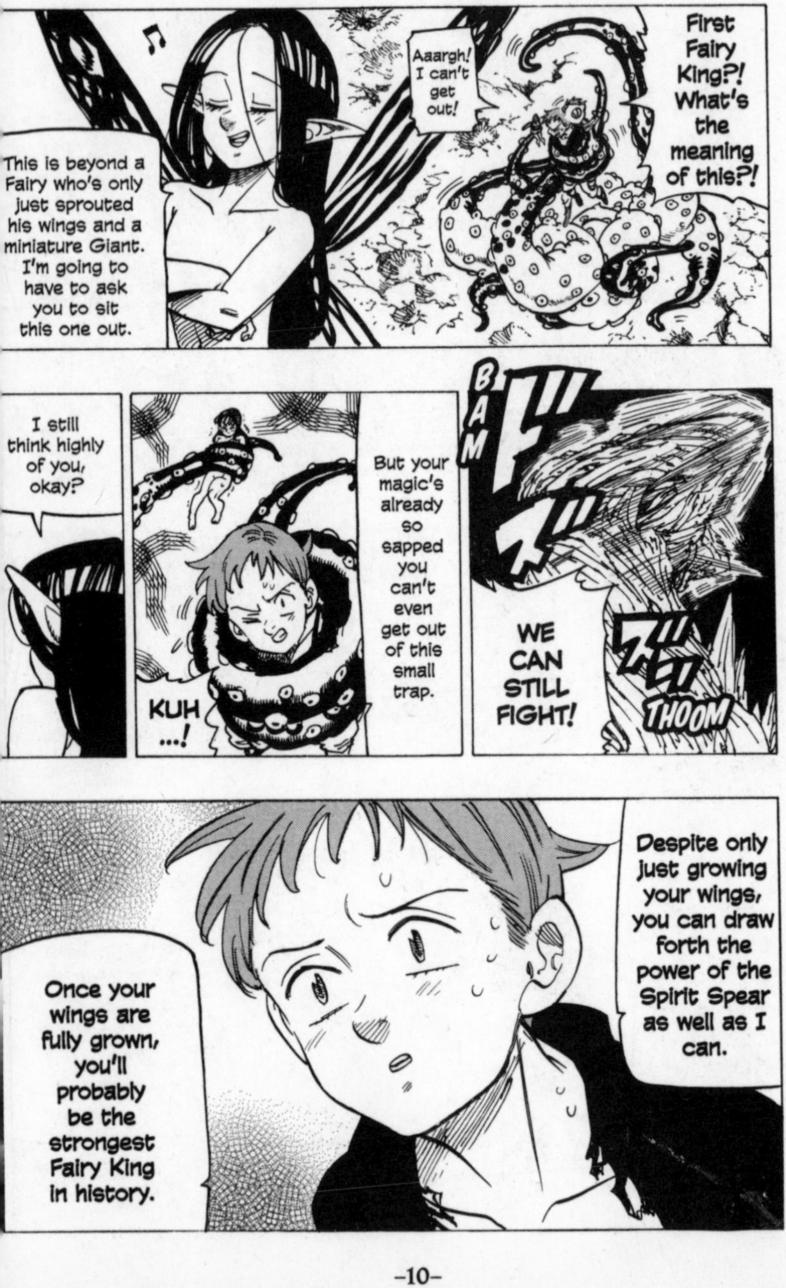
First Fairy King?! What's the meaning of this?!
Aaargh! I can't get out!
This is beyond a Fairy who's only just sprouted his wings and a miniature Giant. I'm going to have to ask you to sit this one out.
BAM
WE CAN STILL FIGHT!
THOOM
But your magic's already so sapped you can't even get out of this small trap.
KUH ...!
I still think highly of you, okay?
Despite only just growing your wings, you can draw forth the power of the Spirit Spear as well as I can.
Once your wings are fully grown, you'll probably be the strongest Fairy King in history.

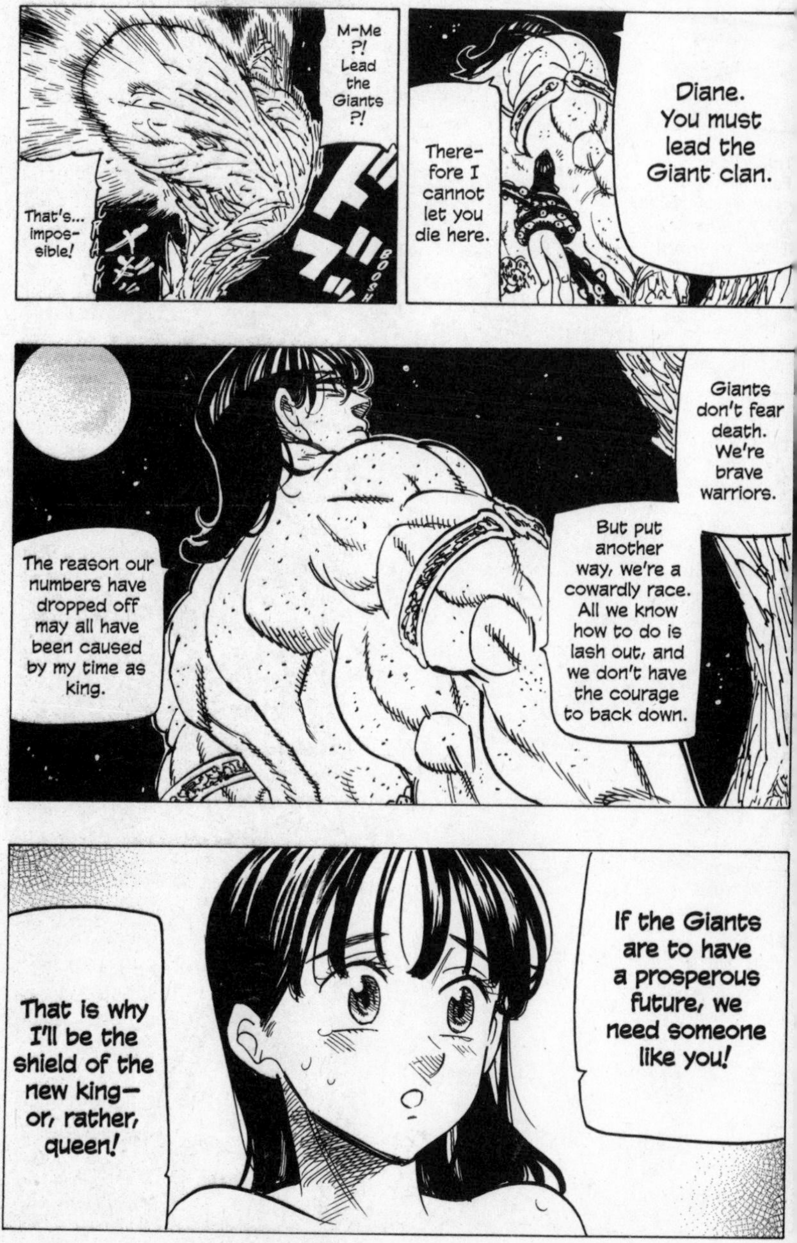
Diane. You must lead the Giant clan.
Therefore I cannot let you die here.
M-Me?! Lead the Giants?!
BOOSH
CRACK
That's... impossible!
Giants don't fear death. We're brave warriors.
But put another way, we're a cowardly race. All we know how to do is lash out, and we don't have the courage to back down.
The reason our numbers have dropped off may all have been caused by my time as king.
If the Giants are to have a prosperous future, we need someone like you!
That is why I'll be the shield of the new king—or, rather, queen!

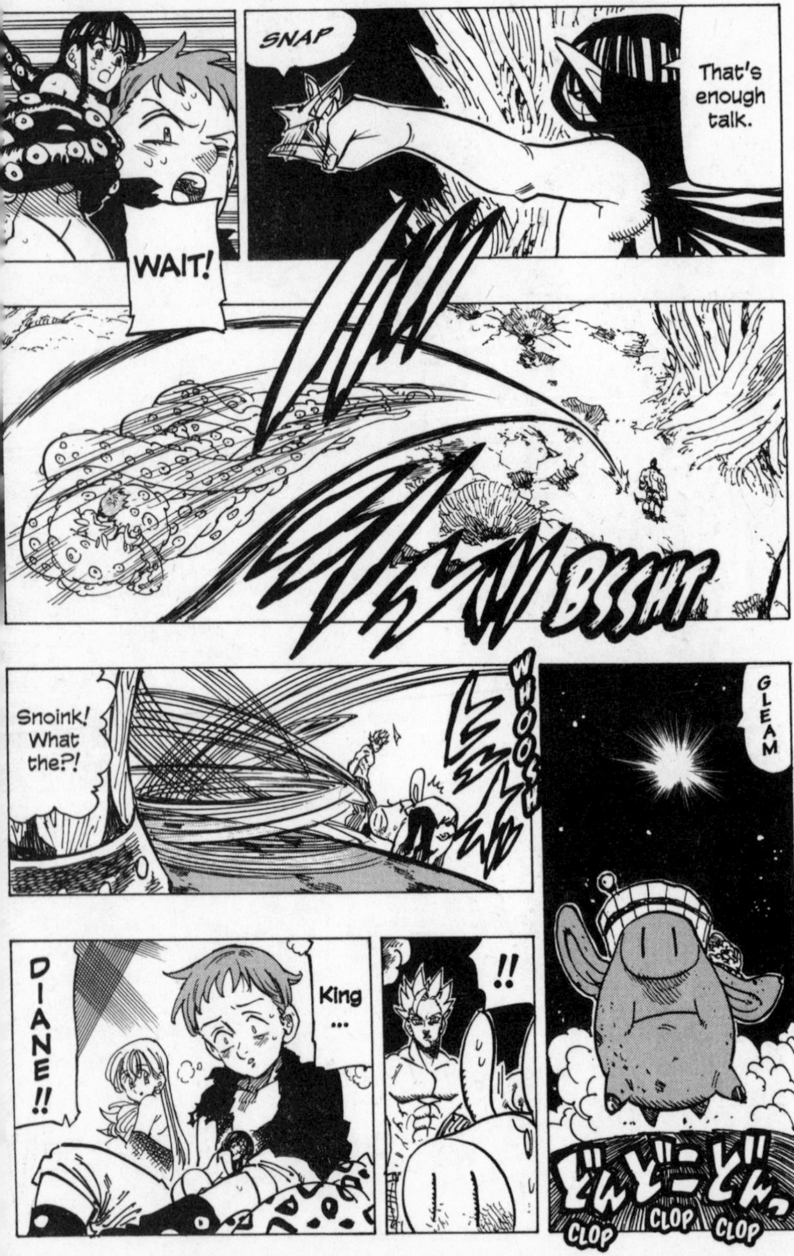
SNAP
That's enough talk.
WAIT!
BSHT
GLEAM
CLOP
CLOP
CLOP
WHOOSH
Snoink! What the?!
!!
King ...
DIANE!!

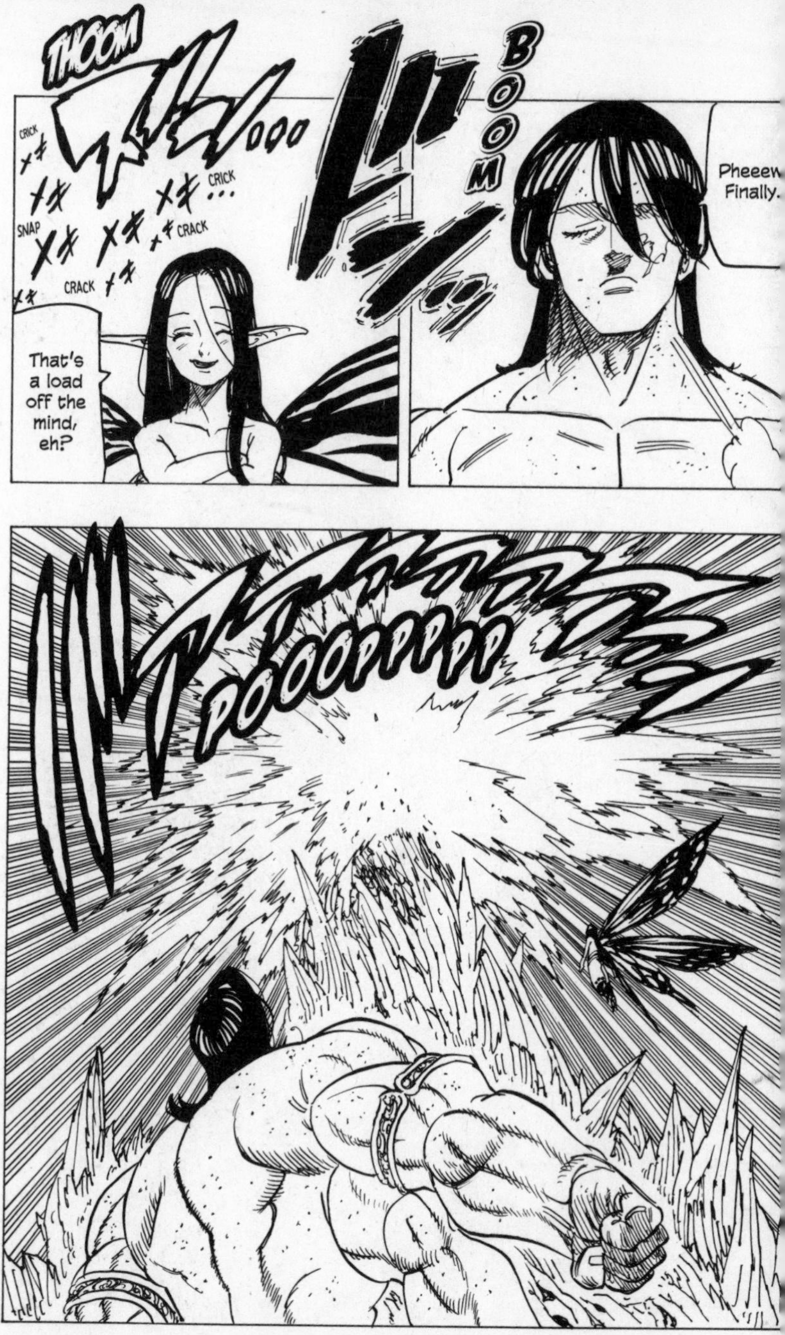

Pheeew Finally.
BOOOM
THOOM
CRICK
CRICK...
SNAP
CRACK
CRACK
That's a load off the mind, eh?
POOOPPPPPP

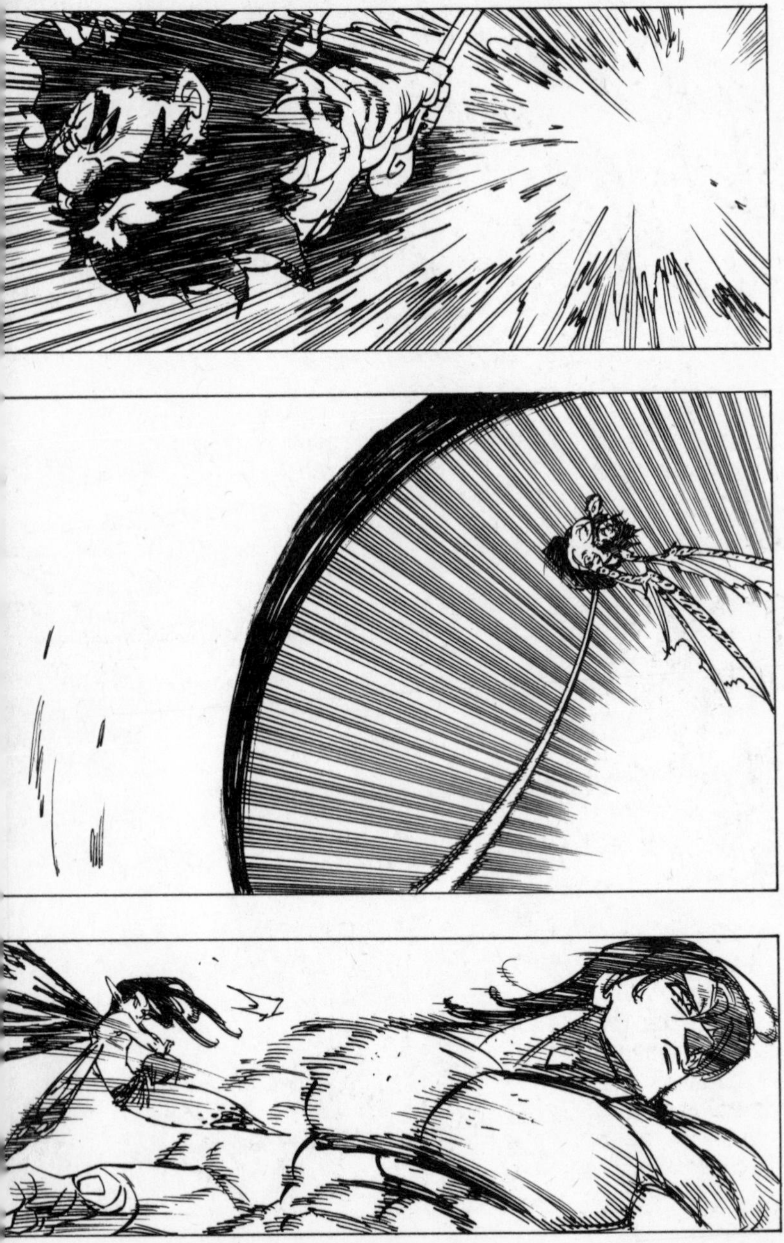

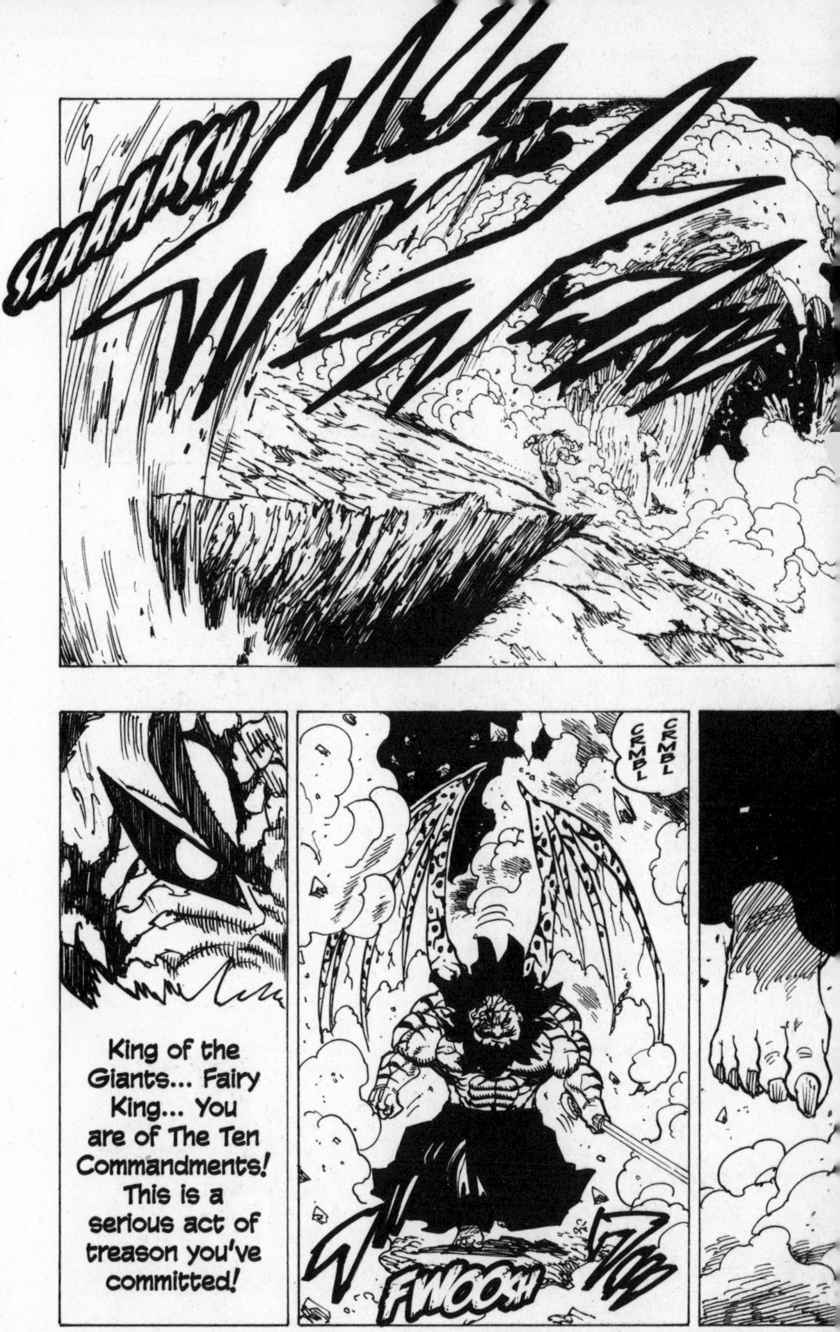
SLAAAASH
CRMBL CRMBL
FWOOSH
King of the Giants... Fairy King... You are of The Ten Commandments! This is a serious act of treason you've committed!

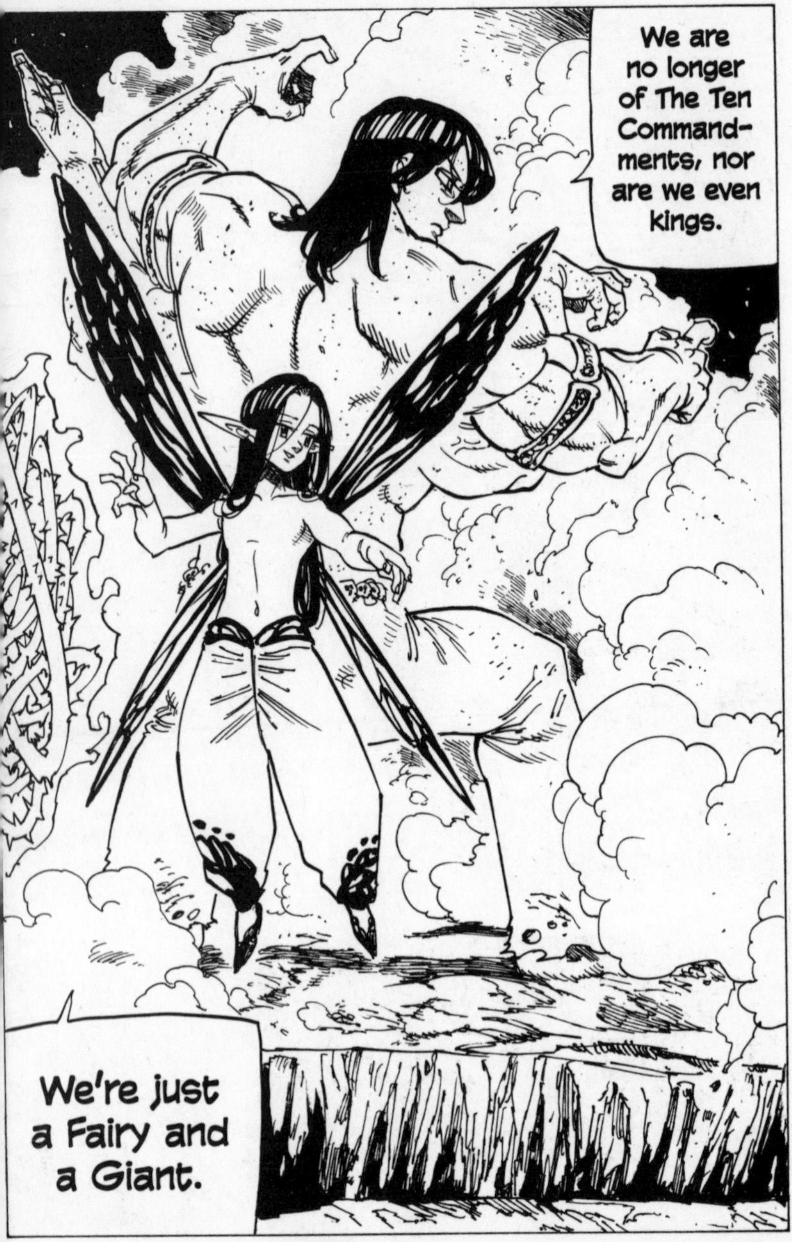

We are no longer of The Ten Command-ments, nor are we even kings.
We're just a Fairy and a Giant.

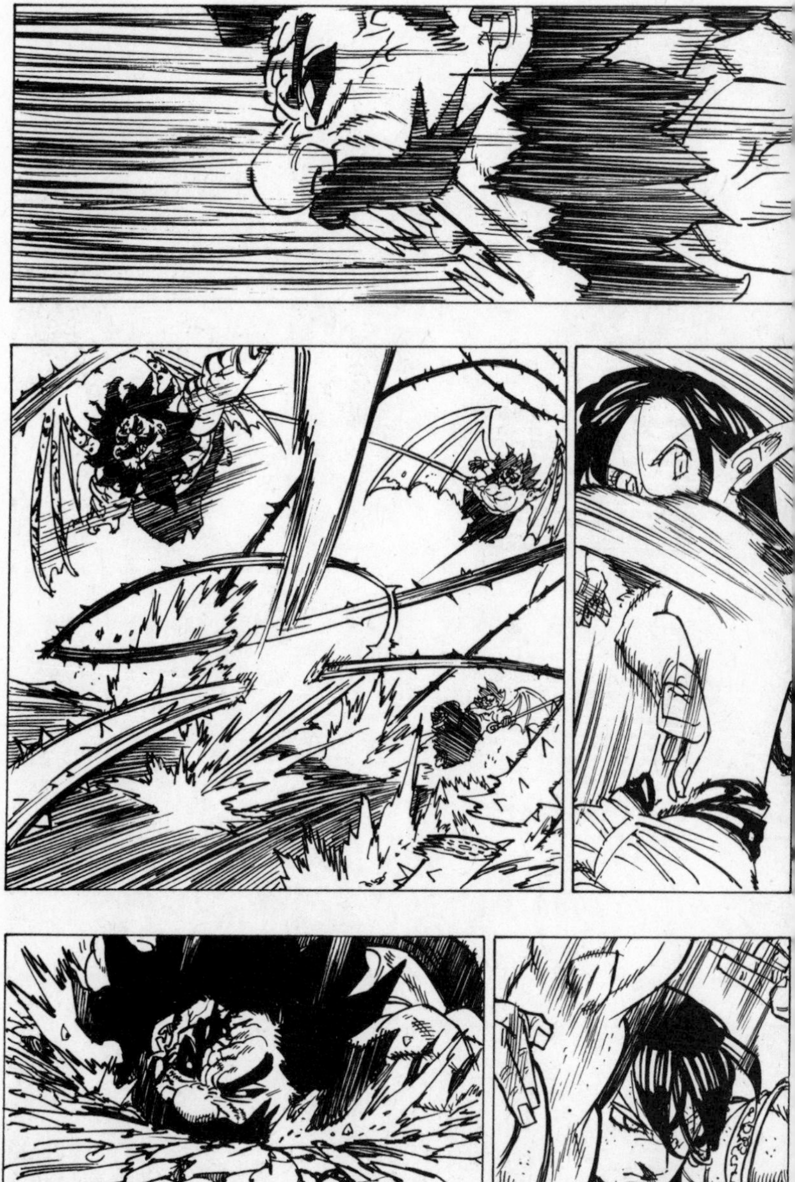

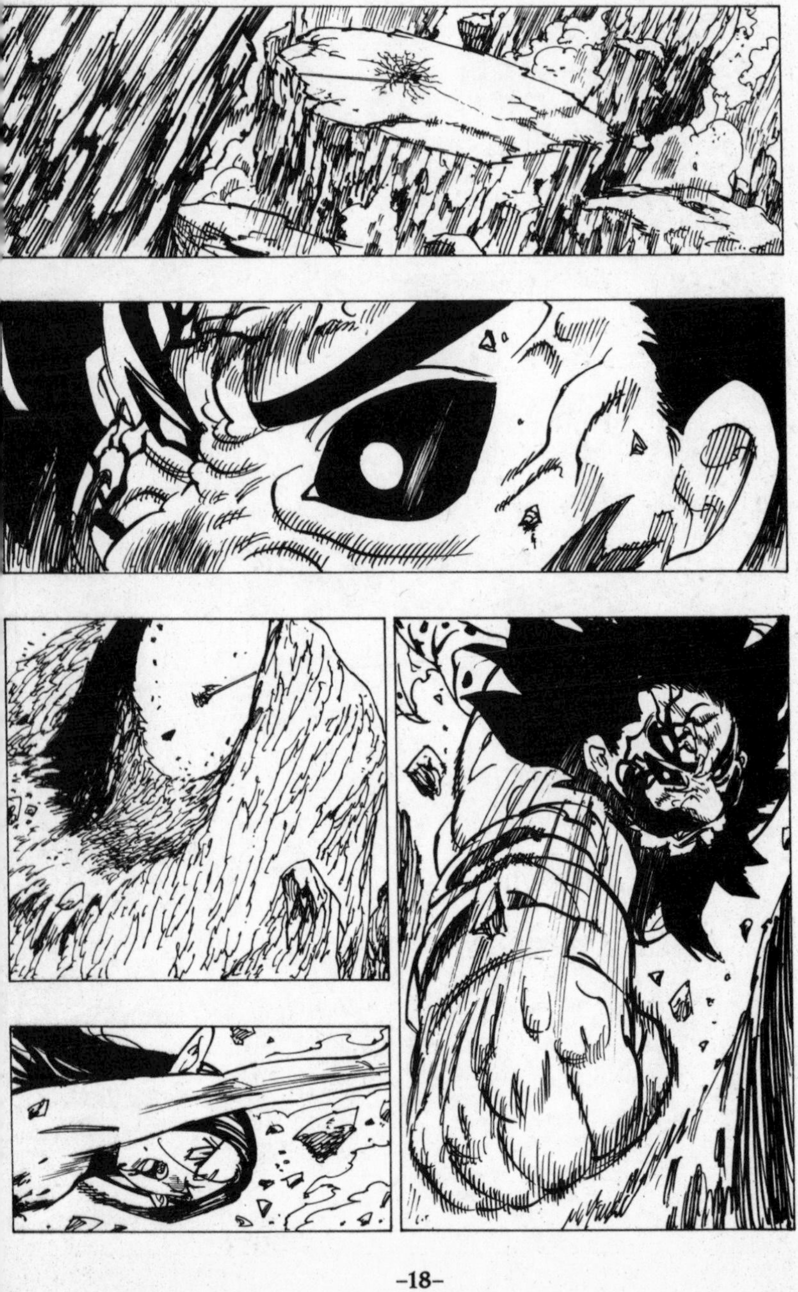

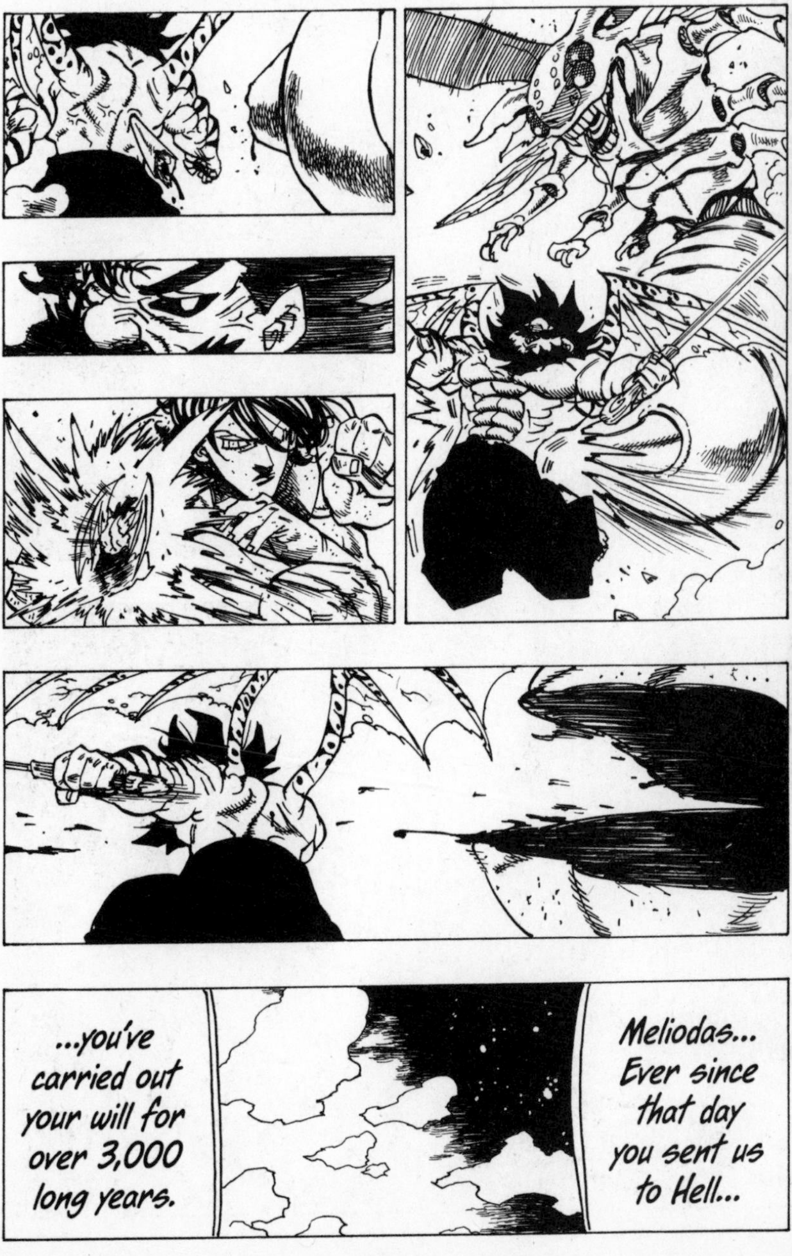
Meliodas... Ever since that day you sent us to Hell...
...you've carried out your will for over 3,000 long years.

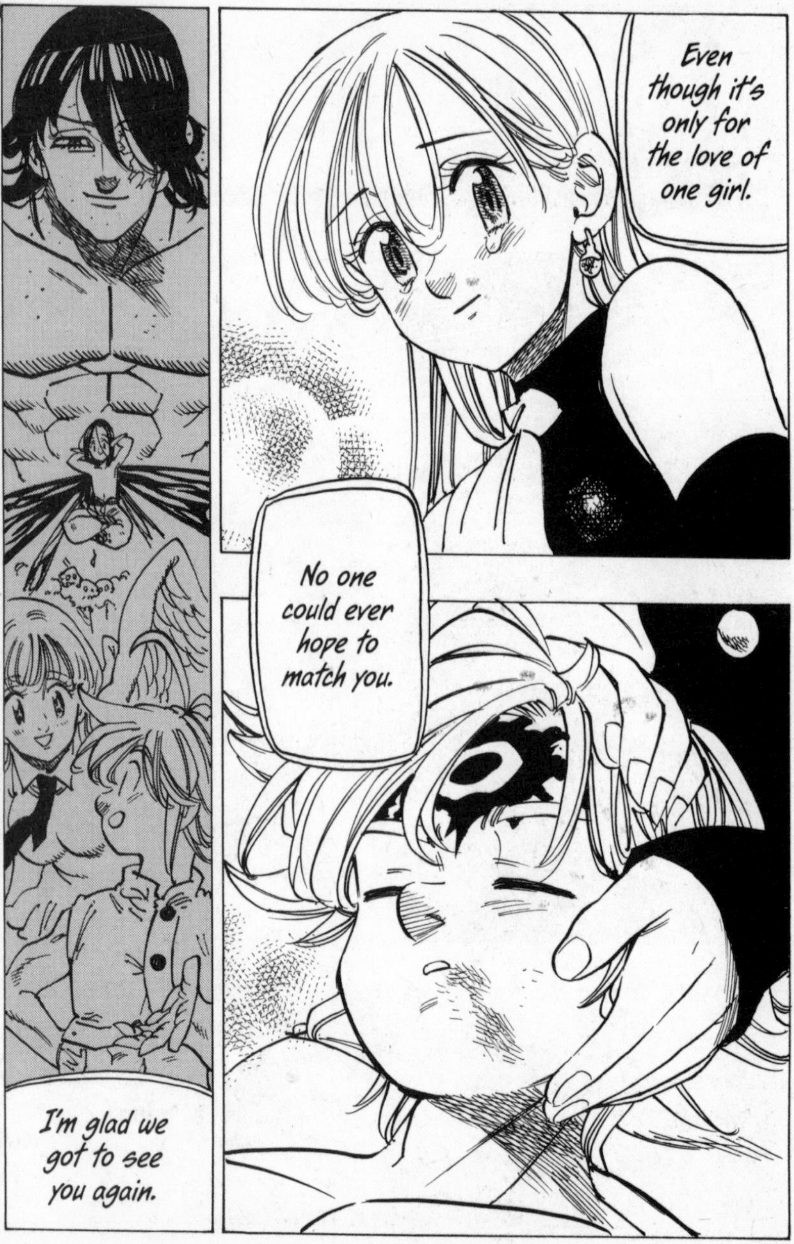
Even though it's only for the love of one girl.
No one could ever hope to match you.
I'm glad we got to see you again.

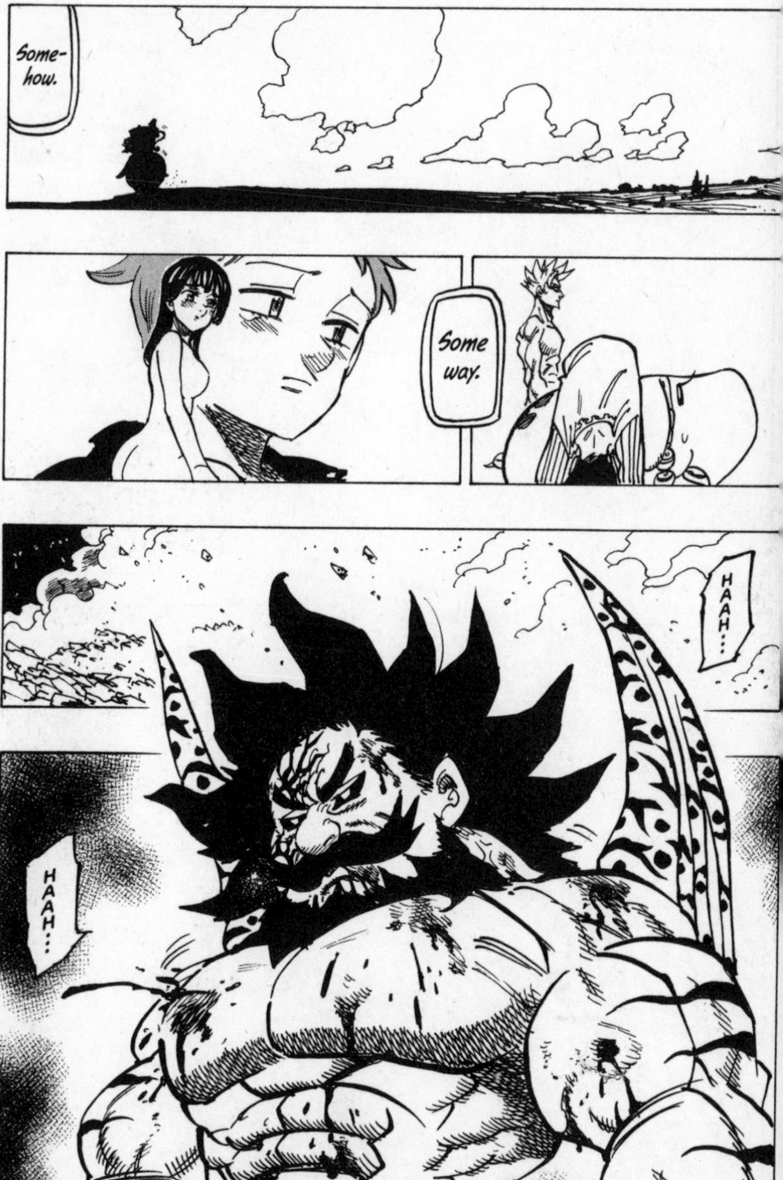
Some-how.
Some way.
HAAH...
HAAH...

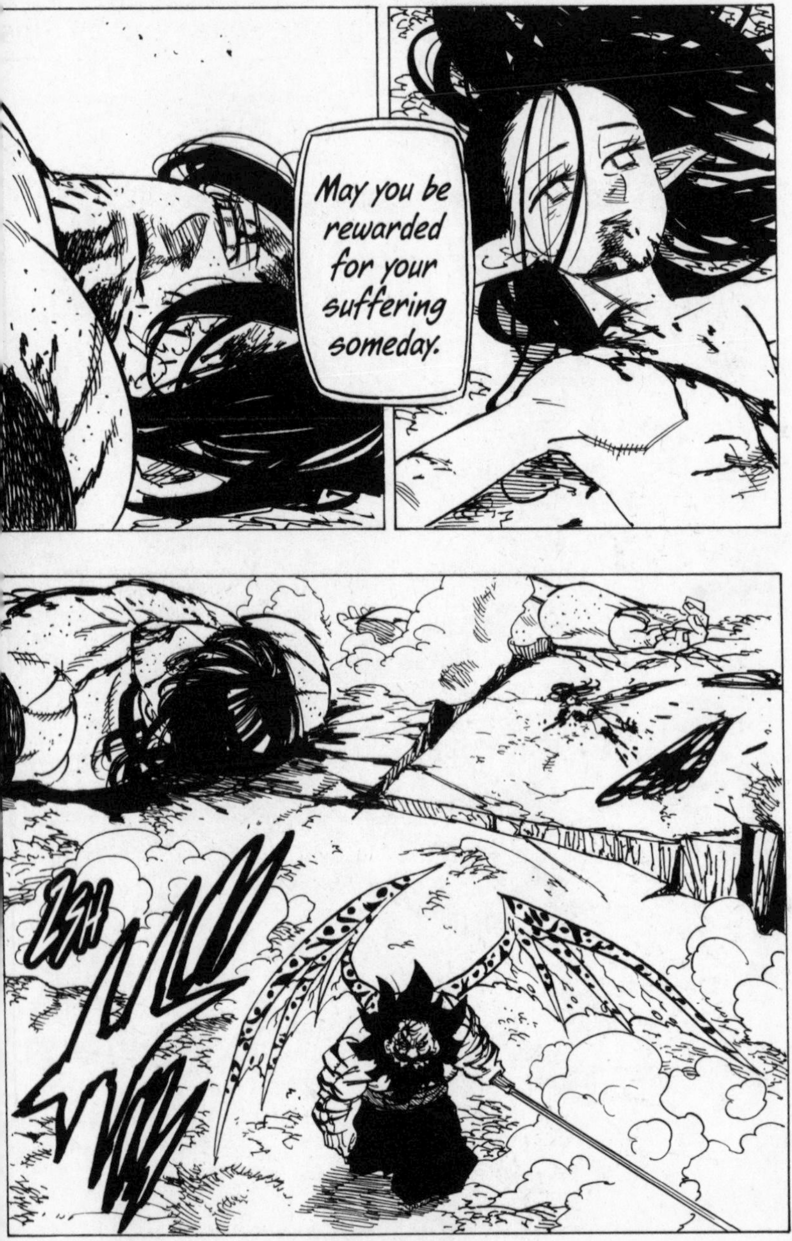
May you be rewarded for your suffering someday.
ZSH

Chapter 242 - The End of The Seven Deadly Sins

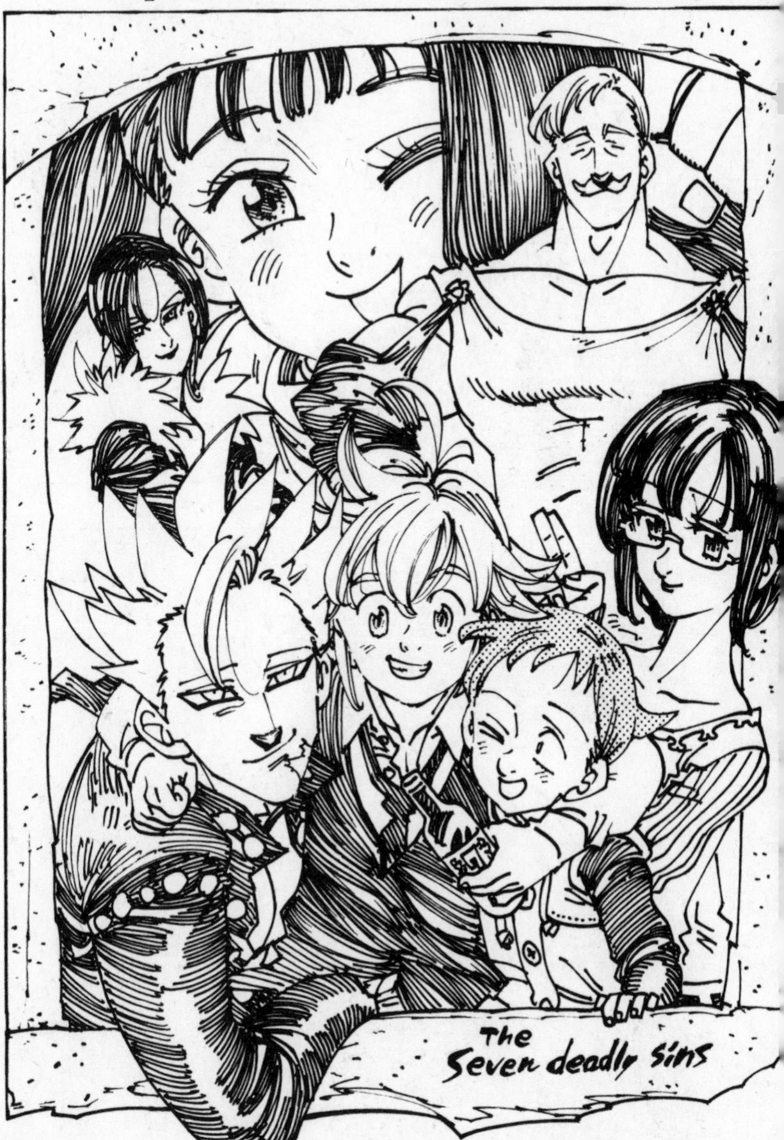
The Seven deadly sins

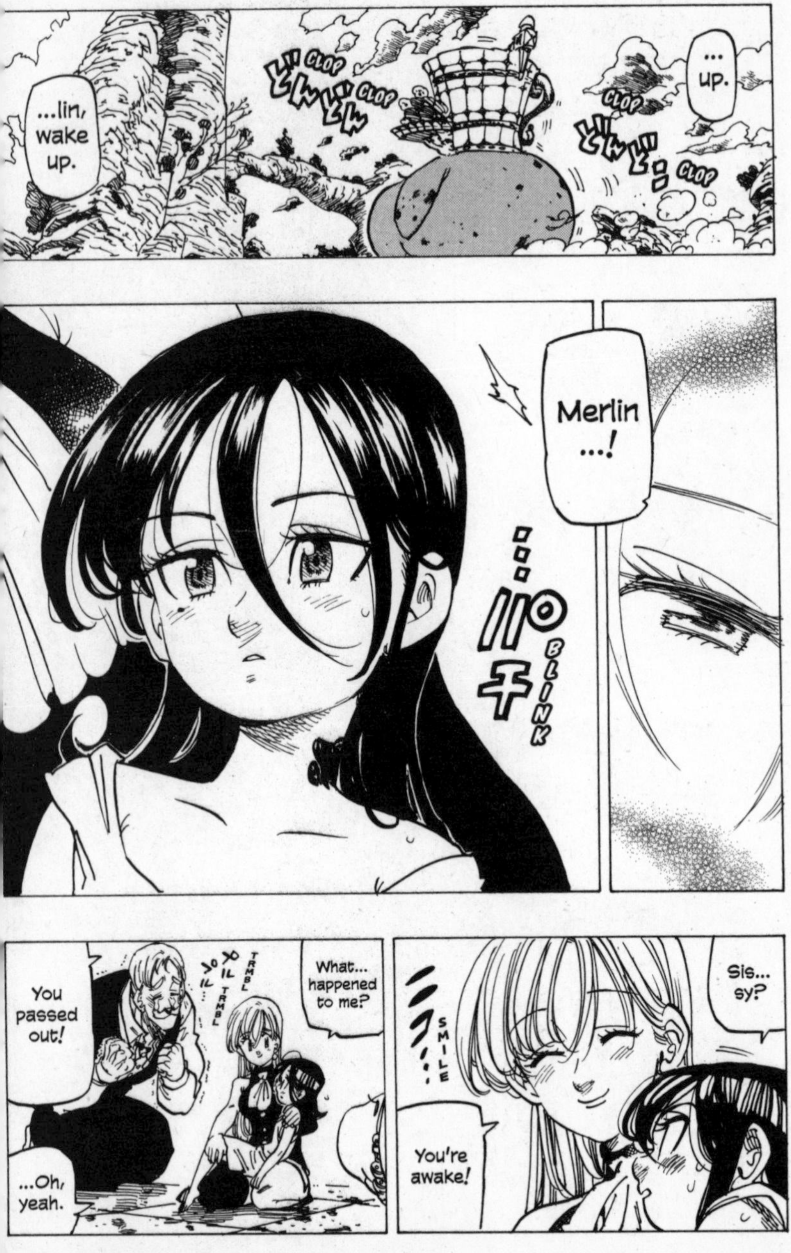
... up.
CLOP
CLOP
CLOP
CLOP
...lin, wake up.
Merlin ...!
BLINK
Sis... sy?
SMILE
You're awake!
What... happened to me?
TRMBL
TRMBL
You passed out!
...Oh, yeah.

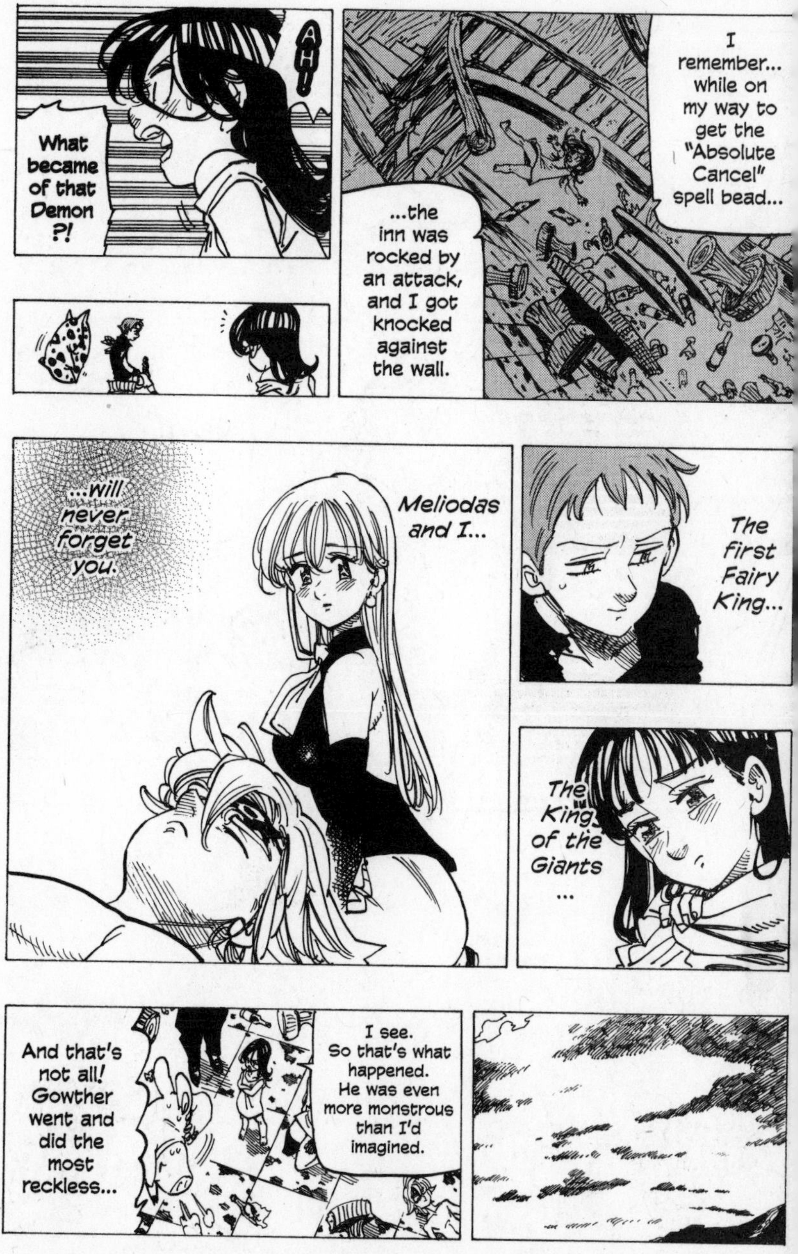
I remember... while on my way to get the "Absolute Cancel" spell bead...
...the inn was rocked by an attack, and I got knocked against the wall.
AH!
What became of that Demon ?!
The first Fairy King...
The King of the Giants ...
Meliodas and I...
...will never forget you.
I see. So that's what happened. He was even more monstrous than I'd imagined.
And that's not all! Gowther went and did the most reckless...

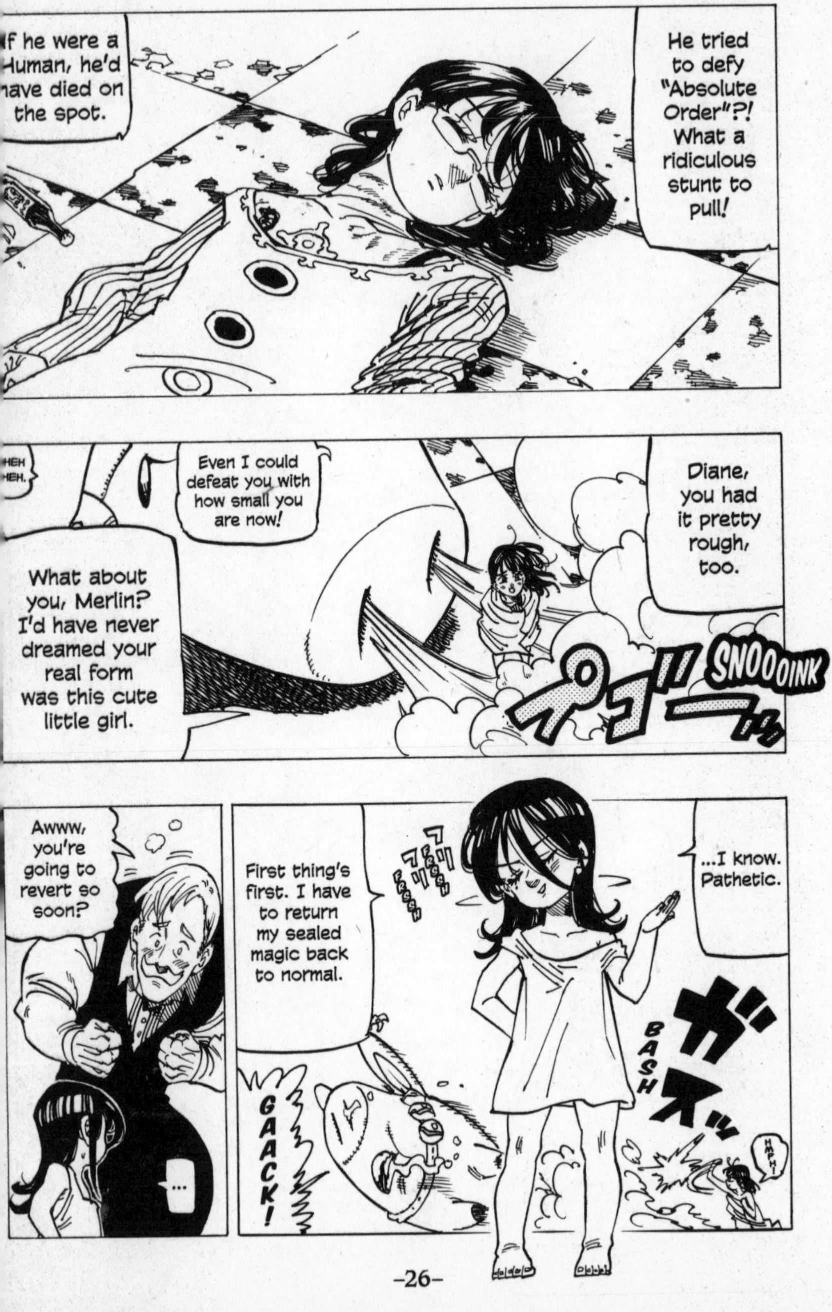
He tried to defy "Absolute Order"?! What a ridiculous stunt to pull!
If he were a Human, he'd have died on the spot.
Diane, you had it pretty rough, too.
SNOOOINK
Even I could defeat you with how small you are now!
HEH HEH.
What about you, Merlin? I'd have never dreamed your real form was this cute little girl.
...I know. Pathetic.
BASH
HMPH!
First thing's first. I have to return my sealed magic back to normal.
FRSSH
FRSSH
GAACK!
Awww, you're going to revert so soon?
...

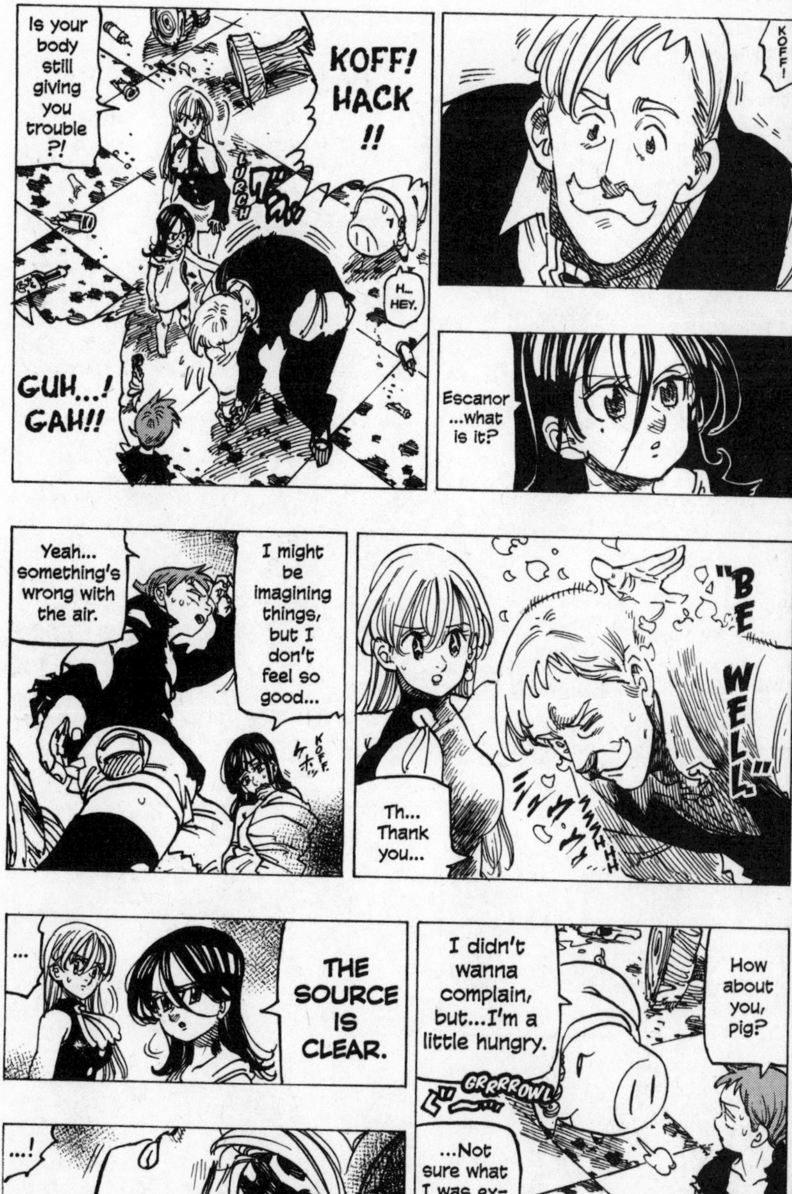
KOFF!
Escanor ...what is it?
KOFF! HACK!!
Is your body still giving you trouble?!
LURCH
H... HEY.
GUH...! GAH!!
"BE WELL"
Th... Thank you...
I might be imagining things, but I don't feel so good...
KOFF
Yeah... something's wrong with the air.
How about you, pig?
I didn't wanna complain, but...I'm a little hungry.
GRRRROWL
...Not sure what I was expecting...
THE SOURCE IS CLEAR.
...
...!

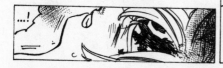

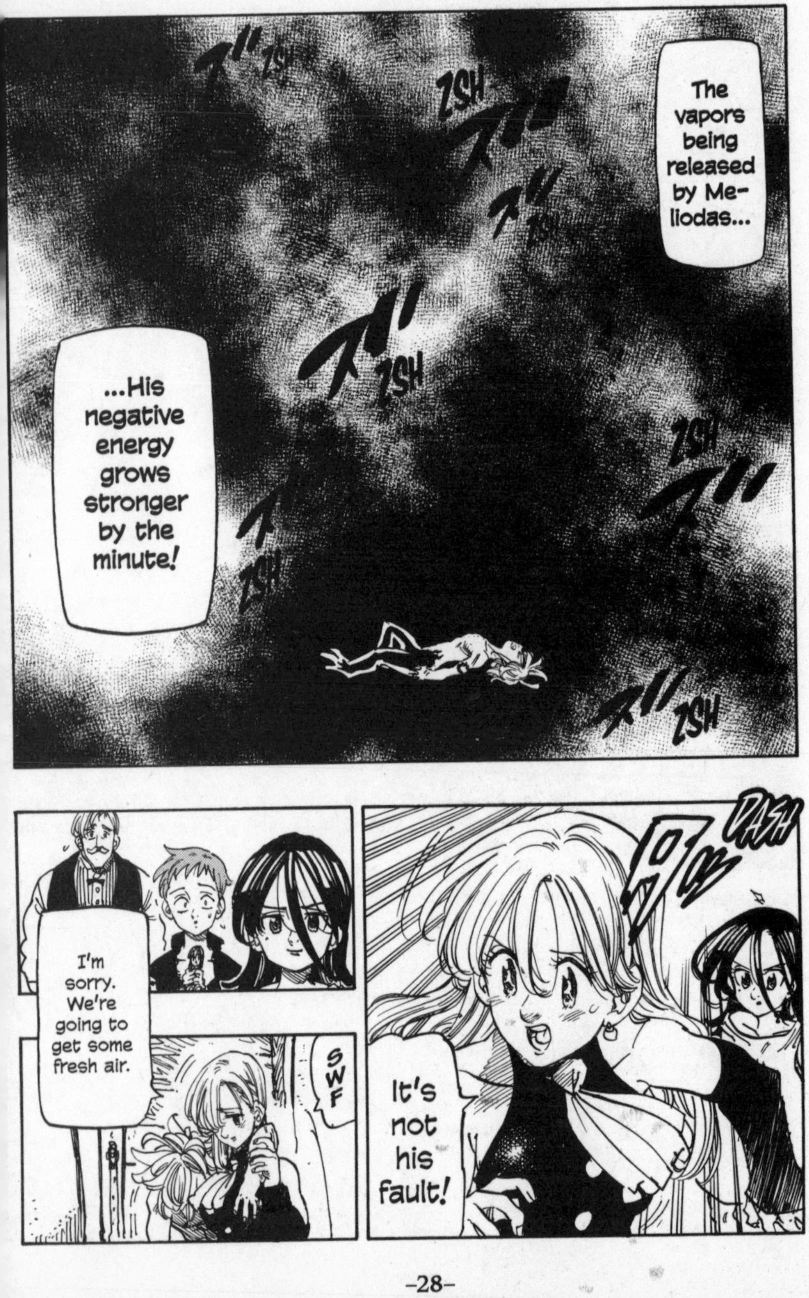
The vapors being released by Me-liodas...
ZSH
ZSH
ZSH
ZSH
...His negative energy grows stronger by the minute!
ZSH
ZSH
ZSH
DASH
It's not his fault!
I'm sorry. We're going to get some fresh air.
SWF

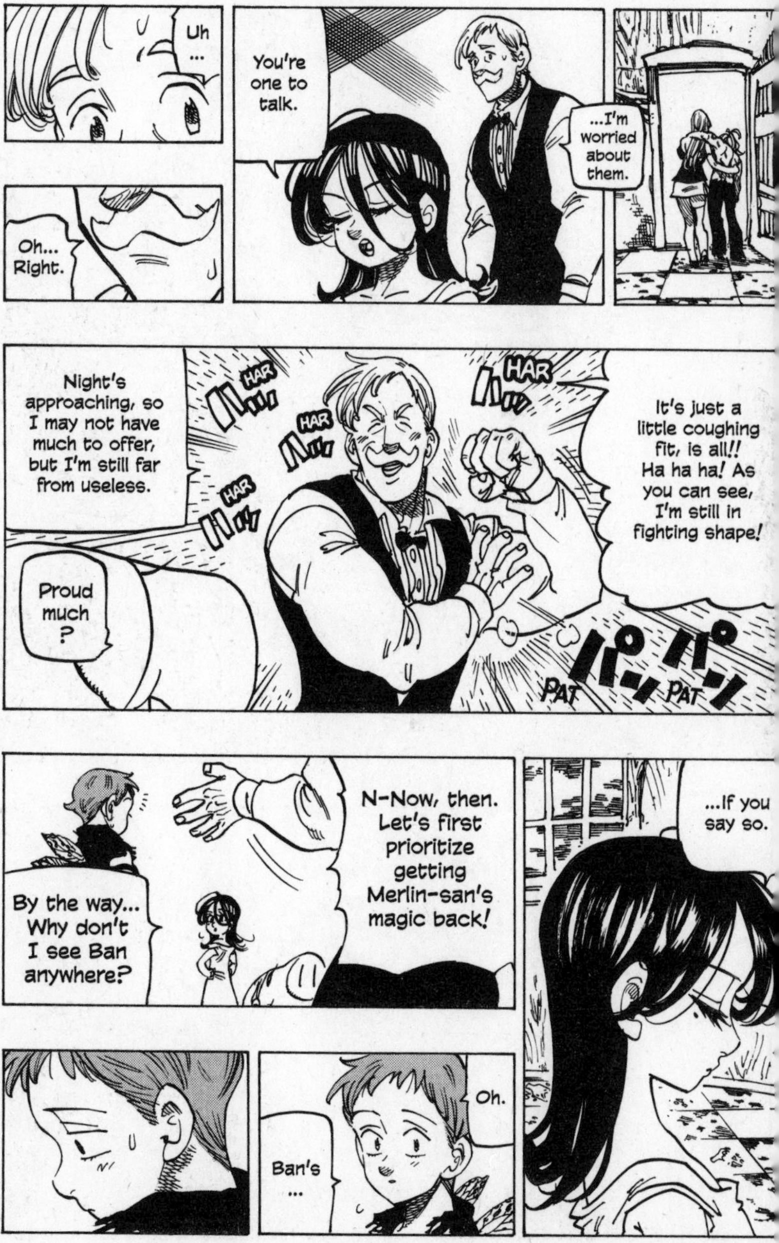
...I'm worried about them.
You're one to talk.
Uh ...
Oh... Right.
It's just a little coughing fit, is all!! Ha ha ha! As you can see, I'm still in fighting shape!
HAR
HAR
HAR
HAR
Night's approaching, so I may not have much to offer, but I'm still far from useless.
PAT
PAT
Proud much ?
...If you say so.
N-Now, then. Let's first prioritize getting Merlin-san's magic back!
By the way... Why don't I see Ban anywhere?
Oh.
Ban's ...

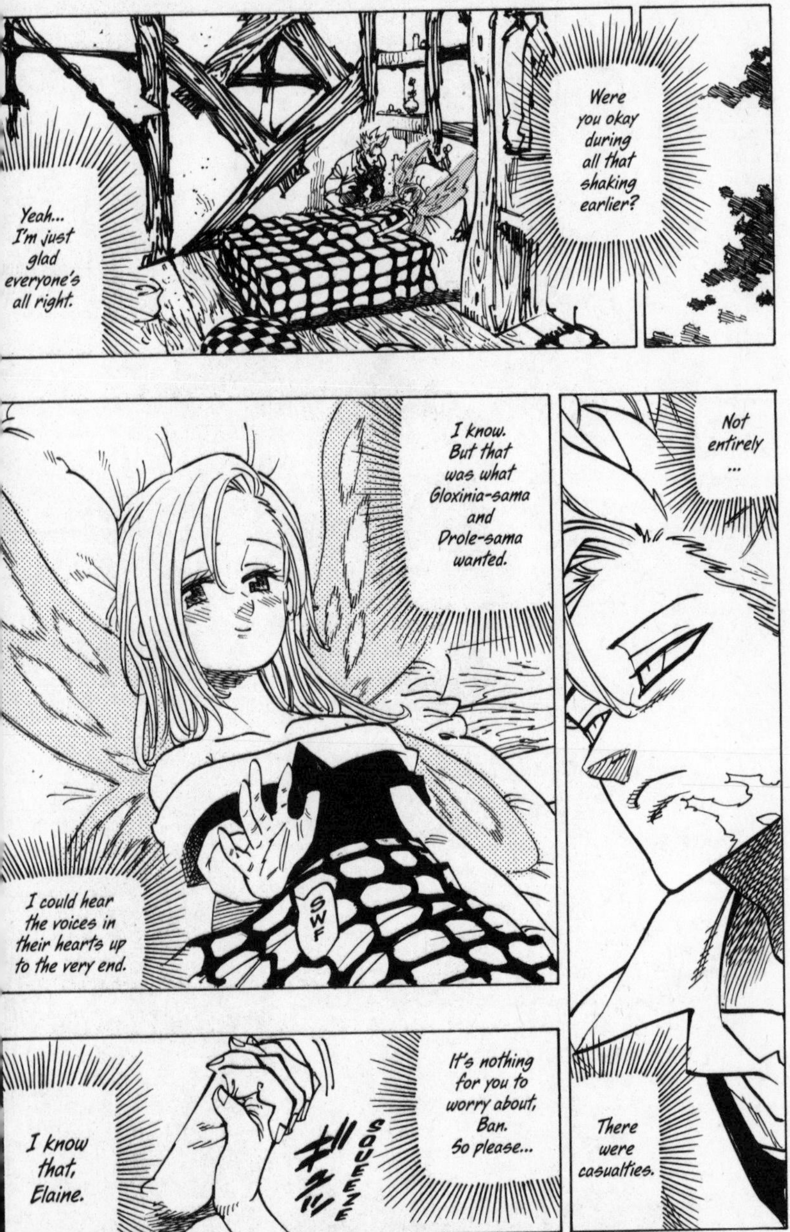
Were you okay during all that shaking earlier?
Yeah... I'm just glad everyone's all right.
Not entirely...
There were casualties.
I know. But that was what Gloxinia-sama and Drole-sama wanted.
SWF
I could hear the voices in their hearts up to the very end.
It's nothing for you to worry about, Ban. So please...
SQUEEZE
I know that, Elaine.

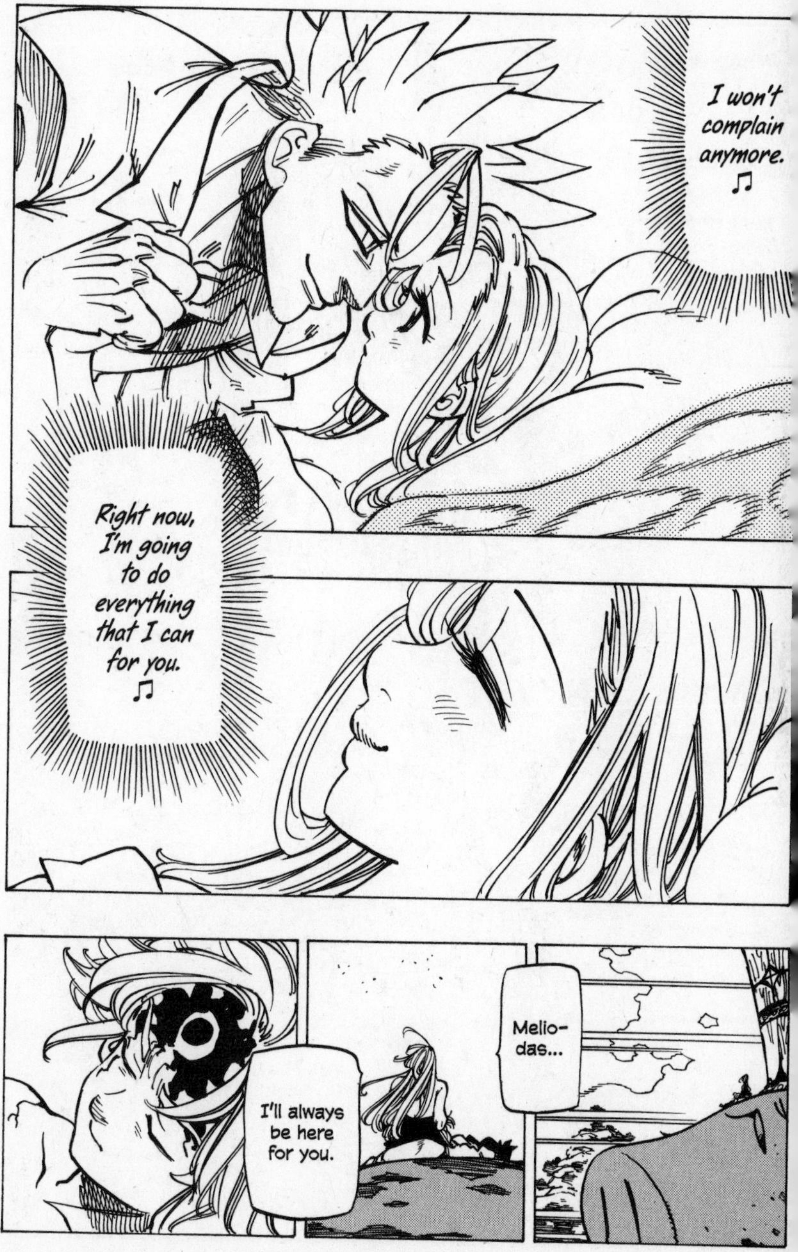
I won't complain anymore. ♫
Right now, I'm going to do everything that I can for you. ♫
Melio-das...
I'll always be here for you.

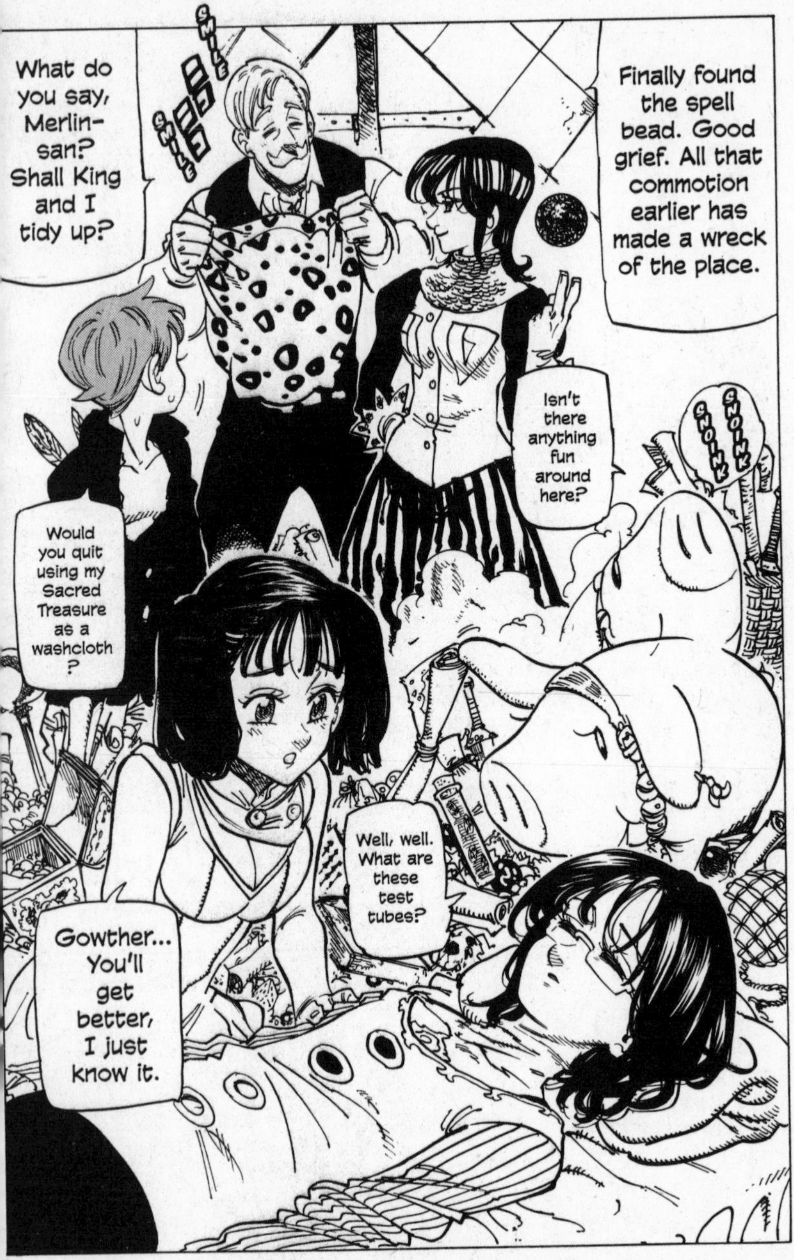
Finally found the spell bead. Good grief. All that commotion earlier has made a wreck of the place.
SMILE SMILE
What do you say, Merlin-san? Shall King and I tidy up?
SNOINK SNOINK
Isn't there anything fun around here?
Would you quit using my Sacred Treasure as a washcloth?
Well, well. What are these test tubes?
Gowther... You'll get better, I just know it.

Anyway, let's hurry and come up with a plan to defend against Chandler!

What about first evacuating the captain and Elizabeth somewhere else?

SNIFF SNIFF

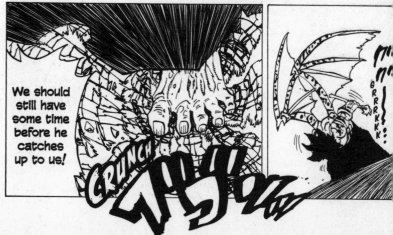

We should still have some time before he catches up to us!

GRUNCH

GRRRKKK

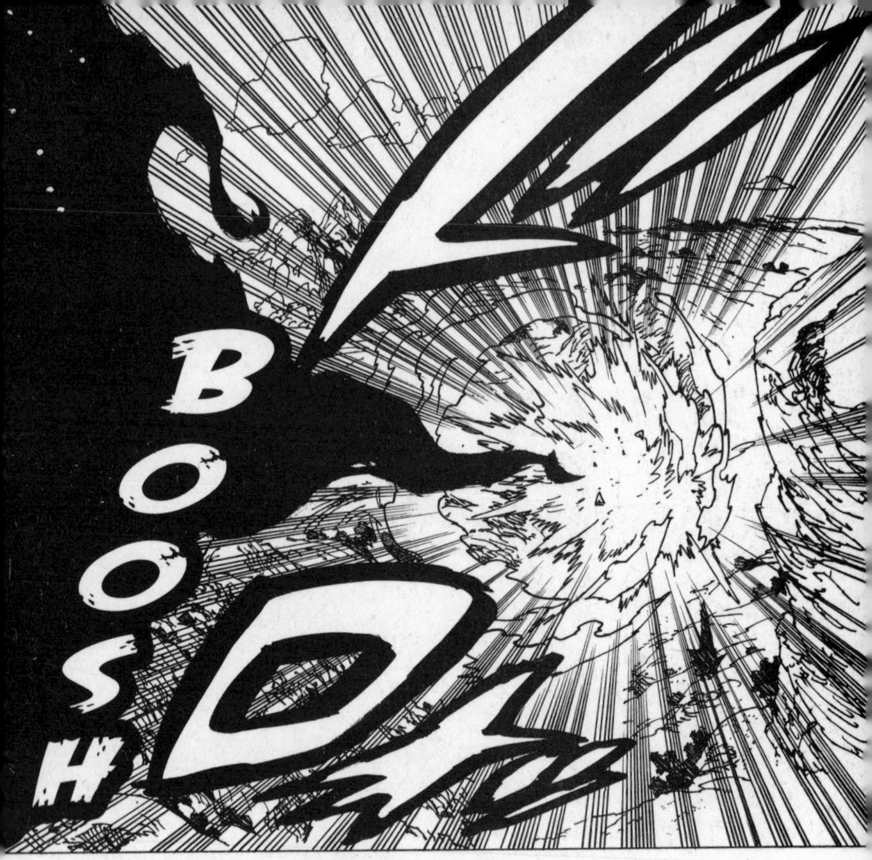
BOOOSH
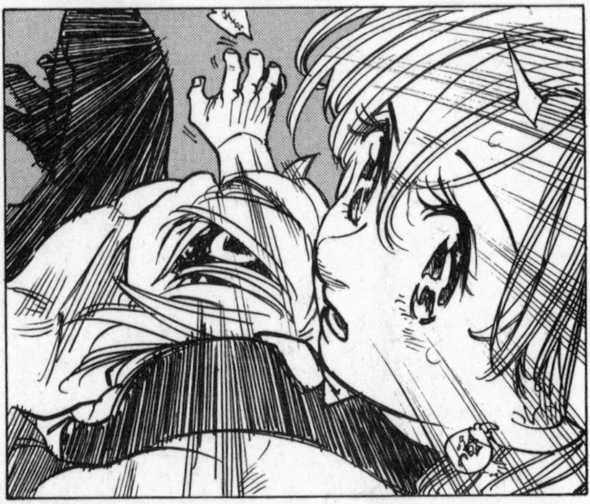
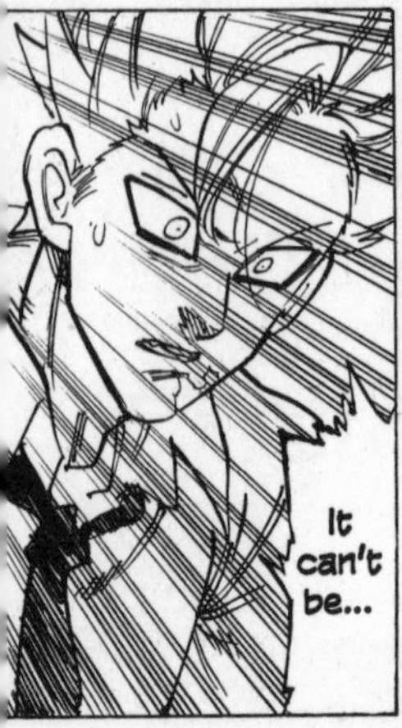
It can't be...

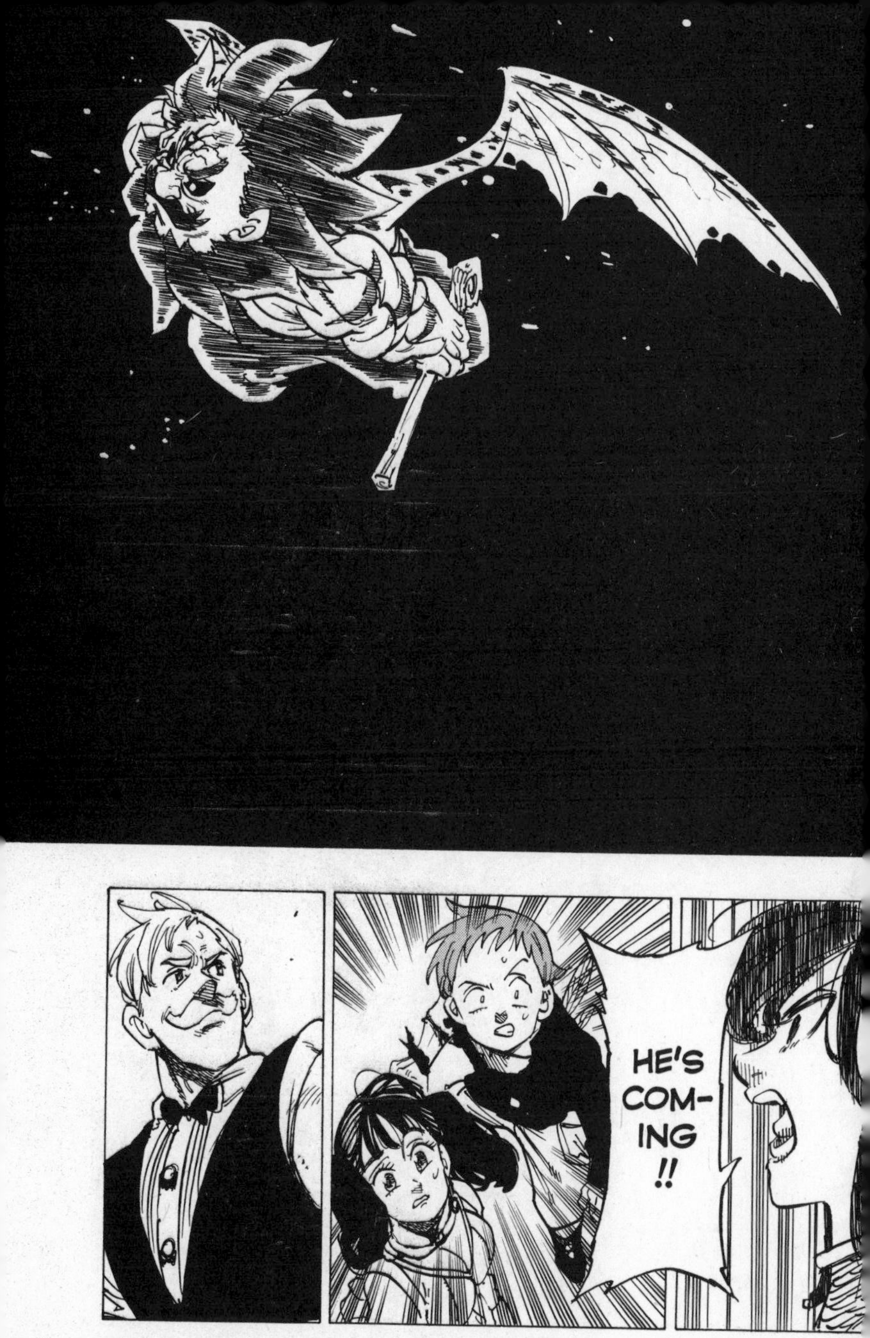
HE'S COMING!!

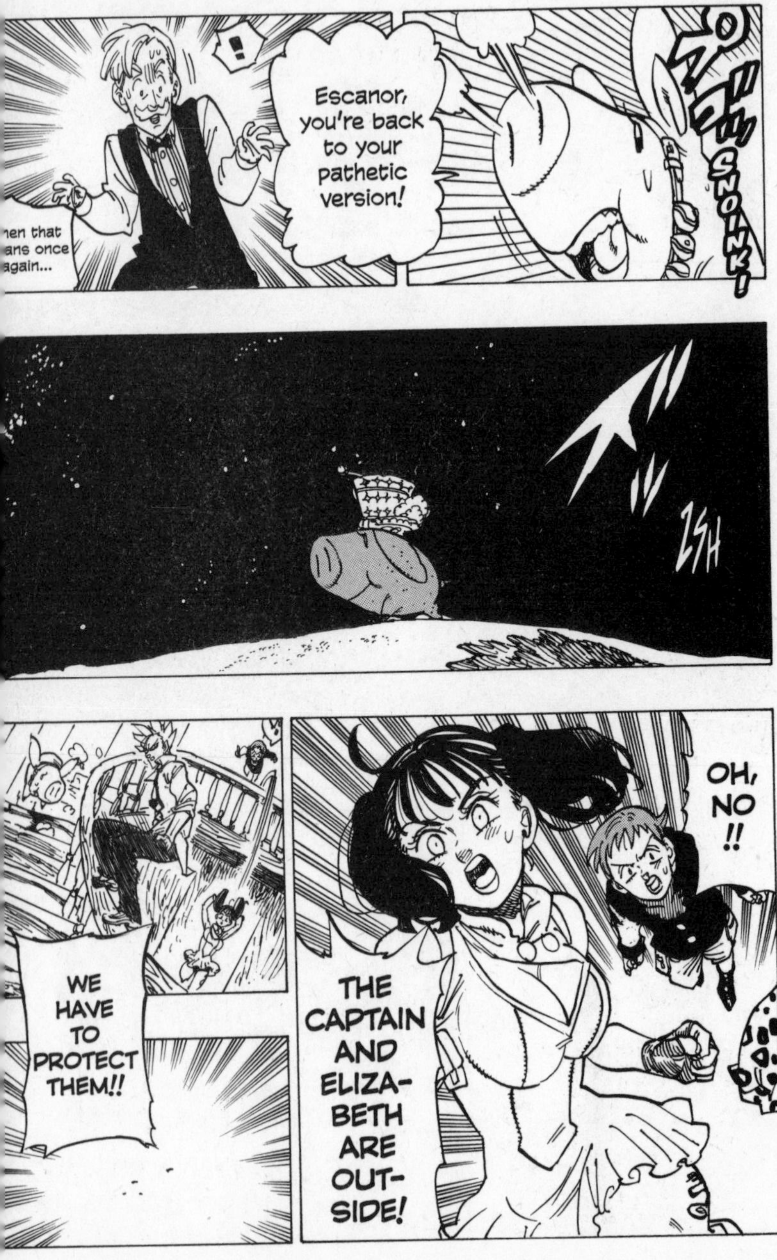
SNOINK!
Escanor, you're back to your pathetic version!
hen that ans once again...
ZSH
OH, NO!!
THE CAPTAIN AND ELIZABETH ARE OUTSIDE!
WE HAVE TO PROTECT THEM!!

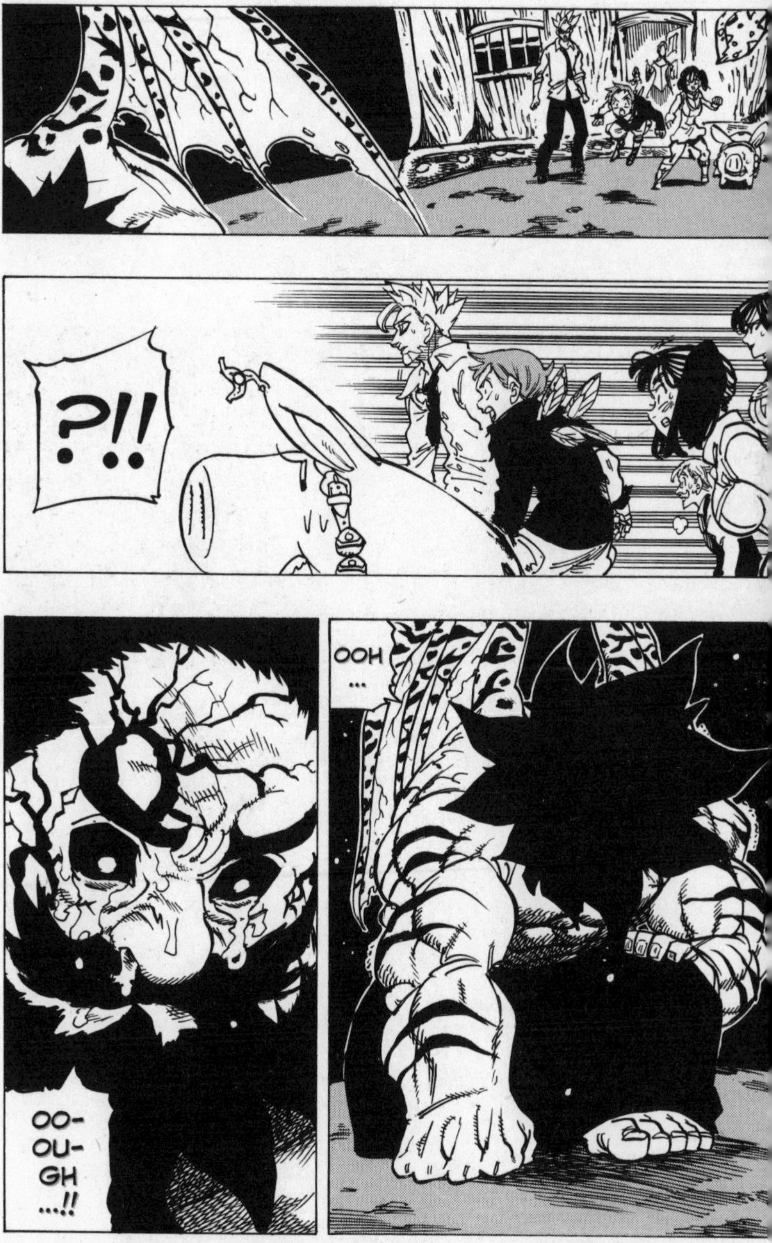
?!!
OOH ...
OO-OU-GH ...!!

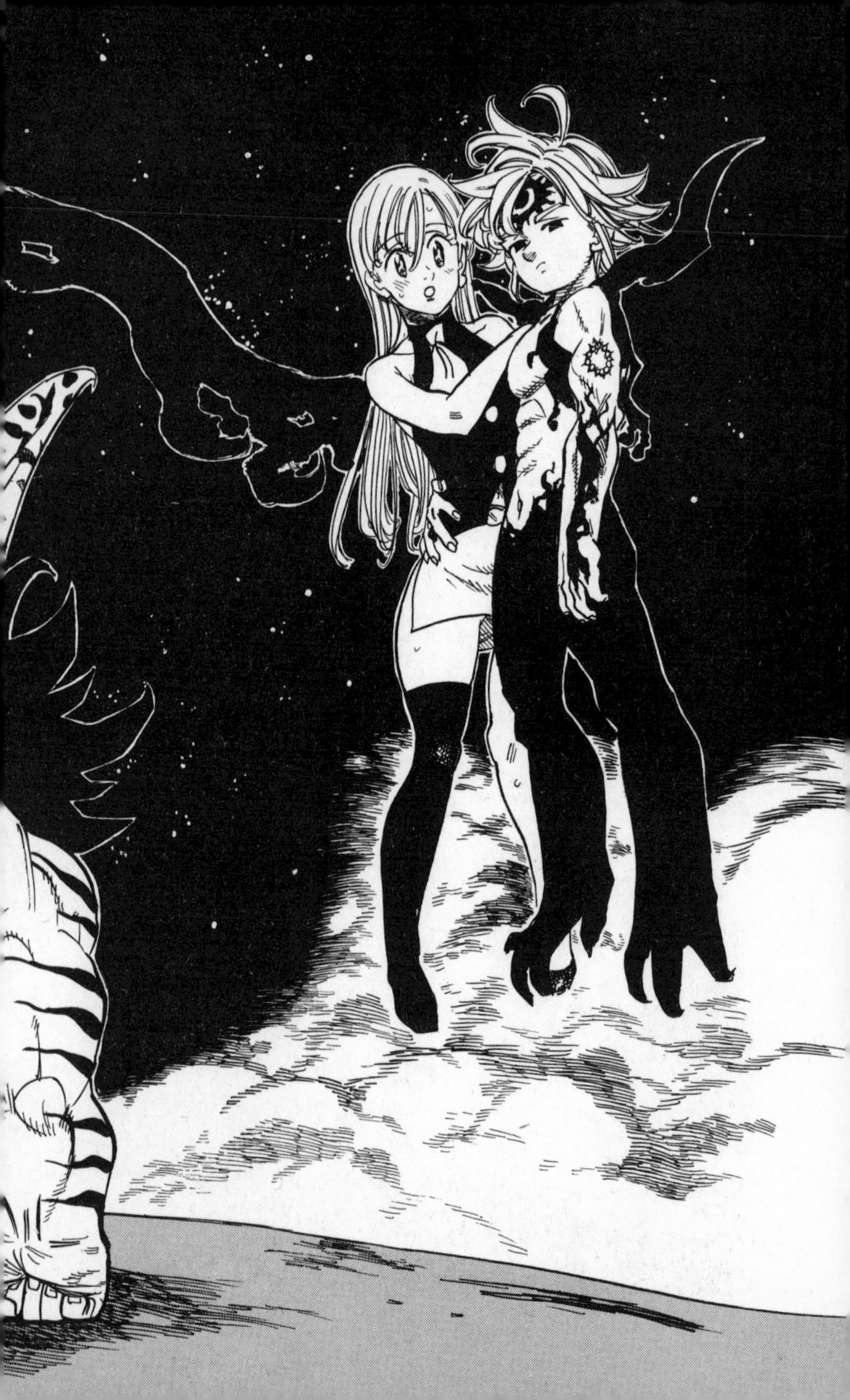

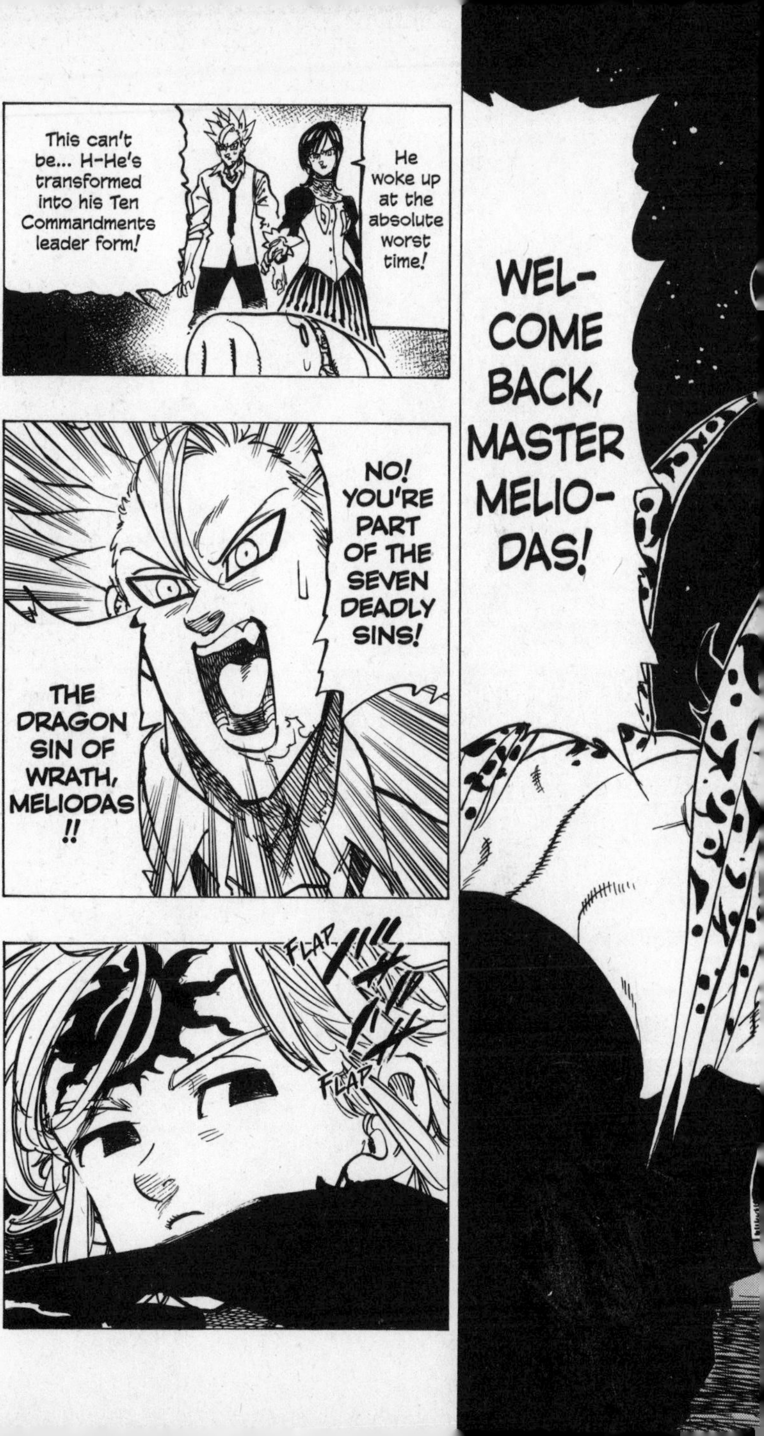
WEL-COME BACK, MASTER MELIO-DAS!
He woke up at the absolute worst time!
This can't be... H-He's transformed into his Ten Commandments leader form!
NO! YOU'RE PART OF THE SEVEN DEADLY SINS!
THE DRAGON SIN OF WRATH, MELIODAS !!
FLAP
FLAP

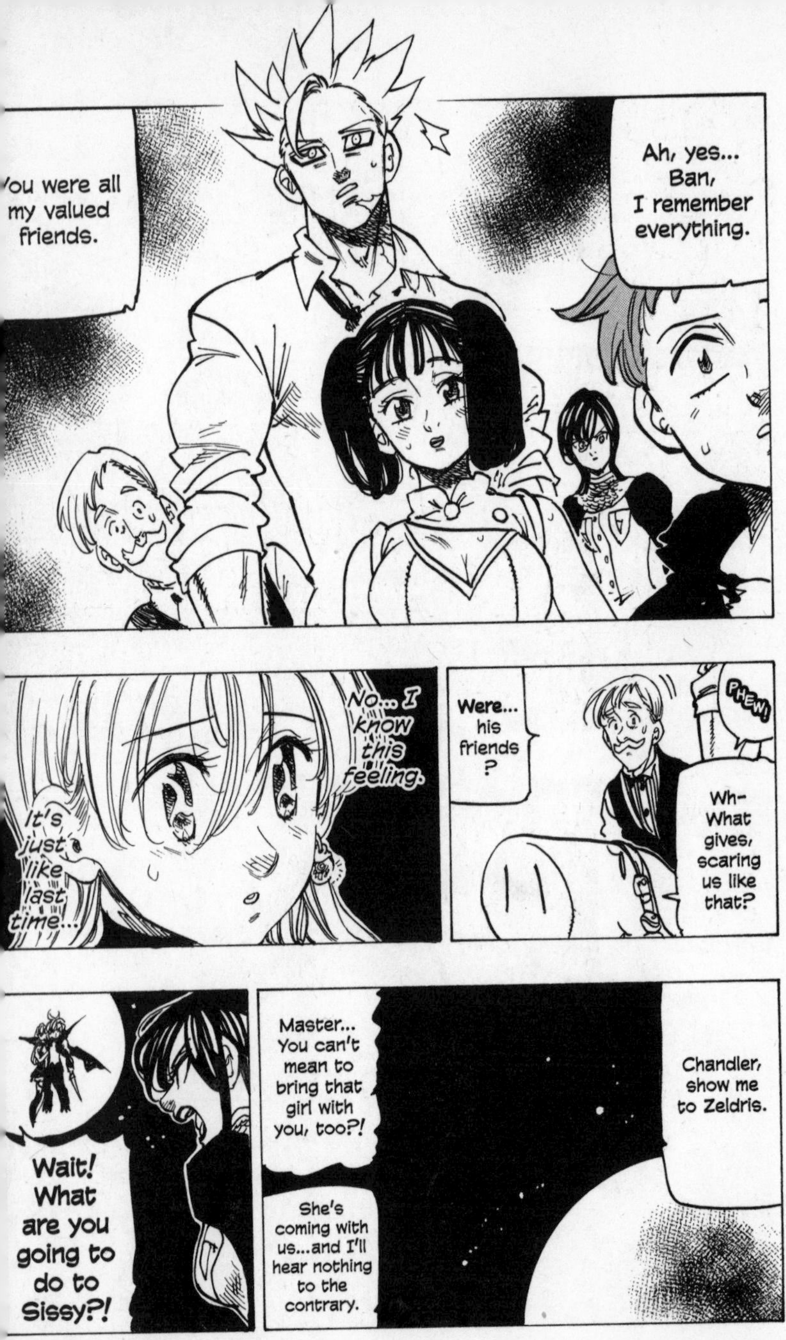
Ah, yes... Ban, I remember everything.
You were all my valued friends.
PHEW!
Were... his friends?
Wh-What gives, scaring us like that?
No... I know this feeling.
It's just like last time...
Chandler, show me to Zeldris.
Master... You can't mean to bring that girl with you, too?!
She's coming with us...and I'll hear nothing to the contrary.
Wait! What are you going to do to Sissy?!

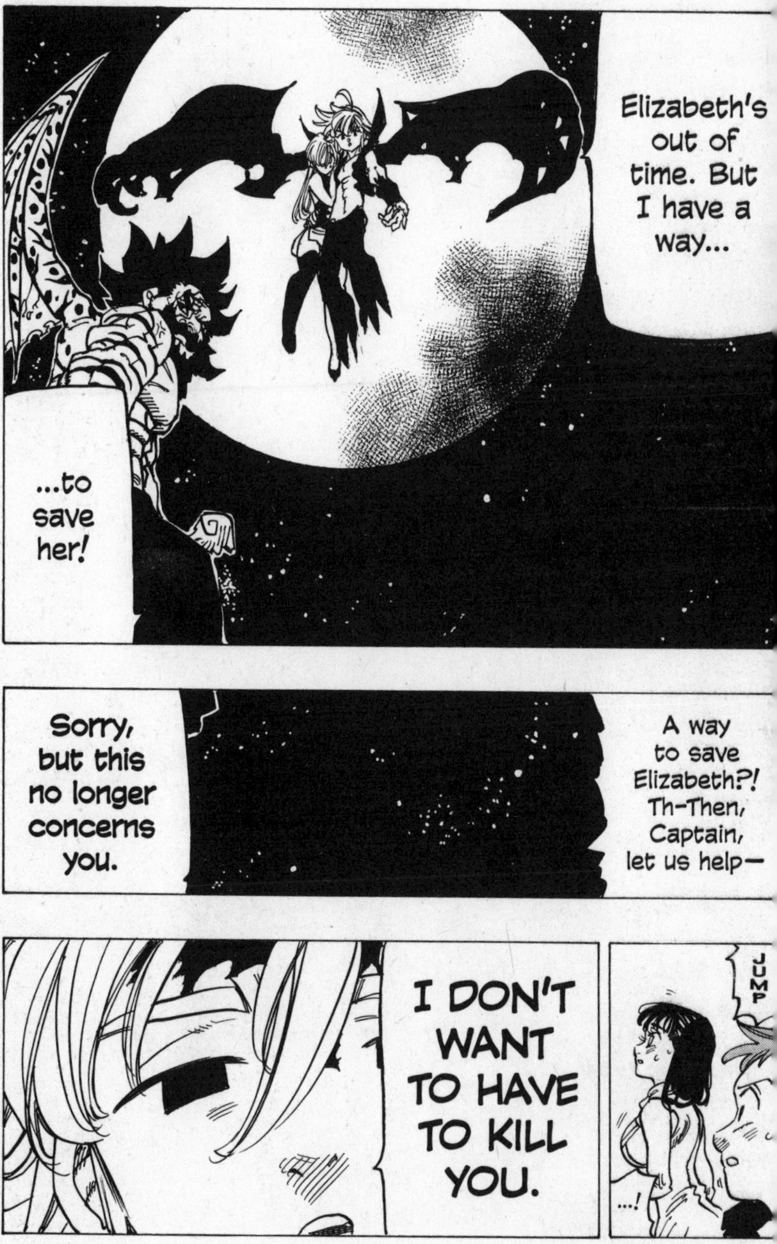

Elizabeth's out of time. But I have a way...
...to save her!
A way to save Elizabeth?! Th-Then, Captain, let us help—
Sorry, but this no longer concerns you.
JUMP
...!
I DON'T WANT TO HAVE TO KILL YOU.

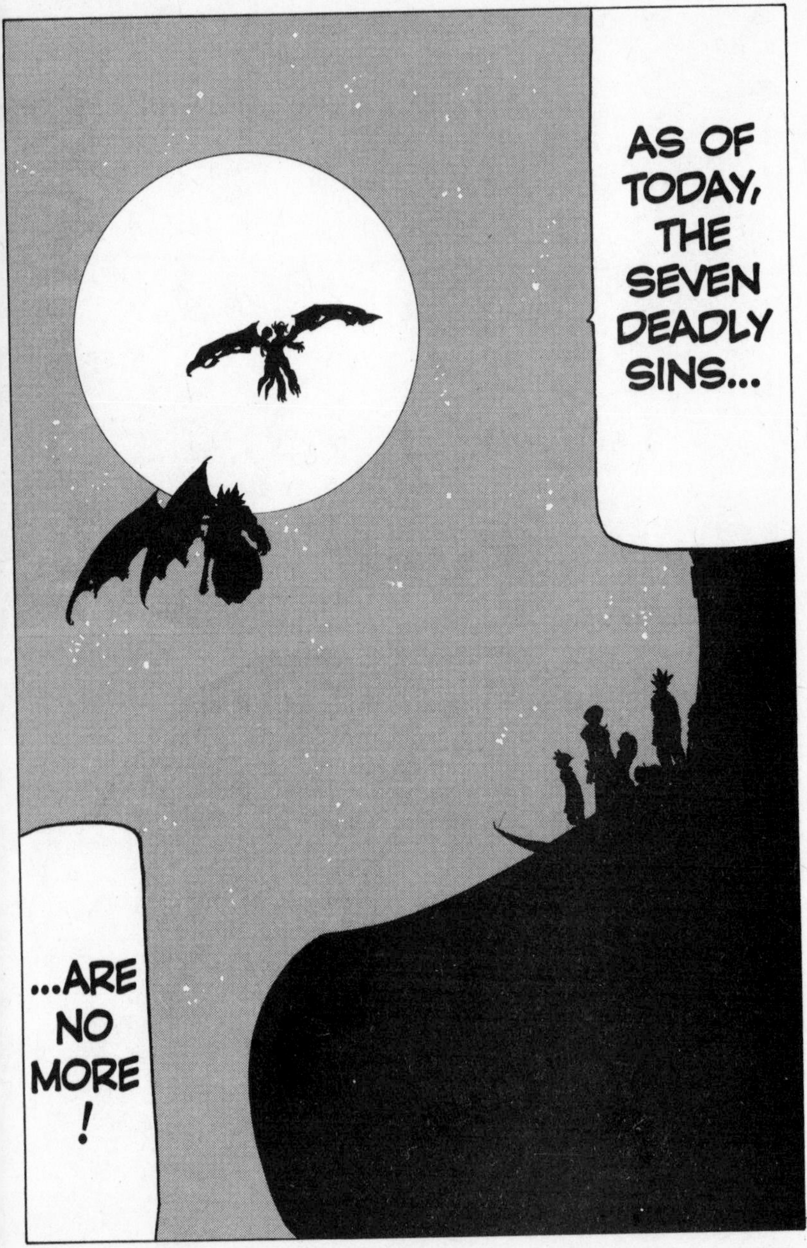
AS OF TODAY, THE SEVEN DEADLY SINS...
...ARE NO MORE !

Chapter 243 - And Then He Leaves on a Trip

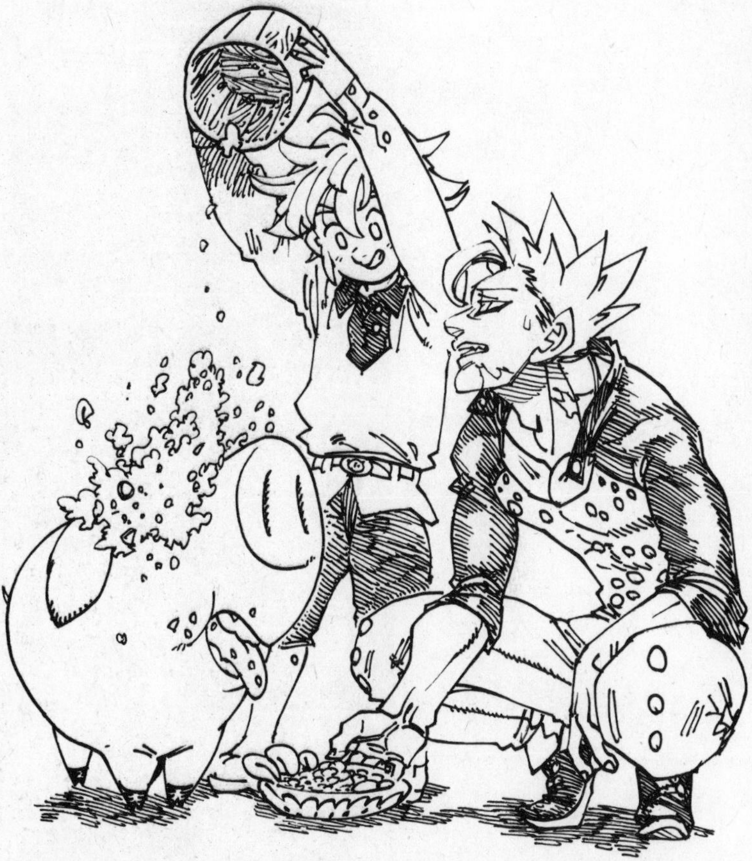

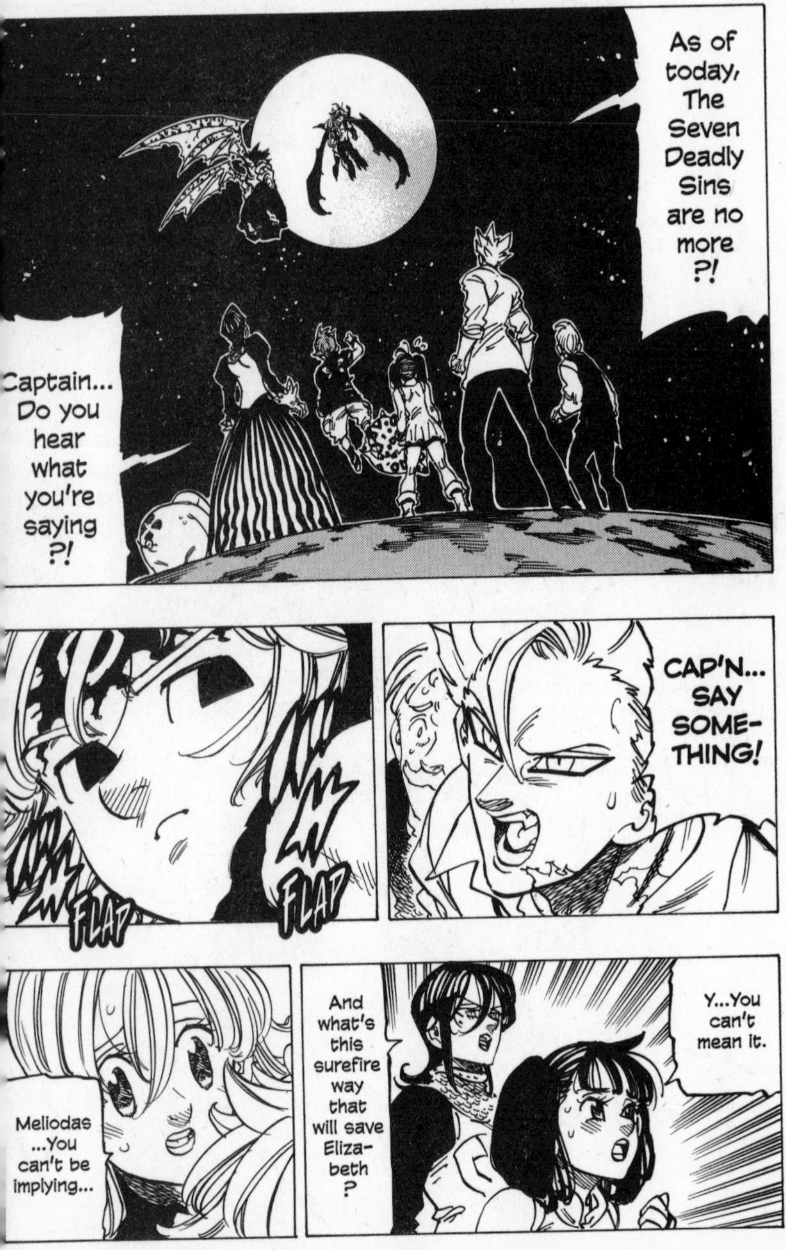
As of today, The Seven Deadly Sins are no more?!
Captain... Do you hear what you're saying?!
CAP'N... SAY SOME-THING!
FLAP
FLAP
Y...You can't mean it.
And what's this surefire way that will save Eliza-beth?
Meliodas ...You can't be implying...

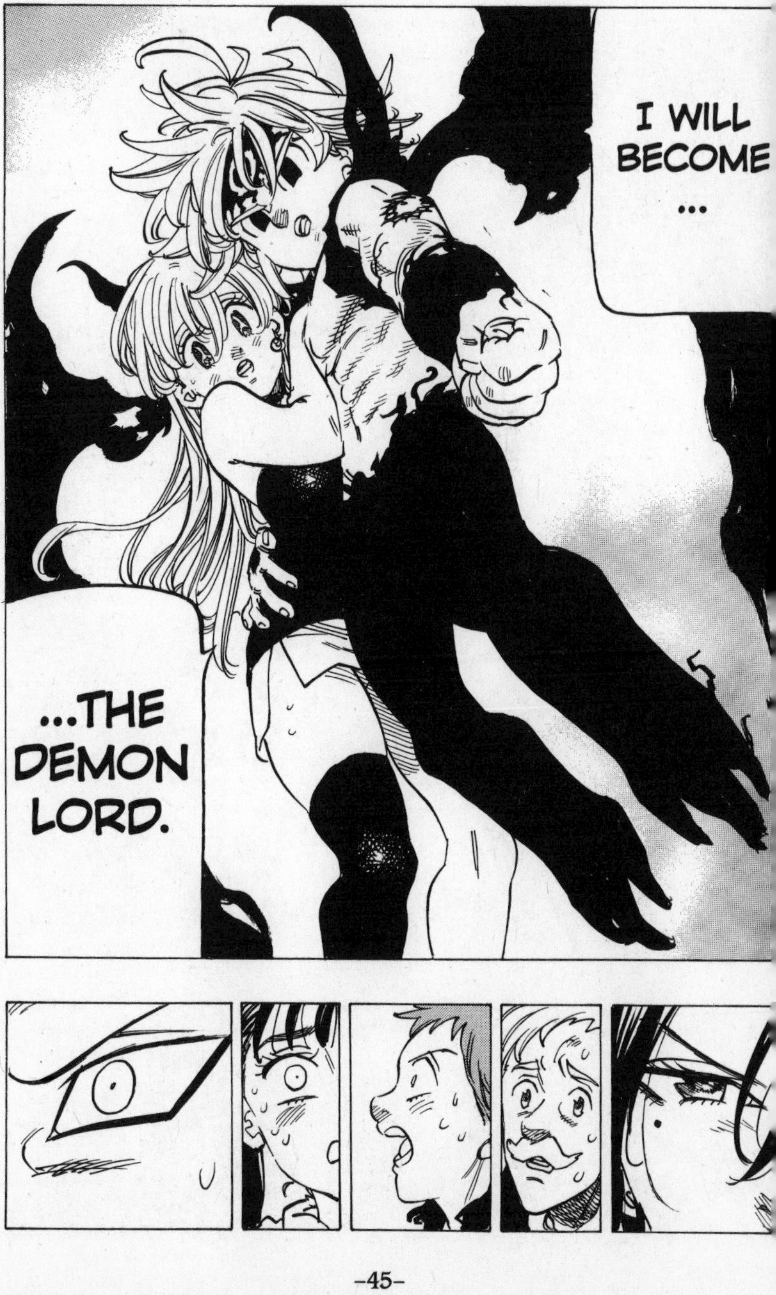
I WILL BECOME ...
...THE DEMON LORD.

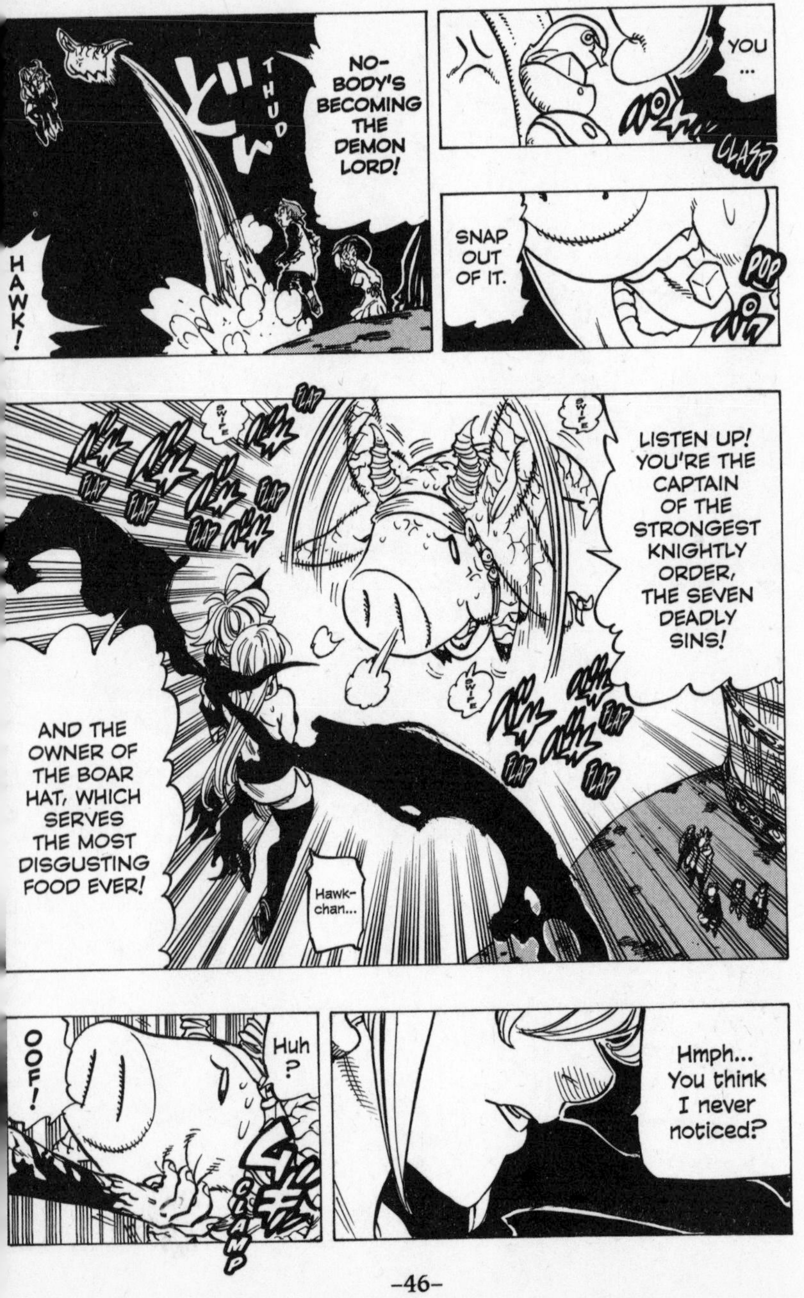
YOU ...
CLASP
SNAP OUT OF IT.
POP
NO-BODY'S BECOMING THE DEMON LORD!
THUD
HAWK!
LISTEN UP! YOU'RE THE CAPTAIN OF THE STRONGEST KNIGHTLY ORDER, THE SEVEN DEADLY SINS!
SWIPE
FLAP
SWIPE
FLAP
AND THE OWNER OF THE BOAR HAT, WHICH SERVES THE MOST DISGUSTING FOOD EVER!
SWIPE
FLAP
Hawk-chan...
Hmph... You think I never noticed?
Huh?
OOF!
CLAMP

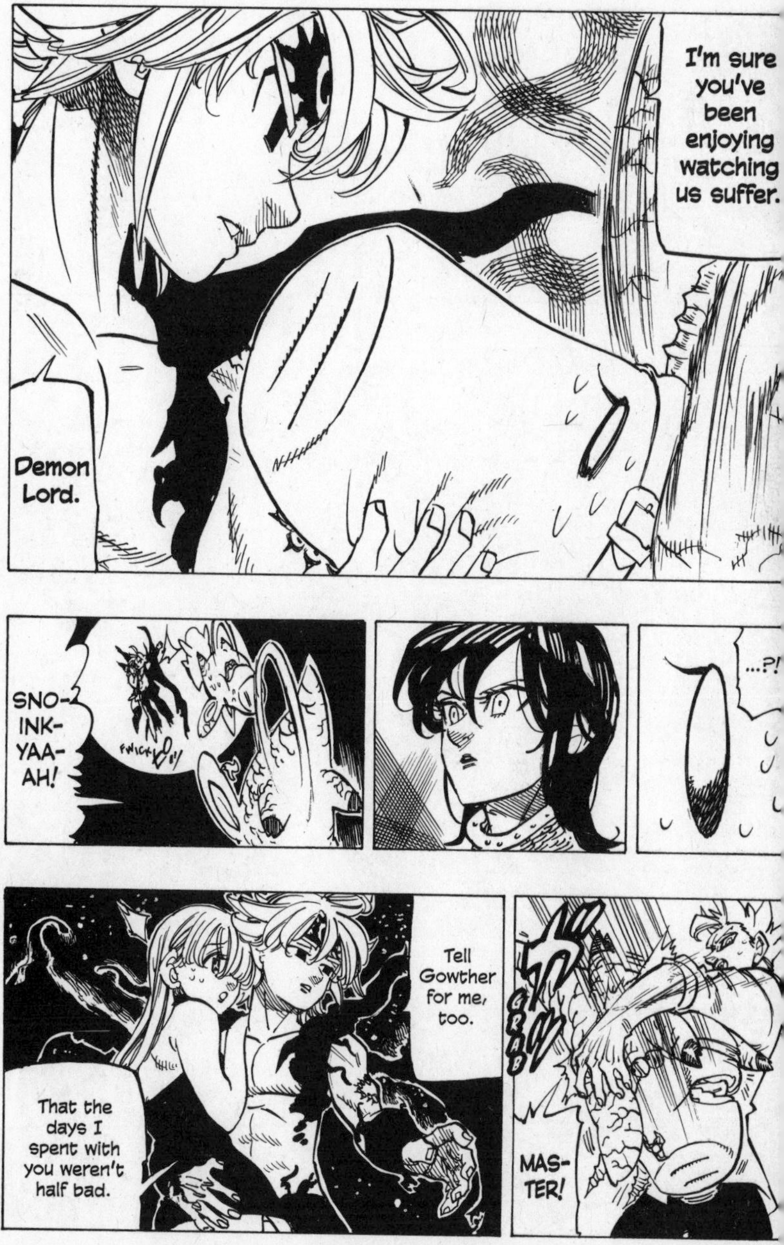
I'm sure you've been enjoying watching us suffer.
Demon Lord.
...?!
SNO-INK-YAA-AH!
GRAB
MAS-TER!
Tell Gowther for me, too.
That the days I spent with you weren't half bad.

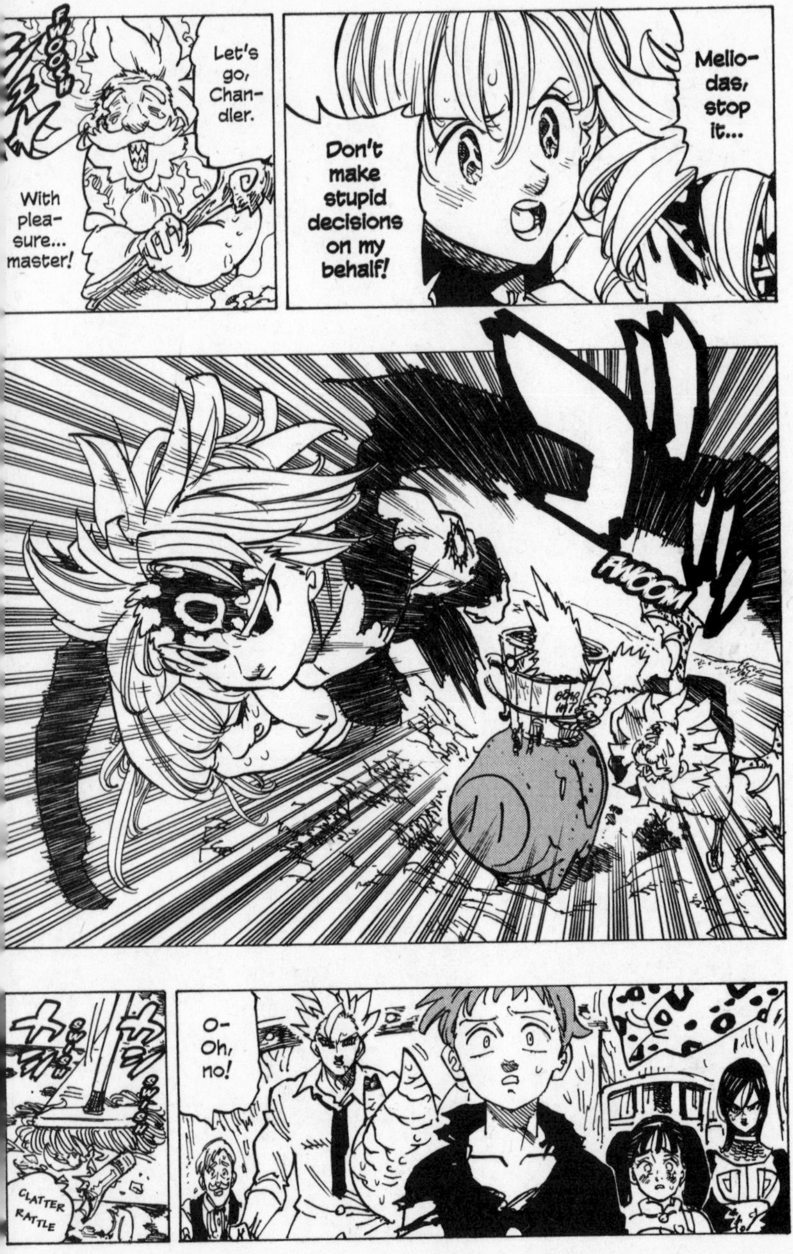
Melio-das, stop it...
Don't make stupid decisions on my behalf!
FWOOSH
Let's go, Chandler.
With plea-sure... master!
FWOOM
O-Oh, no!
SWISH
SWISH
CLATTER RATTLE

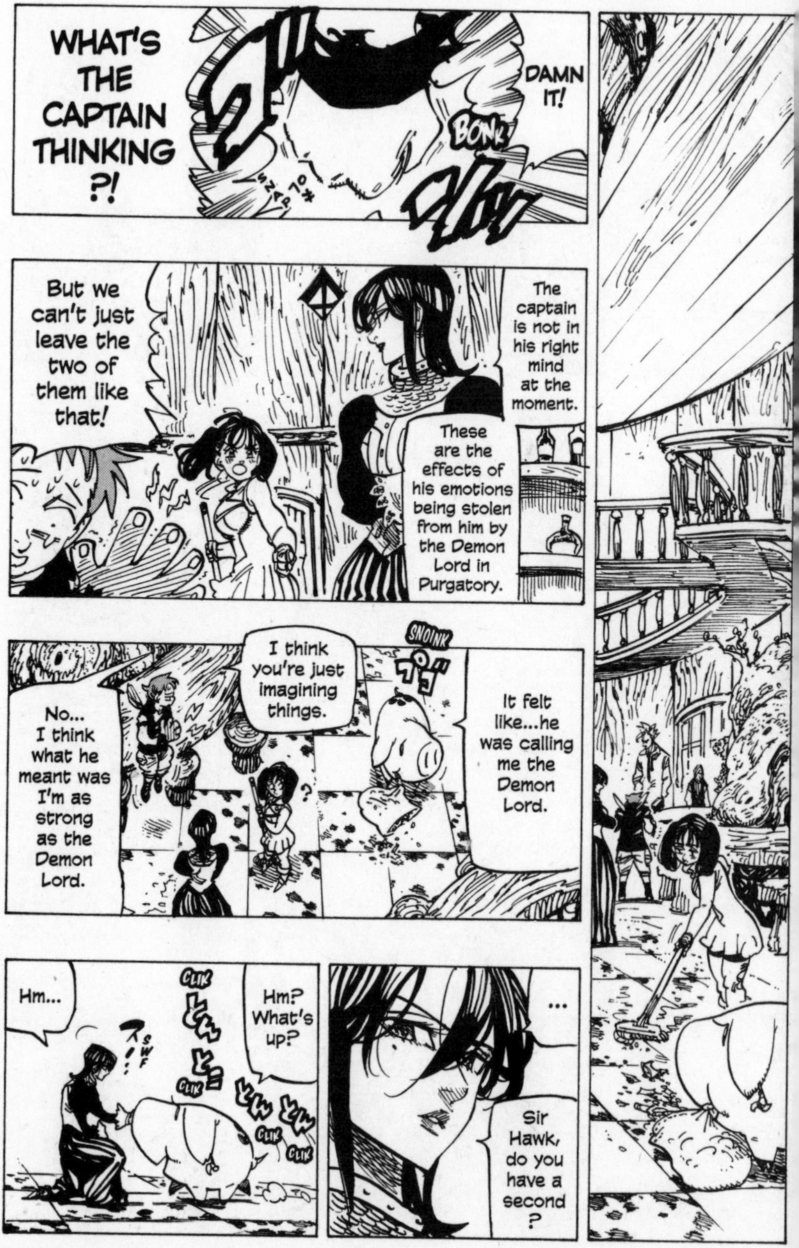
DAMN IT!
BONK
WHAT'S THE CAPTAIN THINKING?!
The captain is not in his right mind at the moment.
These are the effects of his emotions being stolen from him by the Demon Lord in Purgatory.
But we can't just leave the two of them like that!
SNOINK
It felt like...he was calling me the Demon Lord.
I think you're just imagining things.
No... I think what he meant was I'm as strong as the Demon Lord.
...
Sir Hawk, do you have a second?
Hm? What's up?
CLIK
CLIK
CLIK
CLIK
SWF
Hm...

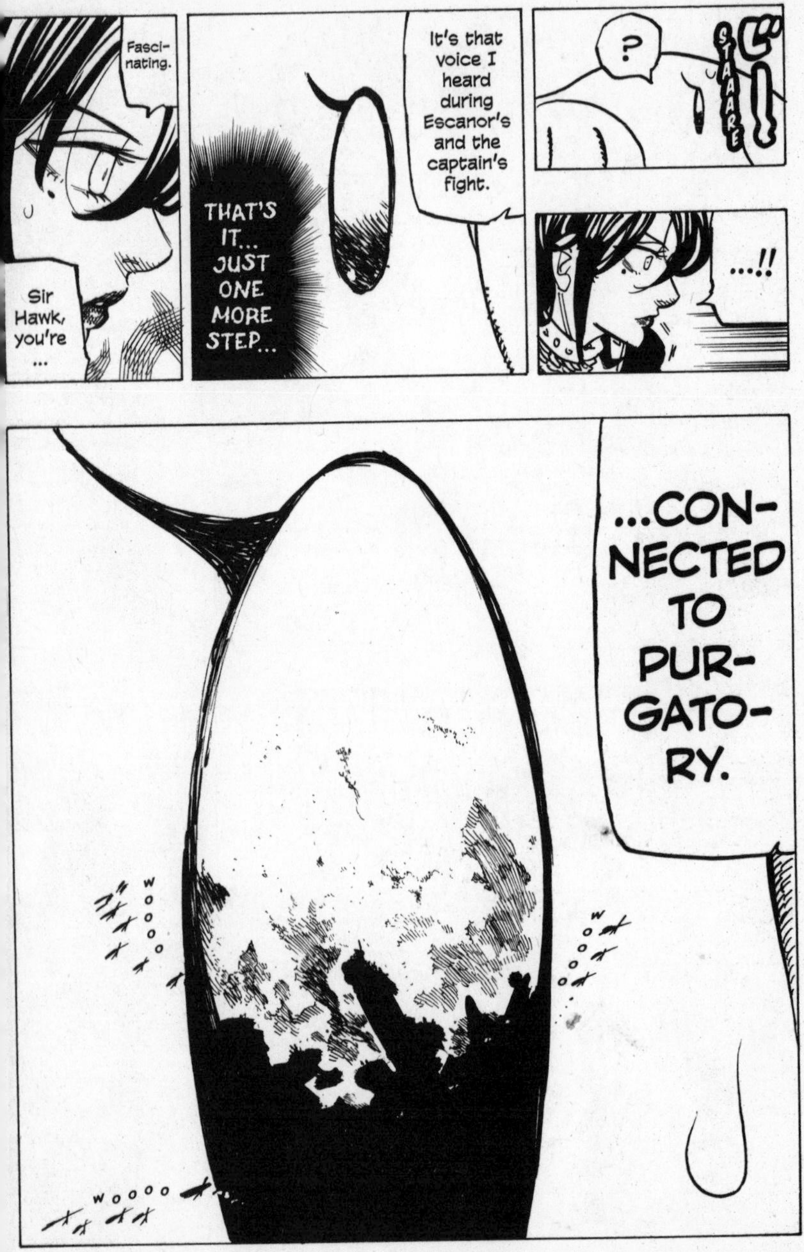
?
STAAARE
...!!
It's that voice I heard during Escanor's and the captain's fight.
THAT'S IT... JUST ONE MORE STEP...
Fascinating.
Sir Hawk, you're ...
...CONNECTED TO PURGATORY.
WOOOO
WOOO
WOOOO

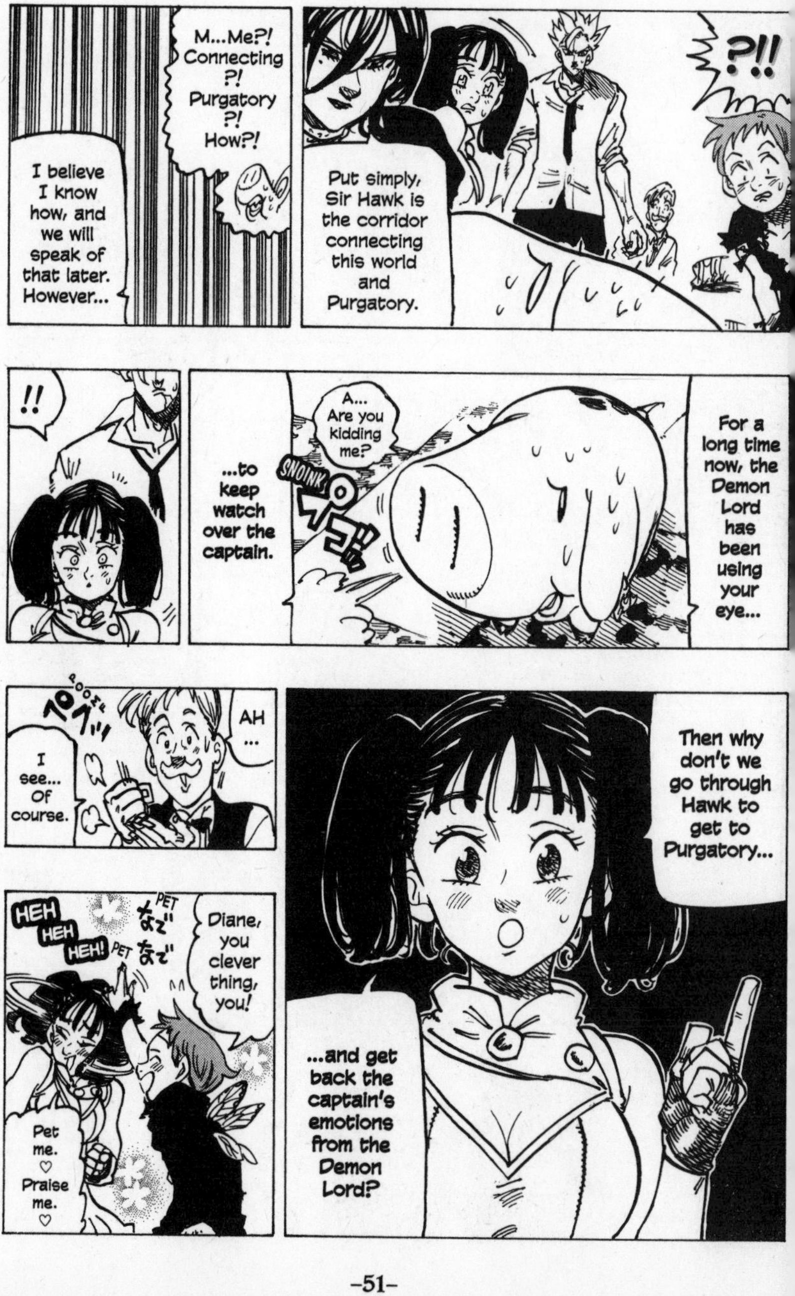
?!!
Put simply, Sir Hawk is the corridor connecting this world and Purgatory.
M...Me?! Connecting?! Purgatory?! How?!
I believe I know how, and we will speak of that later. However...
For a long time now, the Demon Lord has been using your eye...
A... Are you kidding me?
SNOINK
...to keep watch over the captain.
!!
Then why don't we go through Hawk to get to Purgatory...
...and get back the captain's emotions from the Demon Lord?
AH ...
POOF
I see... Of course.
Diane, you clever thing, you!
PET
PET
HEH HEH HEH!
Pet me. ♡ Praise me. ♡

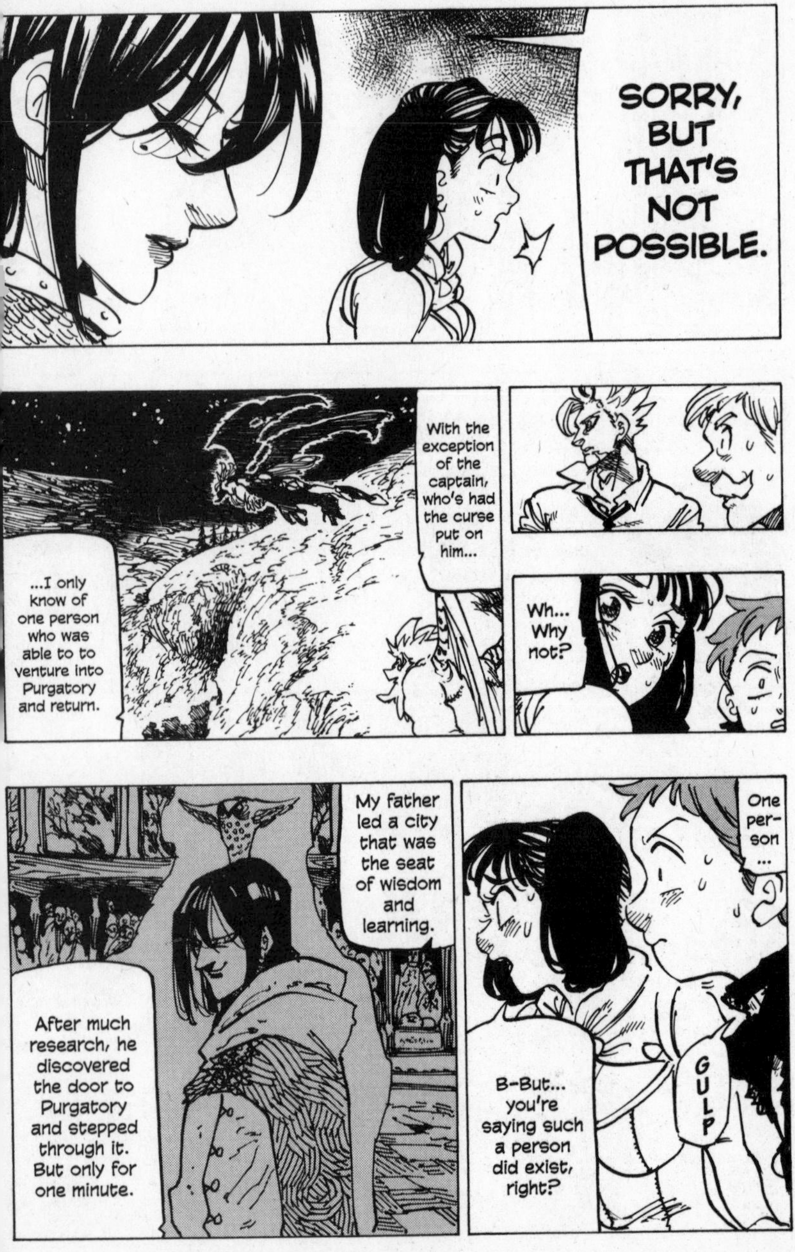
SORRY, BUT THAT'S NOT POSSIBLE.
Wh... Why not?
With the exception of the captain, who's had the curse put on him...
...I only know of one person who was able to to venture into Purgatory and return.
One person...
GULP
B-But... you're saying such a person did exist, right?
My father led a city that was the seat of wisdom and learning.
After much research, he discovered the door to Purgatory and stepped through it. But only for one minute.

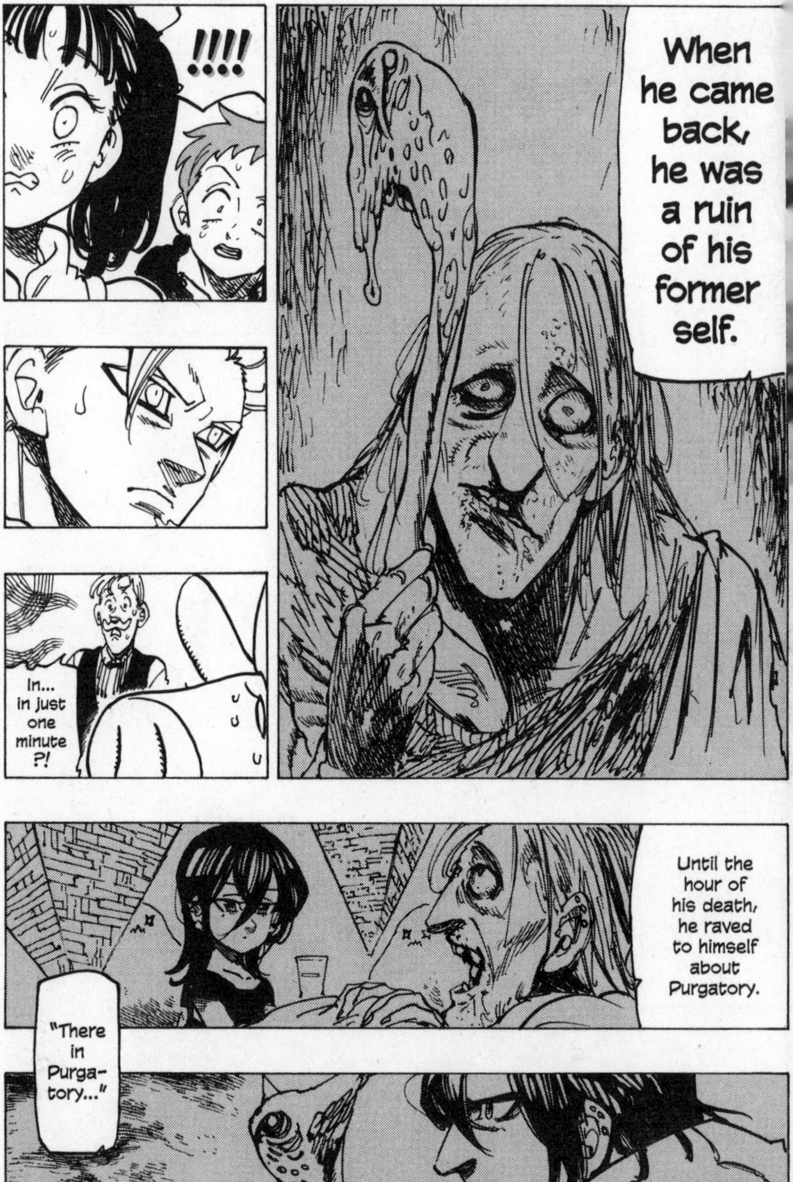
When he came back, he was a ruin of his former self.
!!!!
In... in just one minute ?!
Until the hour of his death, he raved to himself about Purgatory.
"There in Purga-tory..."

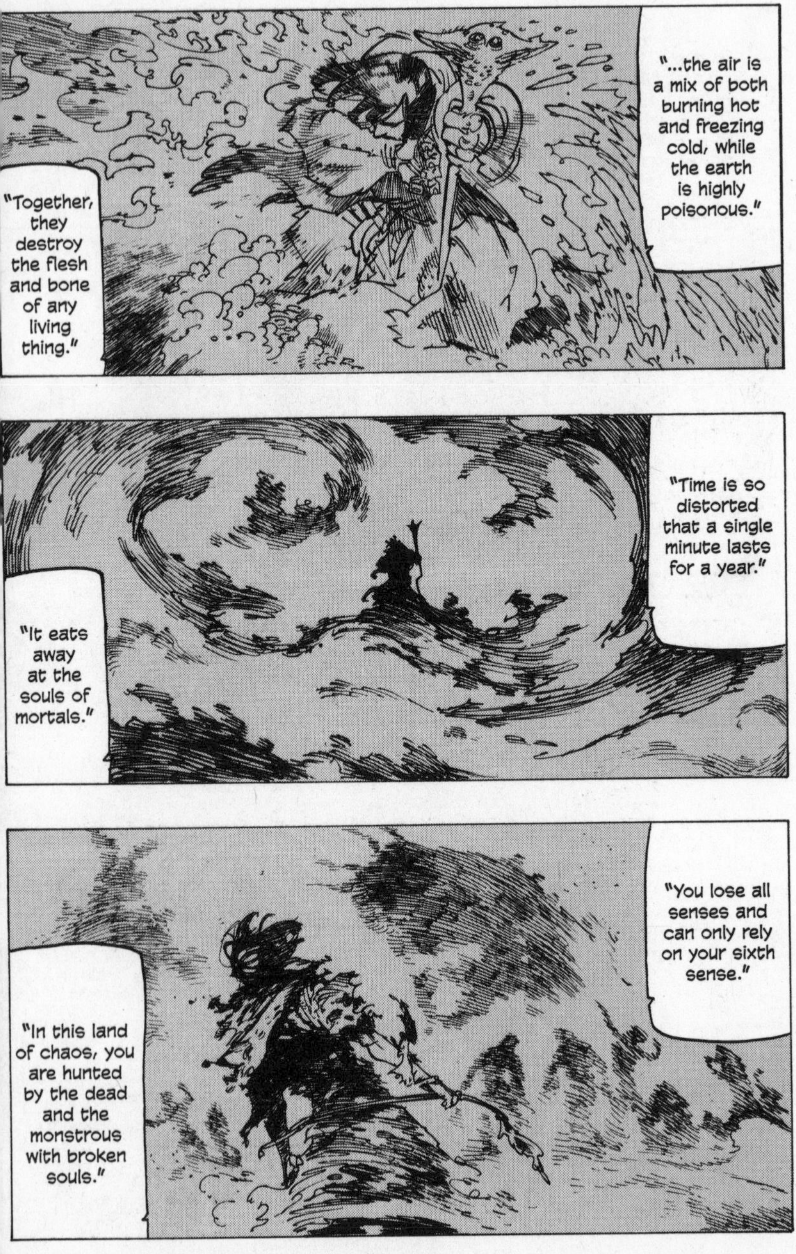
"...the air is a mix of both burning hot and freezing cold, while the earth is highly poisonous."
"Together, they destroy the flesh and bone of any living thing."
"Time is so distorted that a single minute lasts for a year."
"It eats away at the souls of mortals."
"You lose all senses and can only rely on your sixth sense."
"In this land of chaos, you are hunted by the dead and the monstrous with broken souls."

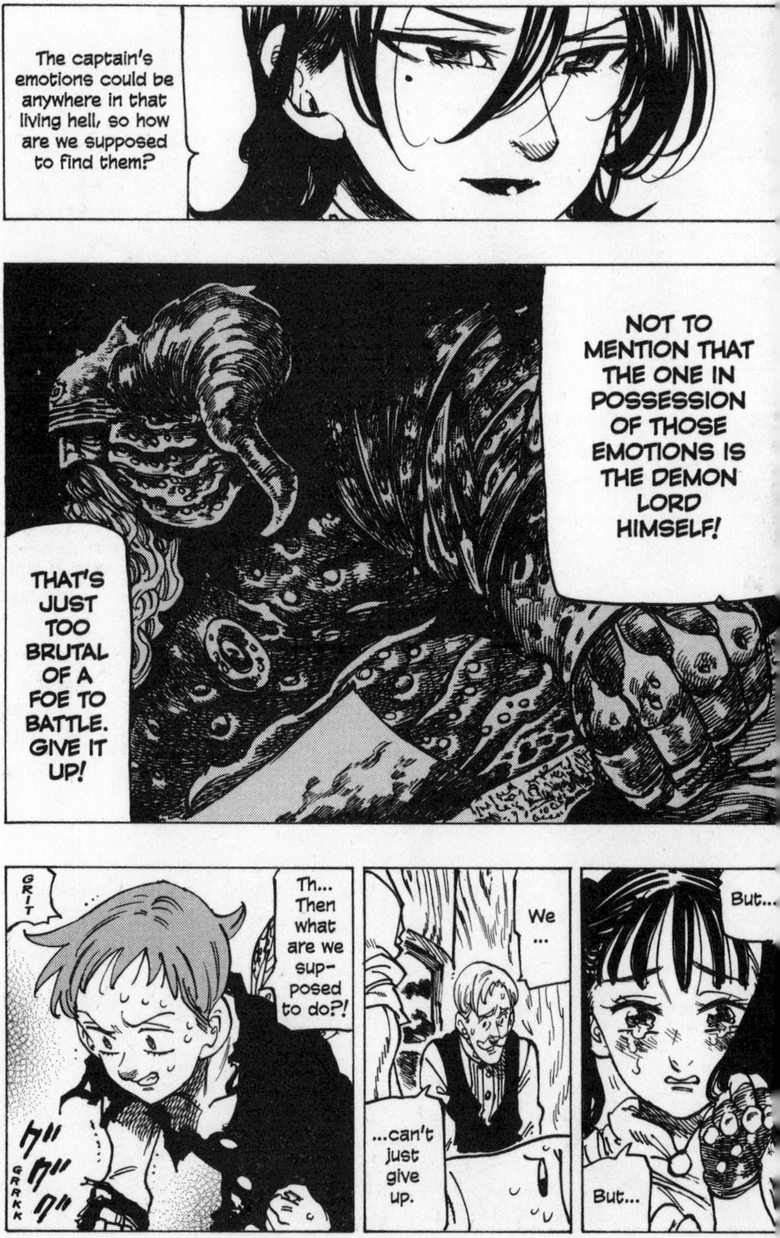
The captain's emotions could be anywhere in that living hell, so how are we supposed to find them?
NOT TO MENTION THAT THE ONE IN POSSESSION OF THOSE EMOTIONS IS THE DEMON LORD HIMSELF!
THAT'S JUST TOO BRUTAL OF A FOE TO BATTLE. GIVE IT UP!
But...
But...
We...
...can't just give up.
GRIT
...
Th... Then what are we sup-posed to do?!
GRRKK

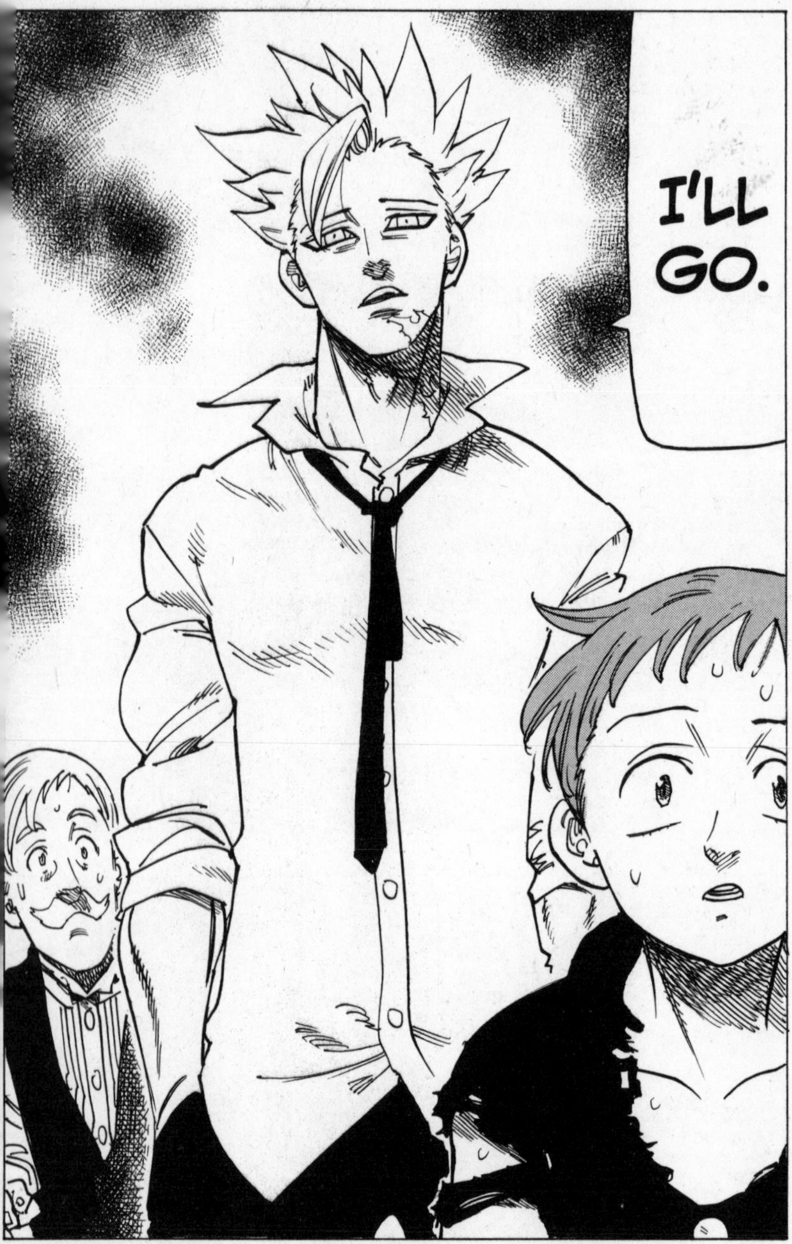
I'LL GO.

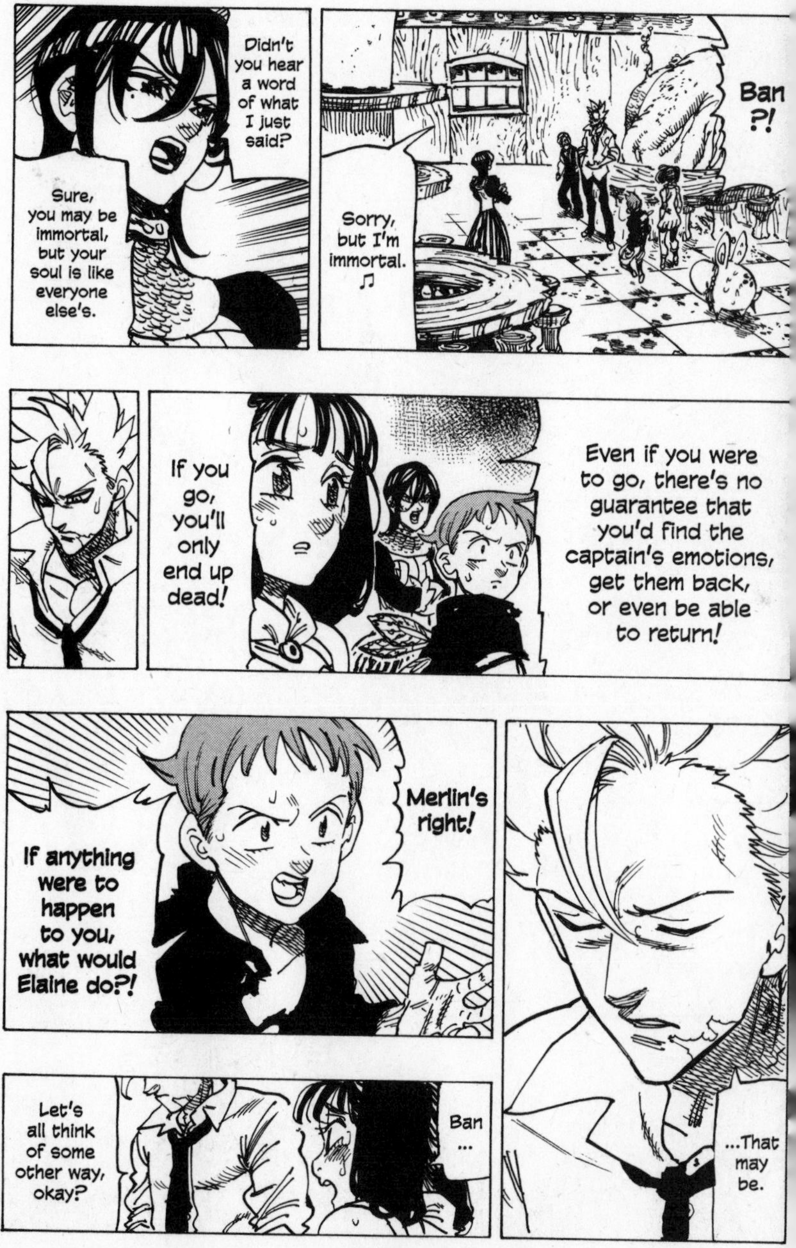
Ban ?!
Sorry, but I'm immortal. ♫
Didn't you hear a word of what I just said?
Sure, you may be immortal, but your soul is like everyone else's.
Even if you were to go, there's no guarantee that you'd find the captain's emotions, get them back, or even be able to return!
If you go, you'll only end up dead!
...That may be.
Merlin's right!
If anything were to happen to you, what would Elaine do?!
Ban ...
Let's all think of some other way, okay?

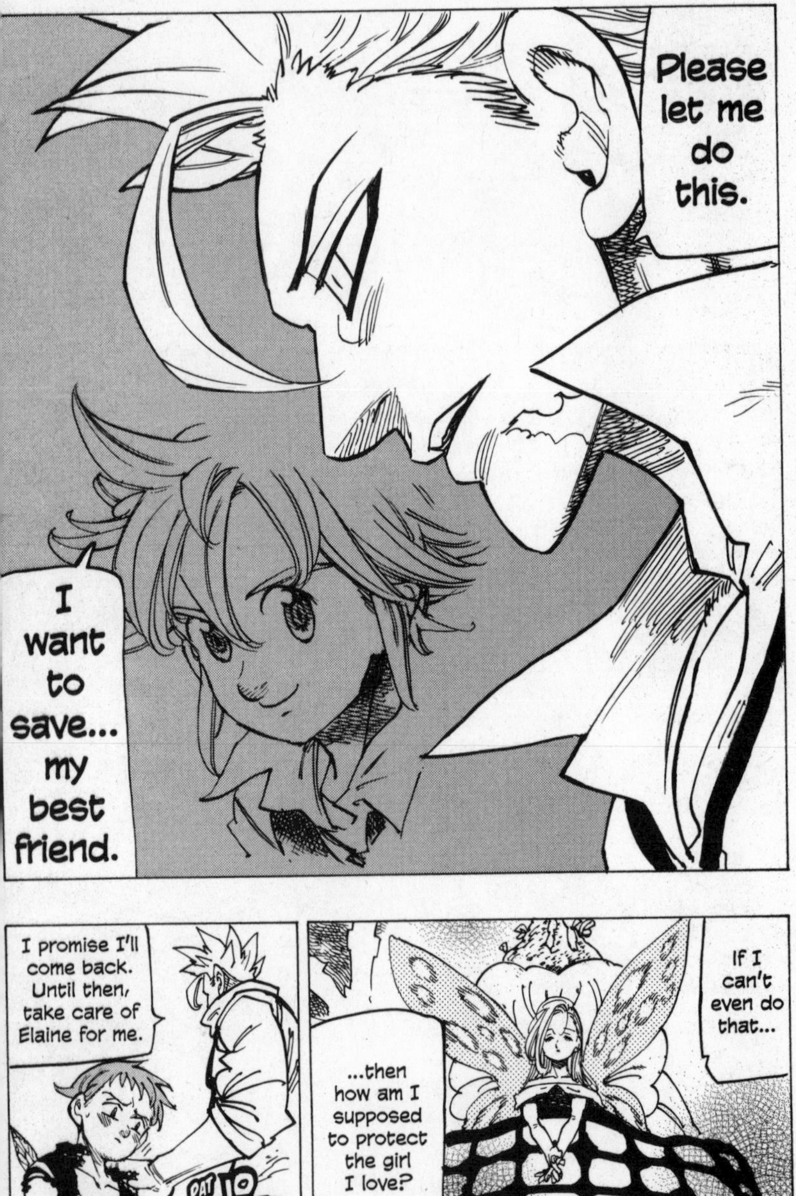
Please let me do this.
I want to save... my best friend.
If I can't even do that...
...then how am I supposed to protect the girl I love?
I promise I'll come back. Until then, take care of Elaine for me.
PAT

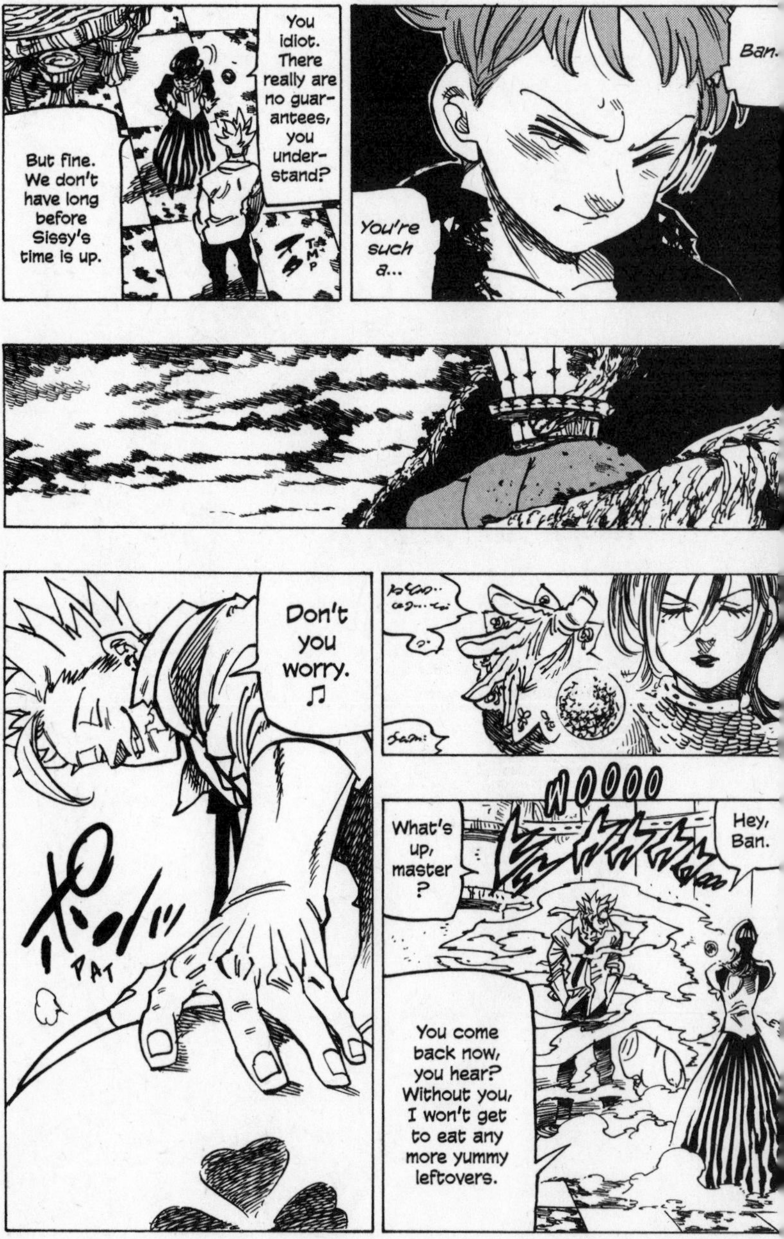

Ban.
You're such a...
You idiot. There really are no guarantees, you understand?
But fine. We don't have long before Sissy's time is up.
TMP
Hey, Ban.
WOOOO
What's up, master?
You come back now, you hear? Without you, I won't get to eat any more yummy leftovers.
Don't you worry. ♫
PAT

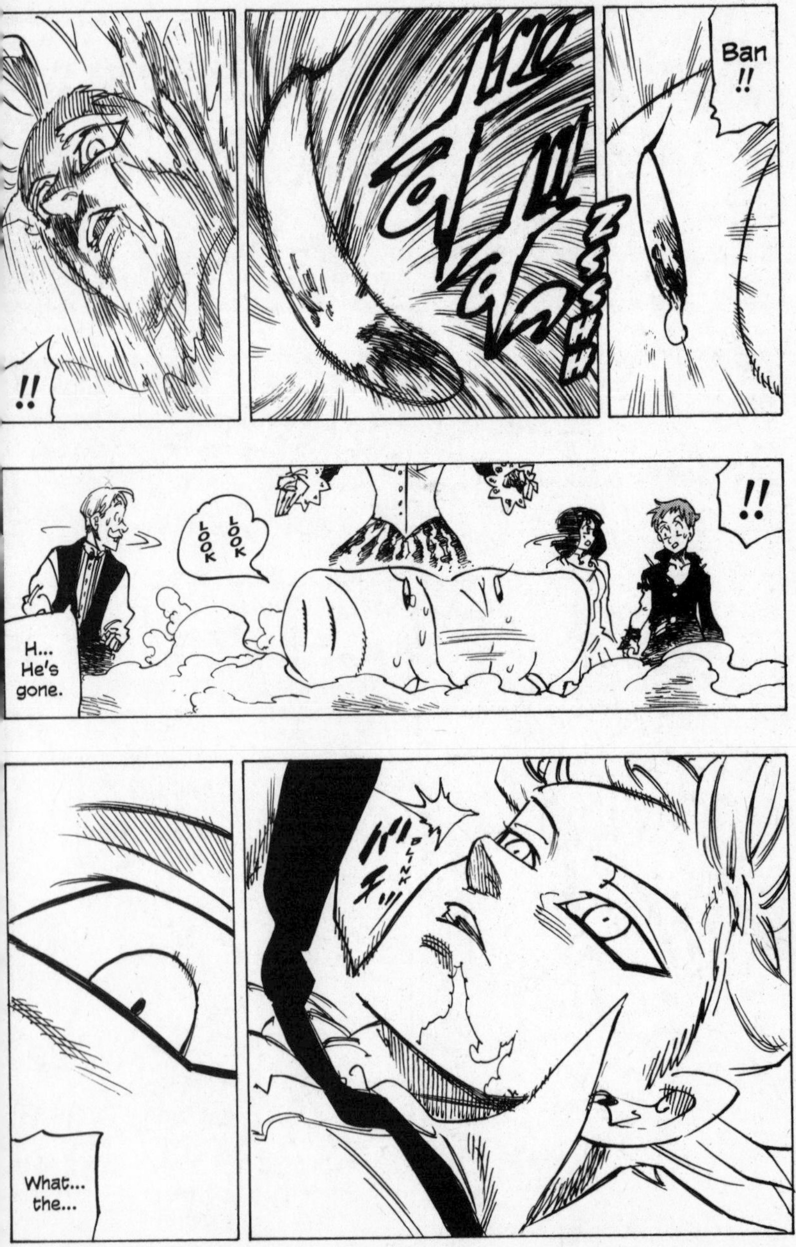
Ban !!
ZSSHH
!!
!!
LOOK LOOK
H... He's gone.
BLINK
What... the...

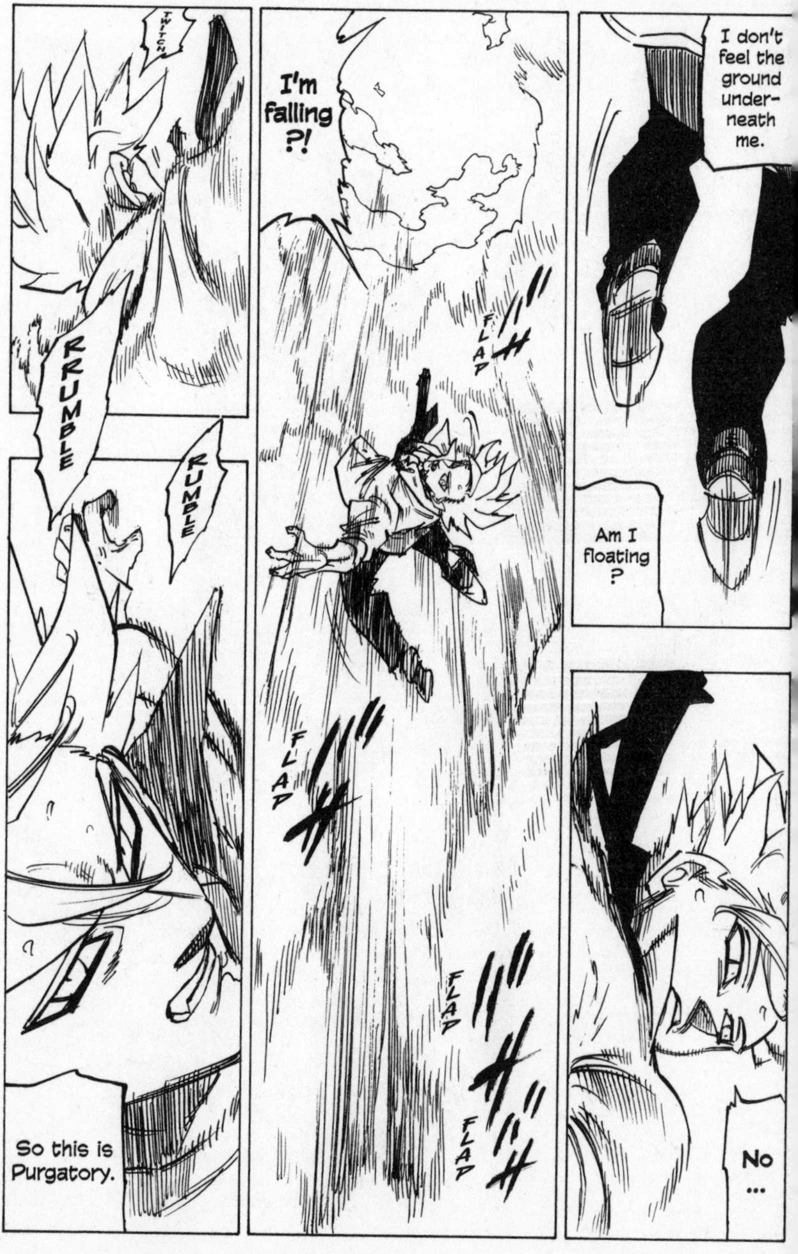
I don't feel the ground underneath me.
Am I floating?
No ...
I'm falling ?!
FLAP
FLAP
FLAP
FLAP
TWITCH
RRUMBLE
RUMBLE
So this is Purgatory.

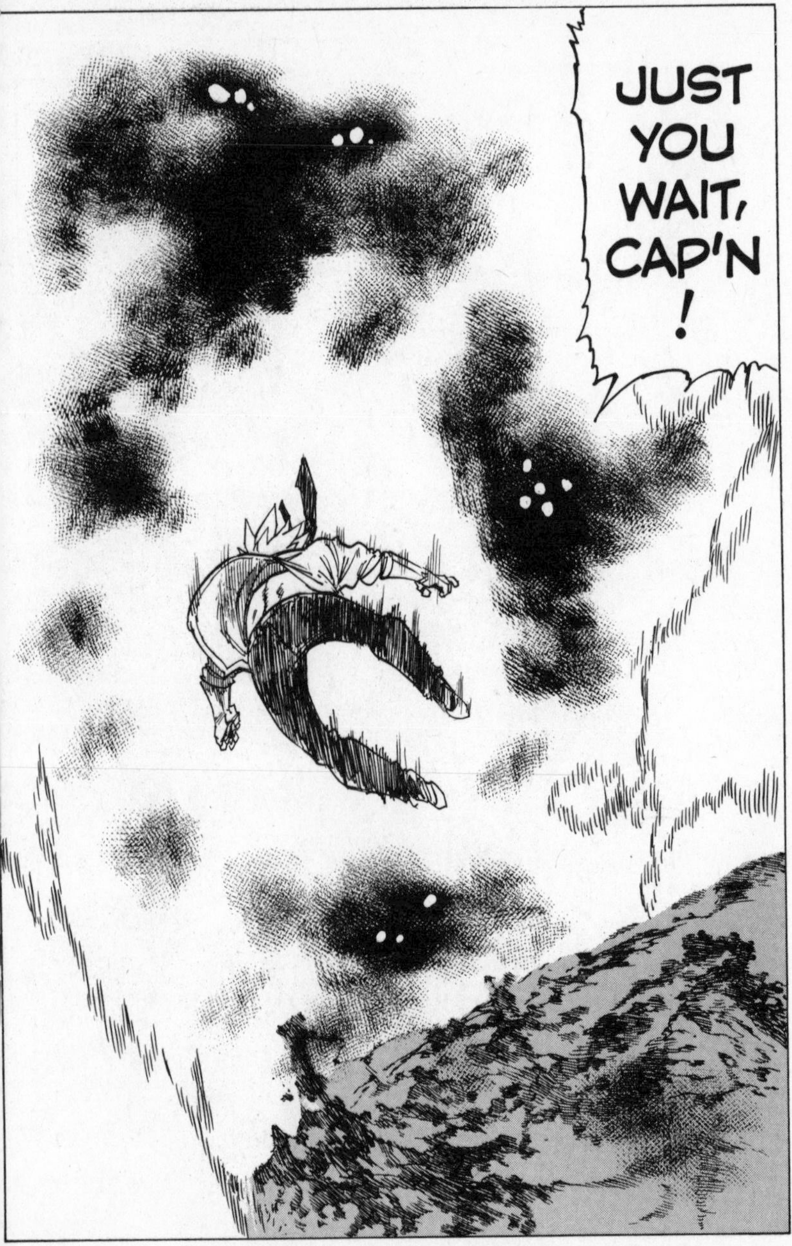
JUST YOU WAIT, CAP'N!

Chapter 244 - The Chosen Queen

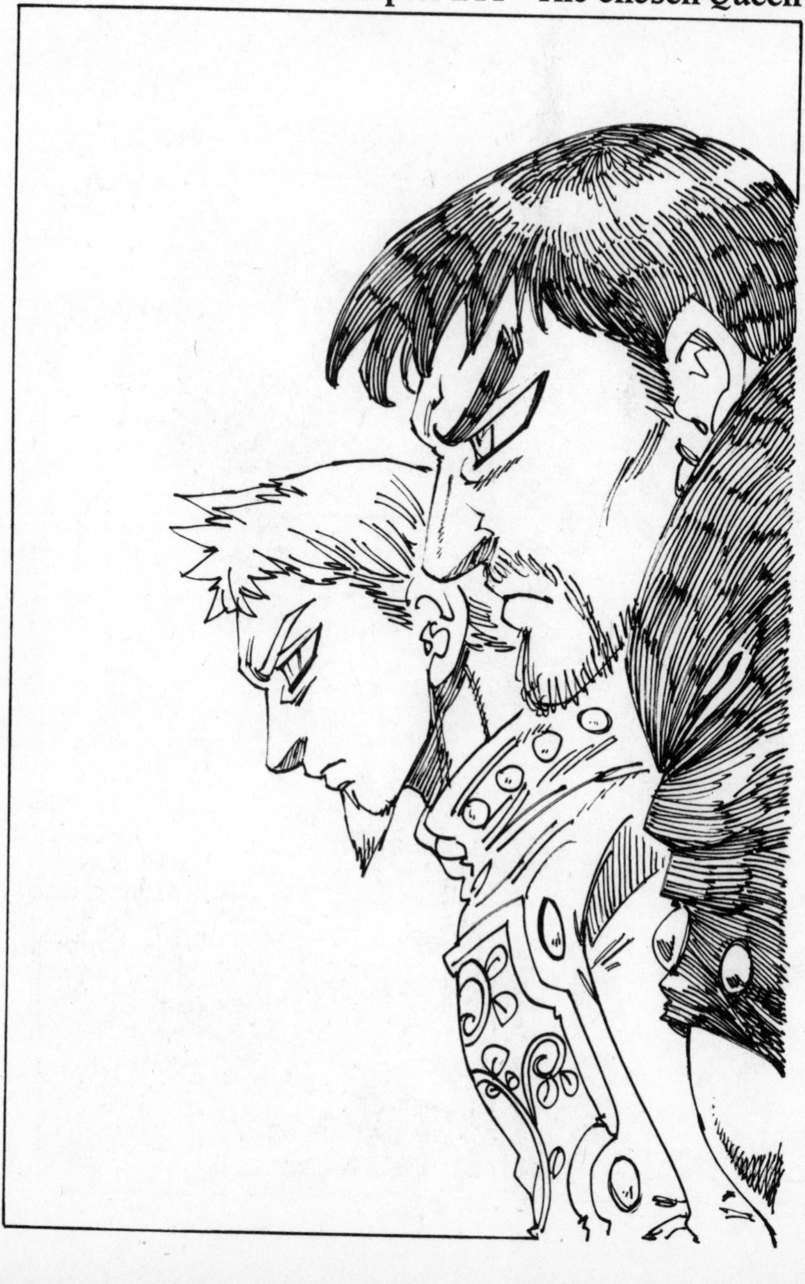

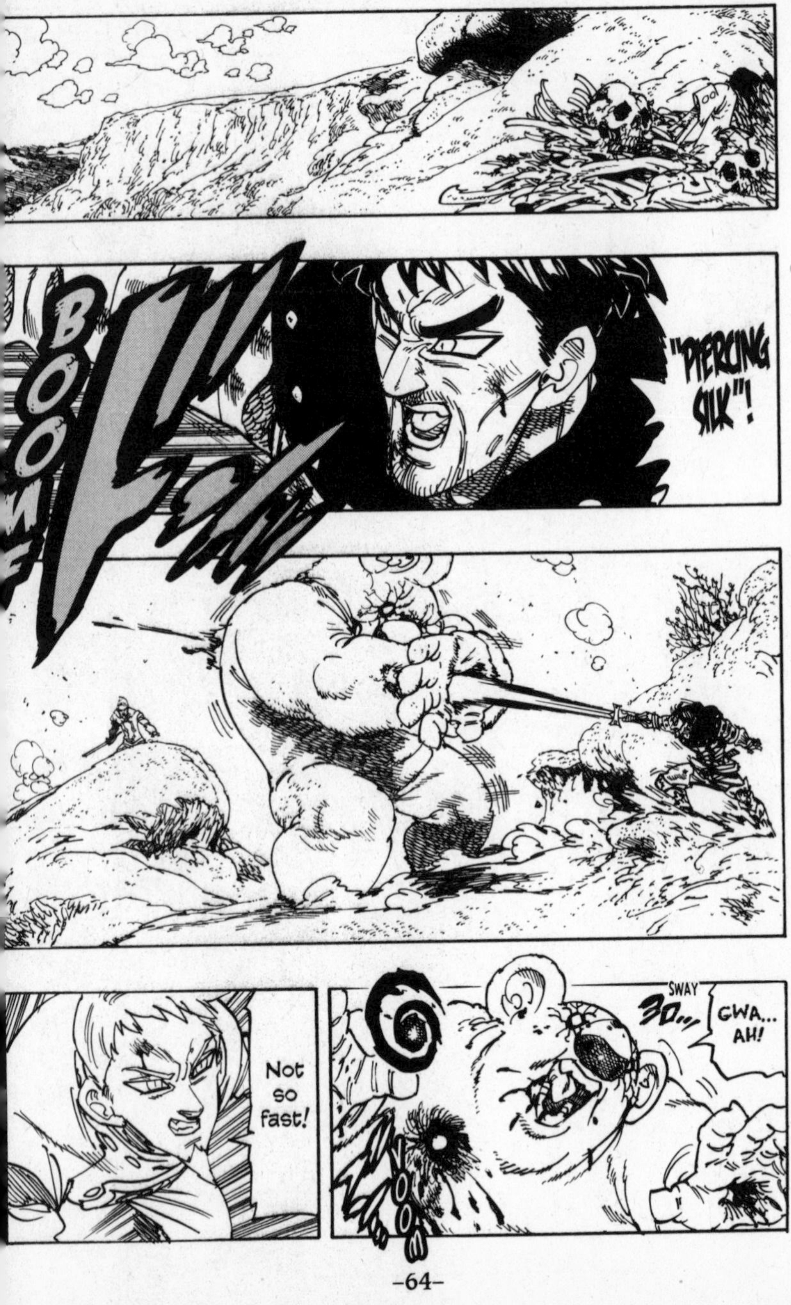
"PIERCING SILK"!
BOOOMF
SWAY
GWA... AH!
VOOOM
Not so fast!

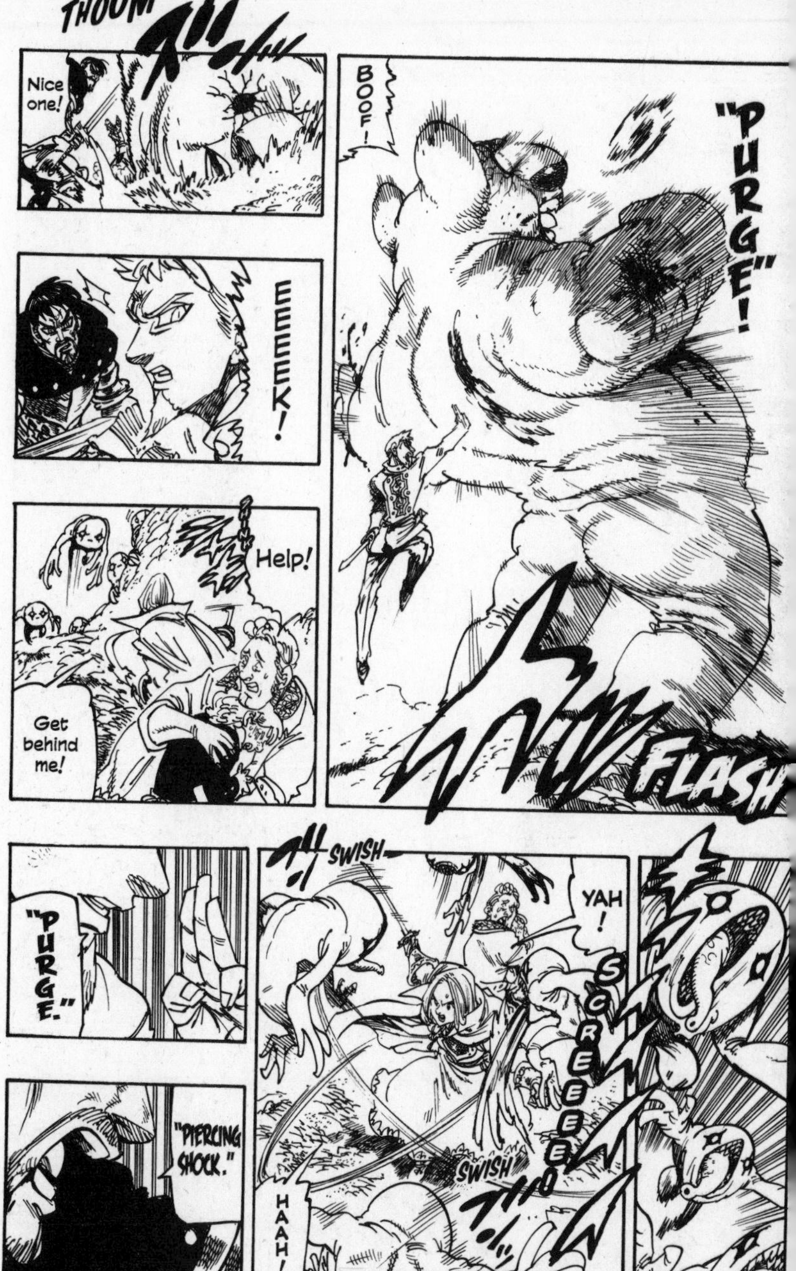
BOOF!
"PURGE"!
FLASH
THOOM
Nice one!
EEEEK!
Help!
Get behind me!
SCREEEEEE!
SWISH
YAH!
SWISH
HAAH!
"PURGE."
"PIERCING SHOCK."

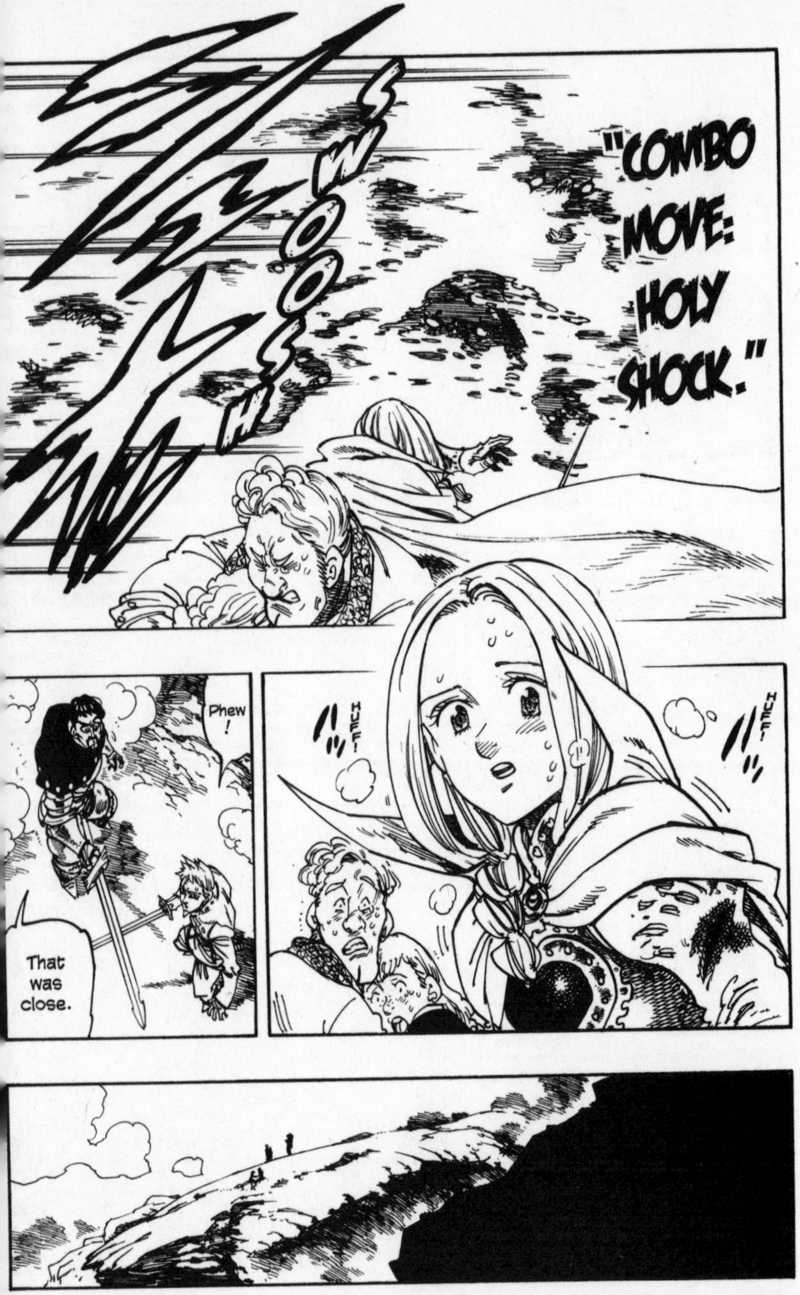
SWOOSH
"COMBO MOVE: HOLY SHOCK."
HUFF!
HUFF!
Phew!
That was close.

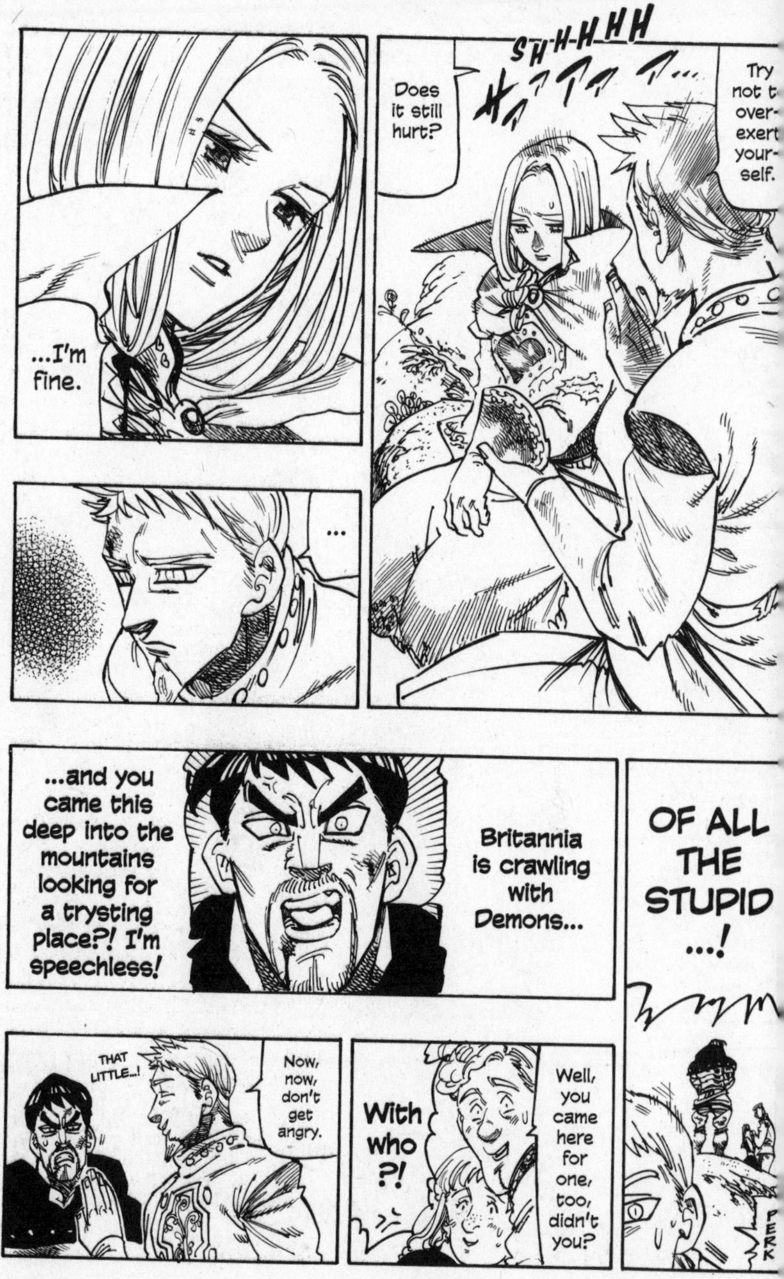
Try not t over-exert your-self.
SH-H-H-H-H
Does it still hurt?
...I'm fine.
...
OF ALL THE STUPID ...!
Britannia is crawling with Demons...
...and you came this deep into the mountains looking for a trysting place?! I'm speechless!
PERK
Well, you came here for one, too, didn't you?
With who?!
Now, now, don't get angry.
THAT LITTLE...!

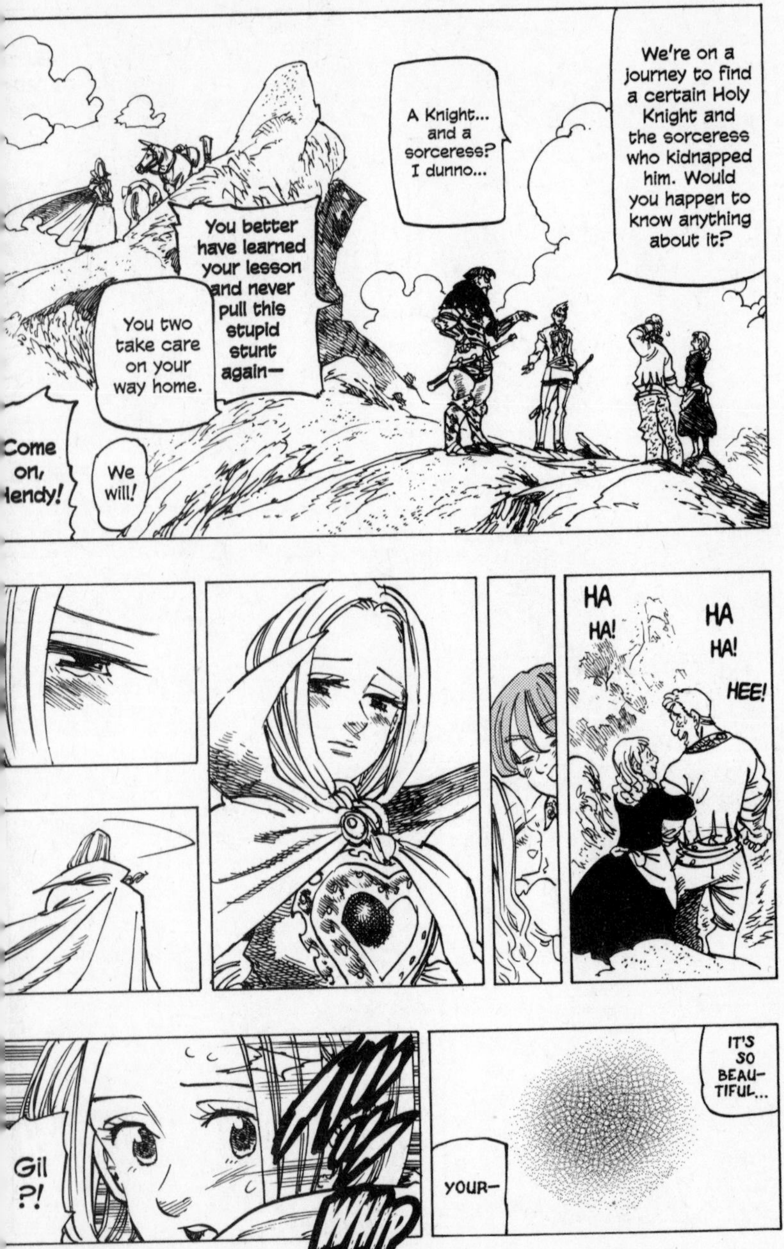
We're on a journey to find a certain Holy Knight and the sorceress who kidnapped him. Would you happen to know anything about it?
A Knight... and a sorceress? I dunno...
You better have learned your lesson and never pull this stupid stunt again—
You two take care on your way home.
We will!
Come on, Hendy!
HA HA!
HA HA!
HEE!
IT'S SO BEAU-TIFUL...
YOUR—
WHIP
Gil ?!

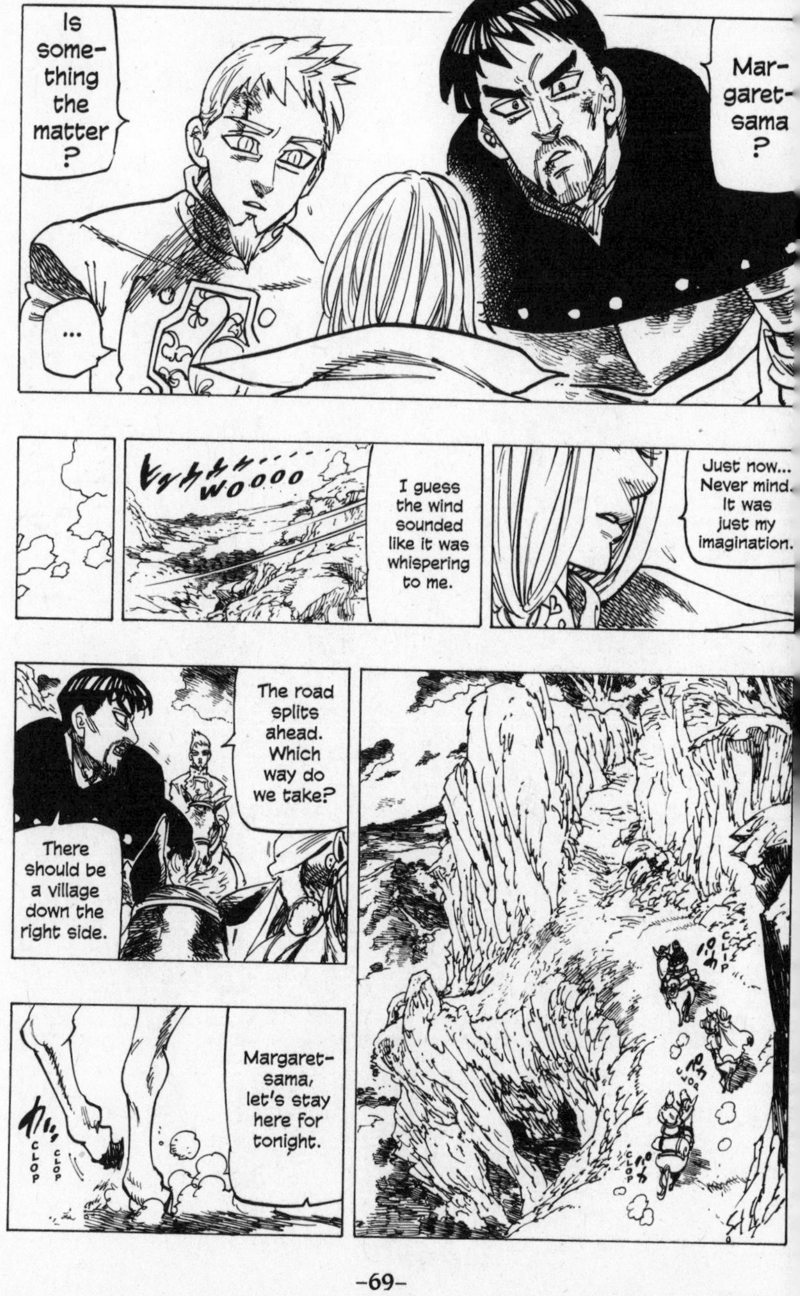

Margaret-sama?
Is something the matter?
...
Just now... Never mind. It was just my imagination.
WOOOO
I guess the wind sounded like it was whispering to me.
CLIP
CLOP
CLOP
The road splits ahead. Which way do we take?
There should be a village down the right side.
Margaret-sama, let's stay here for tonight.
CLOP CLOP

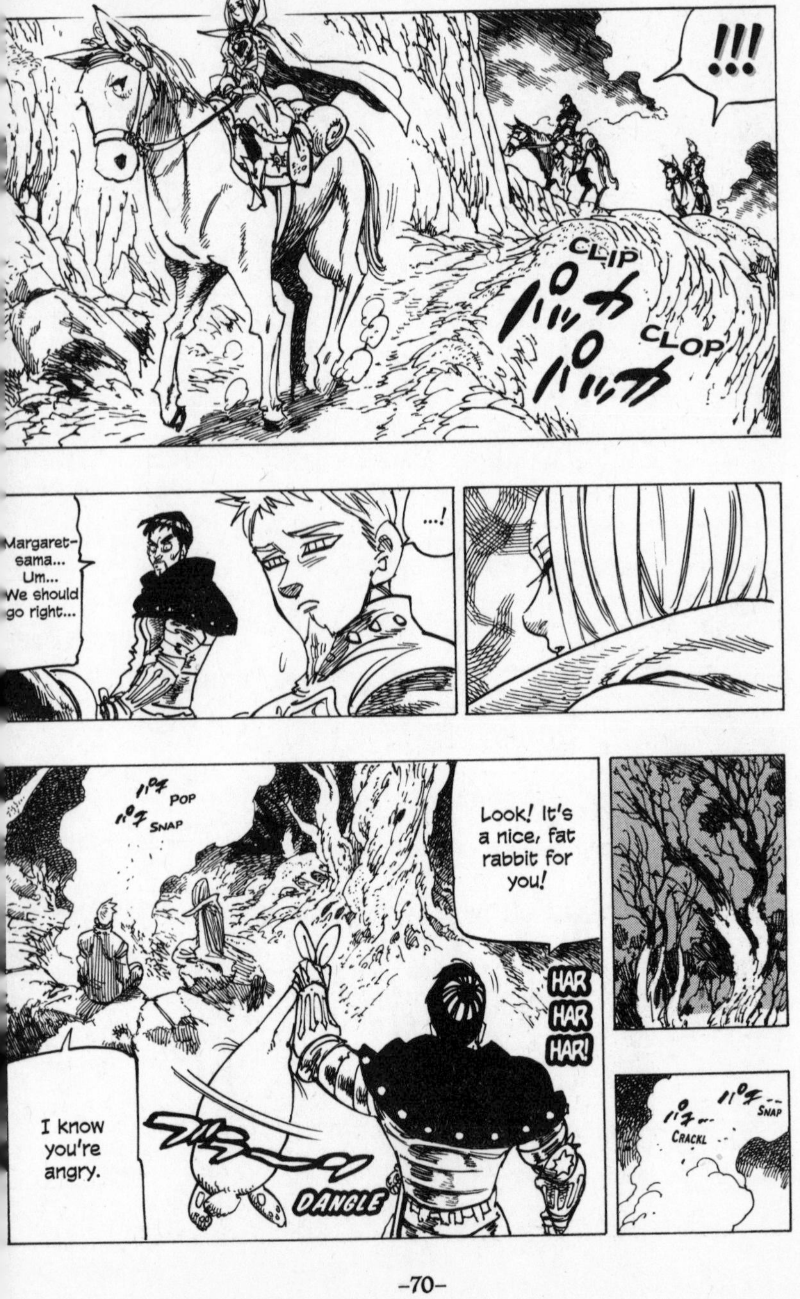
!!!
CLIP
CLOP
...!
Margaret-sama... Um... We should go right...
SNAP
CRACKL
Look! It's a nice, fat rabbit for you!
HAR HAR HAR!
POP
SNAP
DANGLE
I know you're angry.

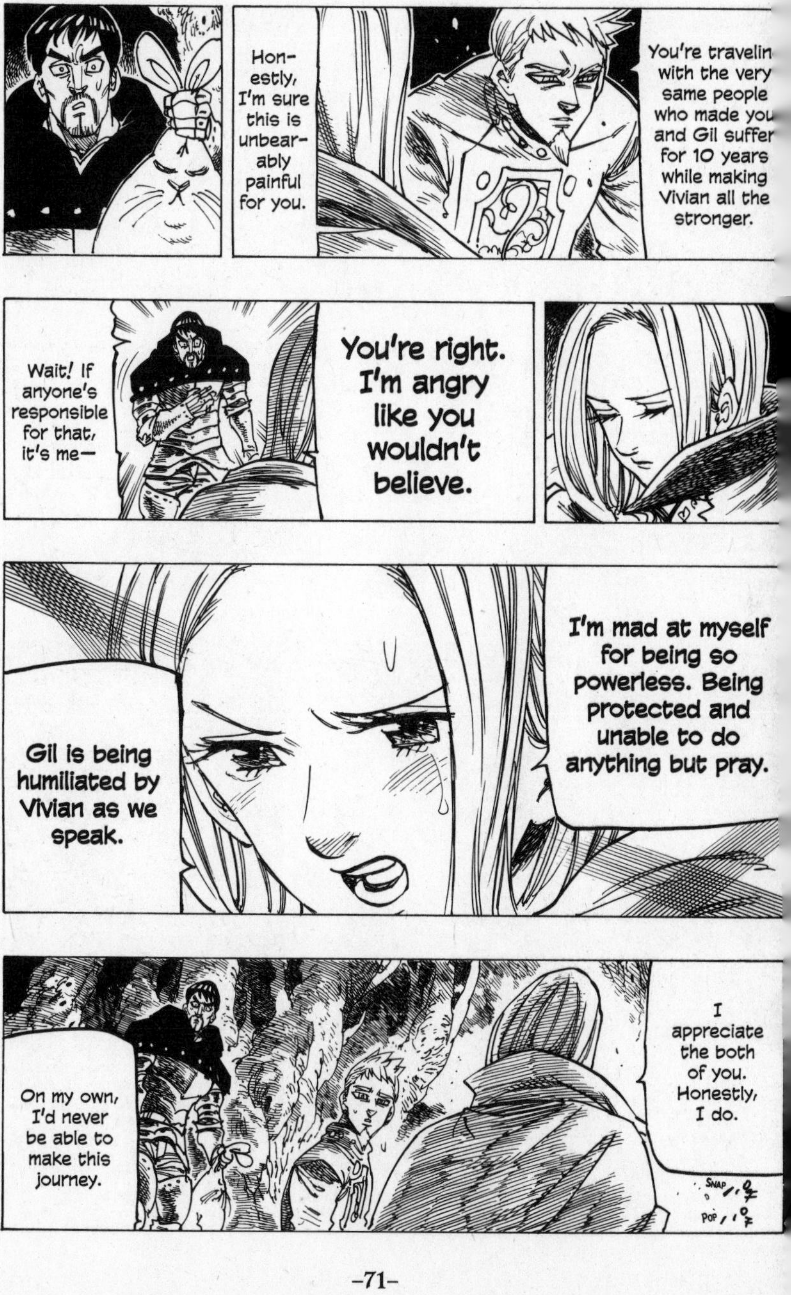
You're travelin with the very same people who made you and Gil suffer for 10 years while making Vivian all the stronger.
Hon-estly, I'm sure this is unbear-ably painful for you.
You're right. I'm angry like you wouldn't believe.
Wait! If anyone's responsible for that, it's me—
I'm mad at myself for being so powerless. Being protected and unable to do anything but pray.
Gil is being humiliated by Vivian as we speak.
I appreciate the both of you. Honestly, I do.
SNAP
POP
On my own, I'd never be able to make this journey.

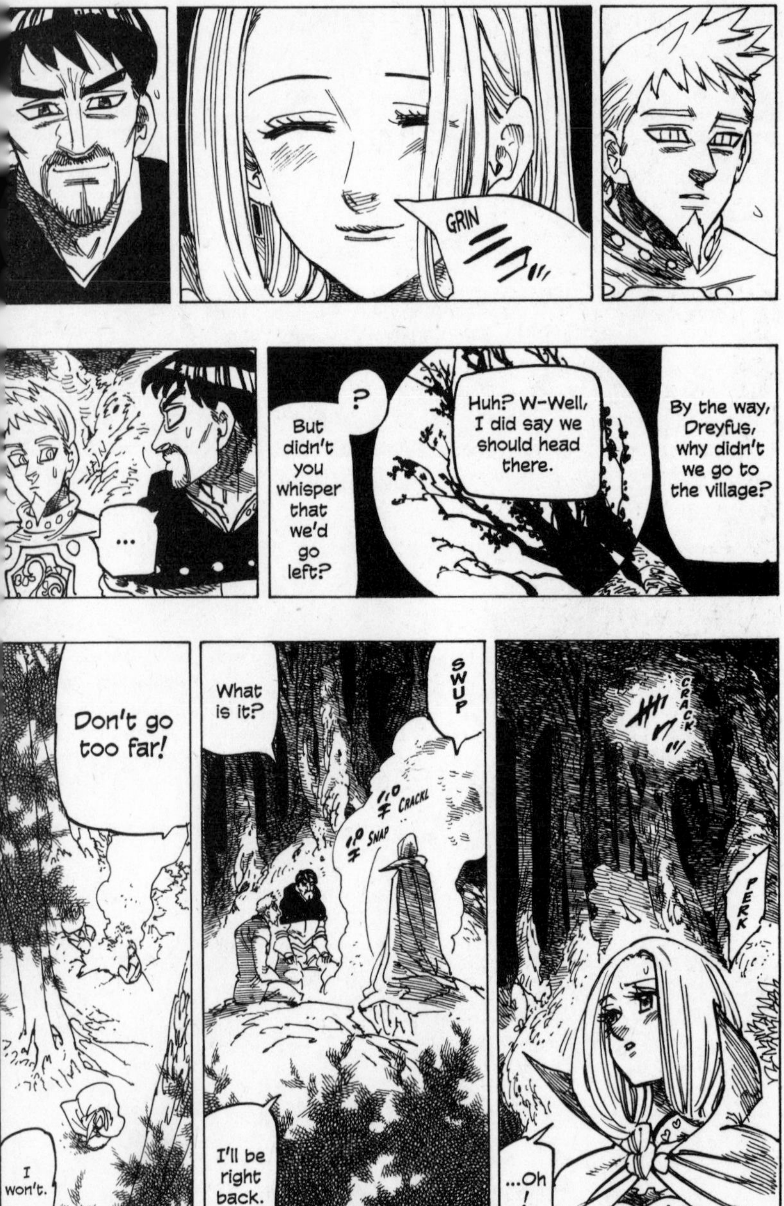
GRIN
By the way, Dreyfus, why didn't we go to the village?
Huh? W-Well, I did say we should head there.
?
But didn't you whisper that we'd go left?
...
CRACK
PERK
...Oh !
SWUP
What is it?
CRACKL
SNAP
I'll be right back.
Don't go too far!
I won't.

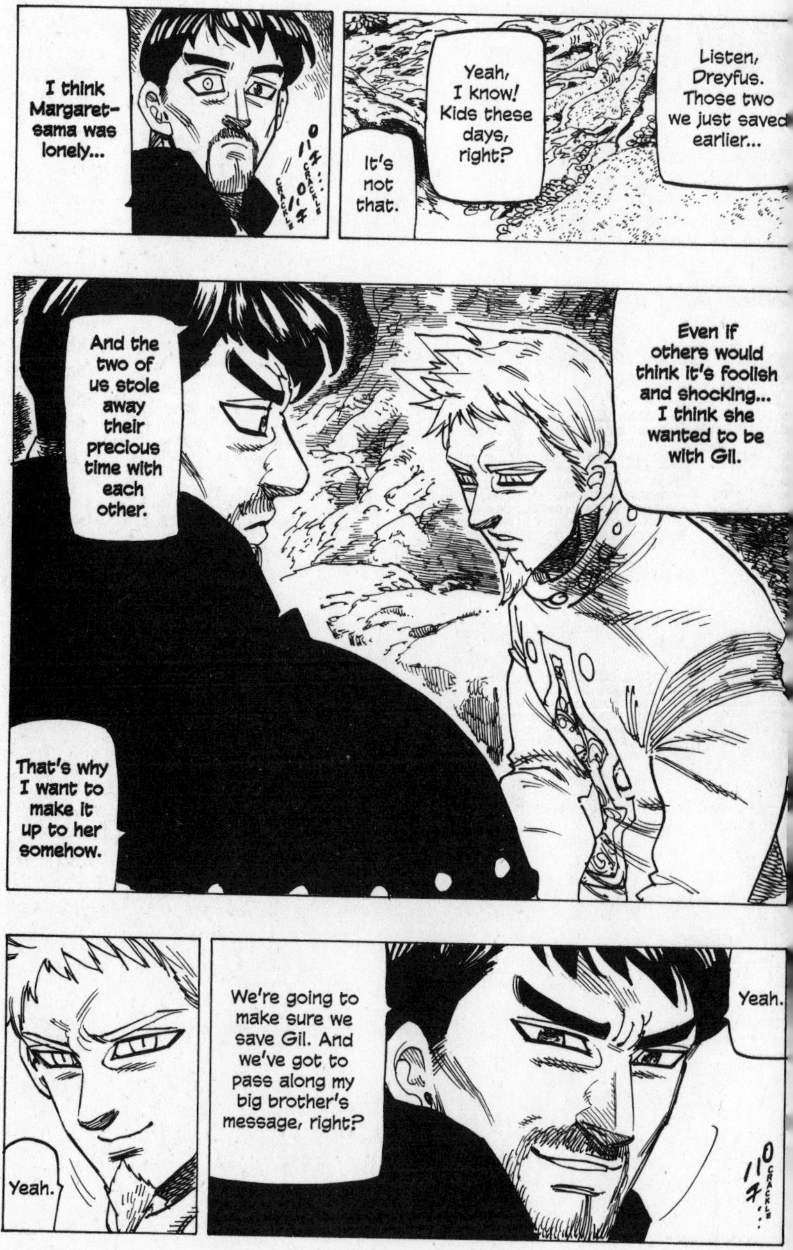
Listen, Dreyfus. Those two we just saved earlier...
Yeah, I know! Kids these days, right?
It's not that.
I think Margaret-sama was lonely...
CRACKLE
Even if others would think it's foolish and shocking... I think she wanted to be with Gil.
And the two of us stole away their precious time with each other.
That's why I want to make it up to her somehow.
Yeah.
We're going to make sure we save Gil. And we've got to pass along my big brother's message, right?
CRACKLE
Yeah.

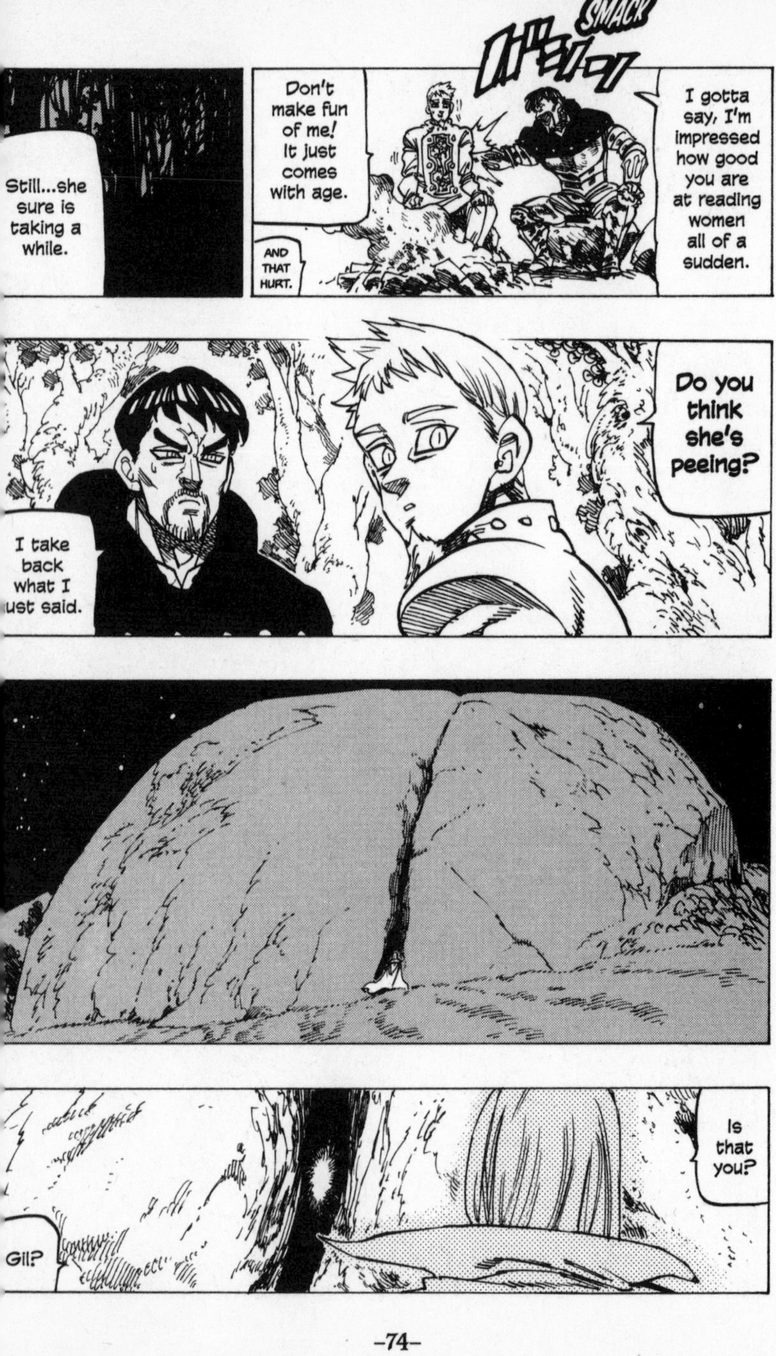
SMACK
I gotta say, I'm impressed how good you are at reading women all of a sudden.
Don't make fun of me! It just comes with age.
AND THAT HURT.
Still...she sure is taking a while.
Do you think she's peeing?
I take back what I ust said.
Is that you?
Gil?

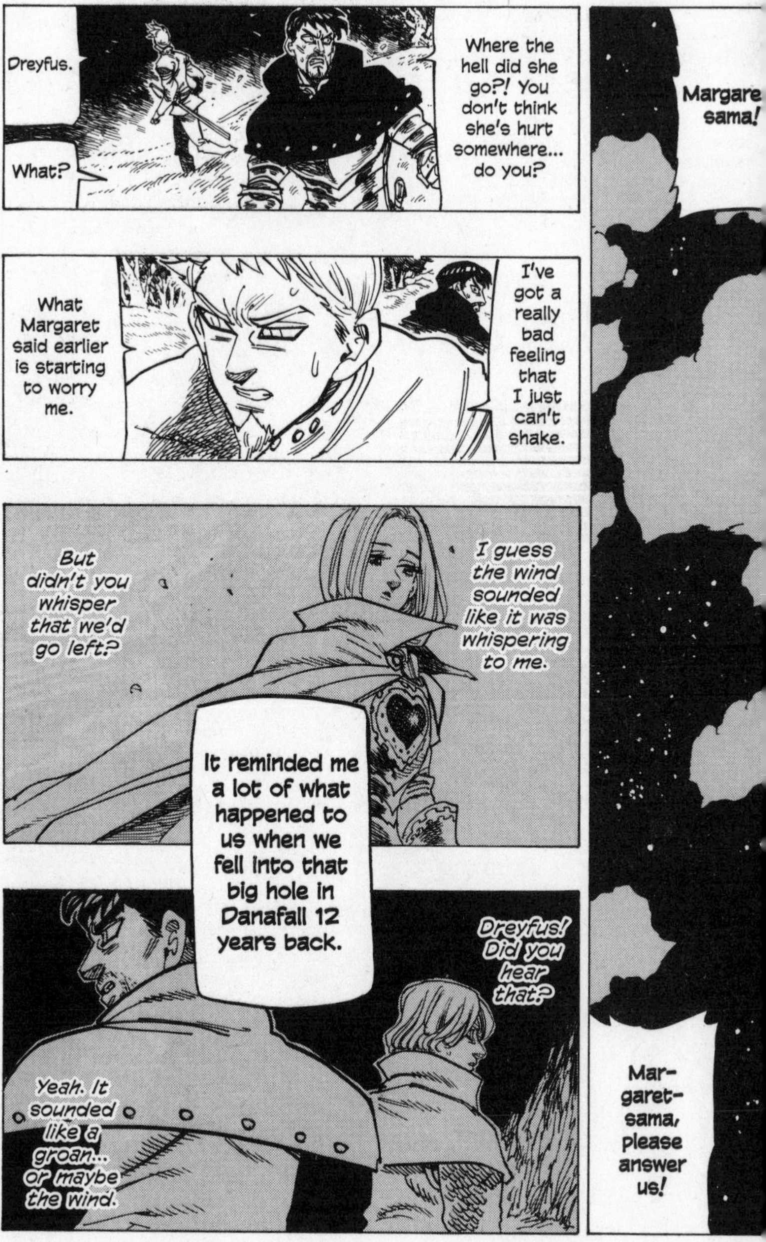
Margare sama!
Mar-garet-sama, please answer us!
Where the hell did she go?! You don't think she's hurt somewhere... do you?
Dreyfus.
What?
I've got a really bad feeling that I just can't shake.
What Margaret said earlier is starting to worry me.
I guess the wind sounded like it was whispering to me.
But didn't you whisper that we'd go left?
It reminded me a lot of what happened to us when we fell into that big hole in Danafall 12 years back.
Dreyfus! Did you hear that?
Yeah. It sounded like a groan... or maybe the wind.

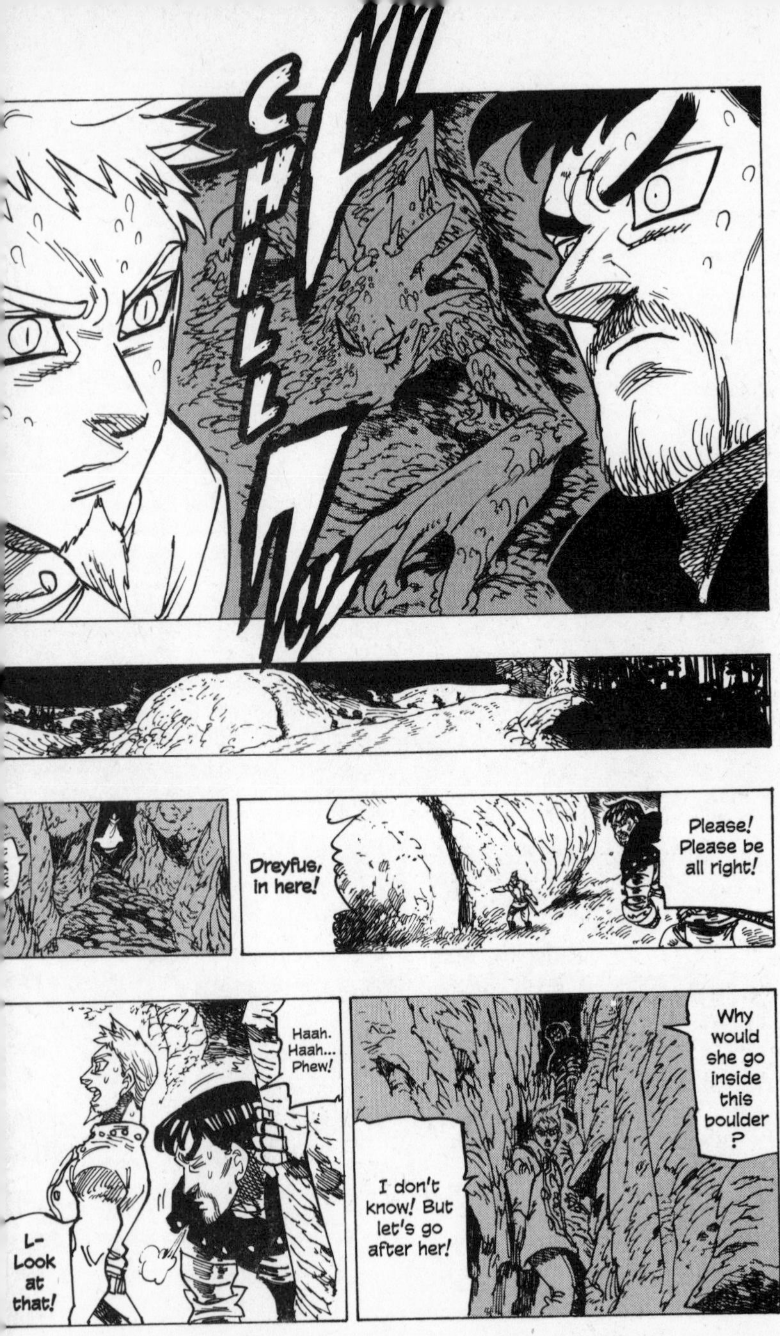
CHILL
Please! Please be all right!
Dreyfus, in here!
Why would she go inside this boulder?
I don't know! But let's go after her!
Haah. Haah... Phew!
L- Look at that!

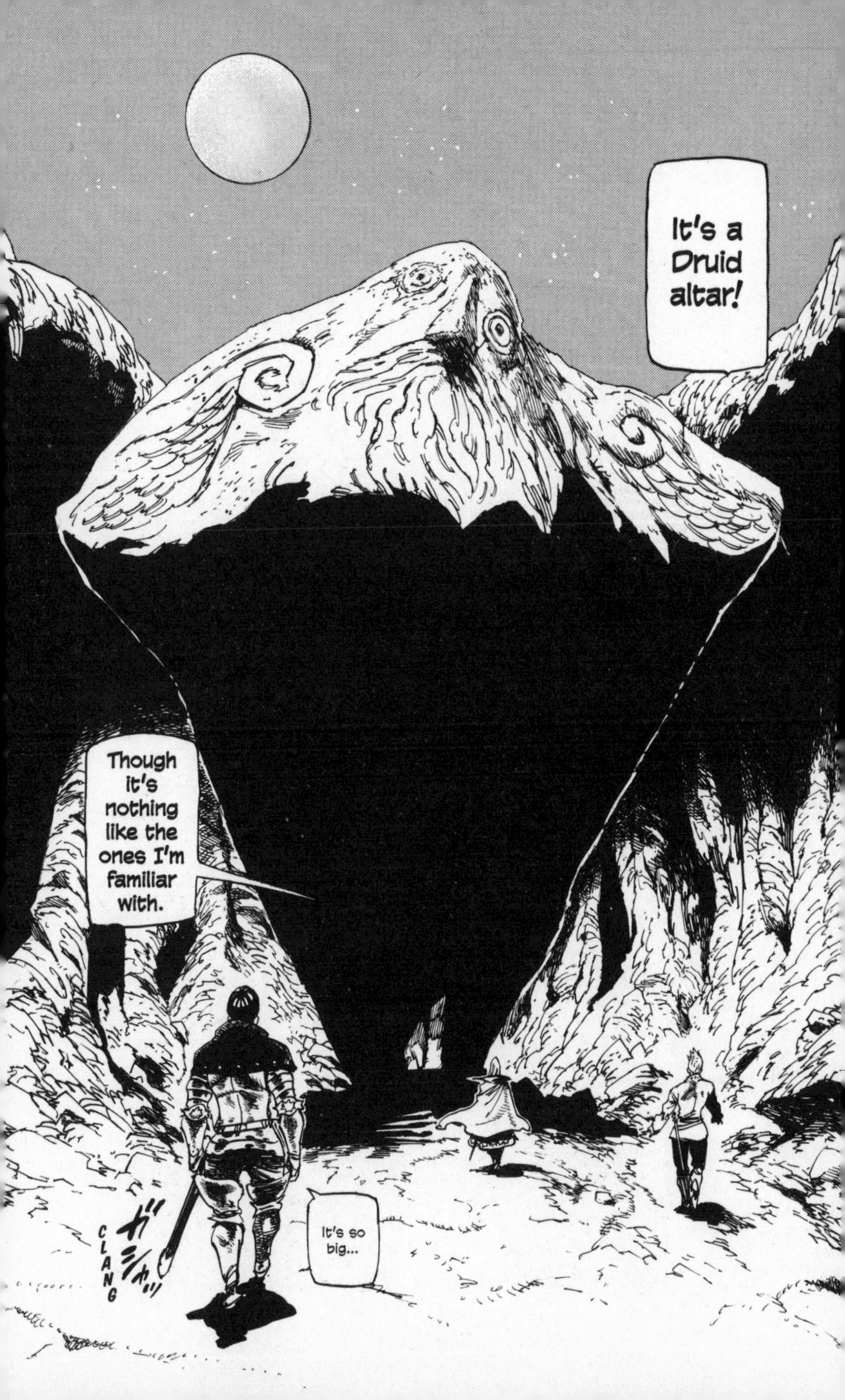
It's a Druid altar!
Though it's nothing like the ones I'm familiar with.
It's so big...
CLANG

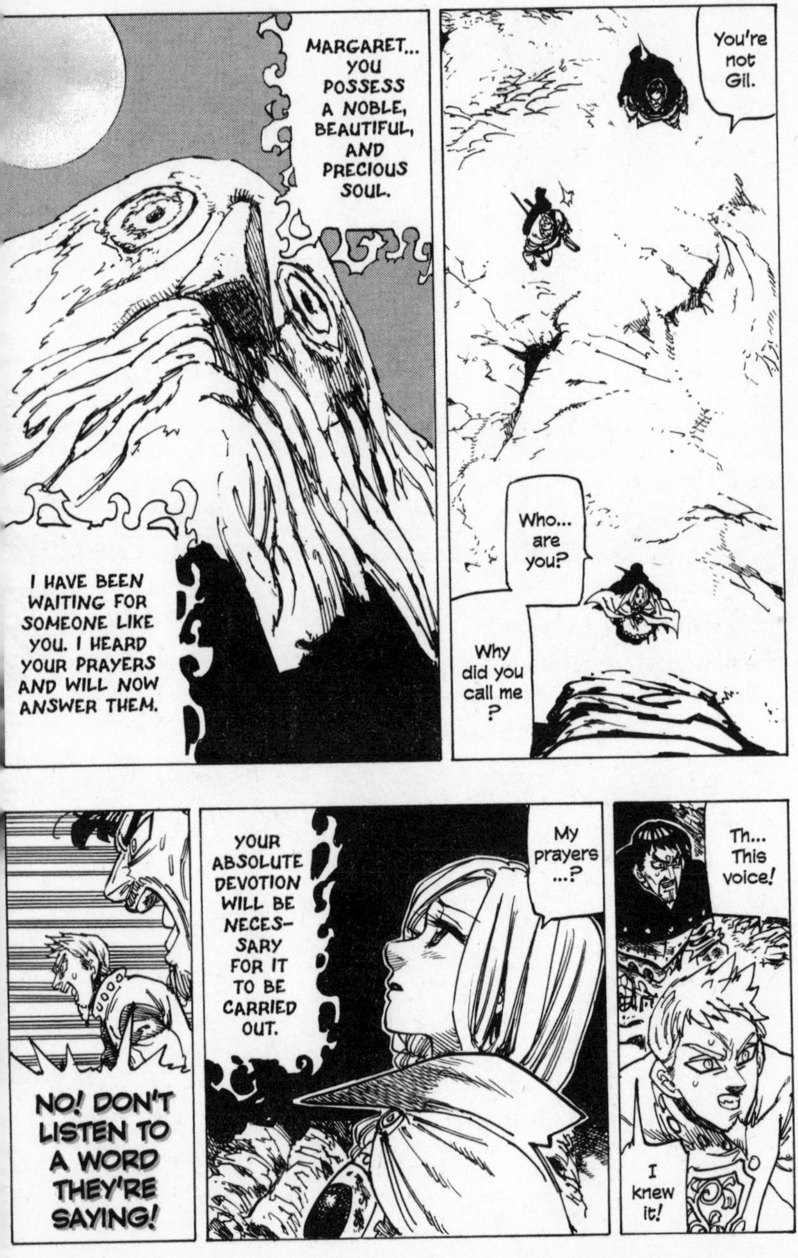
You're not Gil.
Who... are you?
Why did you call me ?
MARGARET... YOU POSSESS A NOBLE, BEAUTIFUL, AND PRECIOUS SOUL.
I HAVE BEEN WAITING FOR SOMEONE LIKE YOU. I HEARD YOUR PRAYERS AND WILL NOW ANSWER THEM.
Th... This voice!
I knew it!
My prayers ...?
YOUR ABSOLUTE DEVOTION WILL BE NECES-SARY FOR IT TO BE CARRIED OUT.
NO! DON'T LISTEN TO A WORD THEY'RE SAYING!

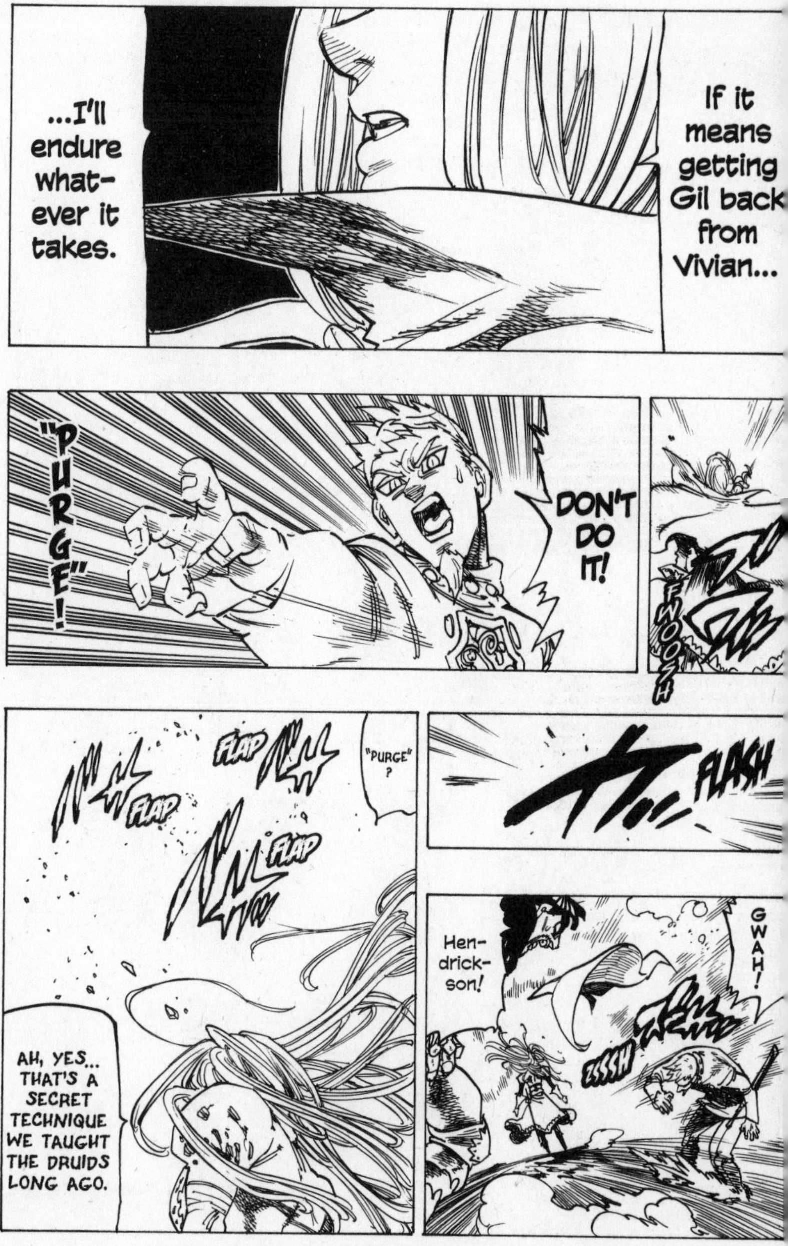
If it means getting Gil back from Vivian...
...I'll endure whatever it takes.
FWOOSH
DON'T DO IT!
"PURGE"!
FLASH
GWAH!
Hendrickson!
ZSSSH
"PURGE" ?
FLAP
FLAP
FLAP
AH, YES... THAT'S A SECRET TECHNIQUE WE TAUGHT THE DRUIDS LONG AGO.

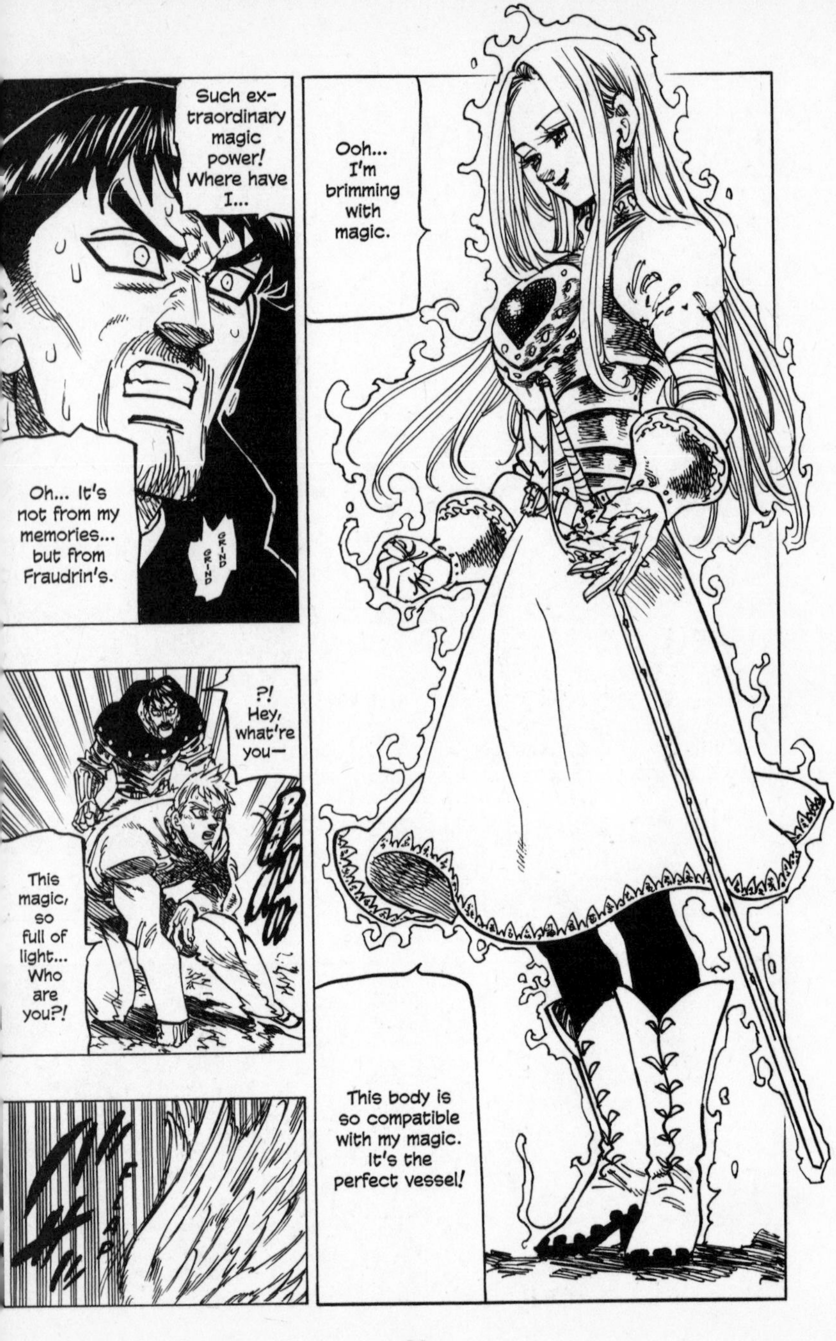
Ooh... I'm brimming with magic.
This body is so compatible with my magic. It's the perfect vessel!
Such extraordinary magic power! Where have I...
Oh... It's not from my memories... but from Fraudrin's.
GRIND GRIND
?! Hey, what're you—
This magic, so full of light... Who are you?!

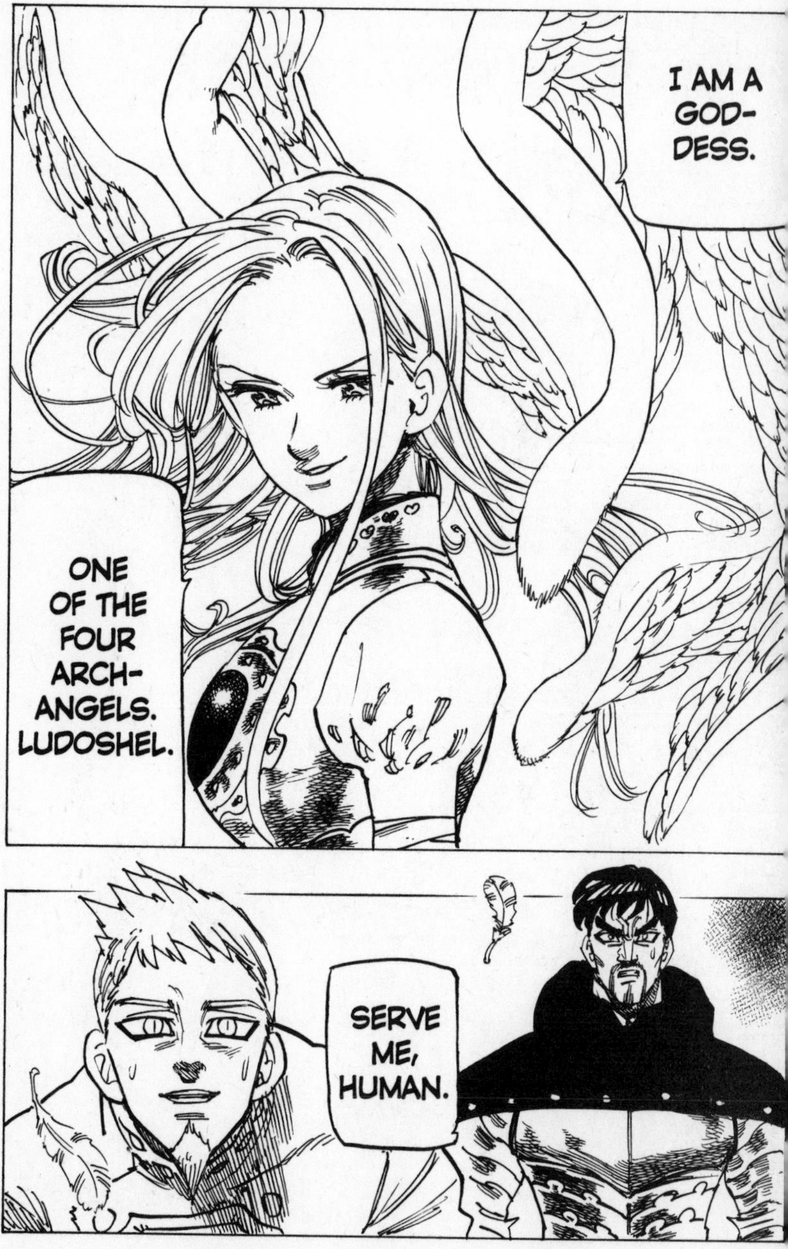
I AM A GOD-DESS.
ONE OF THE FOUR ARCH-ANGELS. LUDOSHEL.
SERVE ME, HUMAN.

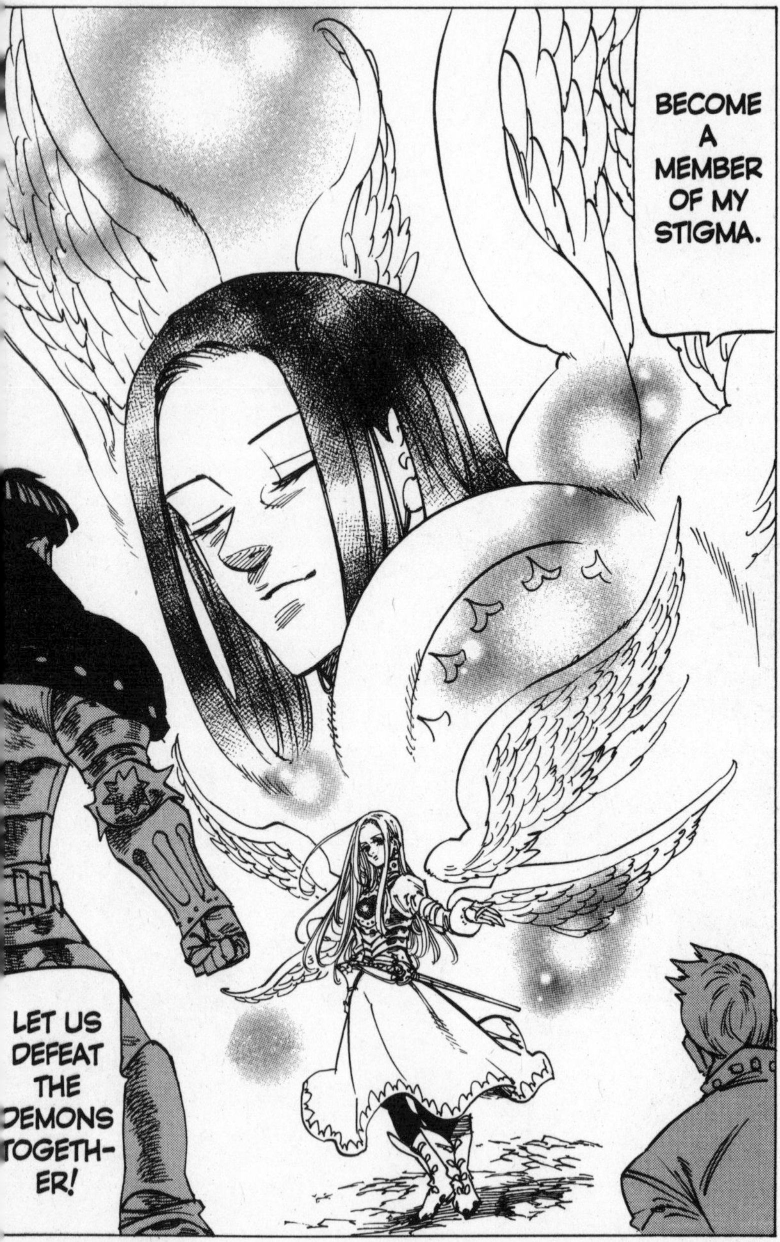
BECOME A MEMBER OF MY STIGMA.
LET US DEFEAT THE DEMONS TOGETH-ER!

Chapter 245 - When The Saints Go Marching In

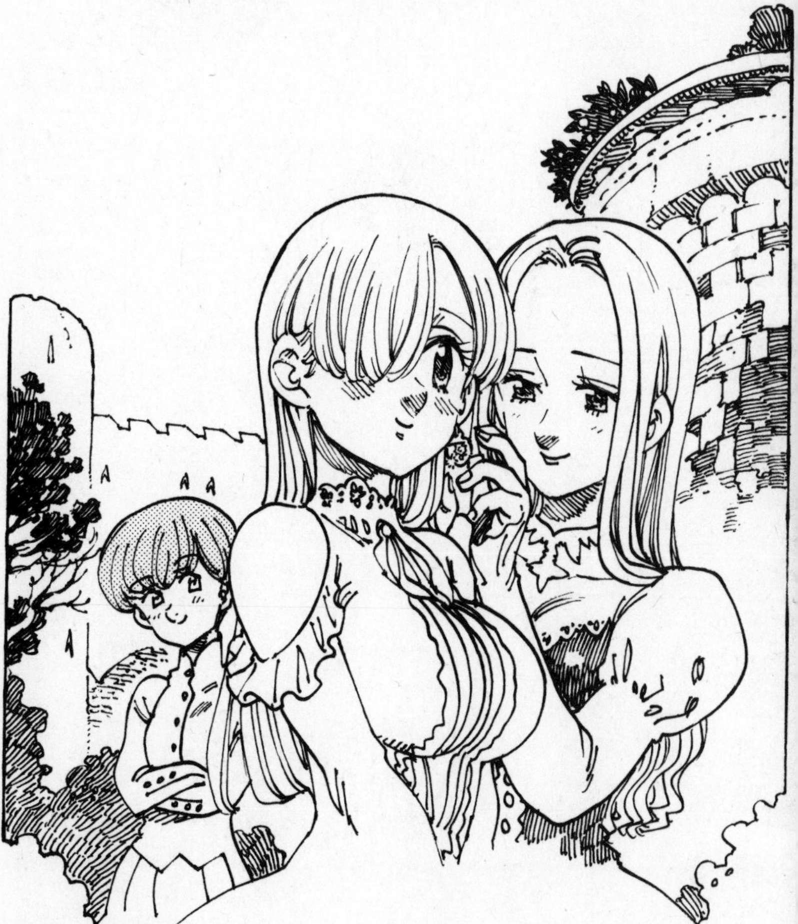

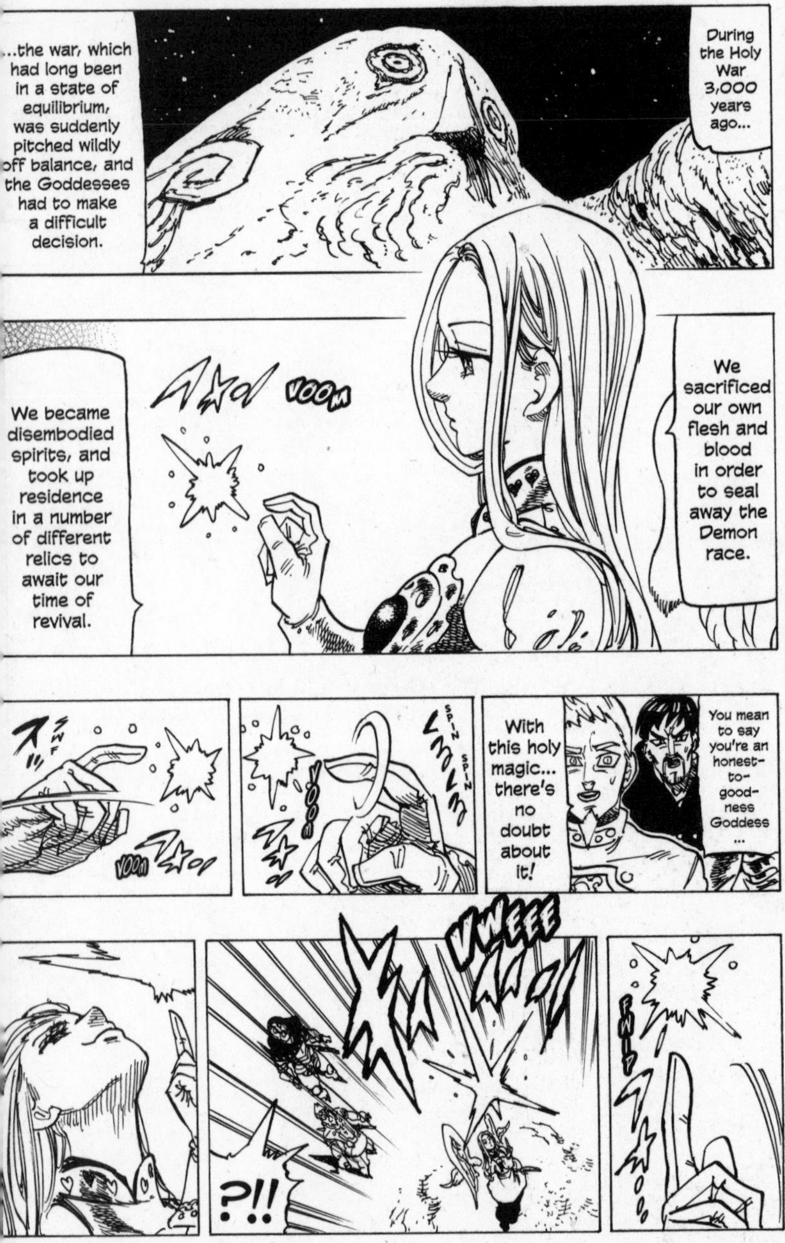
During the Holy War 3,000 years ago...
...the war, which had long been in a state of equilibrium, was suddenly pitched wildly off balance, and the Goddesses had to make a difficult decision.
We sacrificed our own flesh and blood in order to seal away the Demon race.
VOOM
We became disembodied spirits, and took up residence in a number of different relics to await our time of revival.
You mean to say you're an honest-to-goodness Goddess ...
With this holy magic... there's no doubt about it!
SPIN SPIN
VOOM
SWF
VOOM
FWIP
VWEEE
?!!

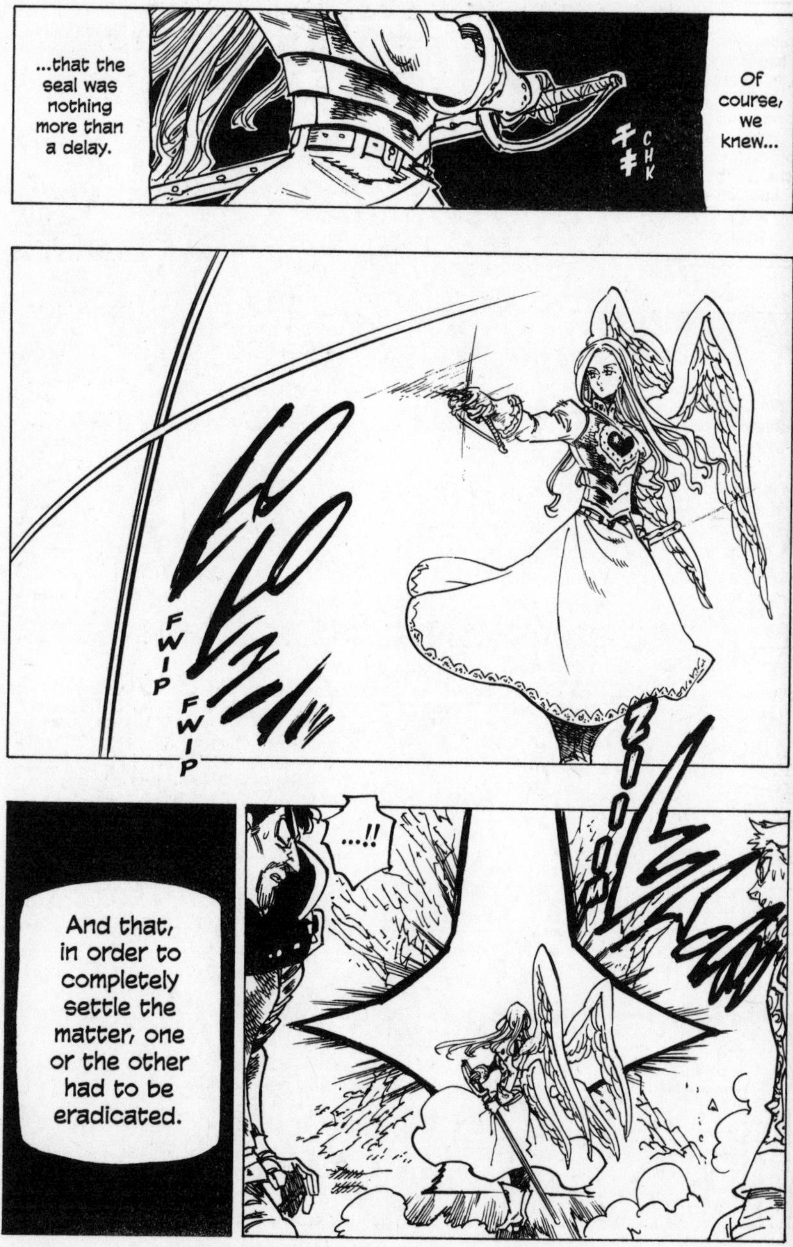
Of course, we knew...
CHK
...that the seal was nothing more than a delay.
FWIP FWIP
...!!
And that, in order to completely settle the matter, one or the other had to be eradicated.

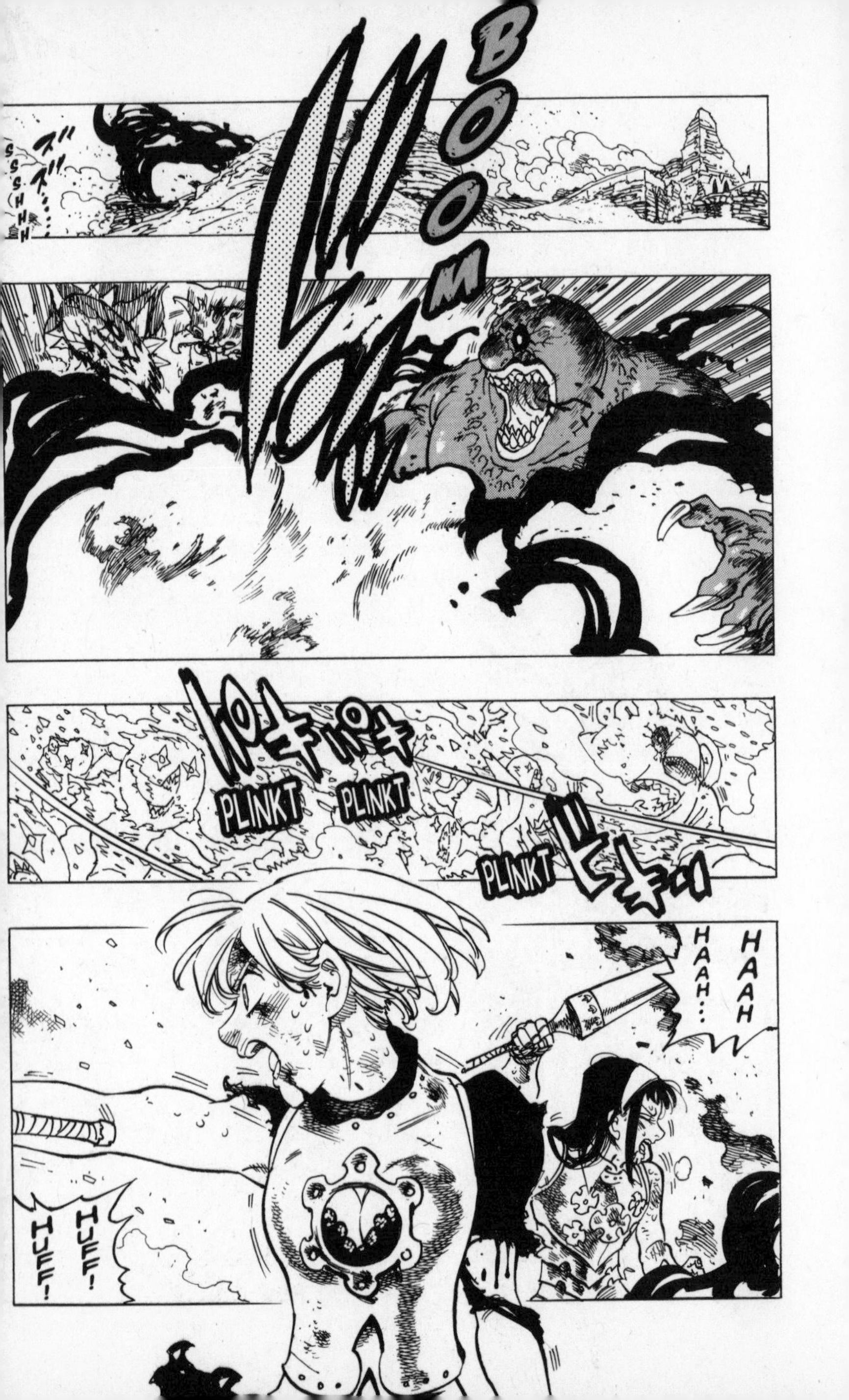
BOOOM
S-S-SHHH
PLINKT
PLINKT
PLINKT
HAAAH
HAAAH...
HUFF!
HUFF!

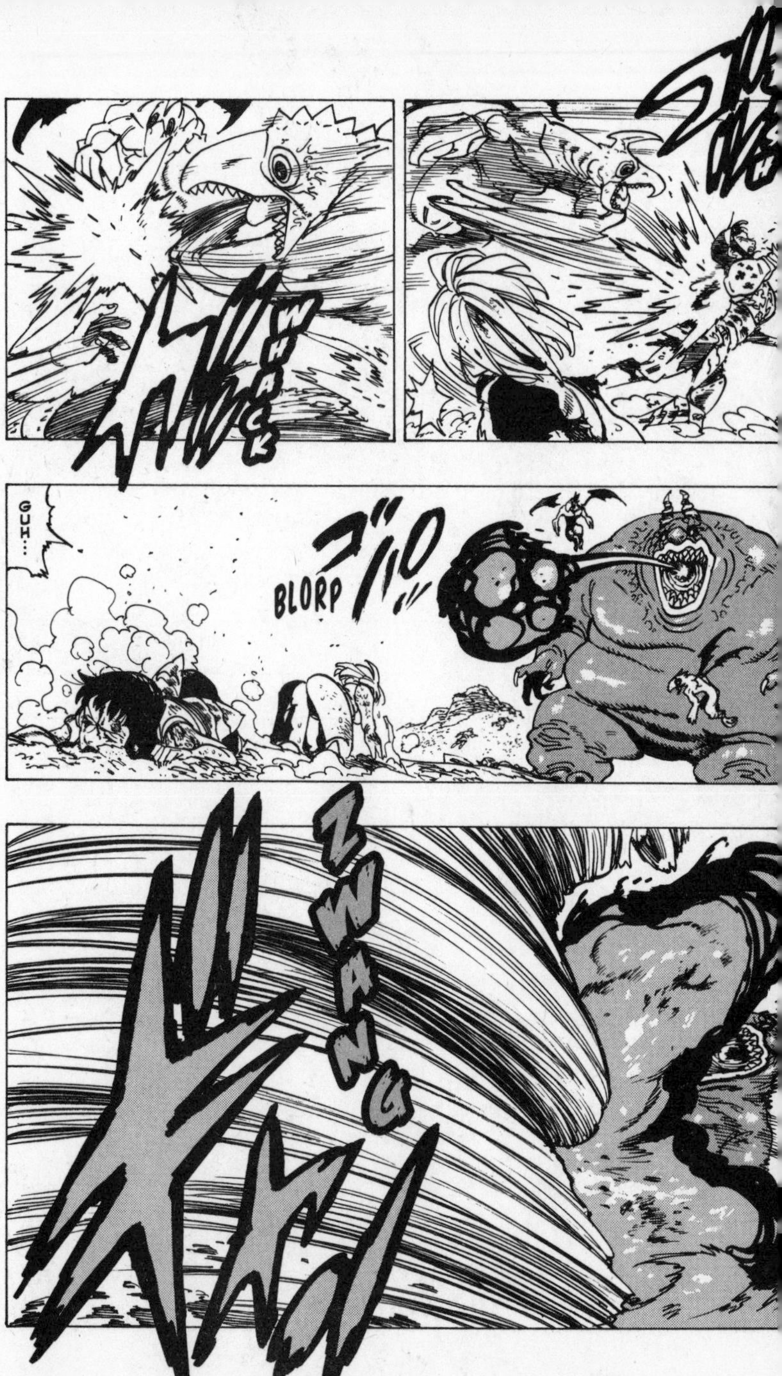
WHACK
BLORP
GUH...
ZWANG

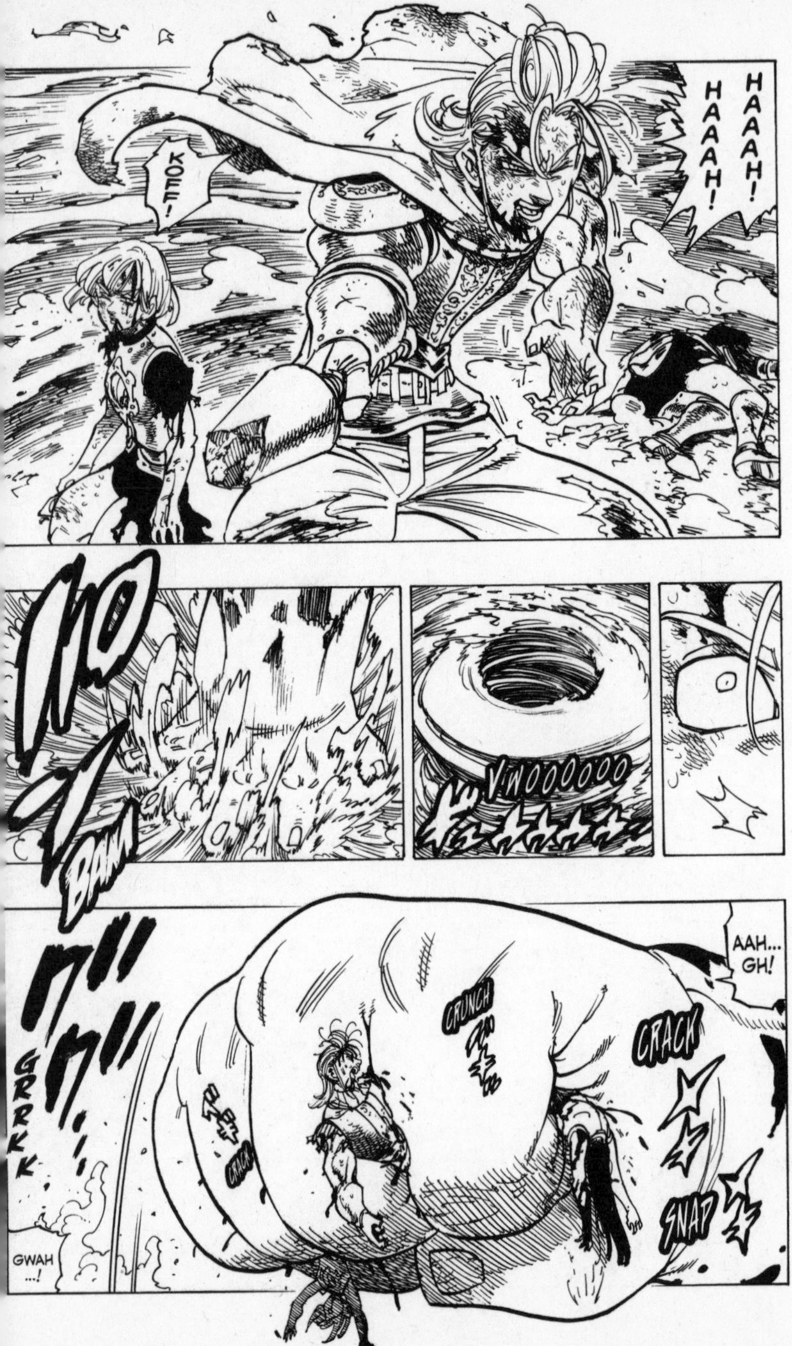
HAAAAH!
HAAAAH!
KOFF!
VWOOOOOO
BAM
AAH... GH!
CRACK
CRUNCH
SNAP
CRACK
GRRRKK
GWAH ...!

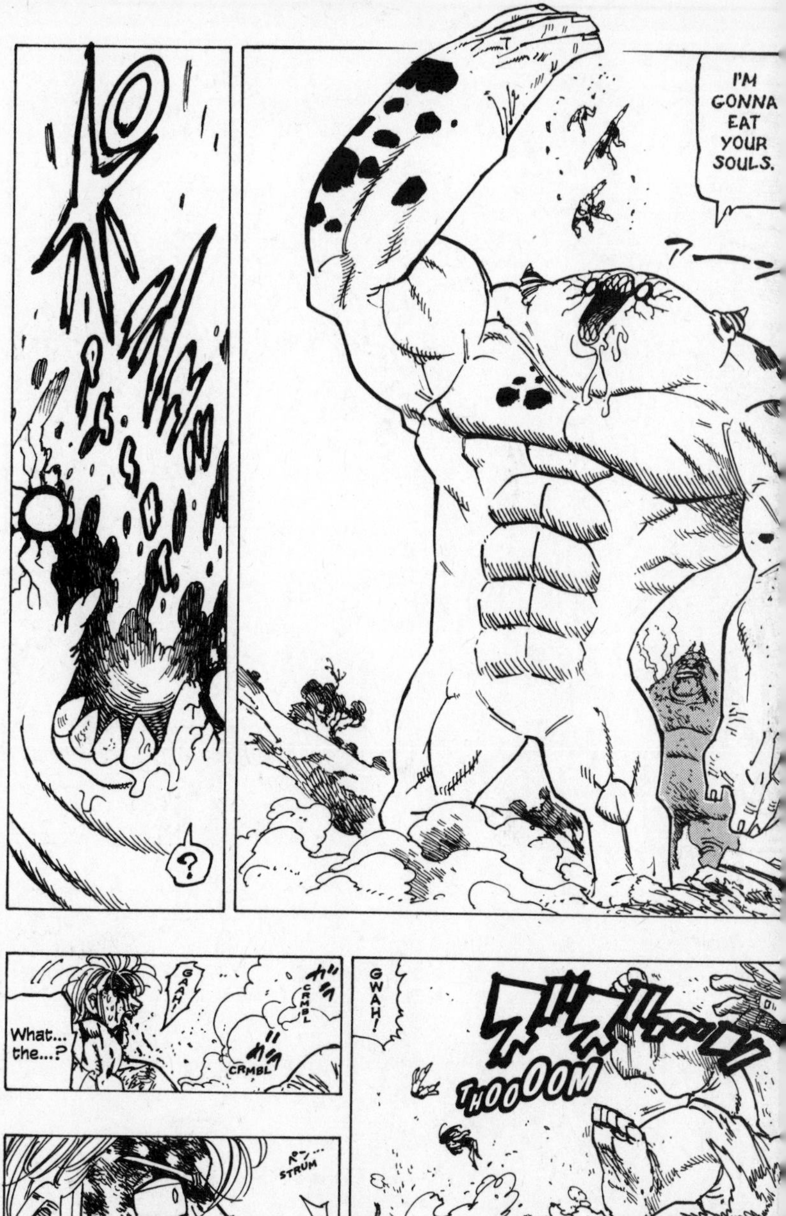
I'M GONNA EAT YOUR SOULS.
?
GWAH!
THOOOOM
GAAH!
CRMBL
CRMBL
What... the...?
STRUM
STRUM
STRUM

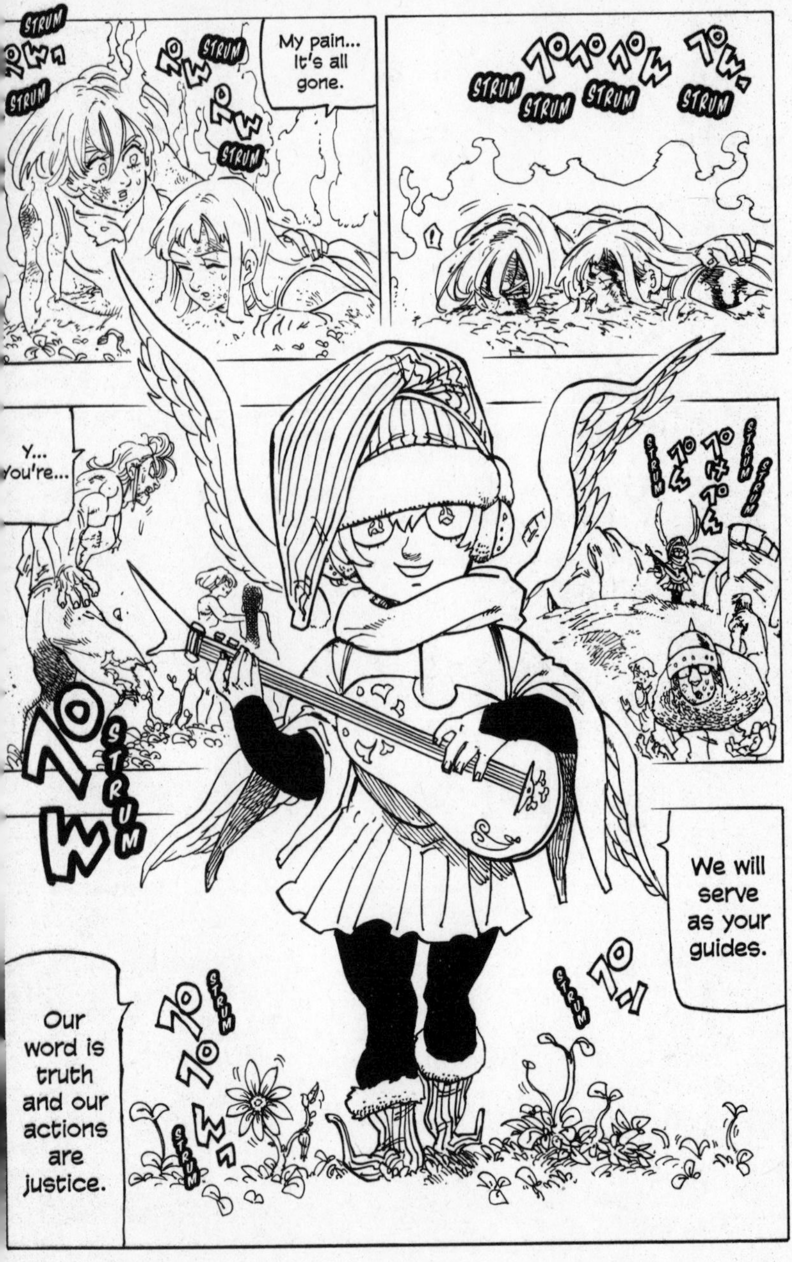
STRUM STRUM STRUM STRUM
!
My pain... It's all gone.
STRUM STRUM STRUM STRUM
STRUM STRUM STRUM
Y... You're...
STRUM
We will serve as your guides.
STRUM
STRUM
Our word is truth and our actions are justice.
STRUM

Follow me, Humans.

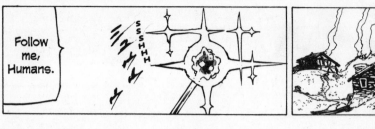

Become a member of my Stigma...

...and join me in crushing the Demons!

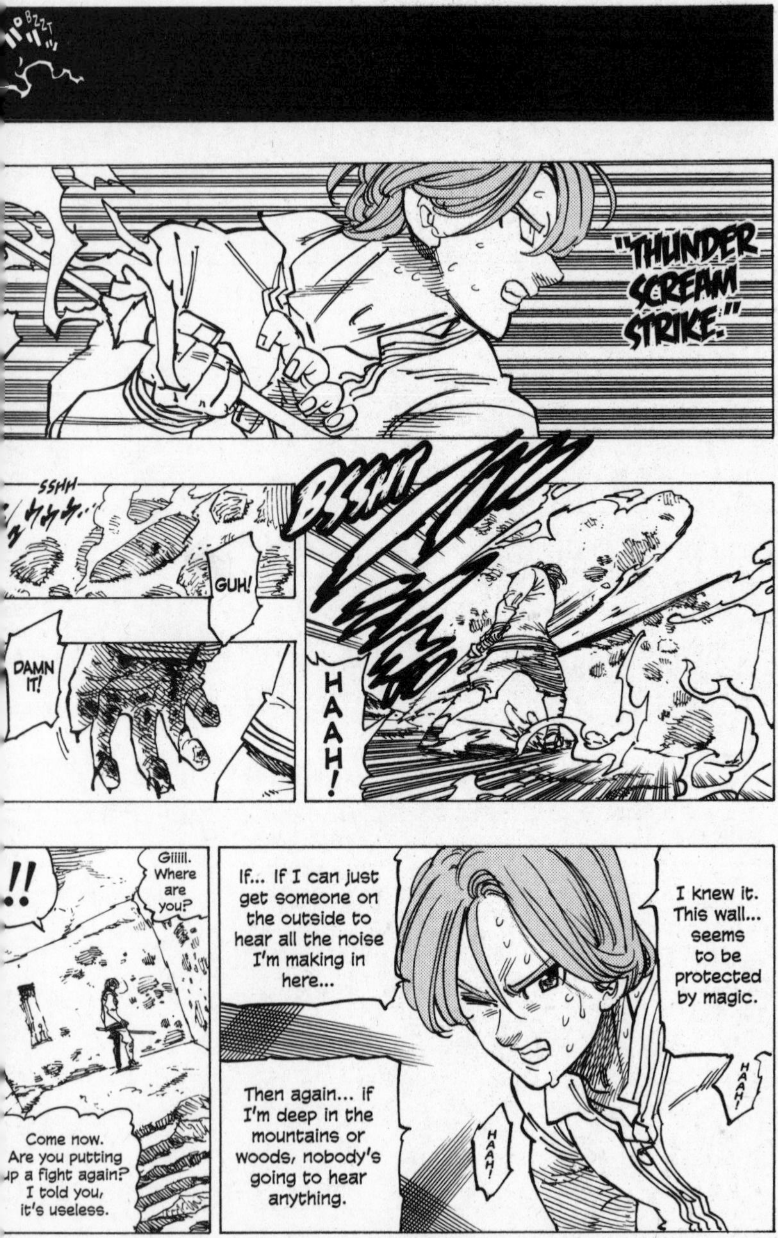
BZZZT
"THUNDER SCREAM STRIKE."
BSSHT
HAAAH!
SSHH
GUH!
DAMN IT!
I knew it. This wall... seems to be protected by magic.
If... If I can just get someone on the outside to hear all the noise I'm making in here...
HAAH!
HAAH!
Then again... if I'm deep in the mountains or woods, nobody's going to hear anything.
Giiiil. Where are you?
!!
Come now. Are you putting up a fight again? I told you, it's useless.

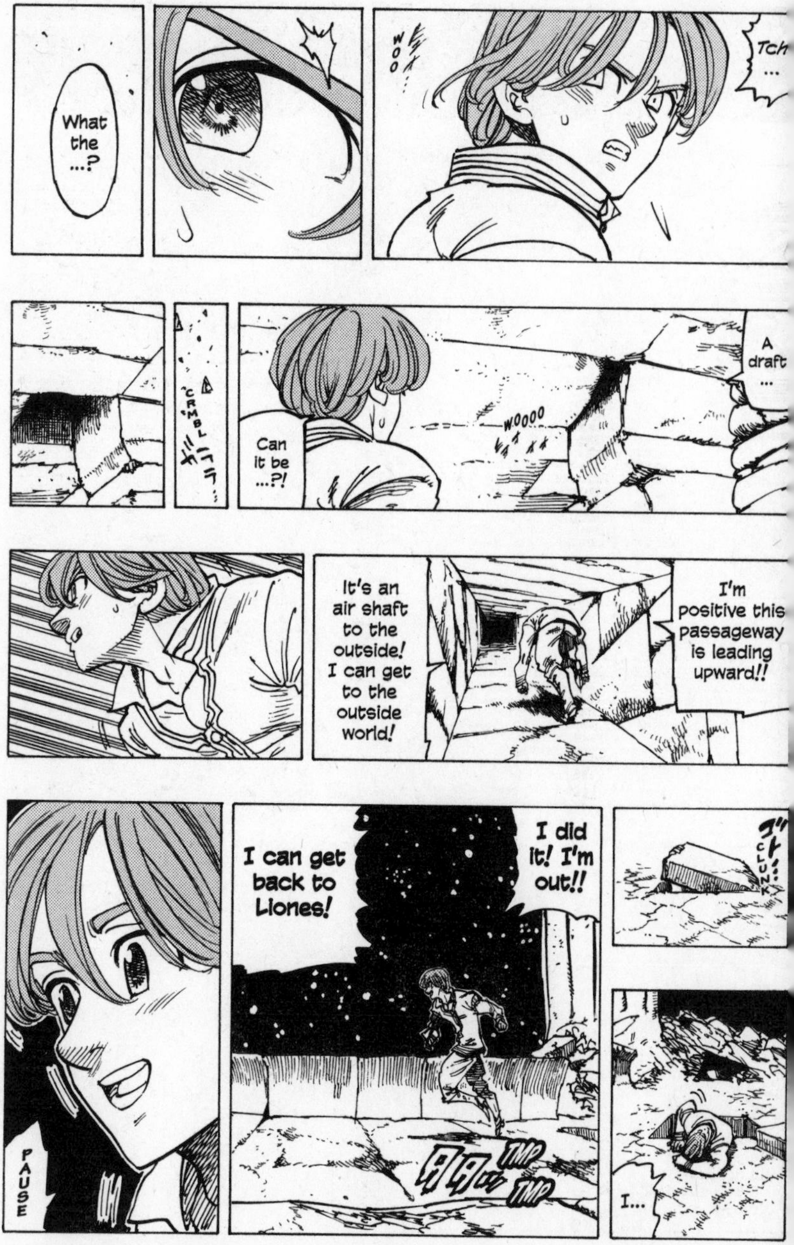

Tch ...
WOOO
What the ...?
A draft ...
WOOOO
Can it be ...?!
CRMBL
I'm positive this passageway is leading upward!!
It's an air shaft to the outside! I can get to the outside world!
CLUNK
I...
I did it! I'm out!!
I can get back to Liones!
TMP TMP
PAUSE

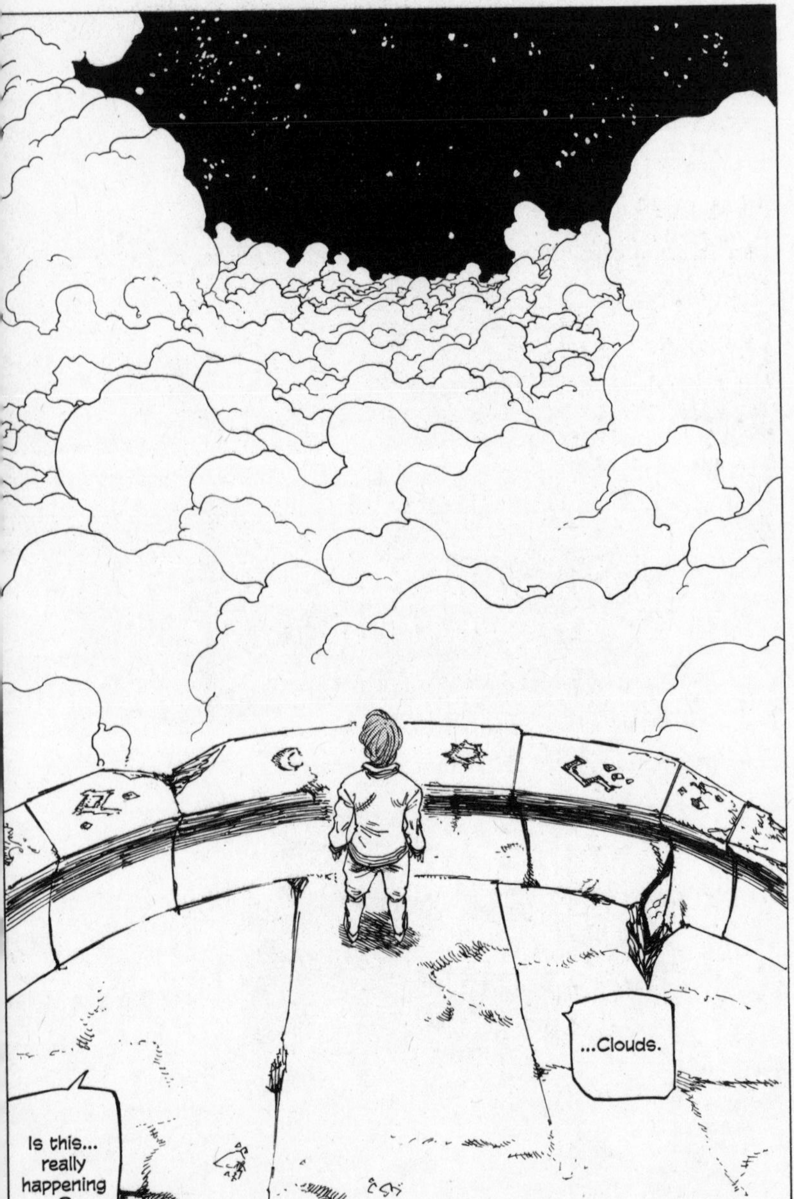
...Clouds.
Is this... really happening ?

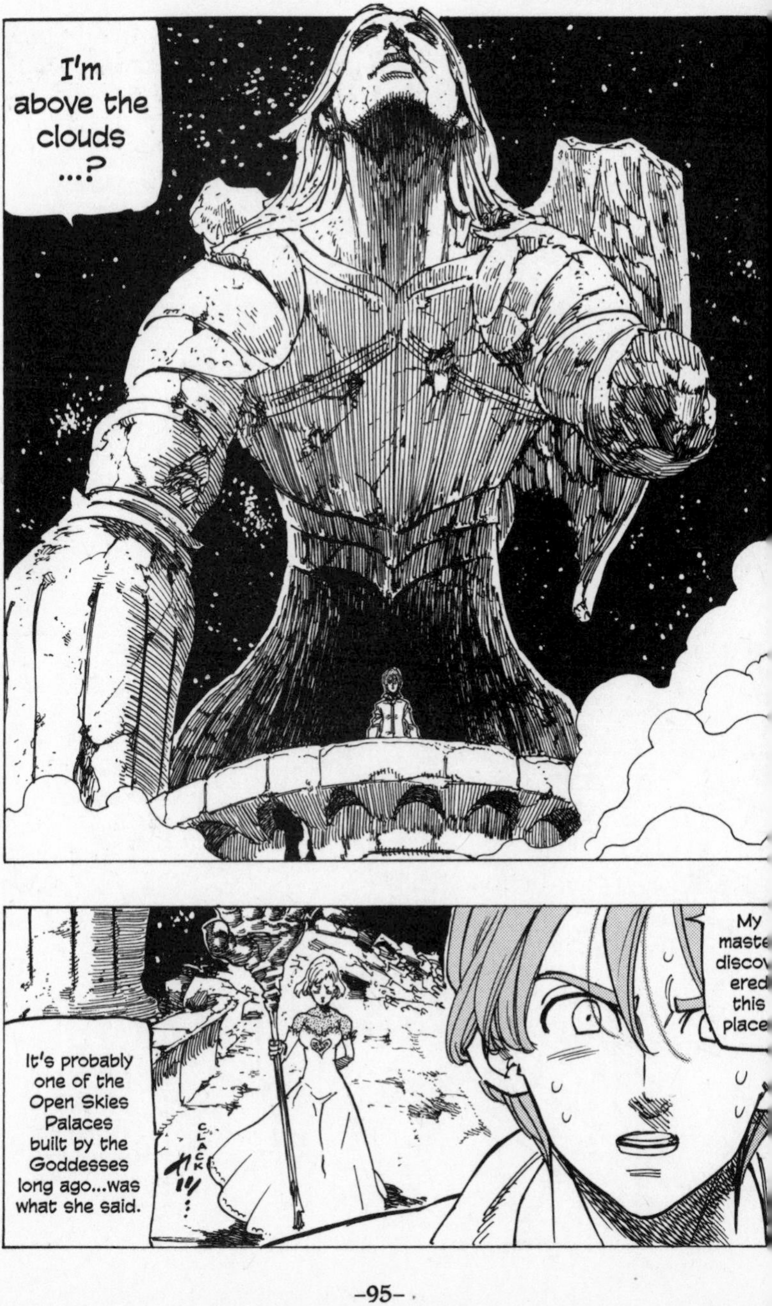
I'm above the clouds ...?
My maste discov ered this place
It's probably one of the Open Skies Palaces built by the Goddesses long ago...was what she said.
CLACK

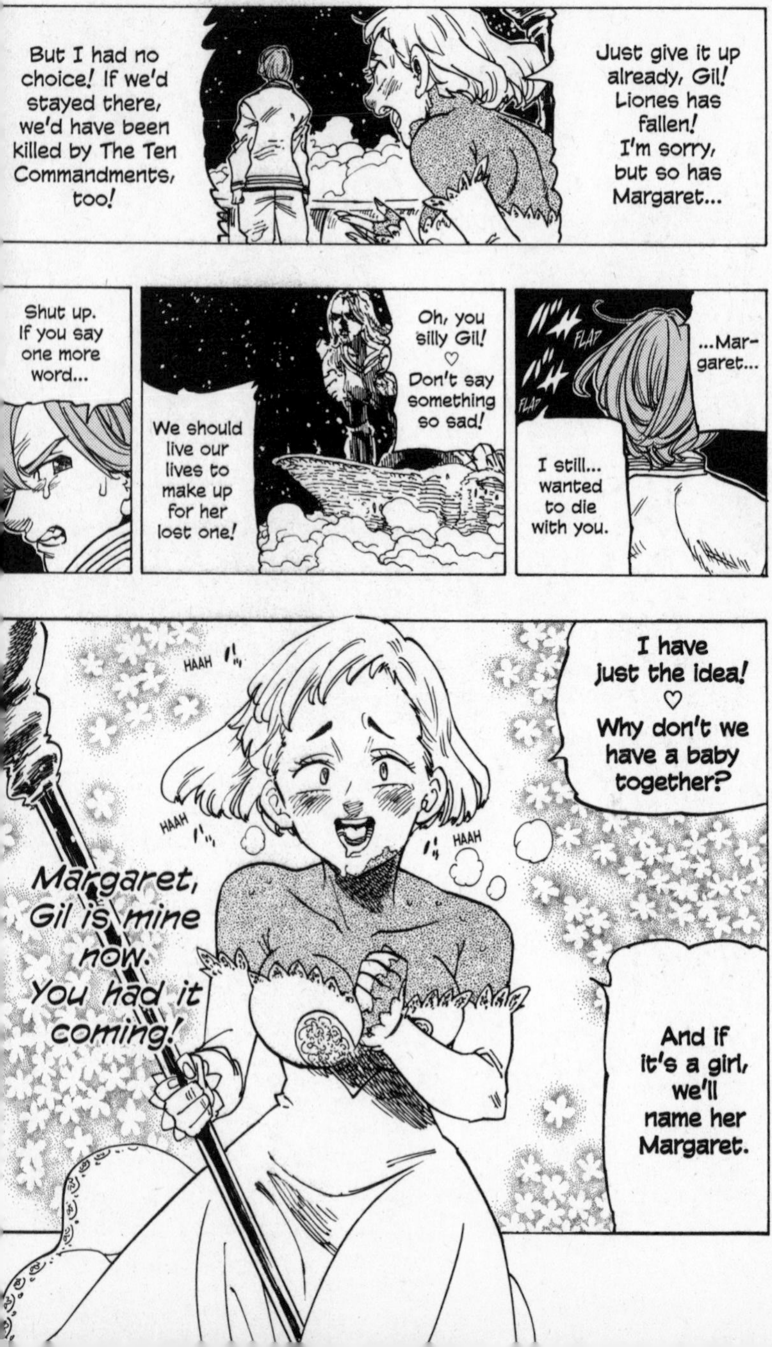
Just give it up already, Gil! Liones has fallen! I'm sorry, but so has Margaret...
But I had no choice! If we'd stayed there, we'd have been killed by The Ten Commandments, too!
...Margaret...
FLAP
FLAP
I still... wanted to die with you.
Oh, you silly Gil! ♡ Don't say something so sad!
We should live our lives to make up for her lost one!
Shut up. If you say one more word...
I have just the idea! ♡ Why don't we have a baby together?
HAAH
HAAH
HAAH
And if it's a girl, we'll name her Margaret.
Margaret, Gil is mine now. You had it coming!

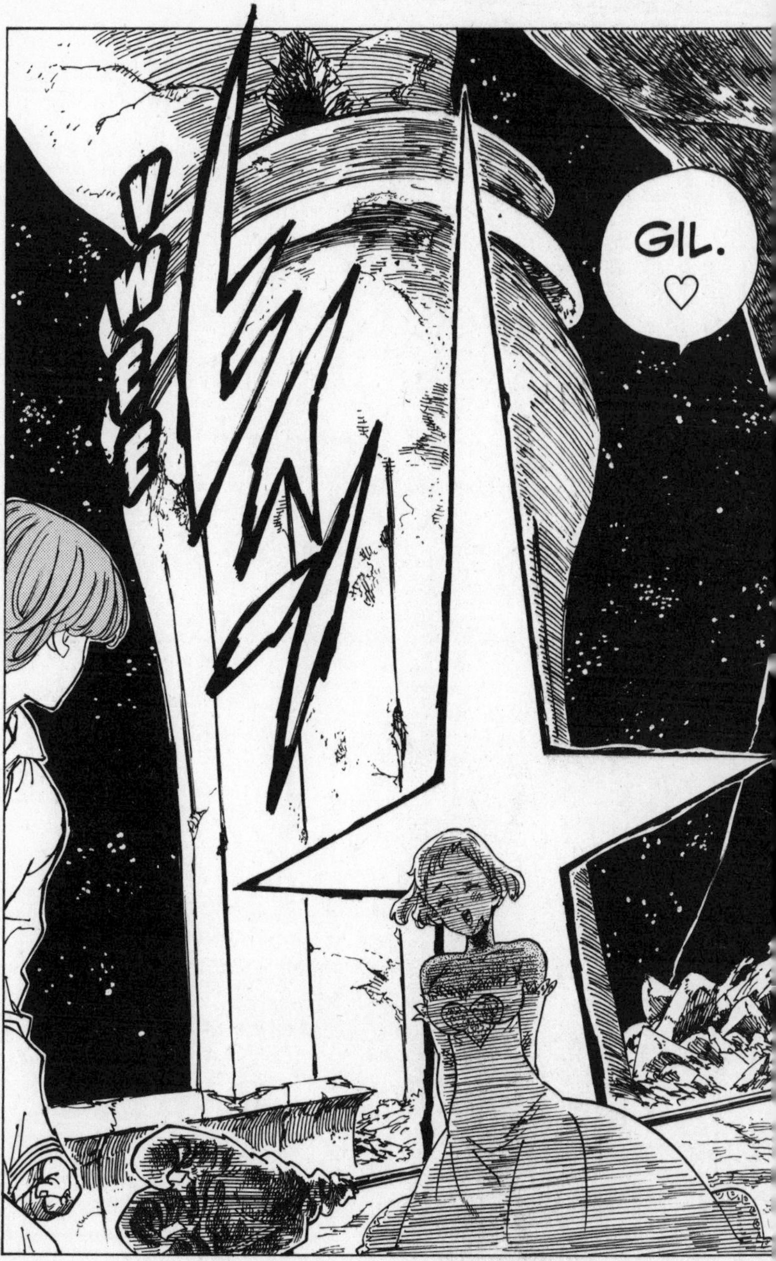
GIL. ♡
VWEEE

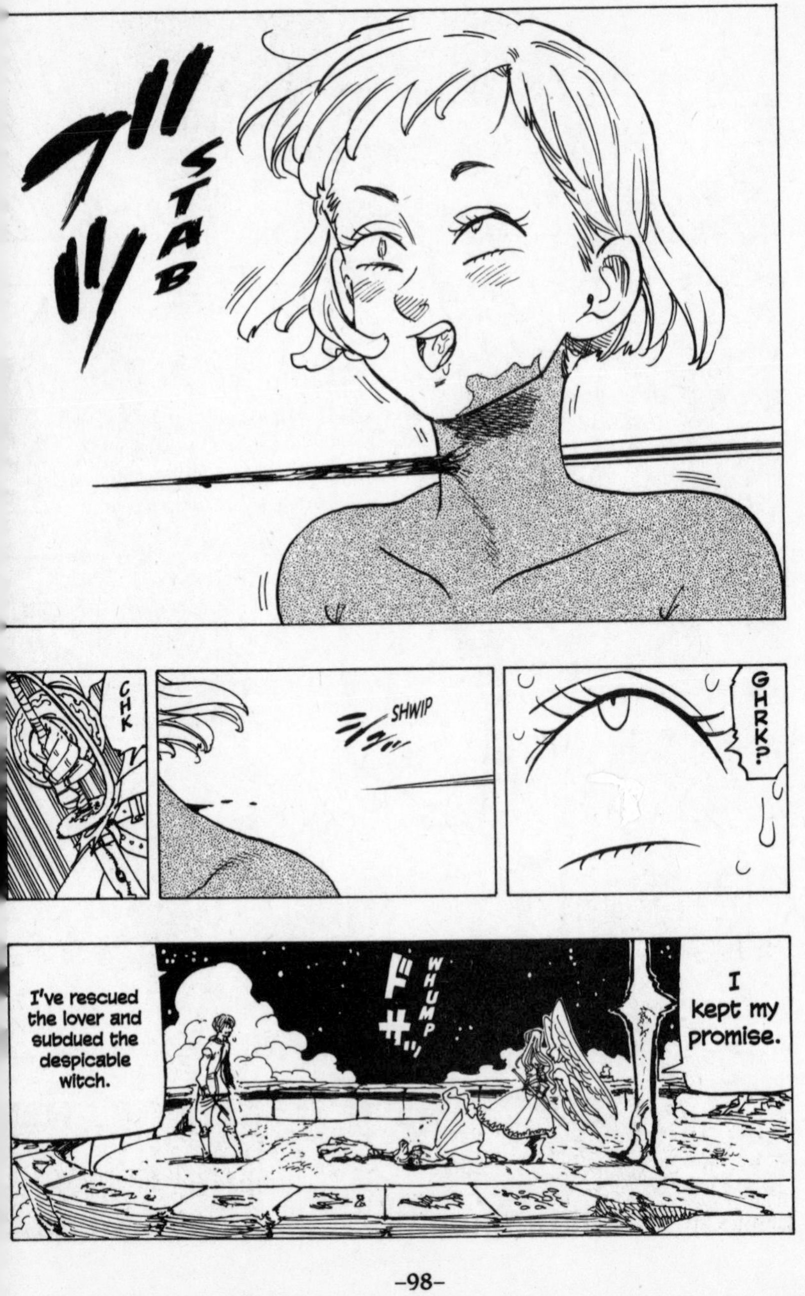
ブッ
STAB
GHRK?
SHWIP
CHK
I kept my promise.
WHUMP
I've rescued the lover and subdued the despicable witch.

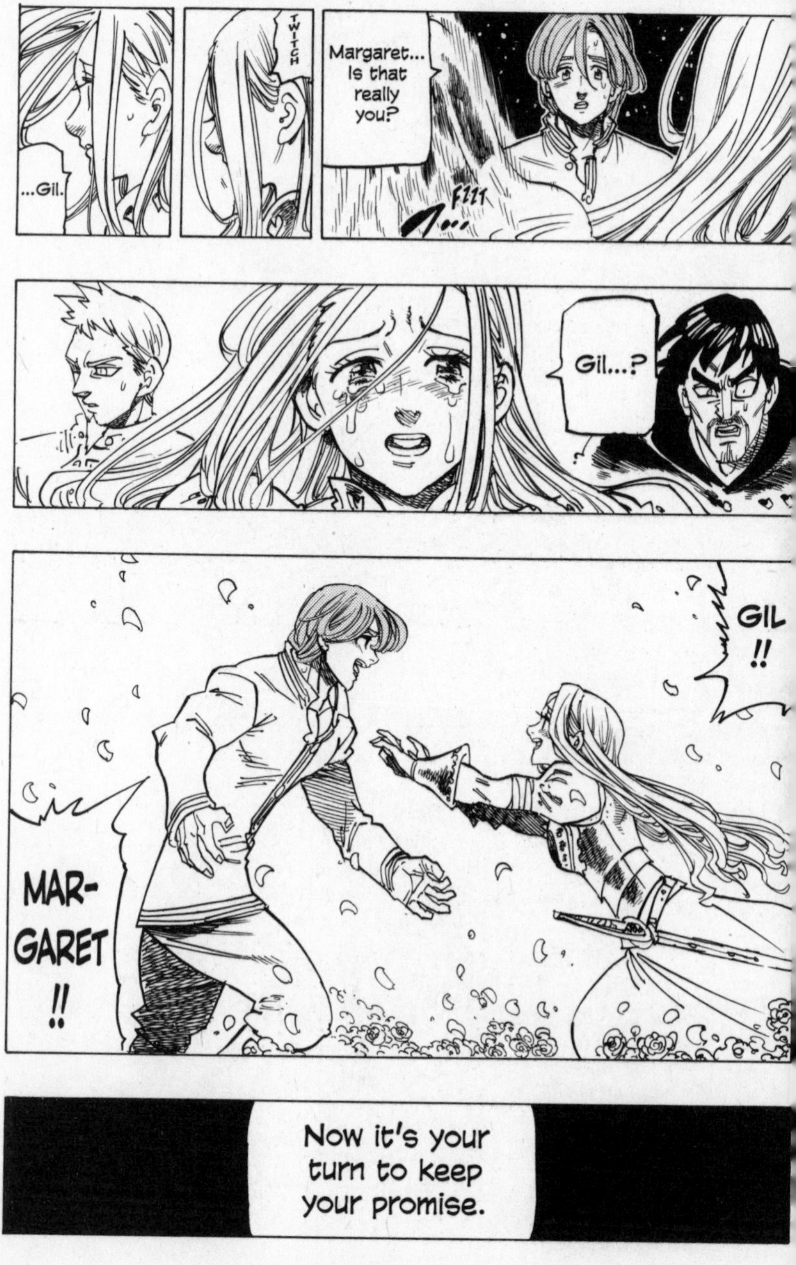
Margaret... Is that really you?
FZZT
TWITCH
...Gil.
Gil...?
GIL !!
MAR-GARET !!
Now it's your turn to keep your promise.

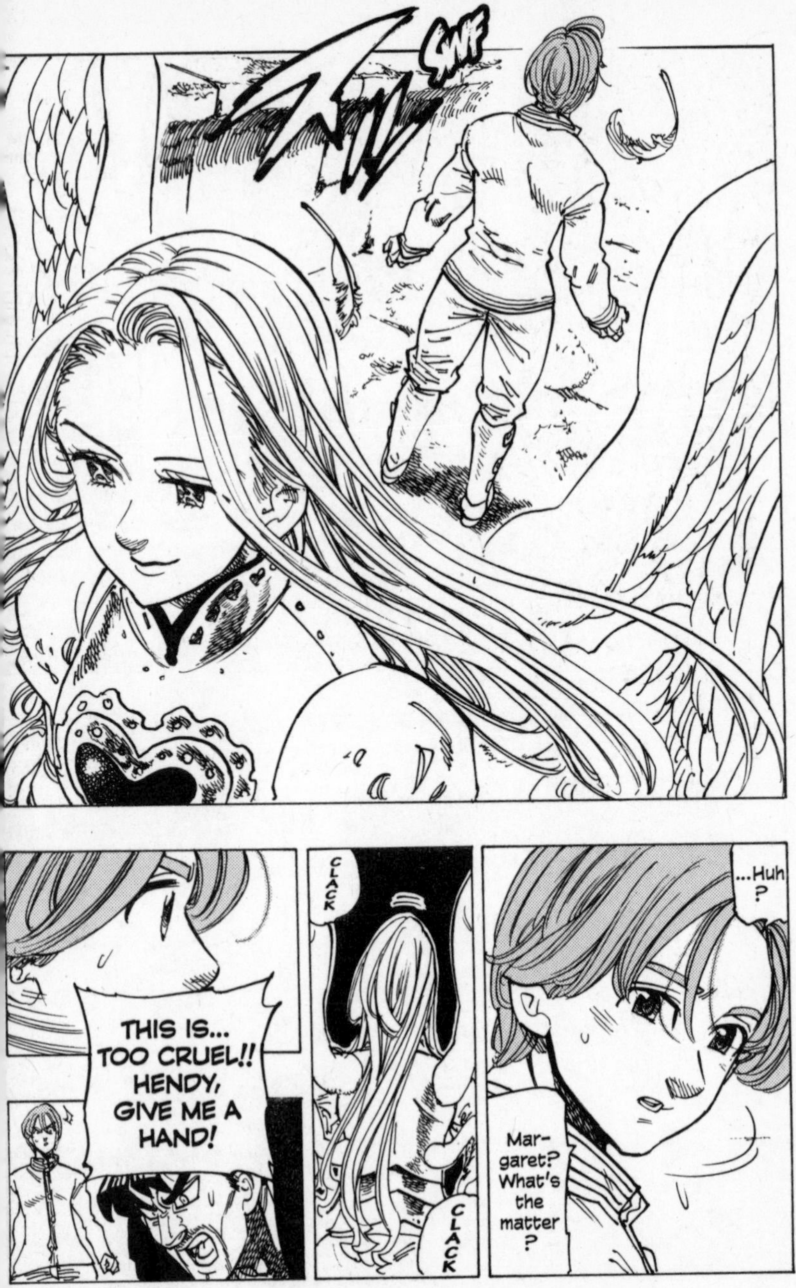
SWIF
...Huh?
Margaret? What's the matter?
CLACK
CLACK
THIS IS... TOO CRUEL!! HENDY, GIVE ME A HAND!

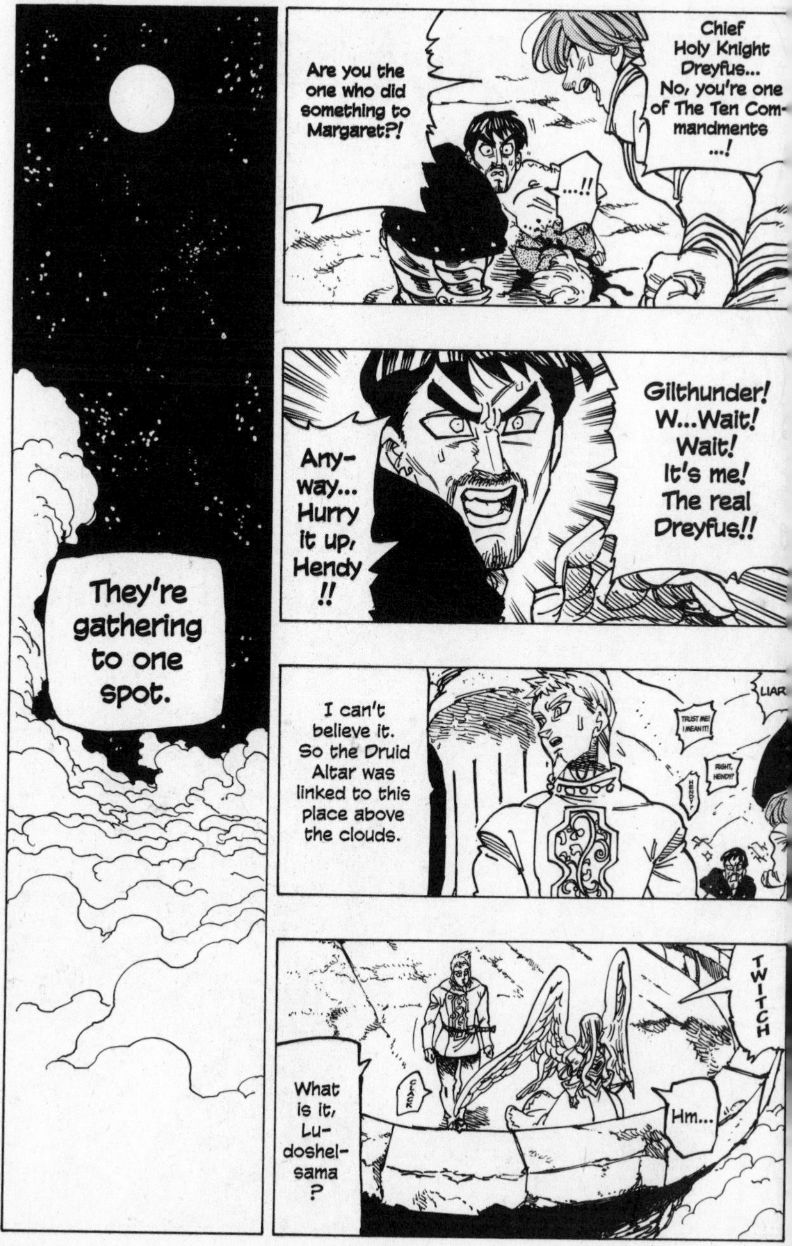

Chief Holy Knight Dreyfus... No, you're one of The Ten Commandments ...!
...!!
Are you the one who did something to Margaret?!
Gilthunder! W...Wait! Wait! It's me! The real Dreyfus!!
Anyway... Hurry it up, Hendy!!
LIAR
TRUST ME! I MEAN IT!
RIGHT, HENDY?
I can't believe it. So the Druid Altar was linked to this place above the clouds.
TWITCH
Hm...
CLACK
What is it, Ludoshel-sama?
They're gathering to one spot.

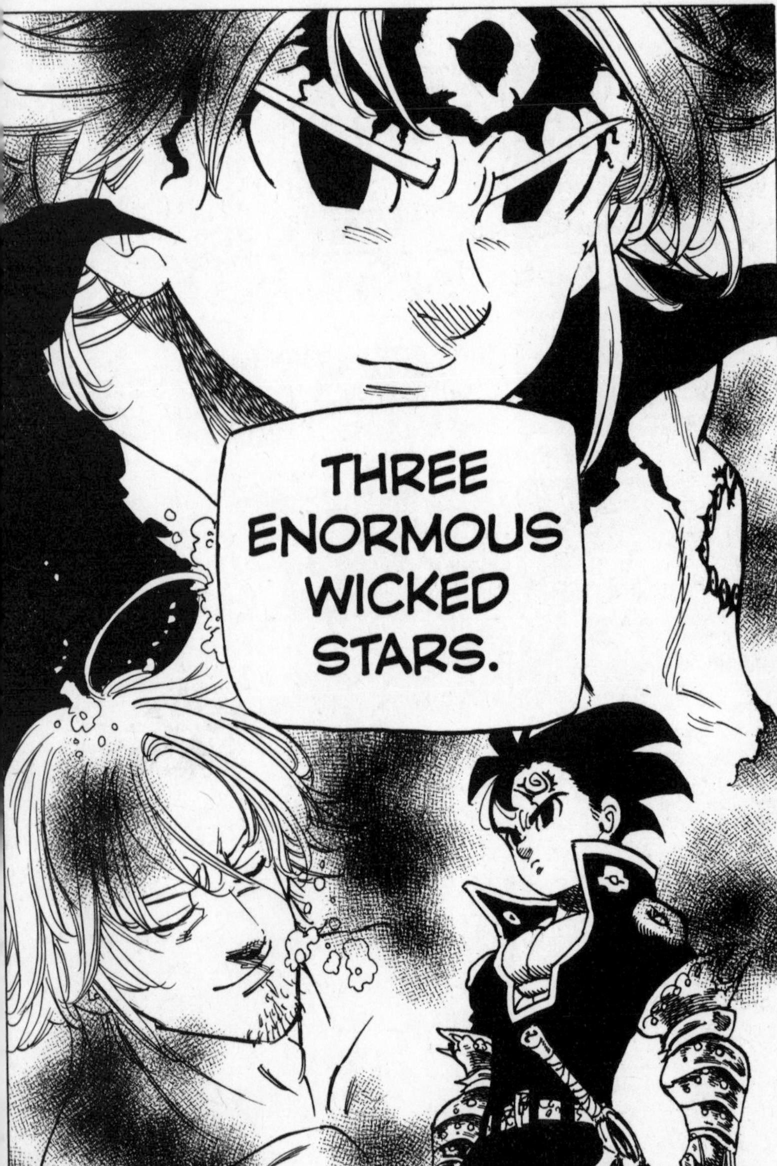
THREE ENORMOUS WICKED STARS.

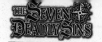

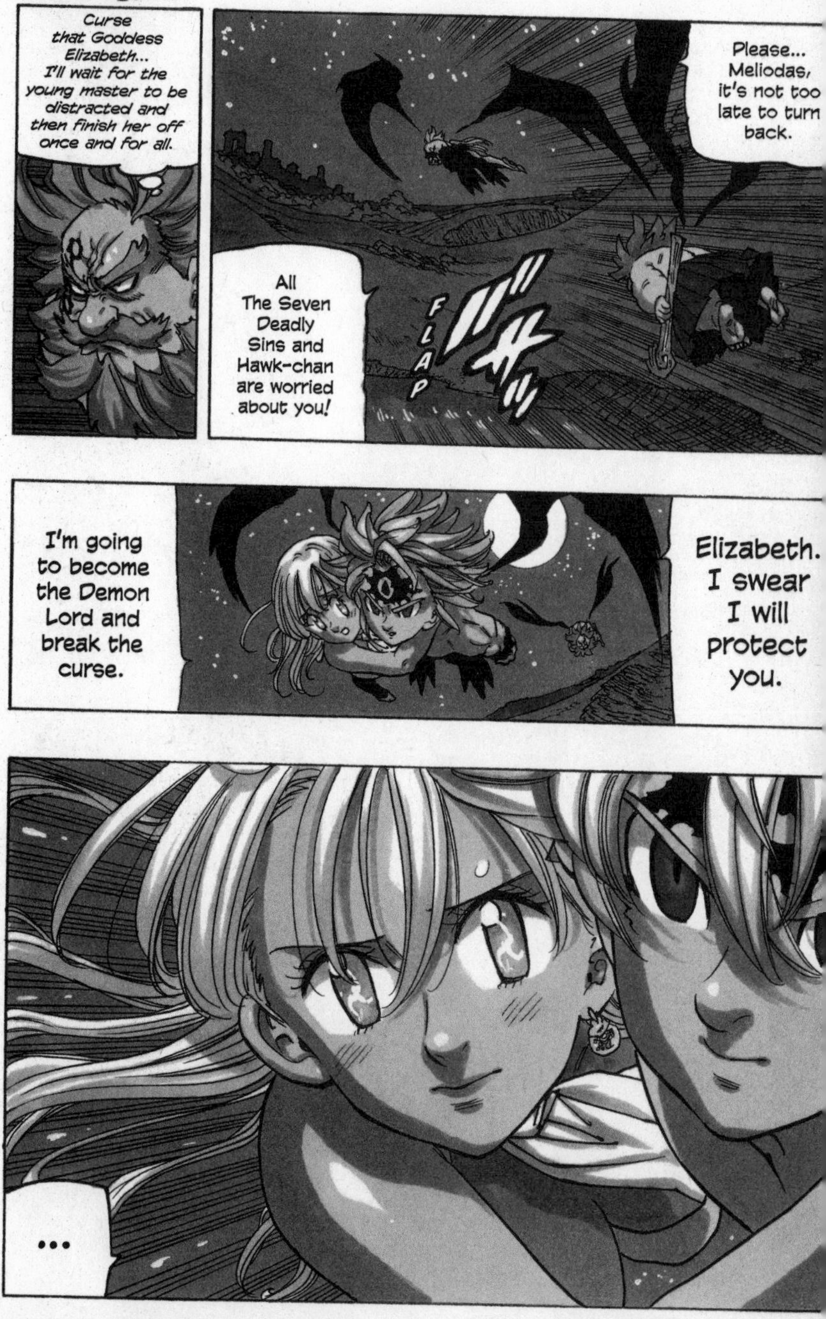
Please... Meliodas, it's not too late to turn back.
All The Seven Deadly Sins and Hawk-chan are worried about you!
FLAP
Curse that Goddess Elizabeth... I'll wait for the young master to be distracted and then finish her off once and for all.
Elizabeth. I swear I will protect you.
I'm going to become the Demon Lord and break the curse.
...

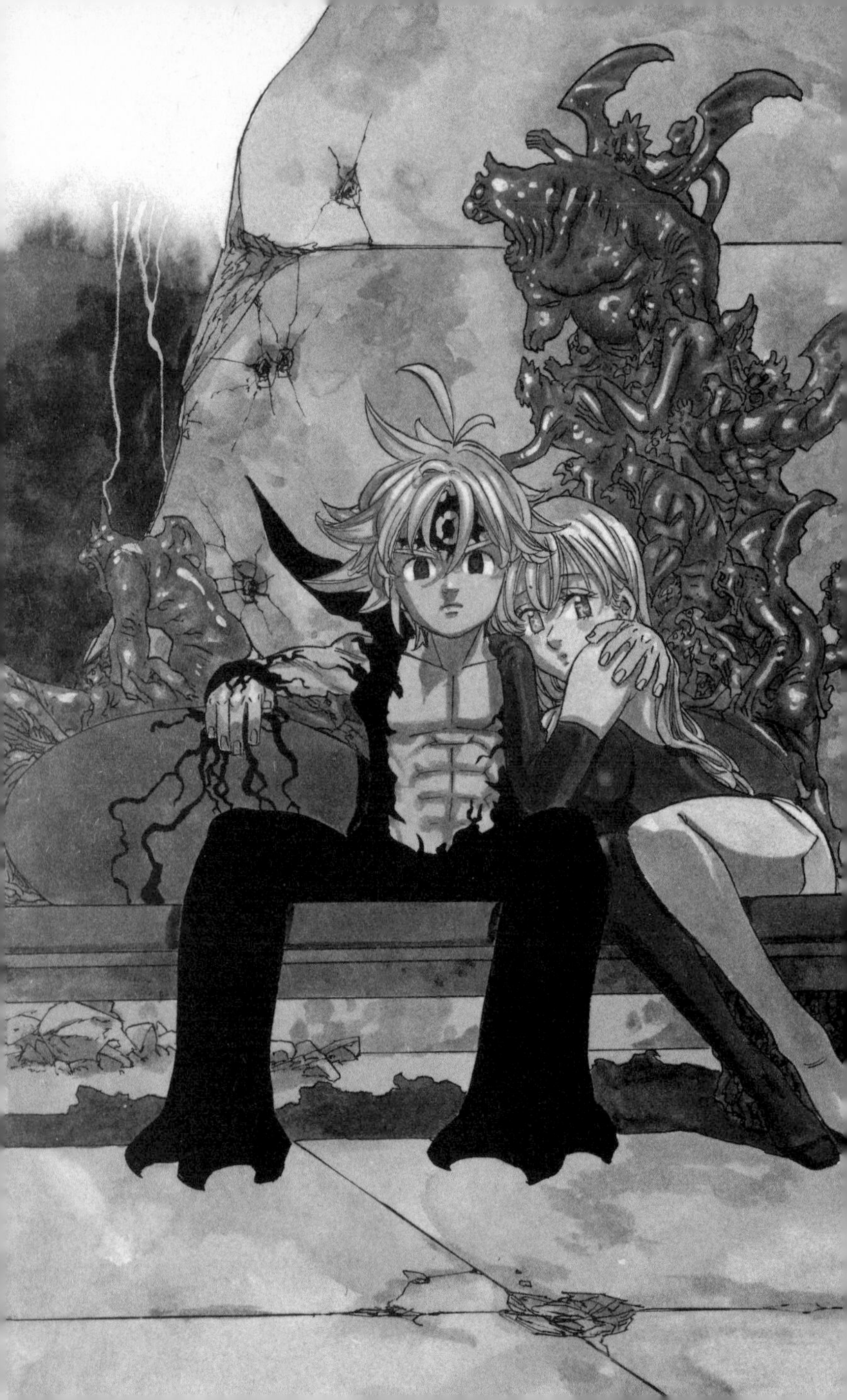

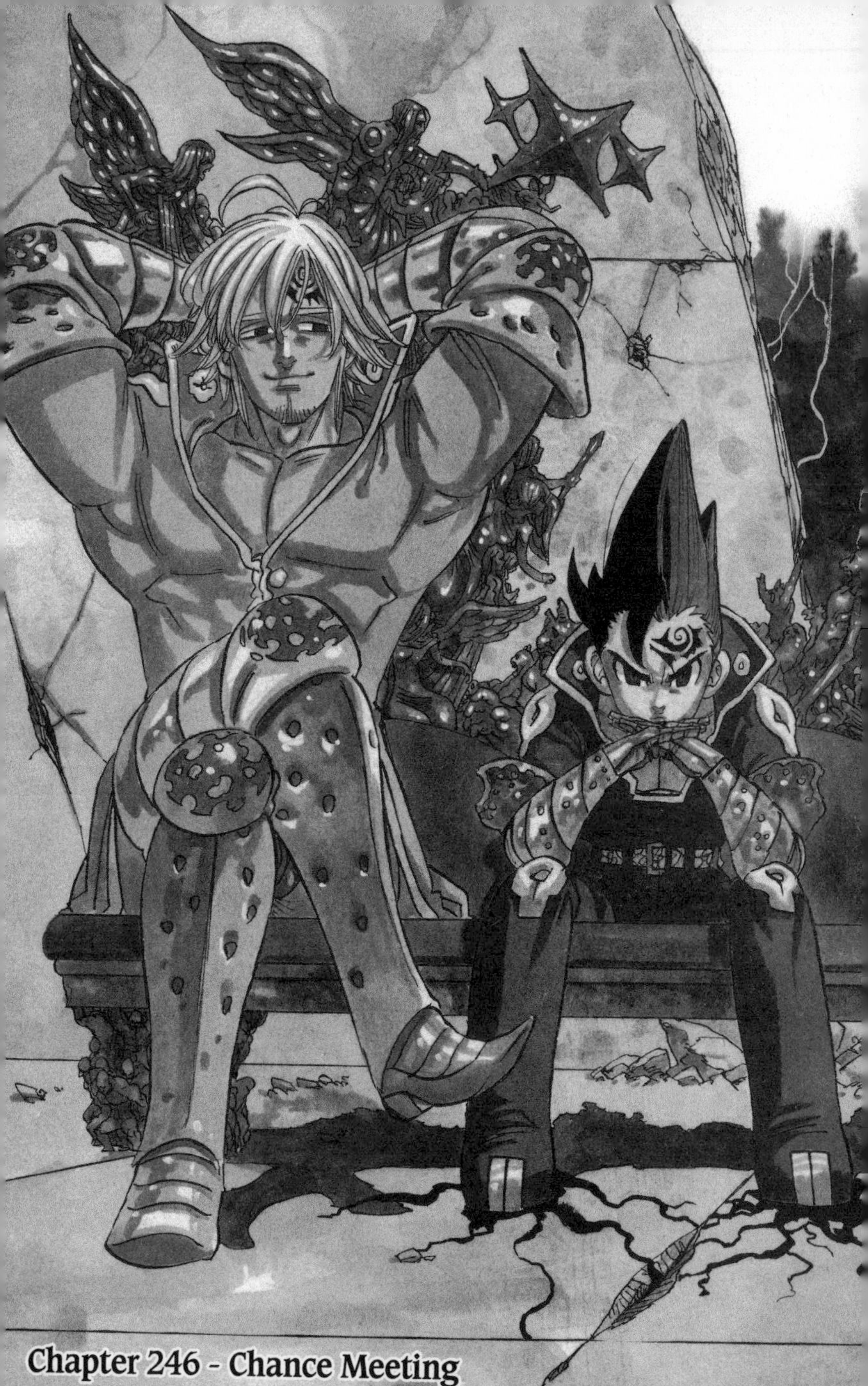

Chapter 246 - Chance Meeting

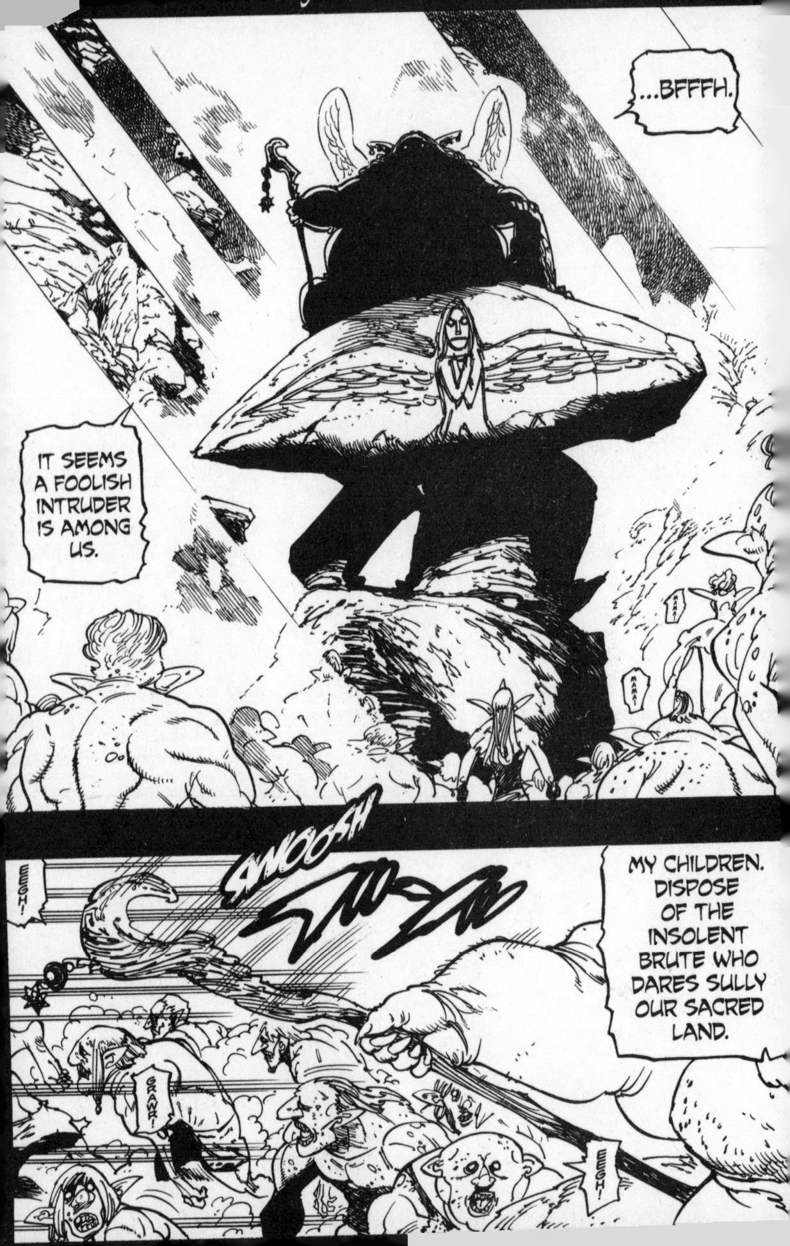
...BFFFH.
IT SEEMS A FOOLISH INTRUDER IS AMONG US.
MAMA!
MAMA!
MY CHILDREN. DISPOSE OF THE INSOLENT BRUTE WHO DARES SULLY OUR SACRED LAND.
SWOOSH
EEGH!
GRAWR!
EEGH!

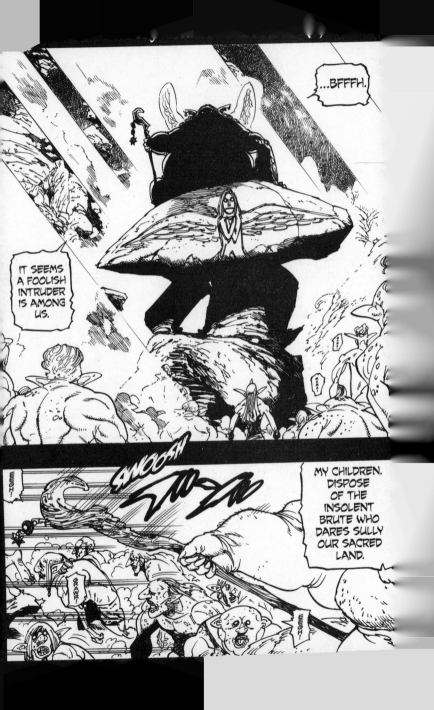

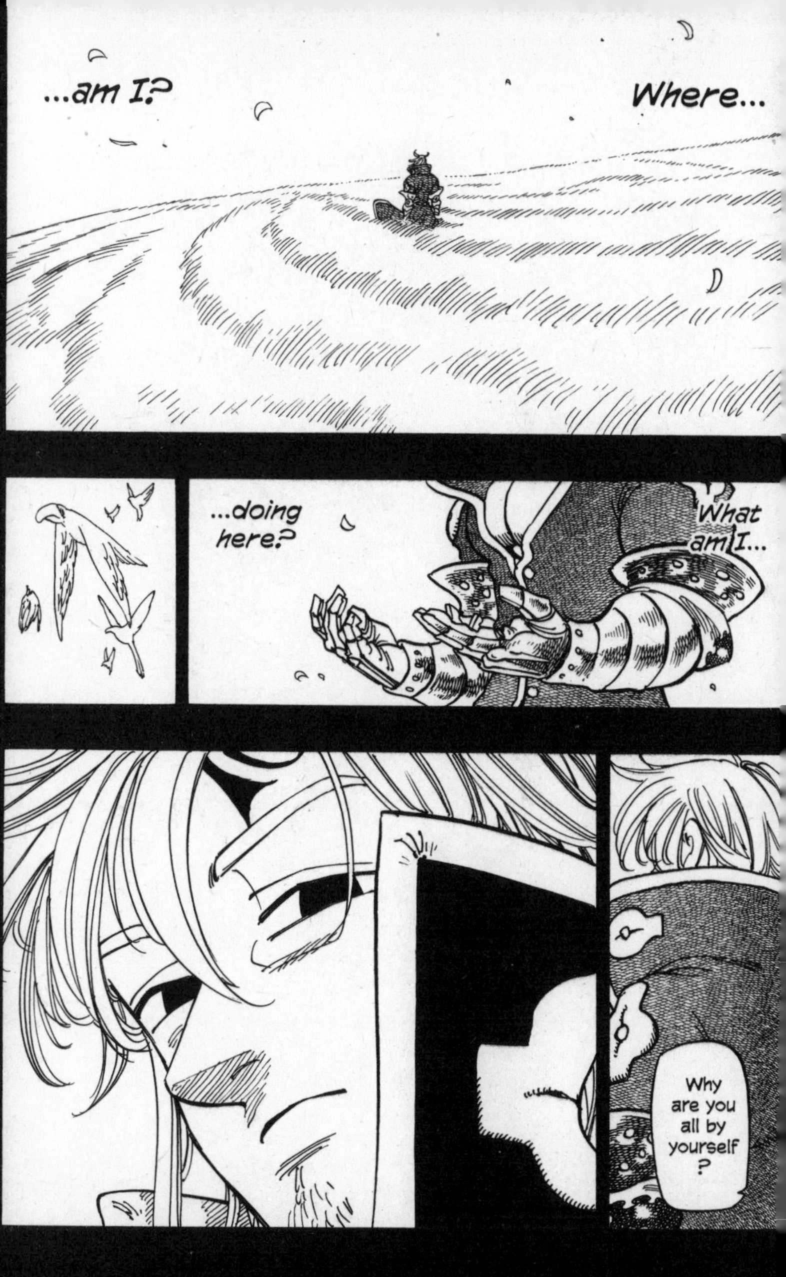
Where...
...am I?
What am I...
...doing here?
Why are you all by yourself?

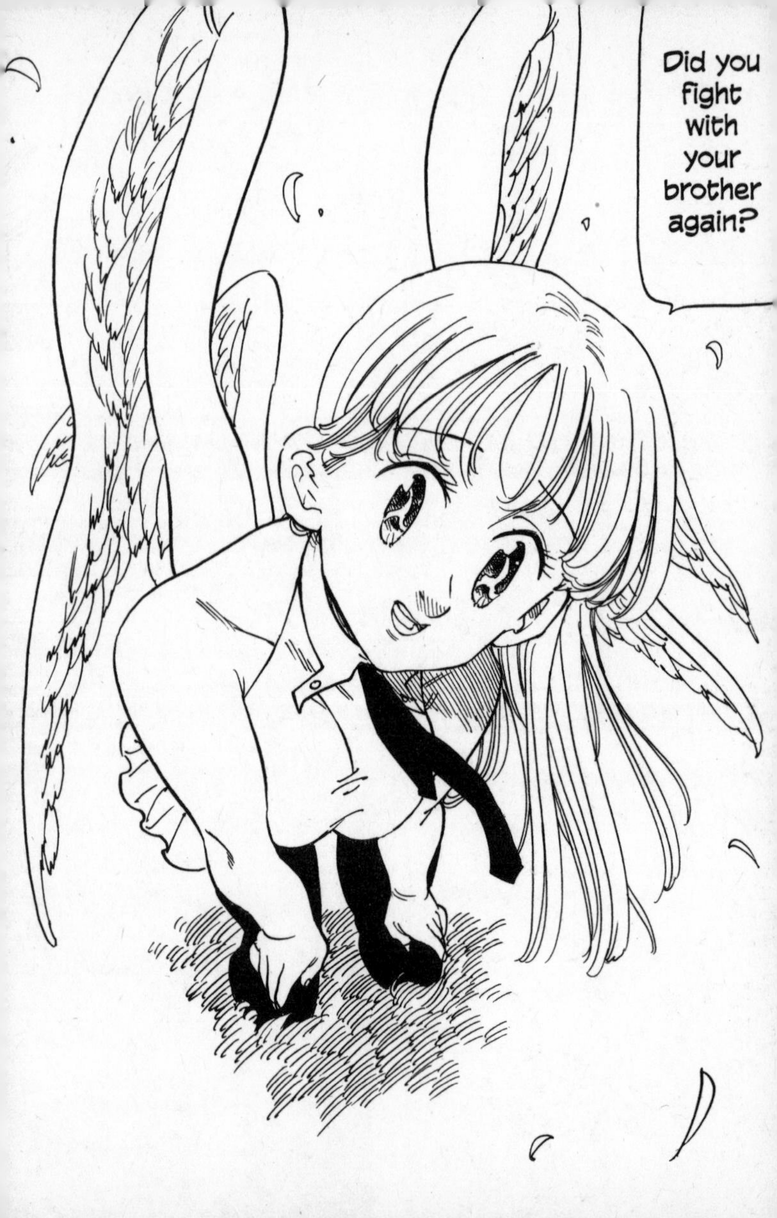
Did you fight with your brother again?

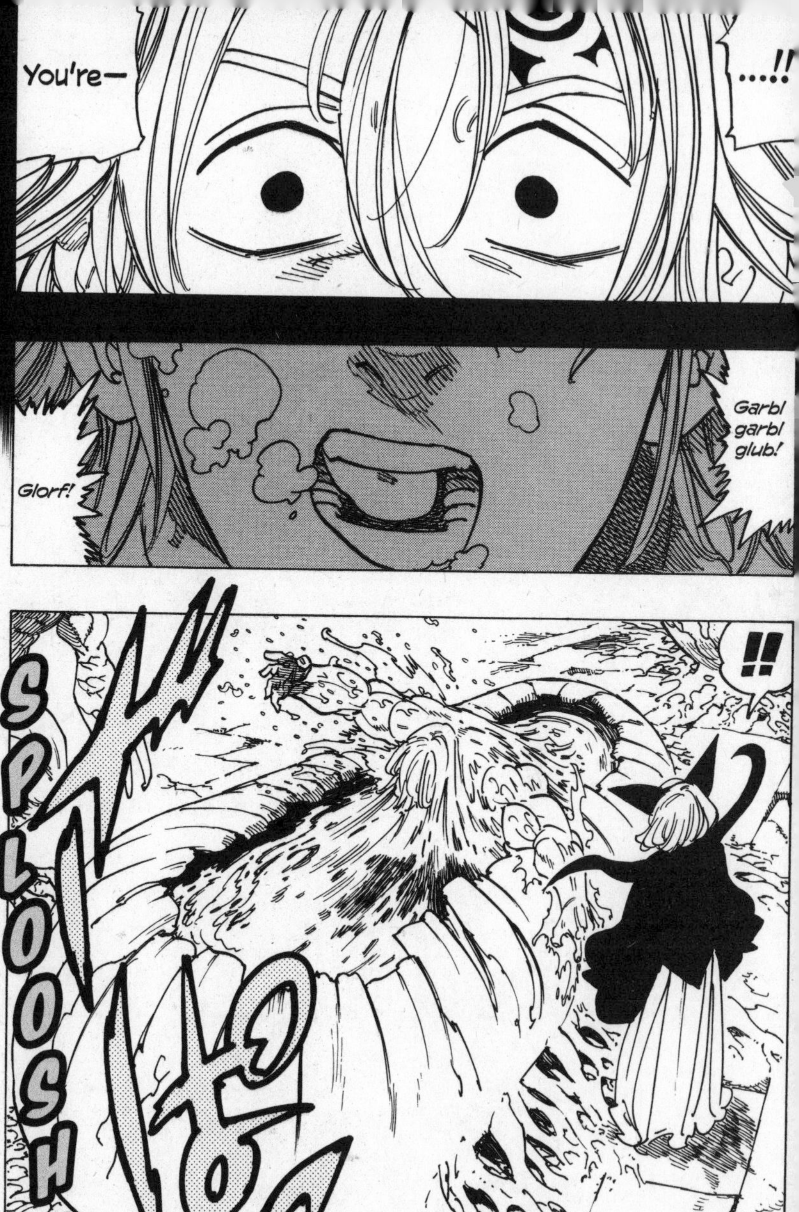
....!!
You're—
Garbl garbl glub!
Glorf!
!!
SPLOOSH

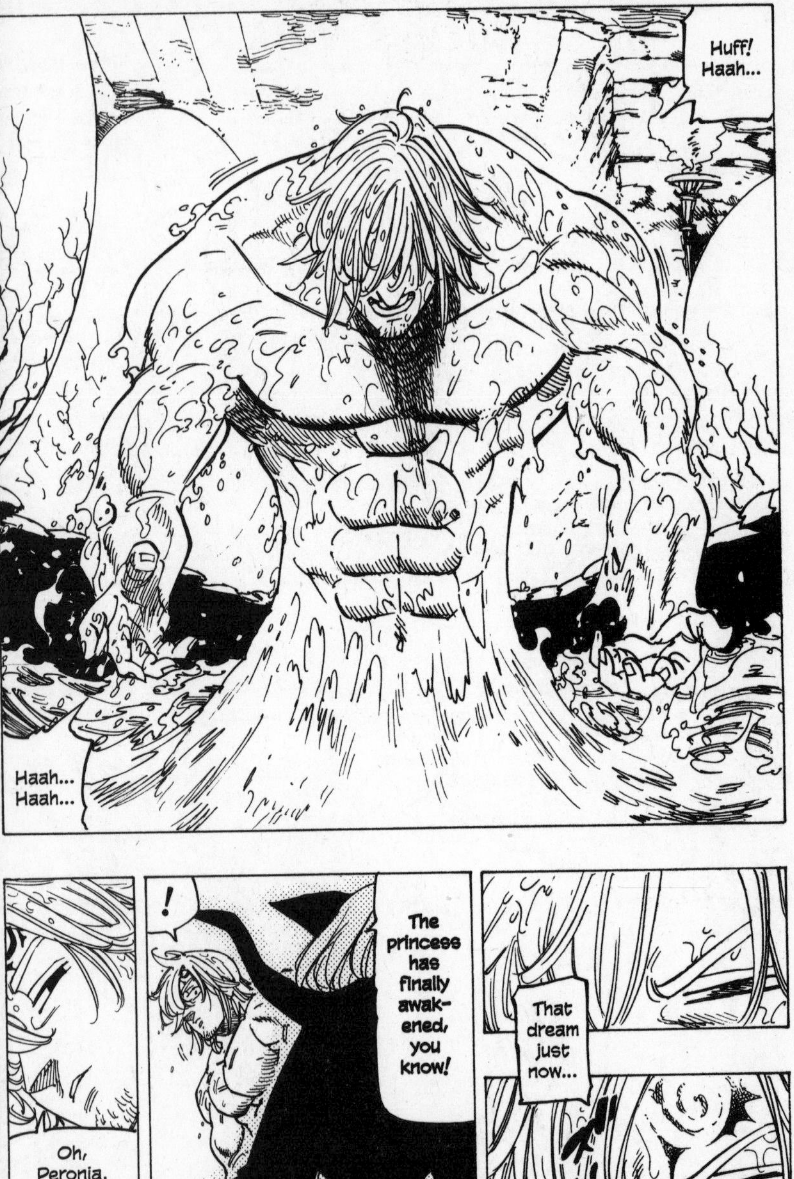
Huff! Haah...
Haah... Haah...
That dream just now...
!
The princess has finally awakened, you know!
Oh, Peronia. Why're you here?

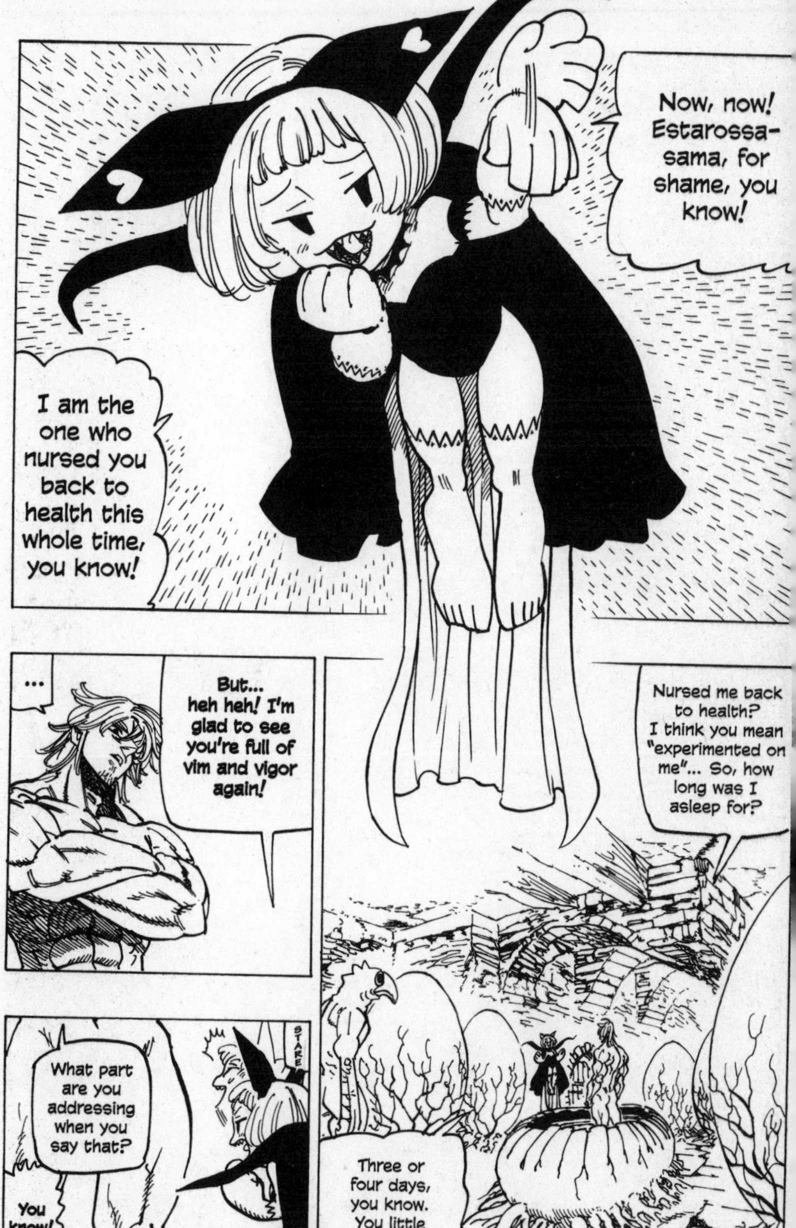
Now, now! Estarossa-sama, for shame, you know!
I am the one who nursed you back to health this whole time, you know!
Nursed me back to health? I think you mean "experimented on me"... So, how long was I asleep for?
Three or four days, you know. You little sleepyhead.
...
But... heh heh! I'm glad to see you're full of vim and vigor again!
STARE
What part are you addressing when you say that?
You know!

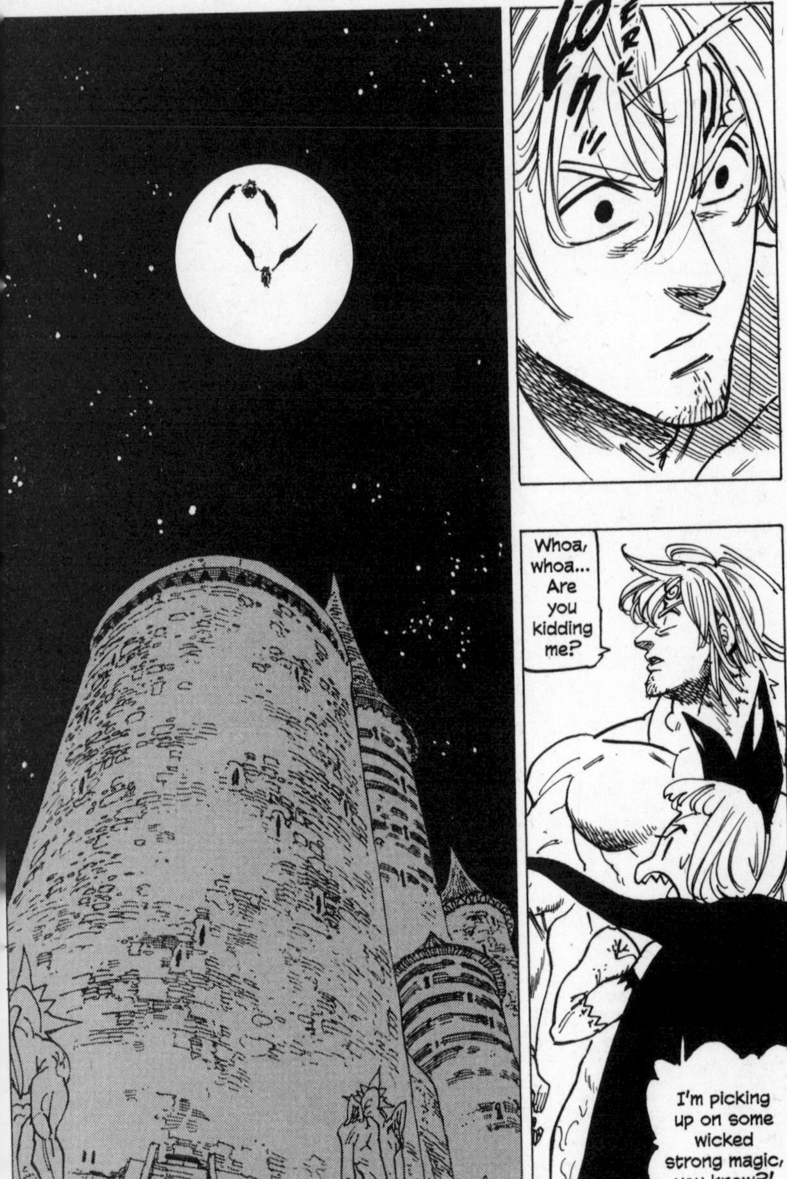
PERK
Whoa, whoa... Are you kidding me?
I'm picking up on some wicked strong magic, you know?!

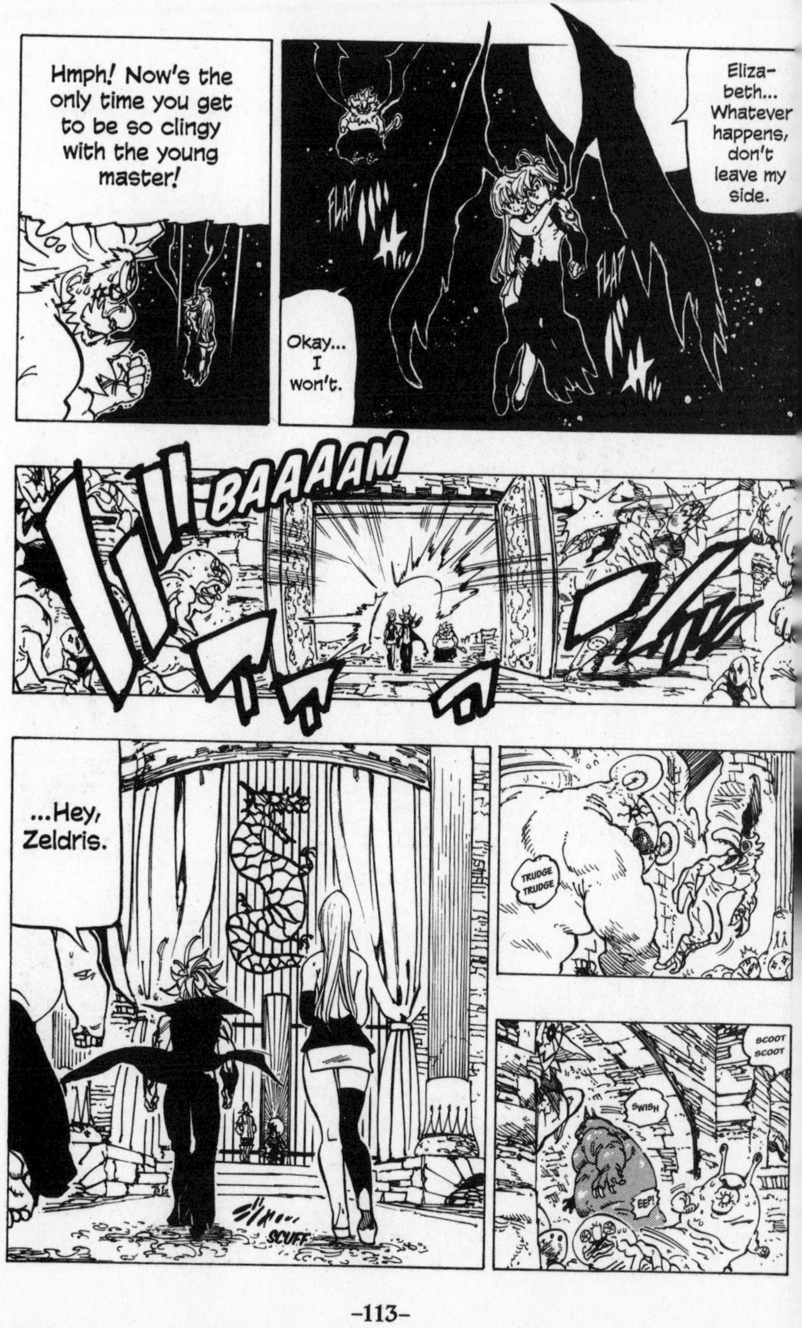
Eliza-beth... Whatever happens, don't leave my side.
FLAP
FLAP
Okay... I won't.
Hmph! Now's the only time you get to be so clingy with the young master!
BAAAAM
TRUDGE TRUDGE
SCOOT SCOOT
SWISH
EEP!
...Hey, Zeldris.
SCUFF

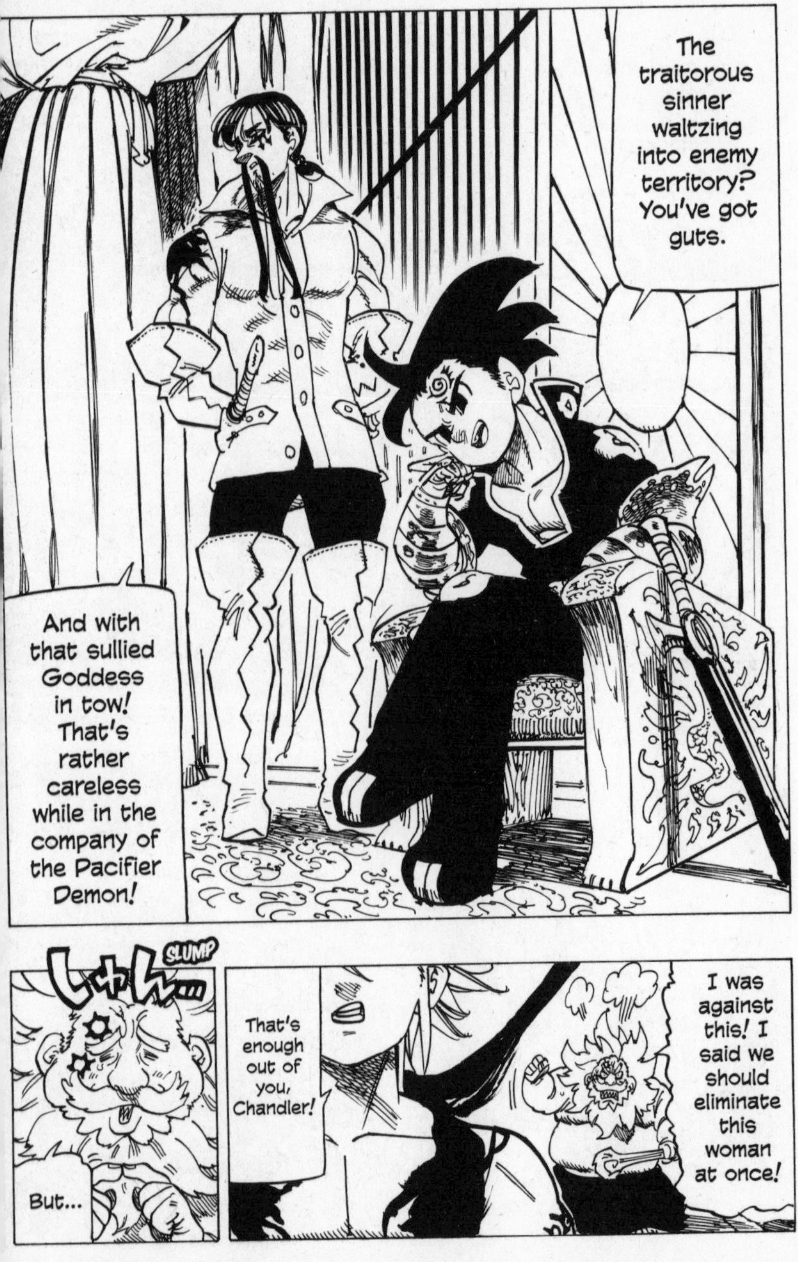
The traitorous sinner waltzing into enemy territory? You've got guts.
And with that sullied Goddess in tow! That's rather careless while in the company of the Pacifier Demon!
I was against this! I said we should eliminate this woman at once!
That's enough out of you, Chandler!
しゅん...
SLUMP
But...

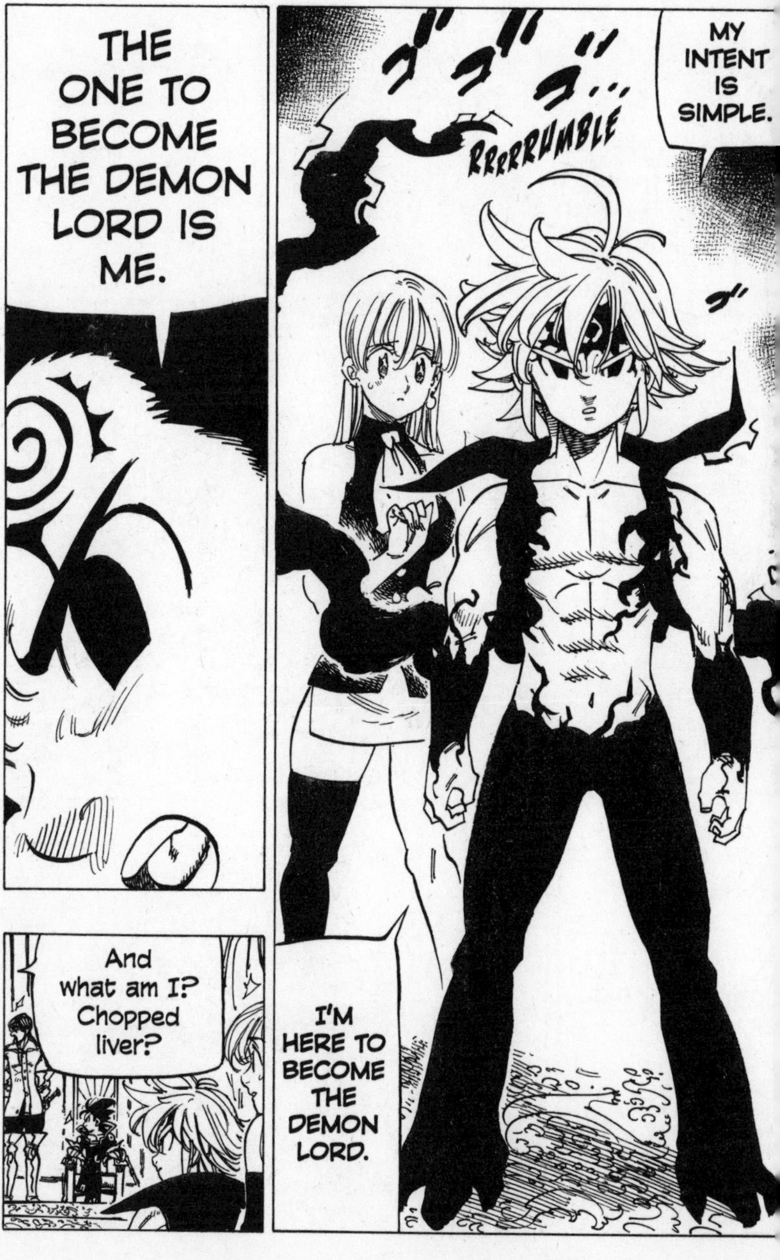
ゴゴゴ…
RRRRRUMBLE
MY INTENT IS SIMPLE.
I'M HERE TO BECOME THE DEMON LORD.
THE ONE TO BECOME THE DEMON LORD IS ME.
And what am I? Chopped liver?

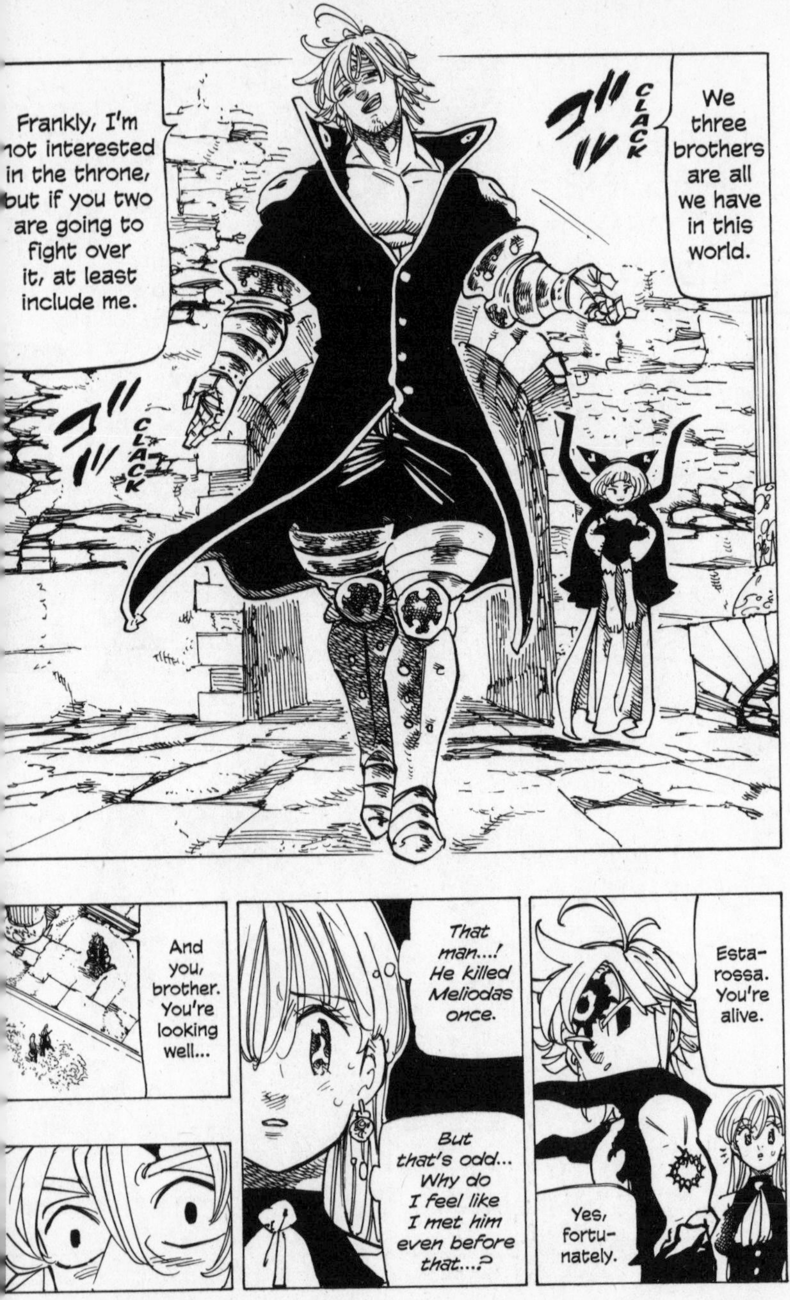
We three brothers are all we have in this world.
CLACK
Frankly, I'm not interested in the throne, but if you two are going to fight over it, at least include me.
CLACK
Esta-rossa. You're alive.
Yes, fortu-nately.
That man...! He killed Meliodas once.
But that's odd... Why do I feel like I met him even before that...?
And you, brother. You're looking well...

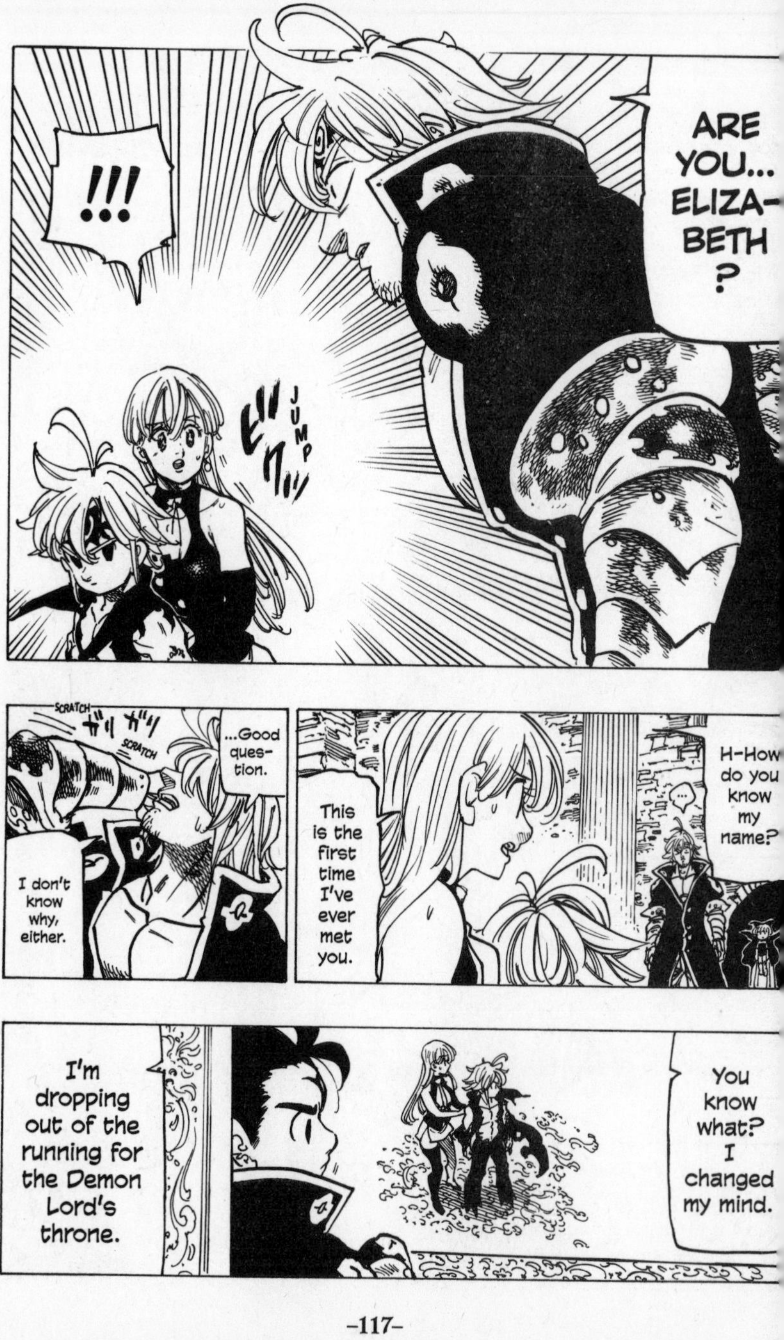
ARE YOU... ELIZA-BETH?
!!!
JUMP
H-How do you know my name?
...
This is the first time I've ever met you.
...Good question.
SCRATCH
SCRATCH
I don't know why, either.
You know what? I changed my mind.
I'm dropping out of the running for the Demon Lord's throne.

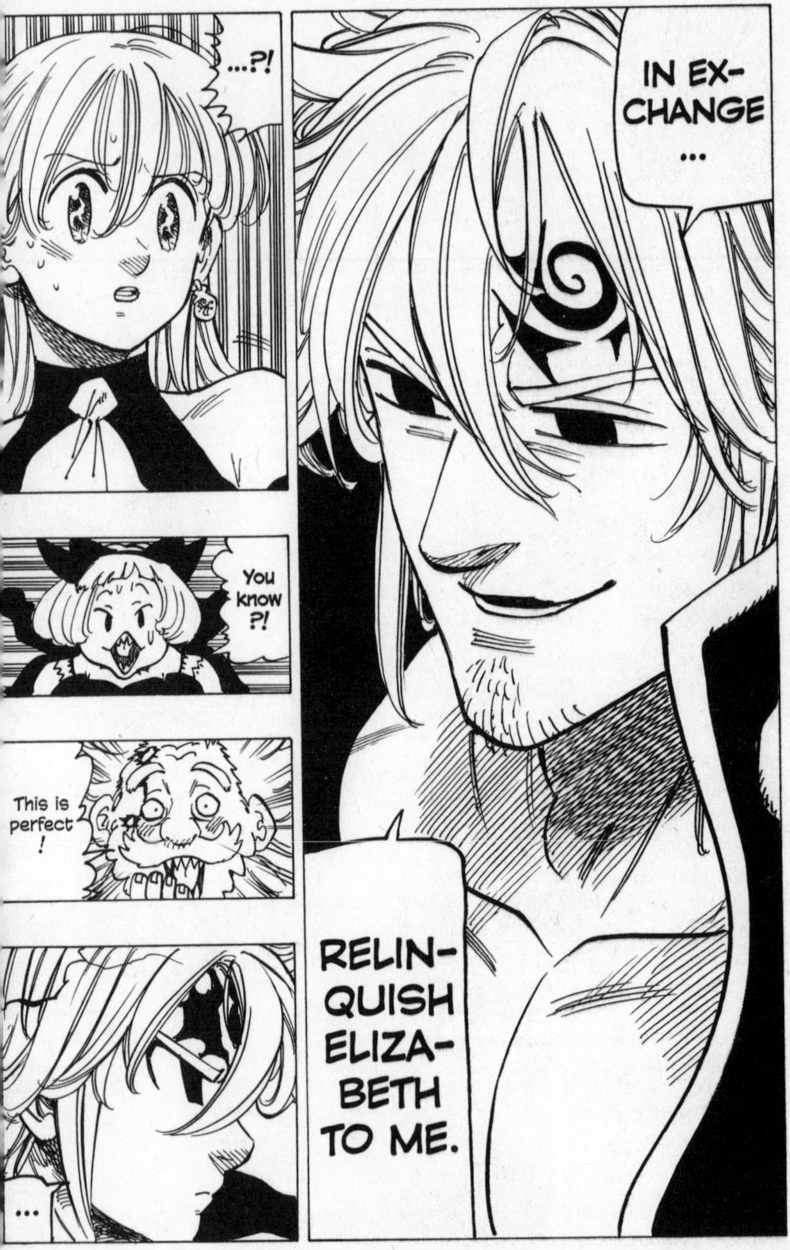
IN EX-CHANGE ...
RELIN-QUISH ELIZA-BETH TO ME.
...?!
You know ?!
This is perfect !
...

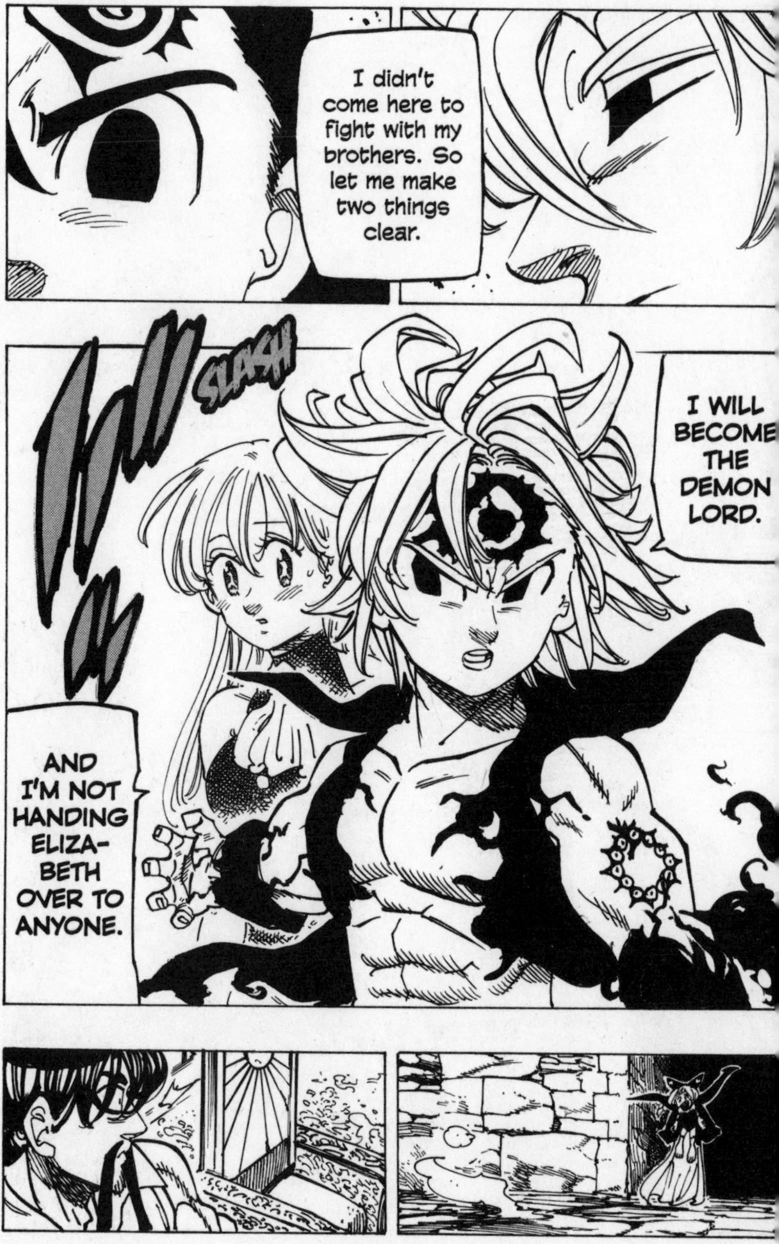
I didn't come here to fight with my brothers. So let me make two things clear.
I WILL BECOME THE DEMON LORD.
SLASH
AND I'M NOT HANDING ELIZA-BETH OVER TO ANYONE.

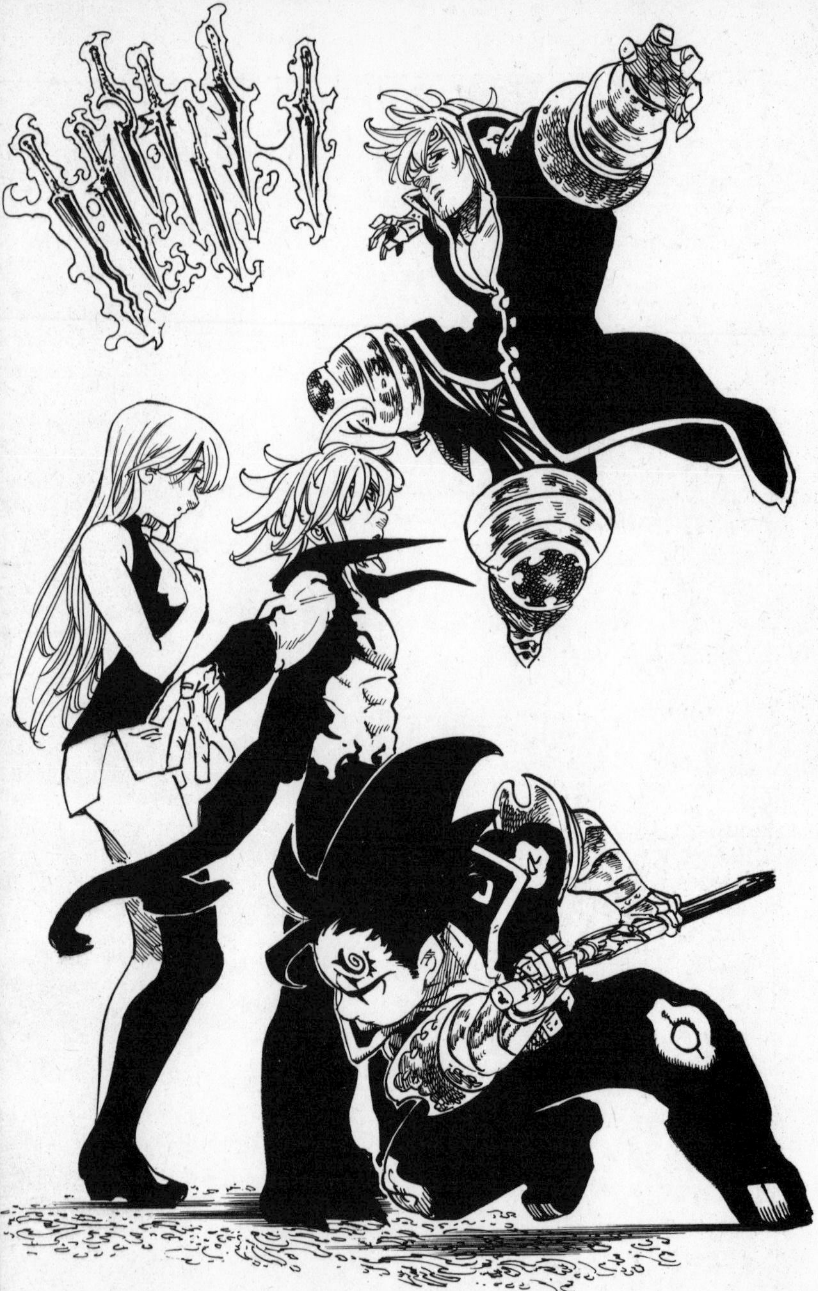

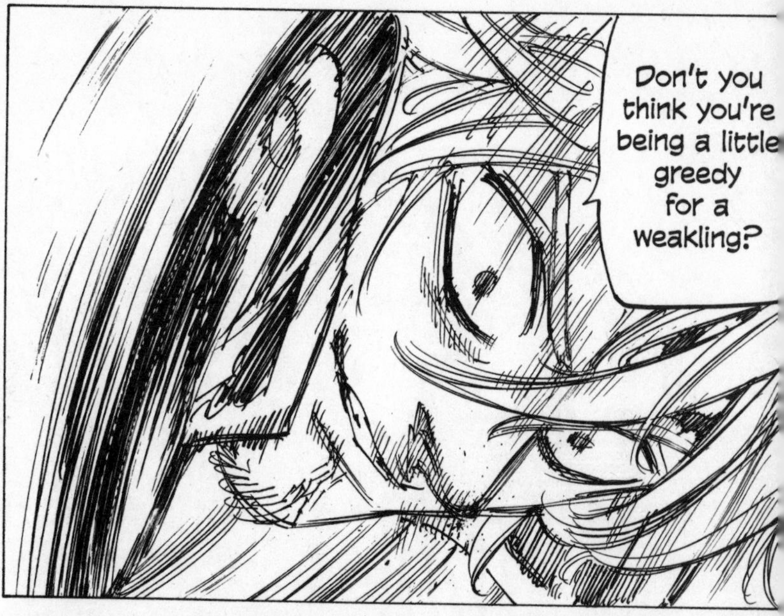
Don't you think you're being a little greedy for a weakling?
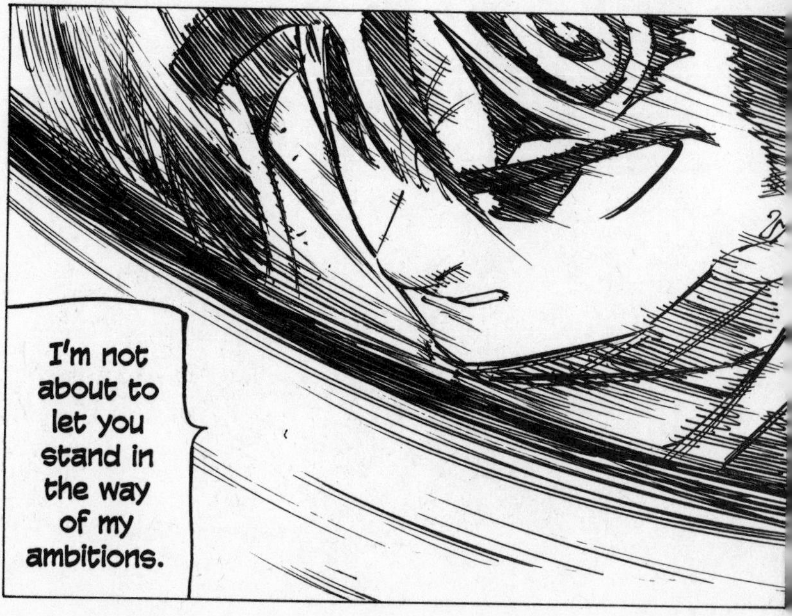
I'm not about to let you stand in the way of my ambitions.

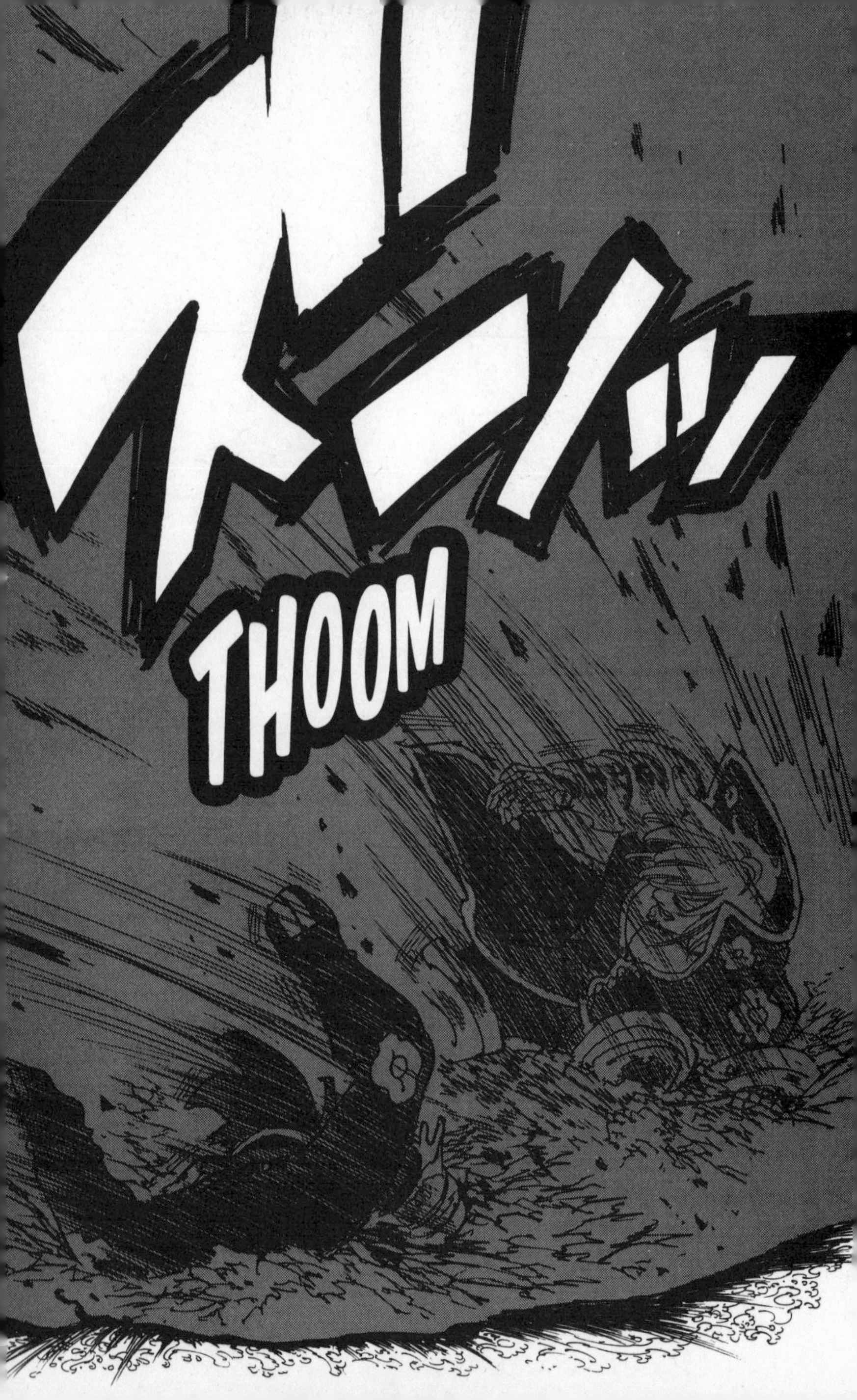
THOOM

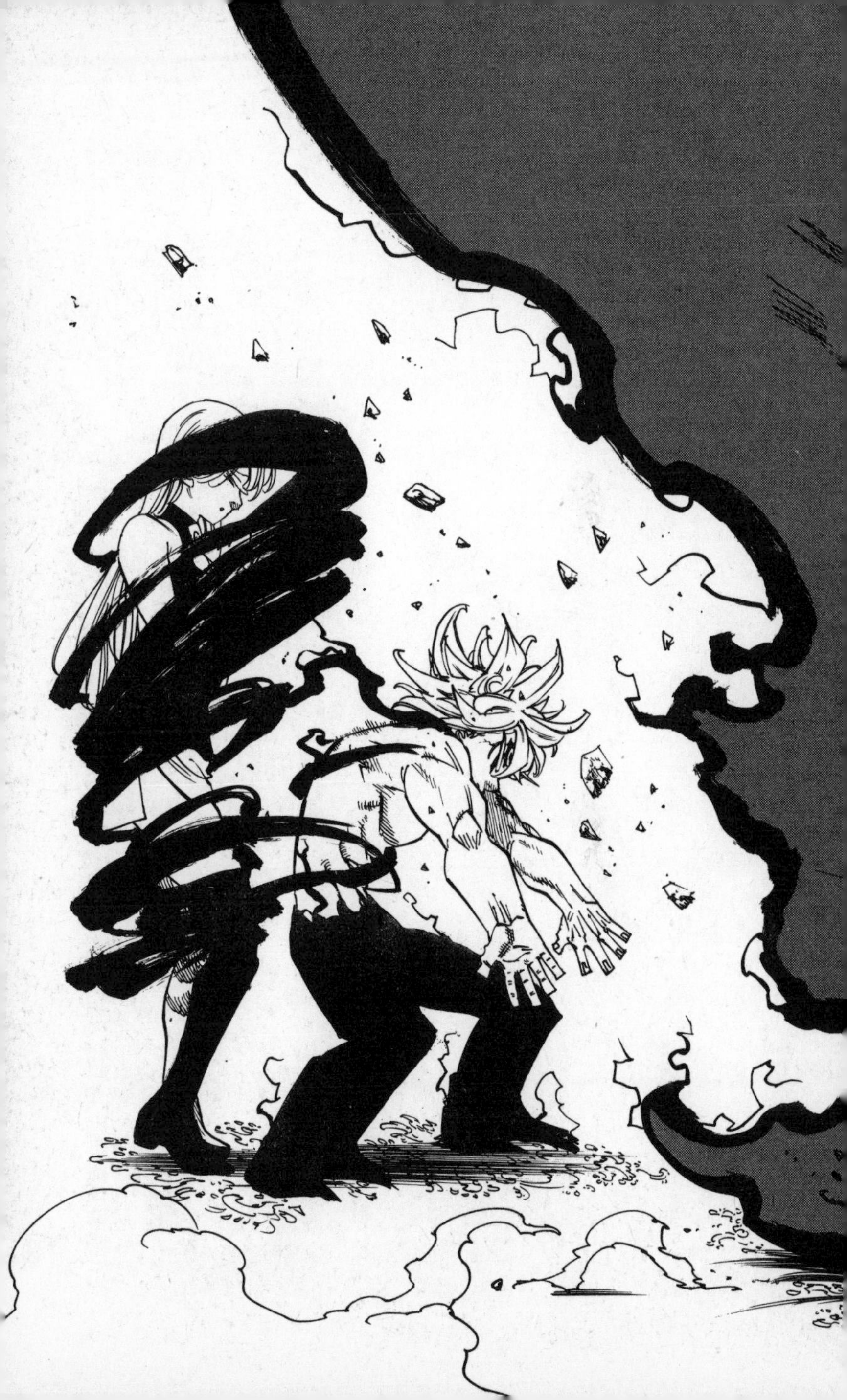

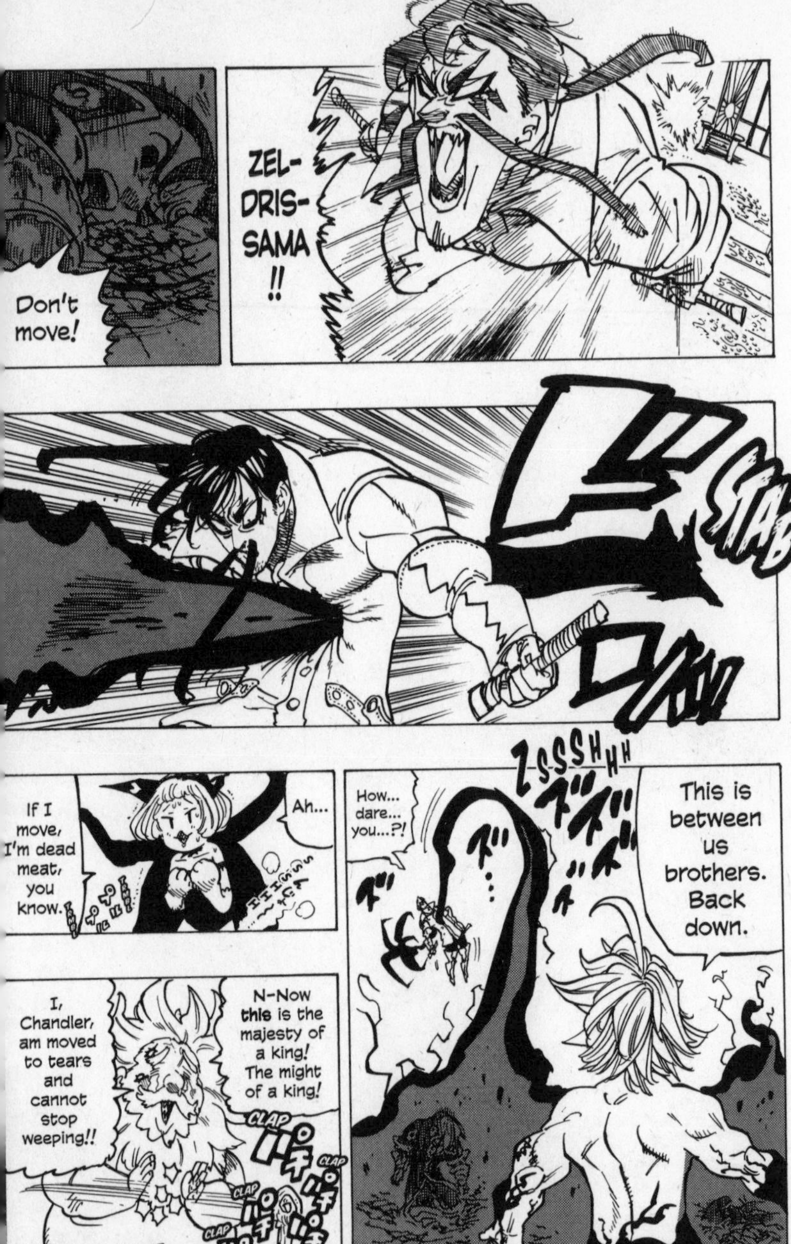
ZEL-DRIS-SAMA!!
Don't move!
STAB
ZSSSHHH
How... dare... you...?!
This is between us brothers. Back down.
Ah...
If I move, I'm dead meat, you know.
N-Now **this** is the majesty of a king! The might of a king!
I, Chandler, am moved to tears and cannot stop weeping!!
CLAP
CLAP
CLAP
CLAP
CLAP

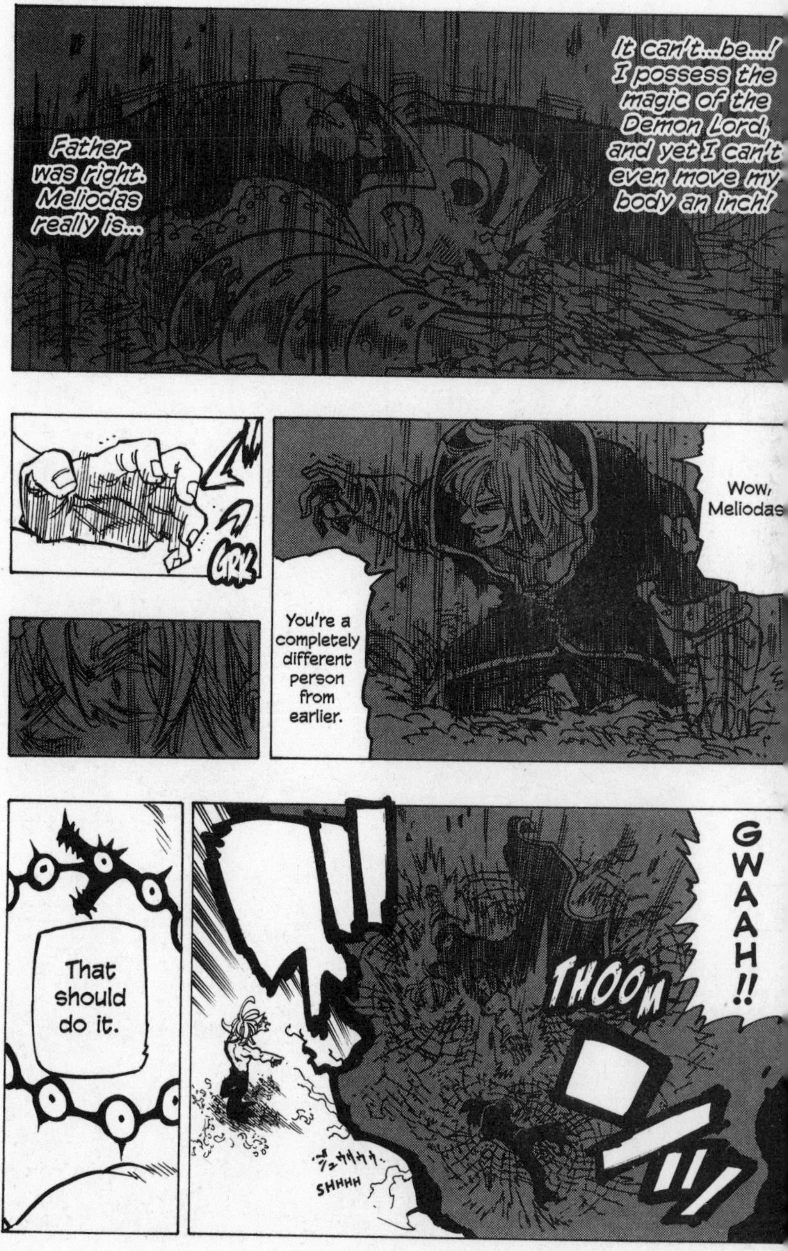
It can't...be...! I possess the magic of the Demon Lord, and yet I can't even move my body an inch!
Father was right. Meliodas really is...
Wow, Meliodas
You're a completely different person from earlier.
GRK
GWAAH!!
THOOM
SHHHH
That should do it.

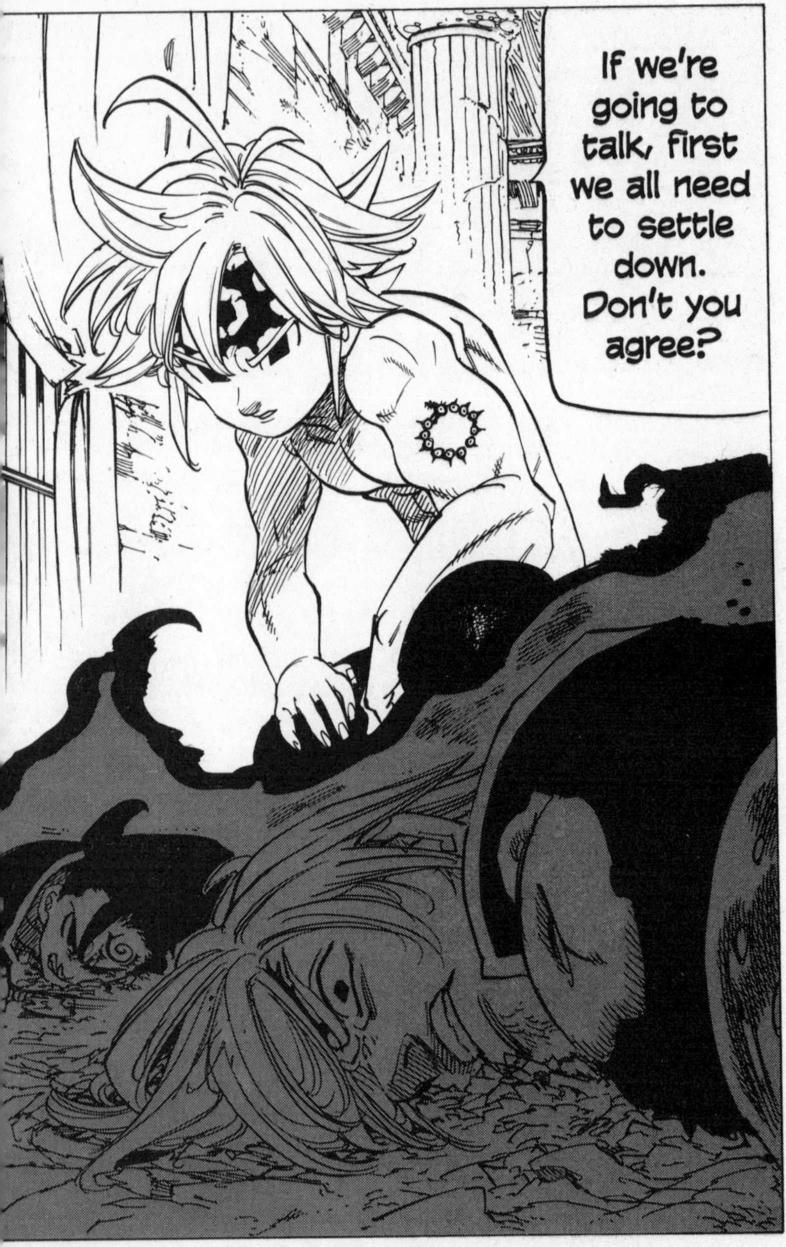
If we're going to talk, first we all need to settle down. Don't you agree?

Chapter 247 - Collectin

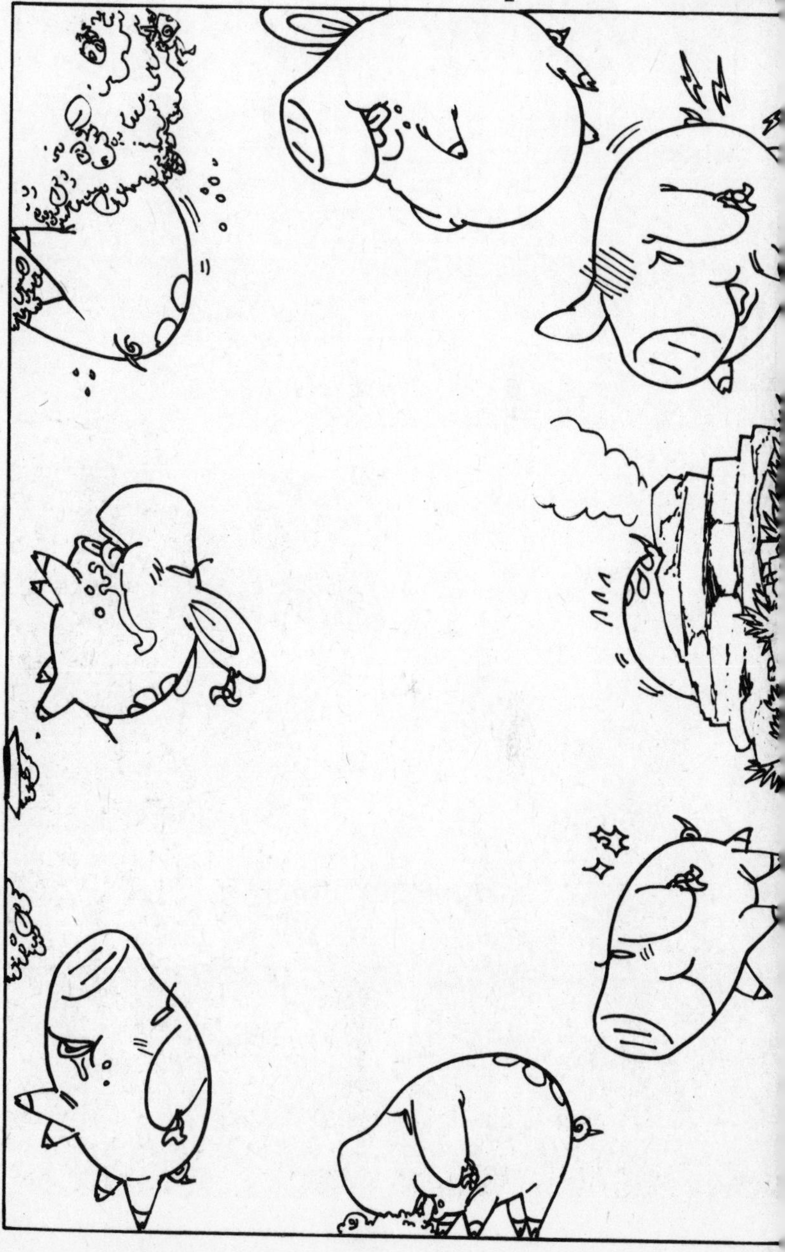

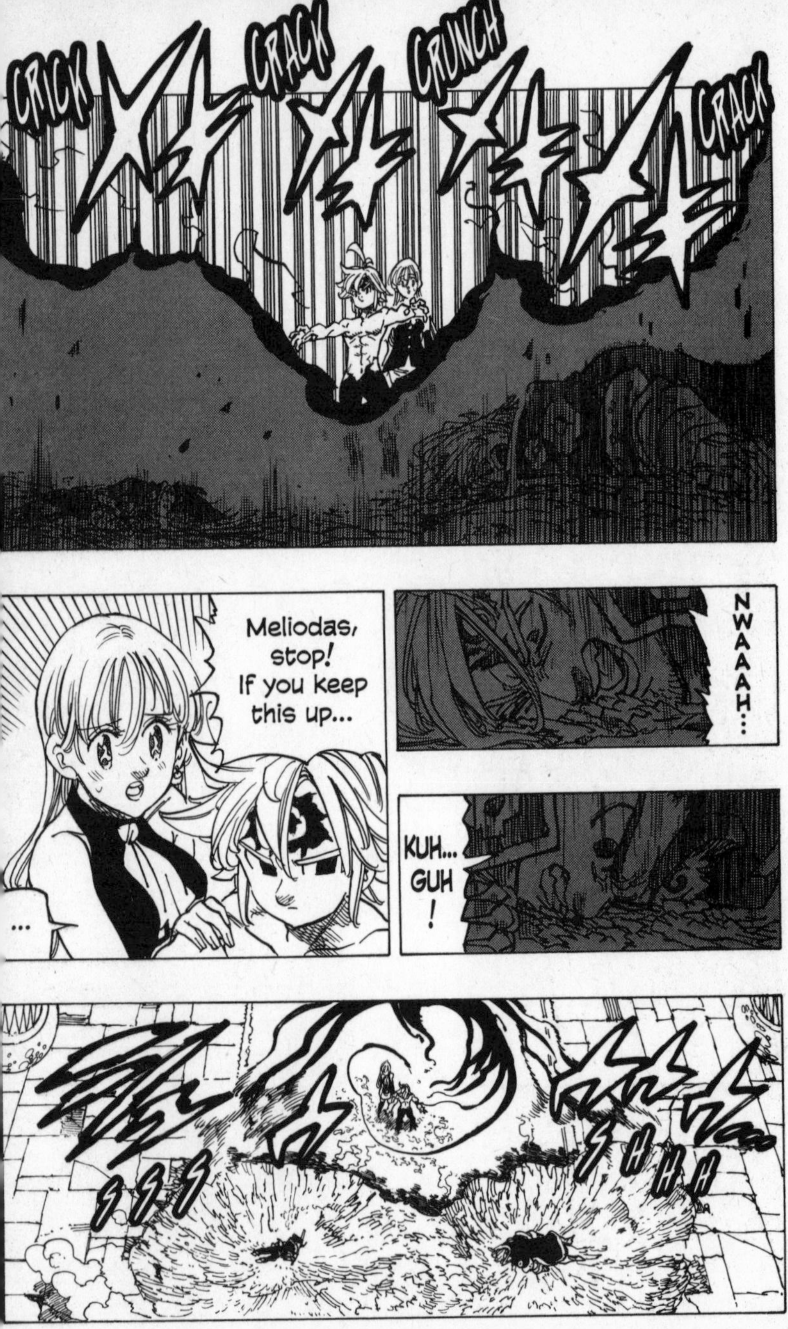
CRACK
CRUNCH
CRACK
CRICK
NWAAAAH...
KUH... GUH!
Meliodas, stop! If you keep this up...
...

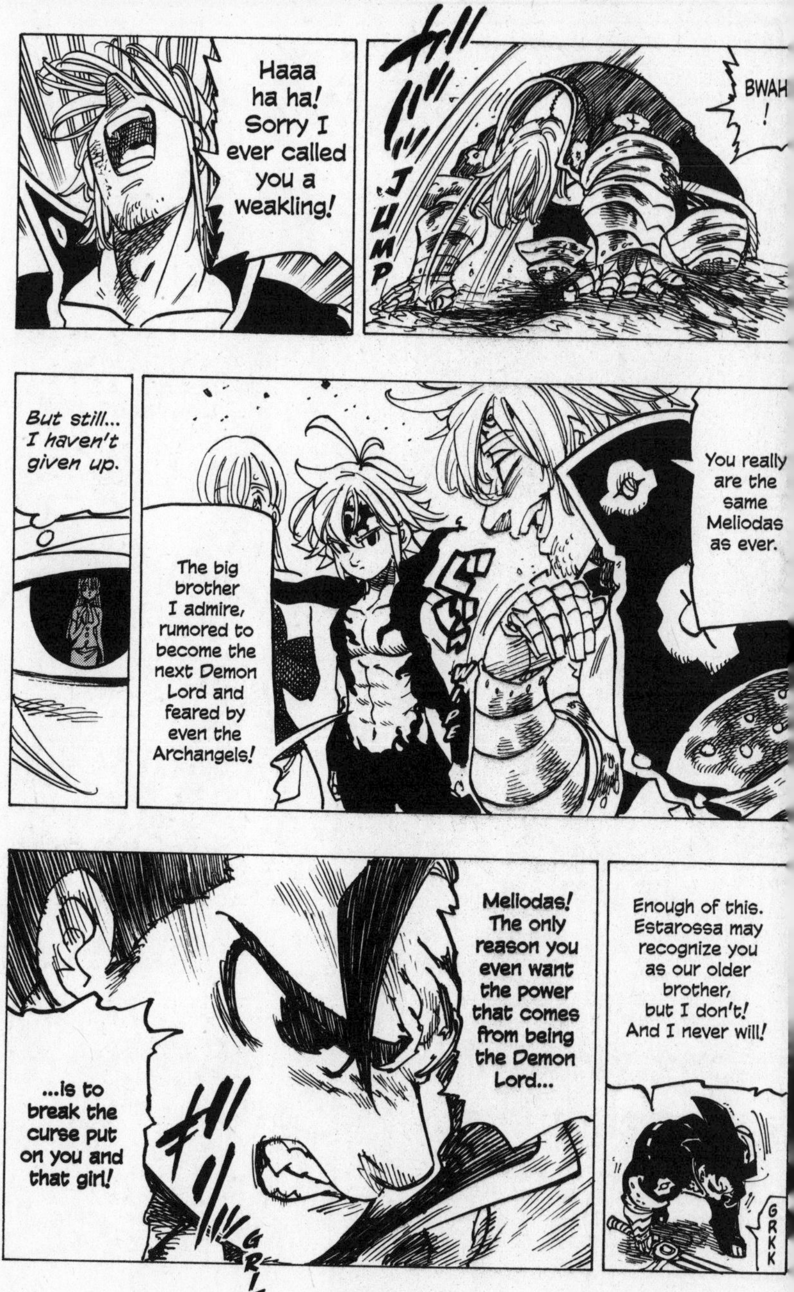
BWAH!
JUMP
Haaa ha ha! Sorry I ever called you a weakling!
You really are the same Meliodas as ever.
The big brother I admire, rumored to become the next Demon Lord and feared by even the Archangels!
WIPE
But still... I haven't given up.
Enough of this. Estarossa may recognize you as our older brother, but I don't! And I never will!
GRKK
Meliodas! The only reason you even want the power that comes from being the Demon Lord...
...is to break the curse put on you and that girl!
GRIT

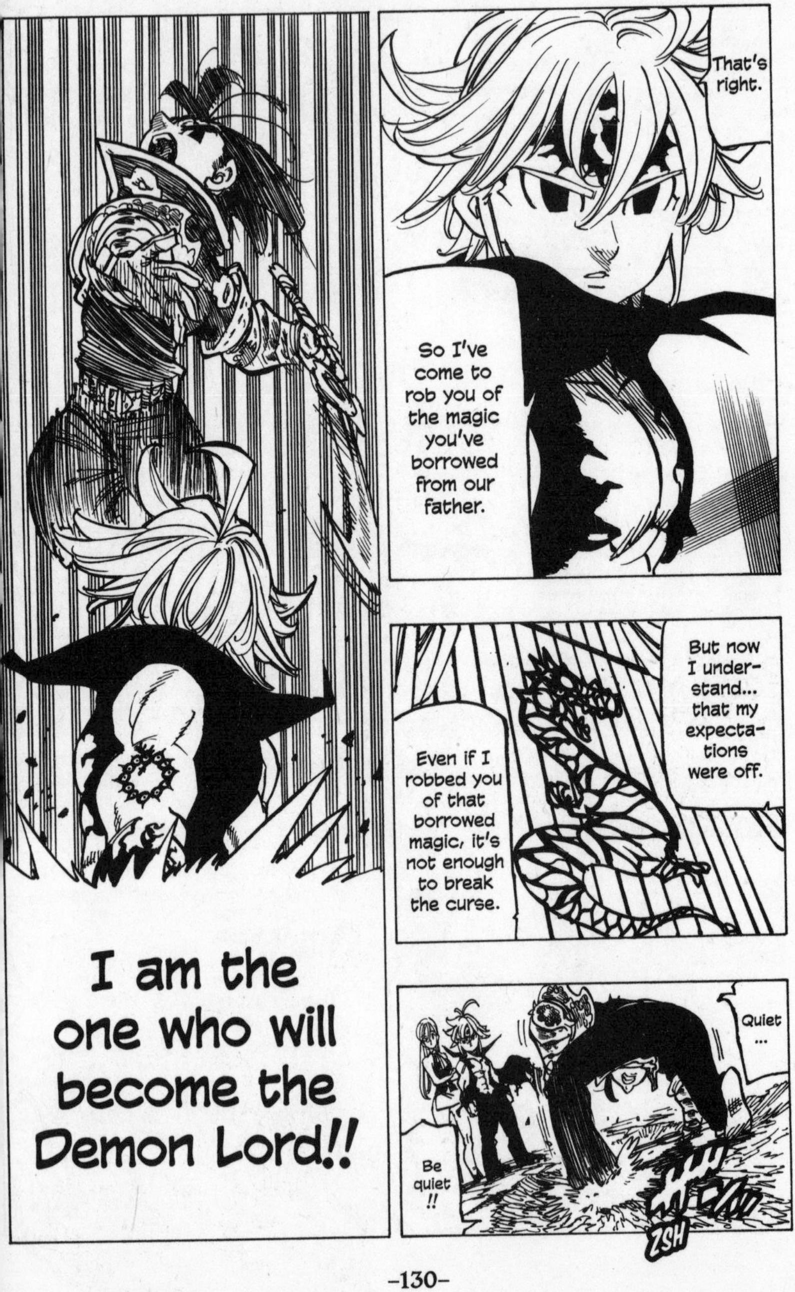
That's right.
So I've come to rob you of the magic you've borrowed from our father.
But now I understand... that my expectations were off.
Even if I robbed you of that borrowed magic, it's not enough to break the curse.
Quiet...
Be quiet!!
ZSH
I am the one who will become the Demon Lord!!

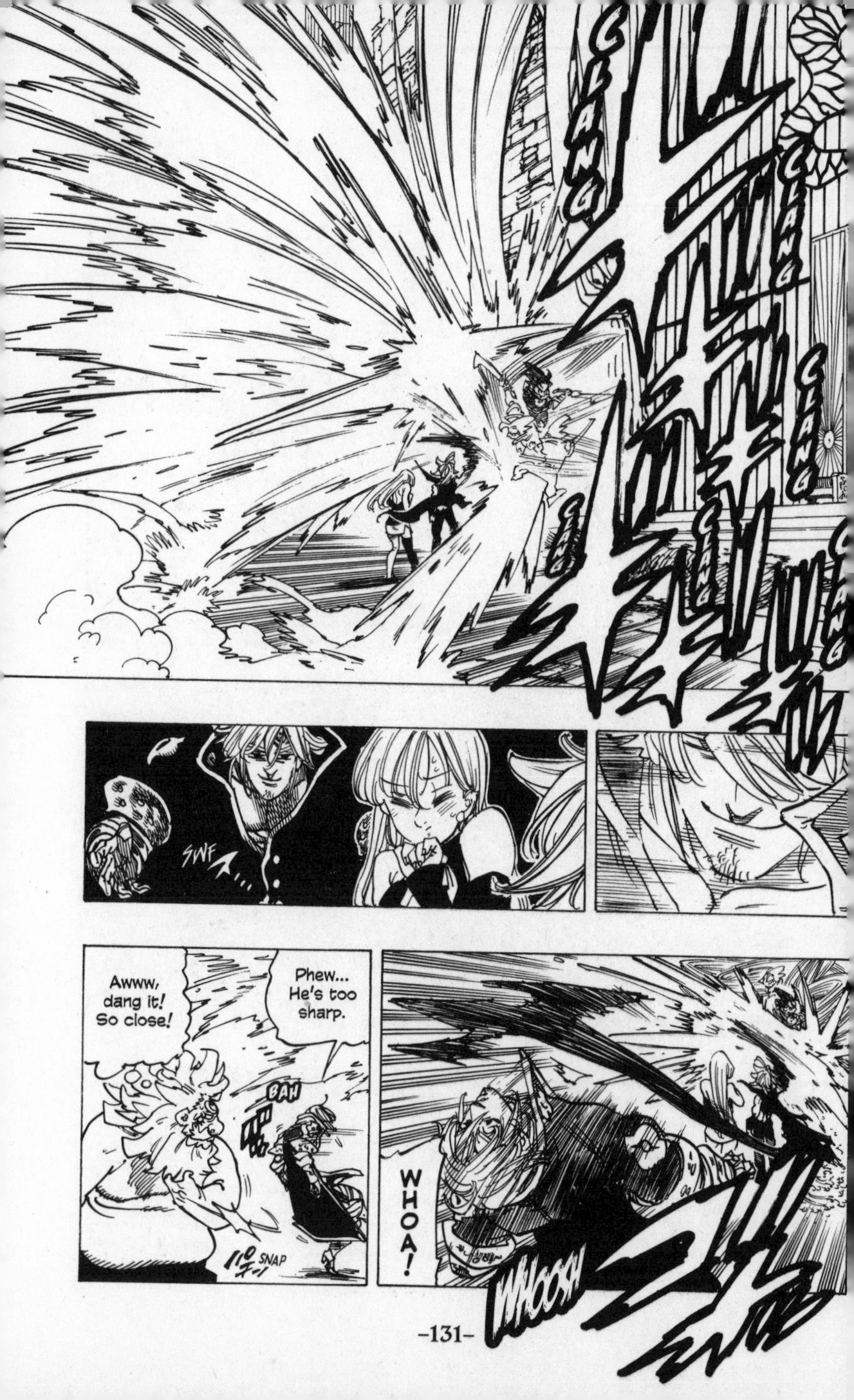

CLANG
CLANG
CLANG
CLANG
CLANG
CLANG
SWF
WHOA!
WHOOSH
Phew... He's too sharp.
Awww, dang it! So close!
BAH
SNAP

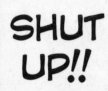

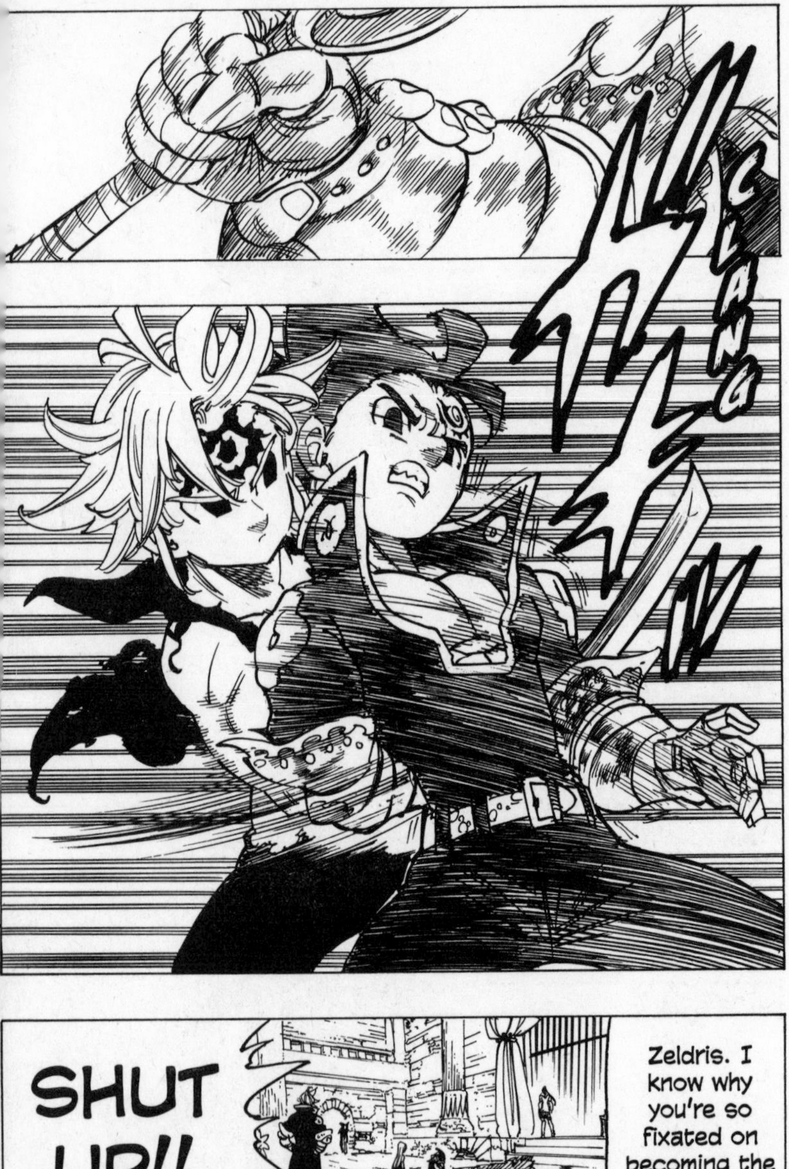
CLANG
Zeldris. I know why you're so fixated on becoming the Demon Lord.
SHUT UP!!

GO...
STAGGER

...?

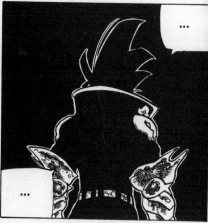

...

...

Zeldris-
sama...
What's
the
matter
?

Z...

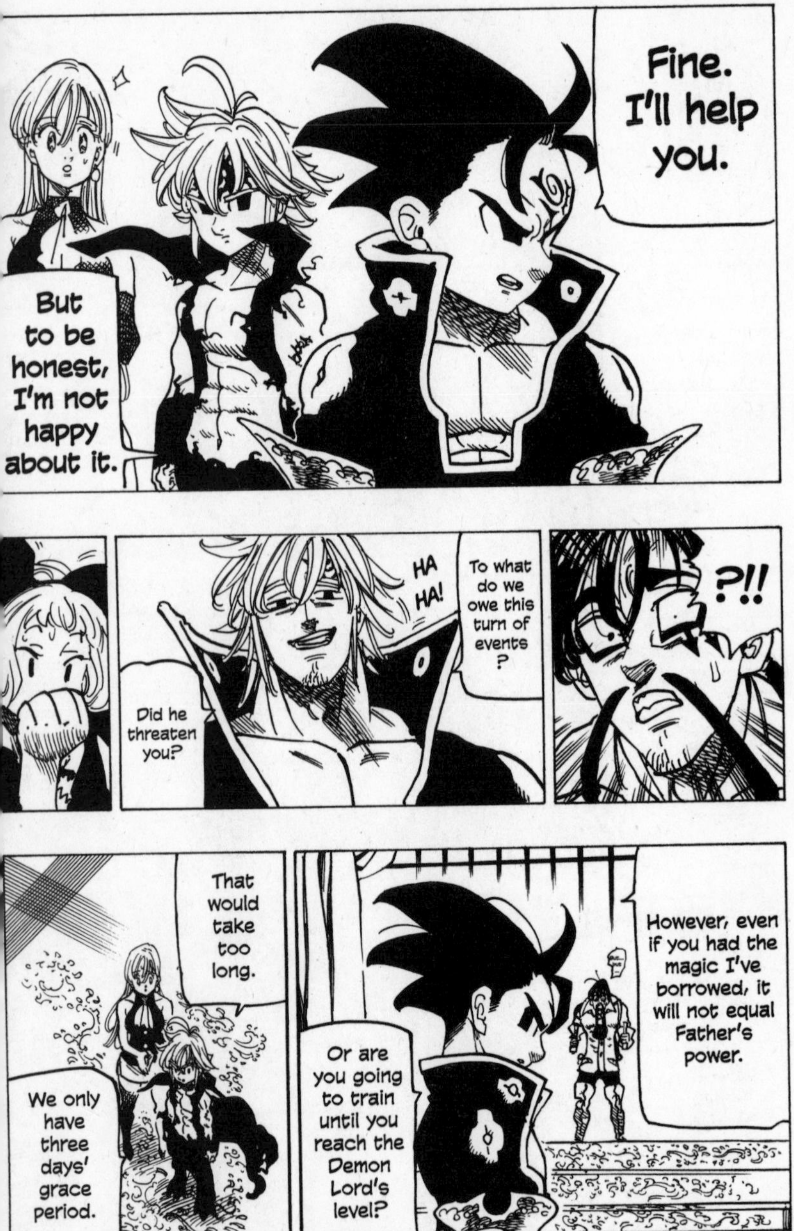
Fine. I'll help you.
But to be honest, I'm not happy about it.
?!!
To what do we owe this turn of events?
HA HA!
Did he threaten you?
However, even if you had the magic I've borrowed, it will not equal Father's power.
Or are you going to train until you reach the Demon Lord's level?
That would take too long.
We only have three days' grace period.

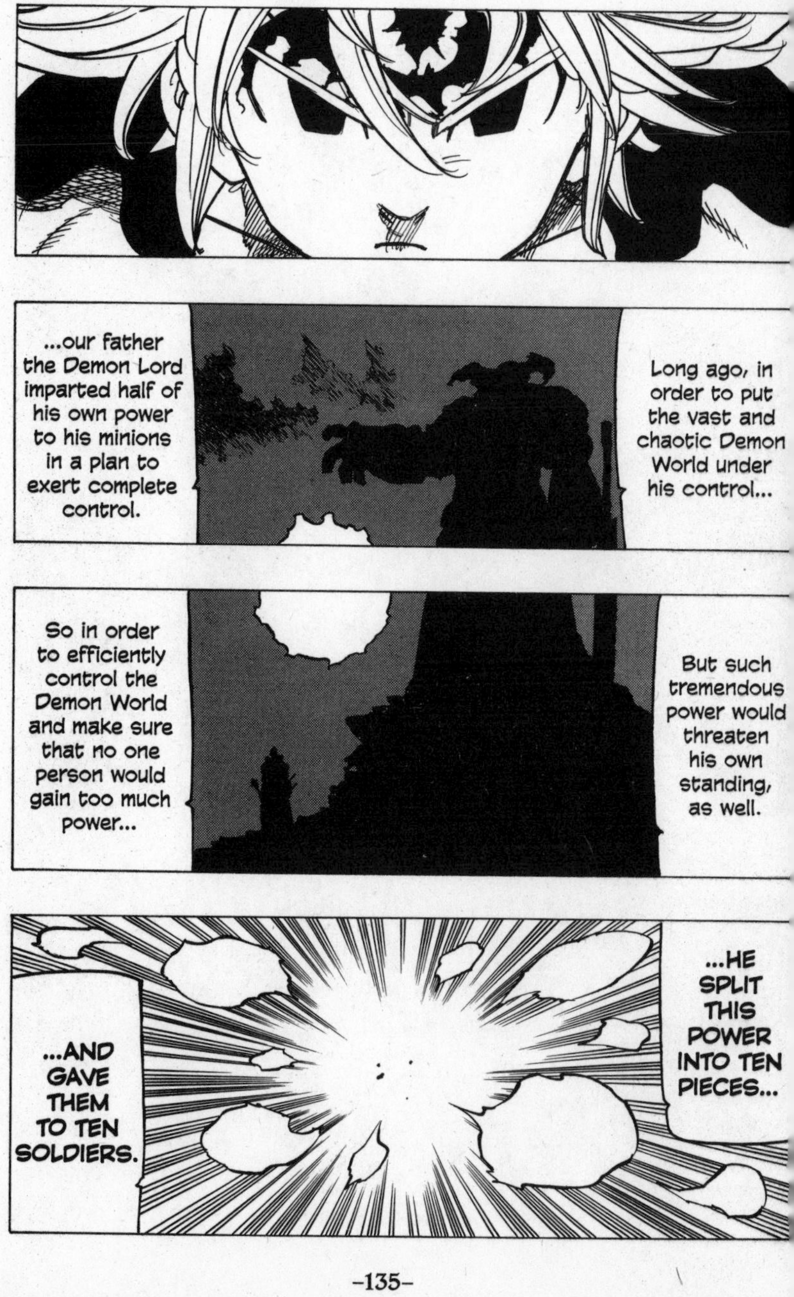
Long ago, in order to put the vast and chaotic Demon World under his control...
...our father the Demon Lord imparted half of his own power to his minions in a plan to exert complete control.
But such tremendous power would threaten his own standing, as well.
So in order to efficiently control the Demon World and make sure that no one person would gain too much power...
...HE SPLIT THIS POWER INTO TEN PIECES...
...AND GAVE THEM TO TEN SOLDIERS.

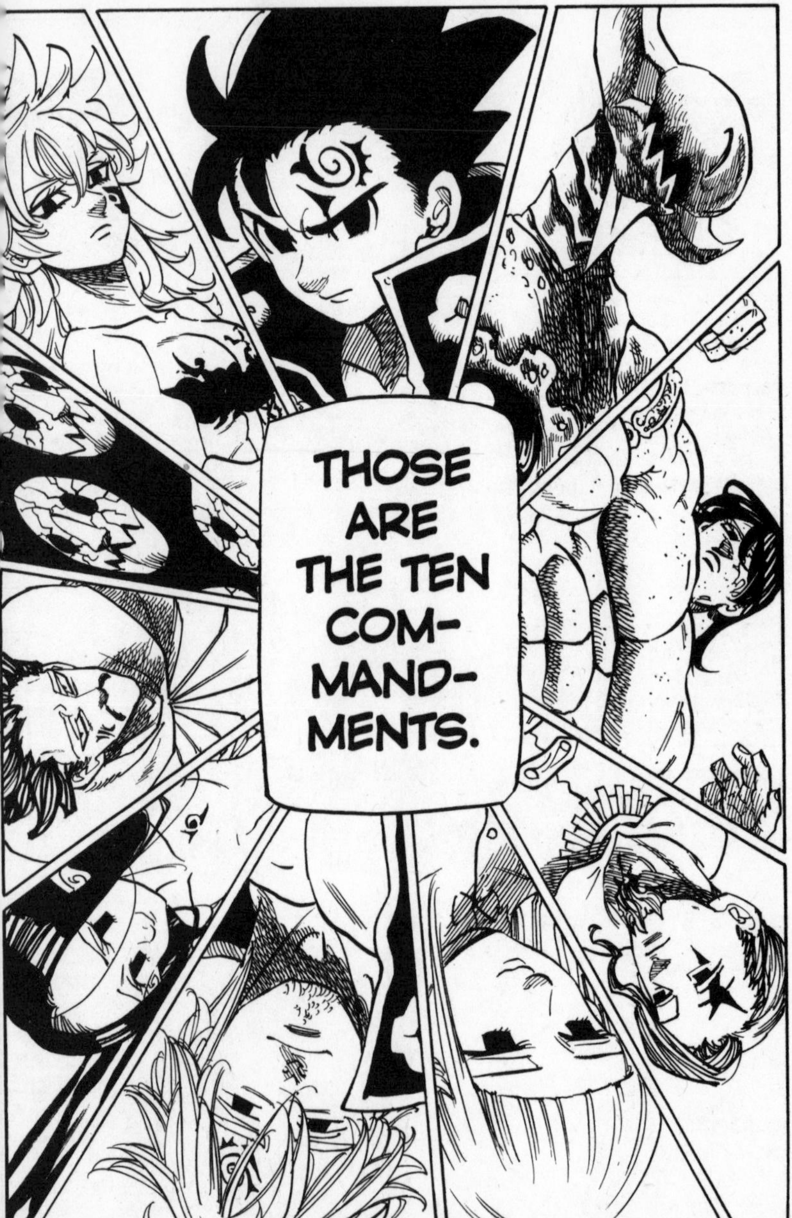
THOSE ARE THE TEN COM-MAND-MENTS.

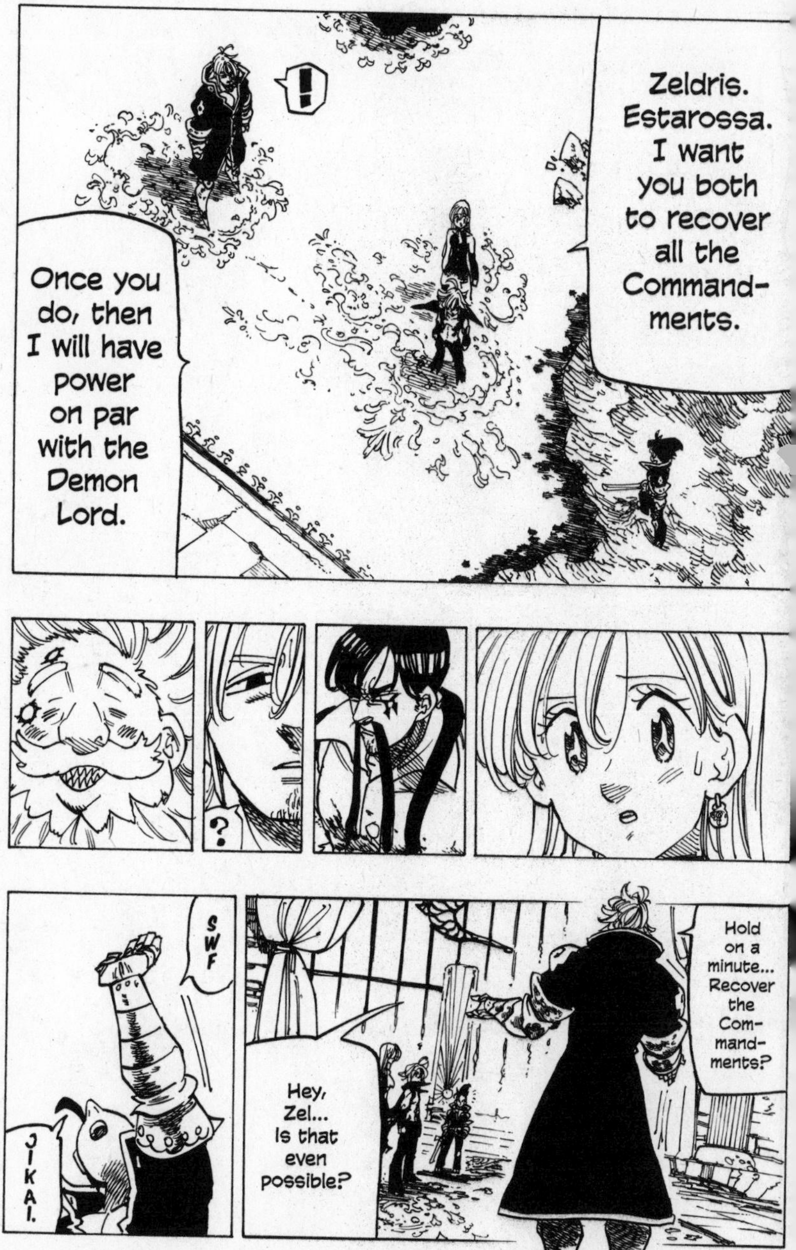
Zeldris. Estarossa. I want you both to recover all the Command-ments.
!
Once you do, then I will have power on par with the Demon Lord.
?
Hold on a minute... Recover the Com-mand-ments?
Hey, Zel... Is that even possible?
SWF
JIKAI.

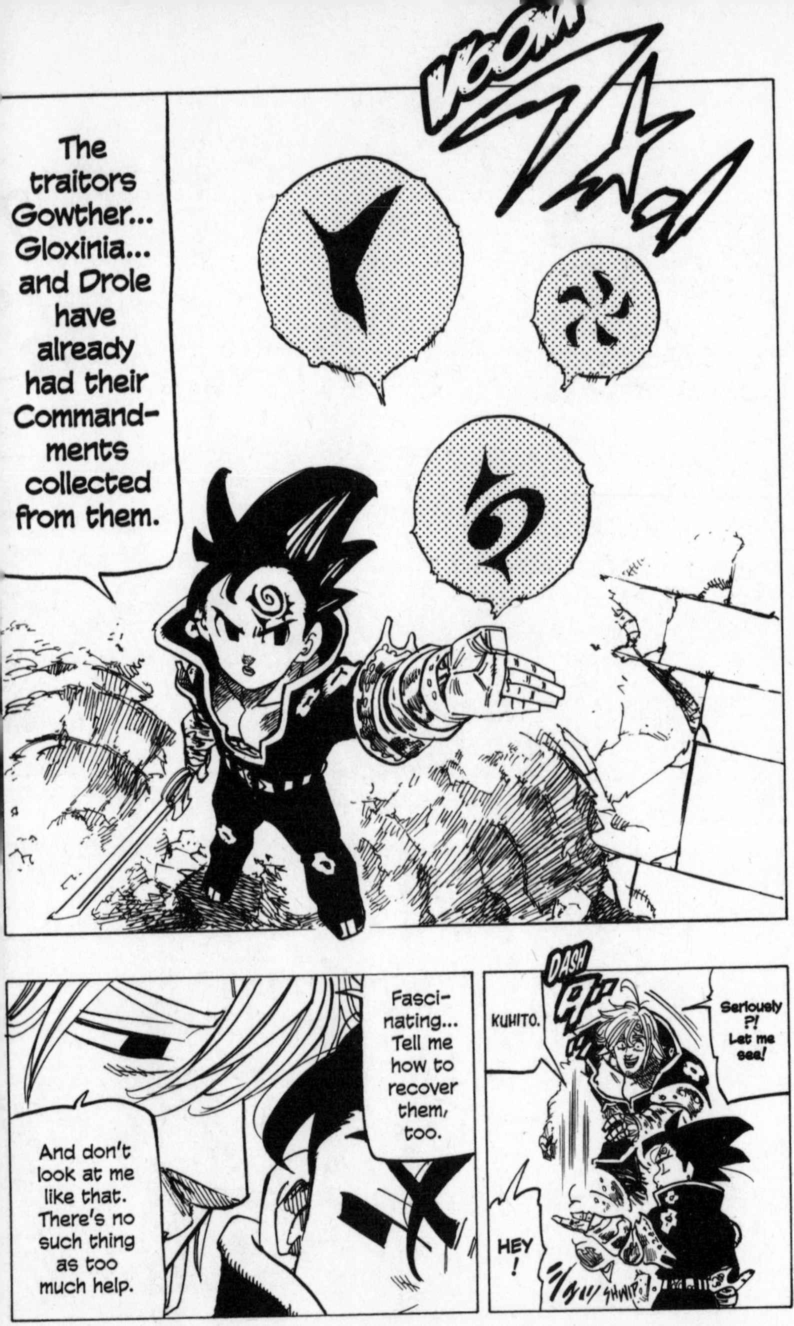
VOOM
The traitors Gowther... Gloxinia... and Drole have already had their Command-ments collected from them.
Seriously ?! Let me see!
DASH
KUHITO.
HEY !
SHWIP
Fasci-nating... Tell me how to recover them, too.
And don't look at me like that. There's no such thing as too much help.

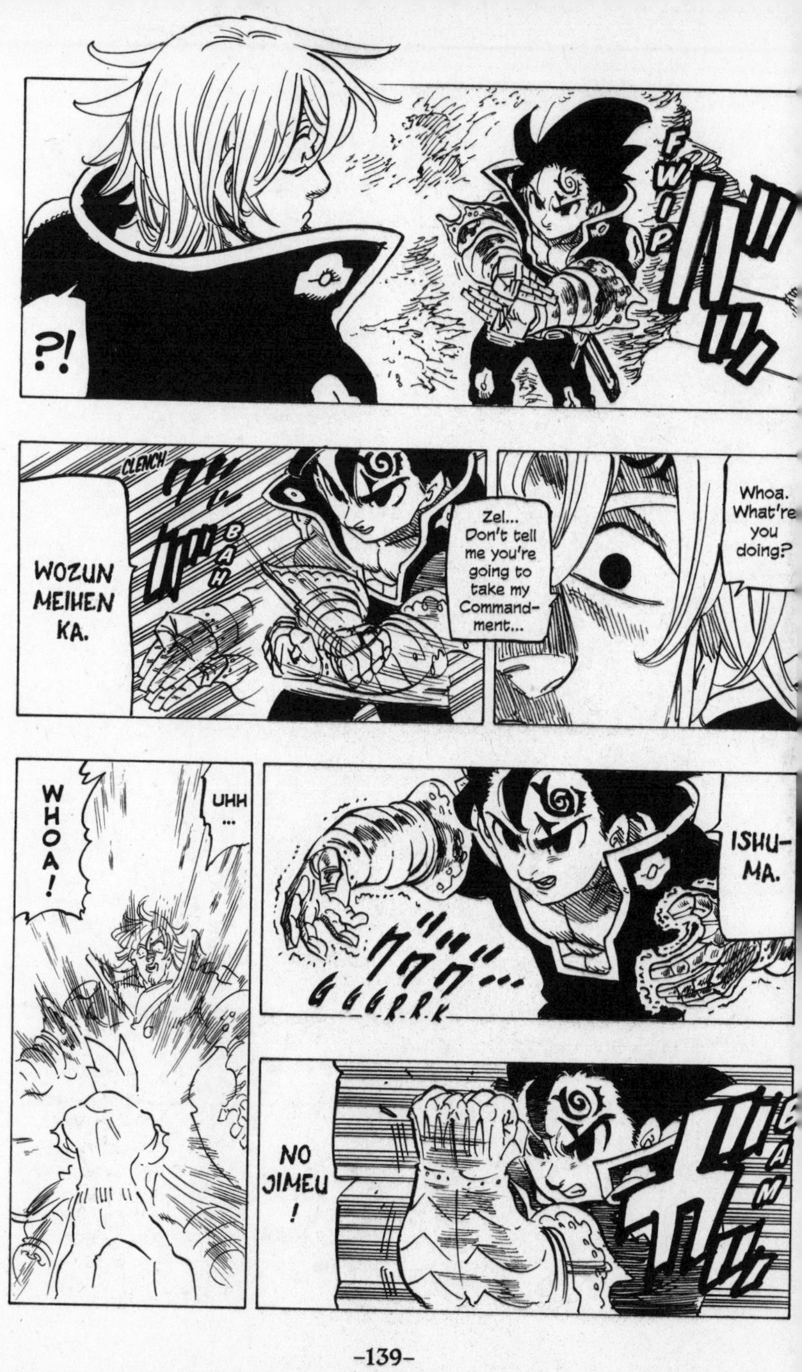
FWIP
?!
Whoa. What're you doing?
Zel... Don't tell me you're going to take my Command-ment...
CLENCH
BAH
WOZUN MEIHEN KA.
ISHU-MA.
GGGRRK
BAM
NO JIMEU!
UHH...
WHOA!

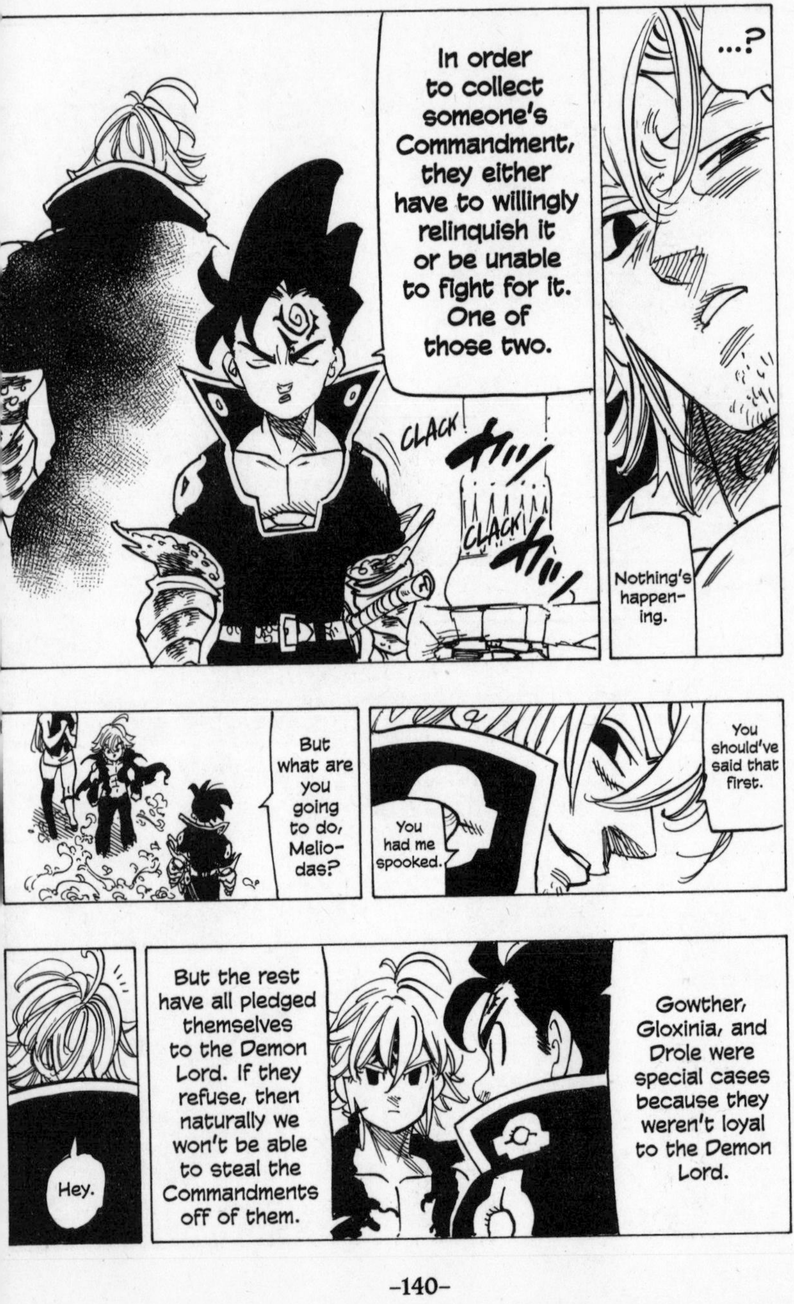
...?
Nothing's happen-ing.
In order to collect someone's Commandment, they either have to willingly relinquish it or be unable to fight for it. One of those two.
CLACK
CLACK
You should've said that first.
You had me spooked.
But what are you going to do, Melio-das?
Gowther, Gloxinia, and Drole were special cases because they weren't loyal to the Demon Lord.
But the rest have all pledged themselves to the Demon Lord. If they refuse, then naturally we won't be able to steal the Commandments off of them.
Hey.

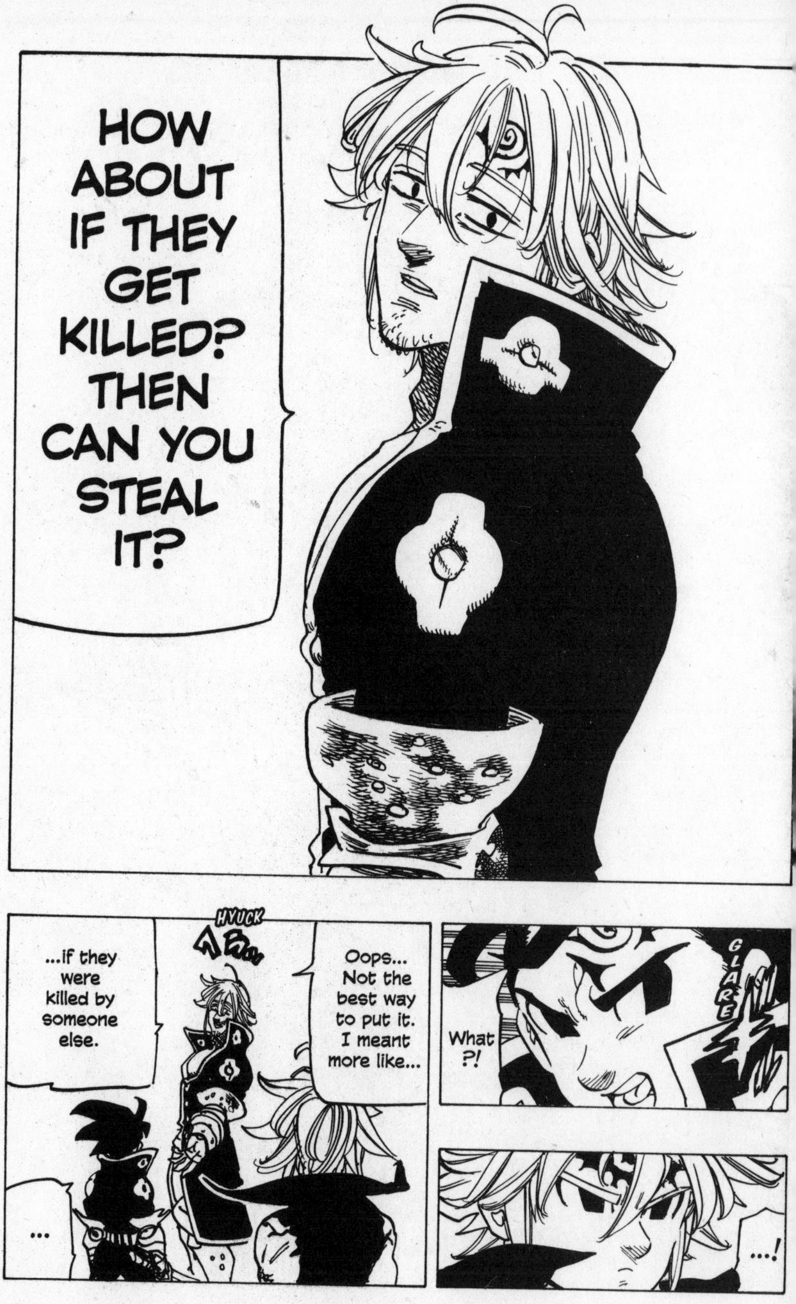
HOW ABOUT IF THEY GET KILLED? THEN CAN YOU STEAL IT?
GLARE
What ?!
...!
Oops... Not the best way to put it. I meant more like...
HYUCK
...if they were killed by someone else.
...

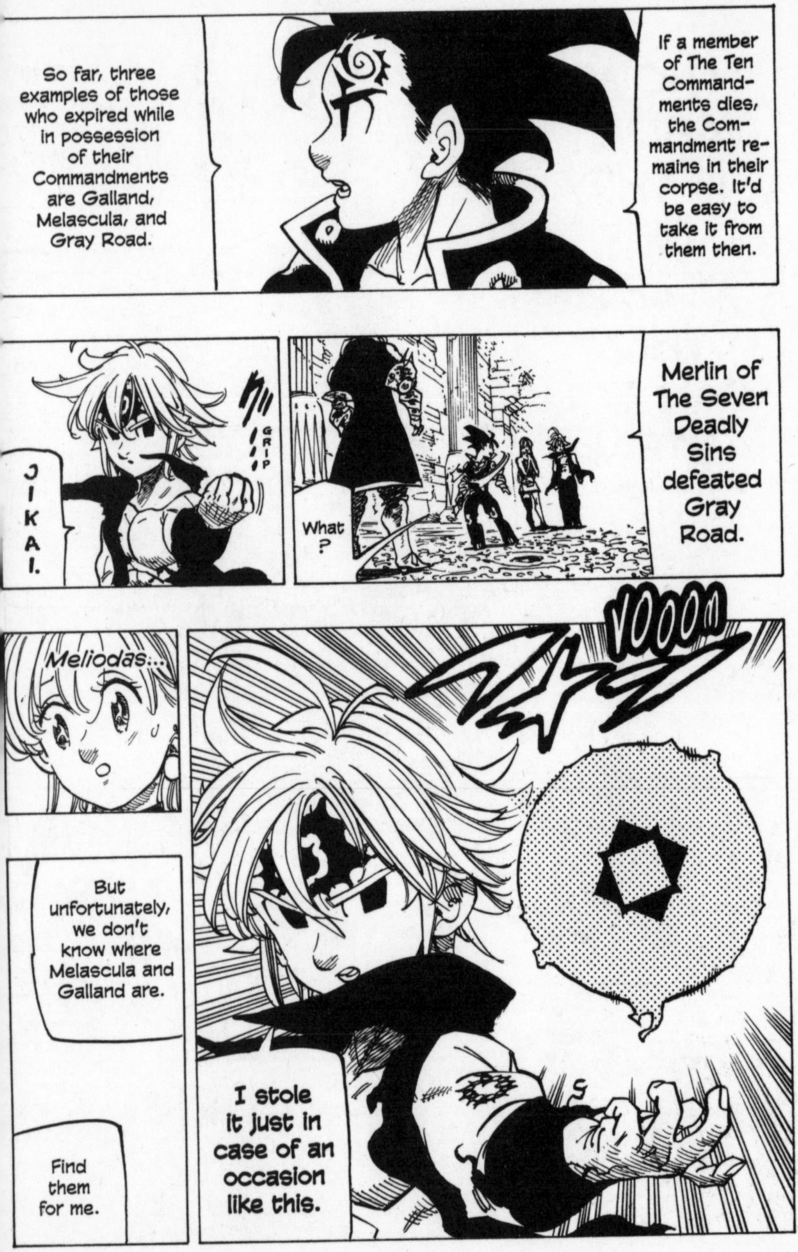
If a member of The Ten Commandments dies, the Commandment remains in their corpse. It'd be easy to take it from them then.
So far, three examples of those who expired while in possession of their Commandments are Galland, Melascula, and Gray Road.
Merlin of The Seven Deadly Sins defeated Gray Road.
What?
GRIP
JIKAI.
VOOOM
I stole it just in case of an occasion like this.
Meliodas...
But unfortunately, we don't know where Melascula and Galland are.
Find them for me.

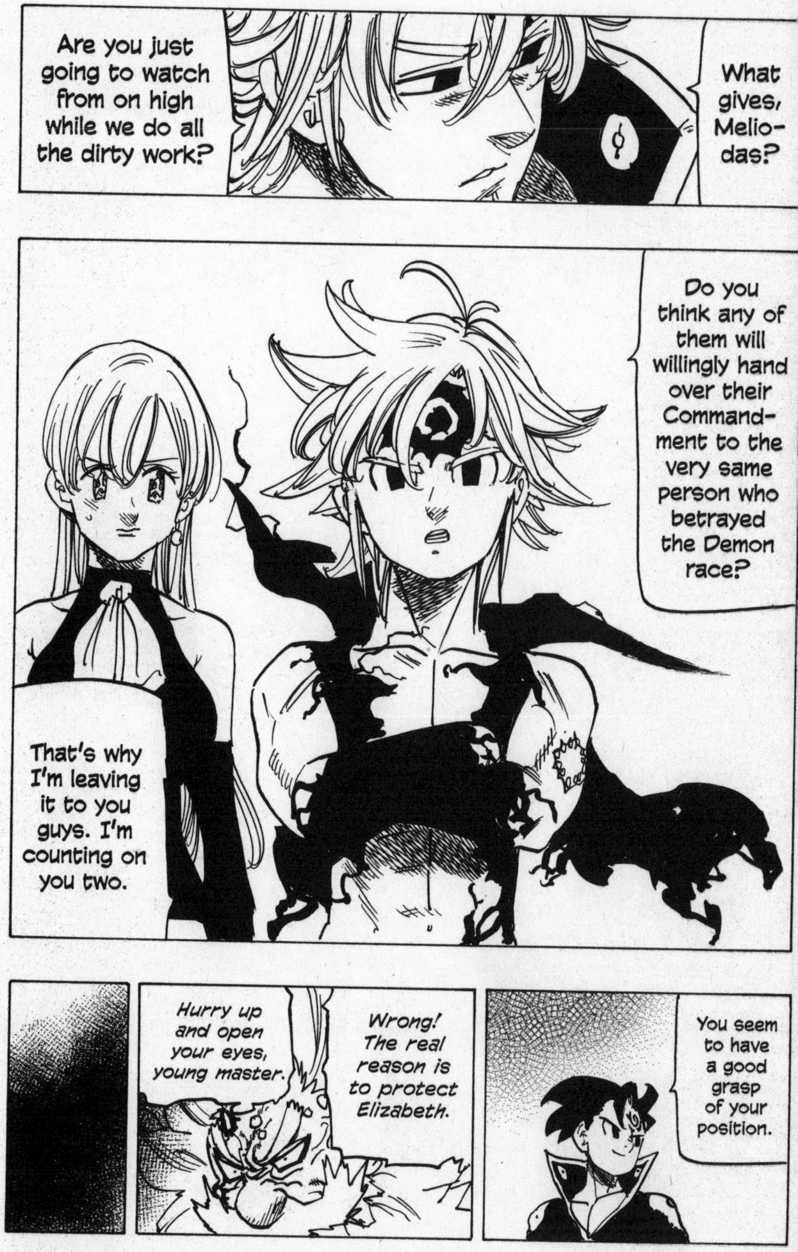
What gives, Melio-das?
Are you just going to watch from on high while we do all the dirty work?
Do you think any of them will willingly hand over their Command-ment to the very same person who betrayed the Demon race?
That's why I'm leaving it to you guys. I'm counting on you two.
You seem to have a good grasp of your position.
Wrong! The real reason is to protect Elizabeth.
Hurry up and open your eyes, young master.

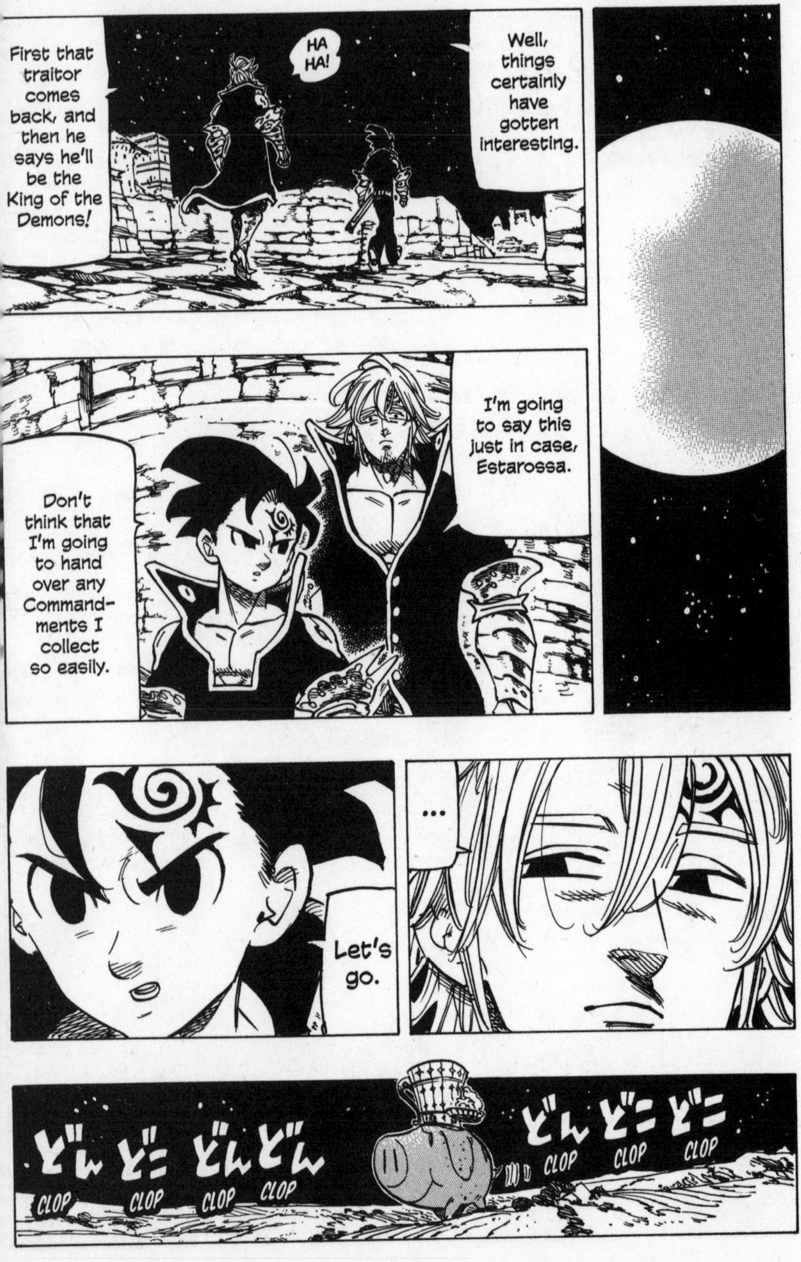
Well, things certainly have gotten interesting.
HA HA!
First that traitor comes back, and then he says he'll be the King of the Demons!
I'm going to say this just in case, Estarossa.
Don't think that I'm going to hand over any Command-ments I collect so easily.
...
Let's go.
どこ CLOP
どこ CLOP
どん CLOP
どん CLOP
どん CLOP
どこ CLOP
どん CLOP

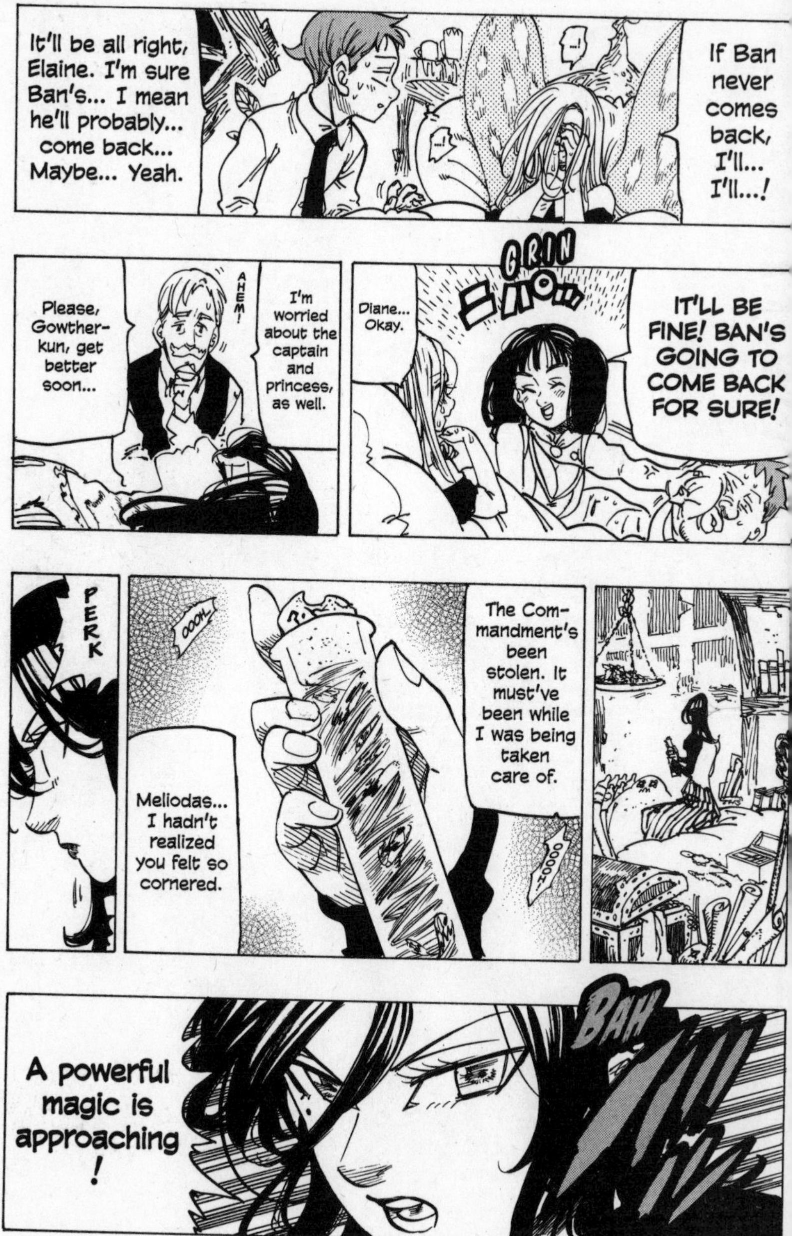
If Ban never comes back, I'll... I'll...!
It'll be all right, Elaine. I'm sure Ban's... I mean he'll probably... come back... Maybe... Yeah.
GRIN
IT'LL BE FINE! BAN'S GOING TO COME BACK FOR SURE!
Diane... Okay.
I'm worried about the captain and princess, as well.
AHEM!
Please, Gowther-kun, get better soon...
The Commandment's been stolen. It must've been while I was being taken care of.
OOOH...
OOOH...
Meliodas... I hadn't realized you felt so cornered.
PERK
BAH
A powerful magic is approaching!

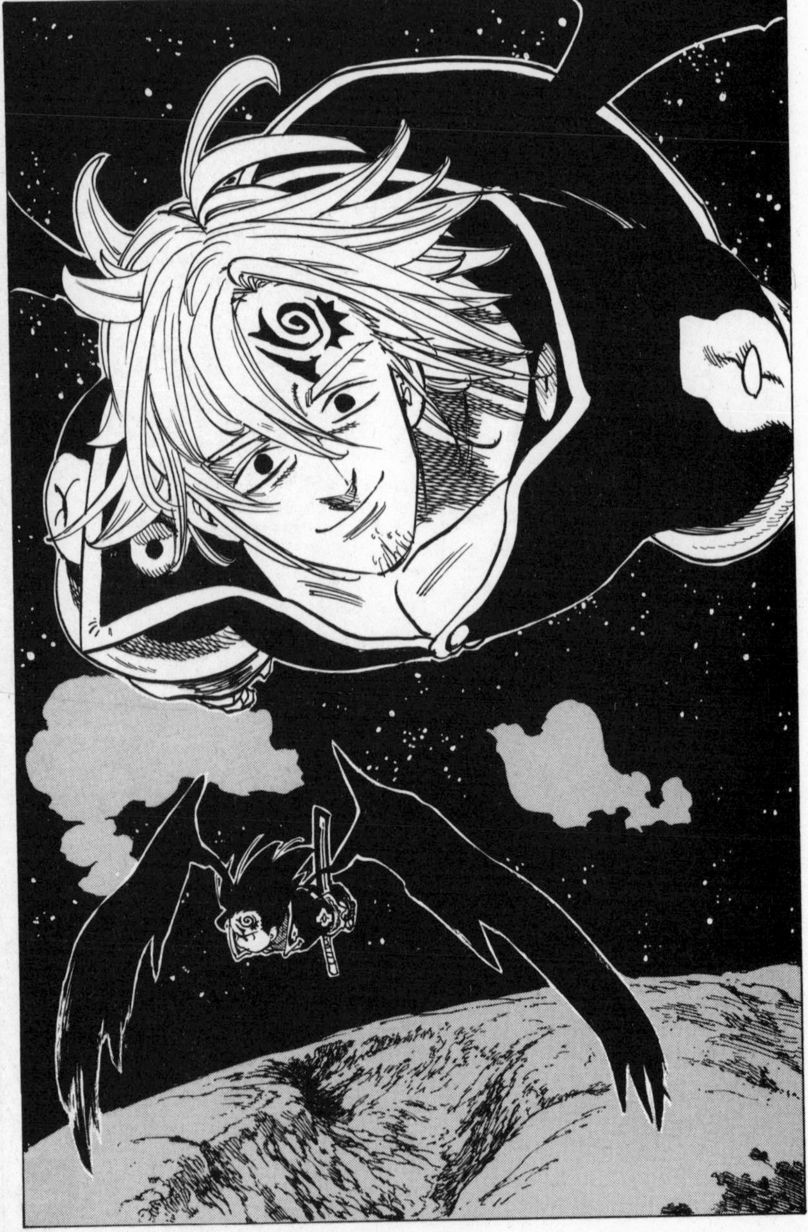

Chapter 248 - Our Choice

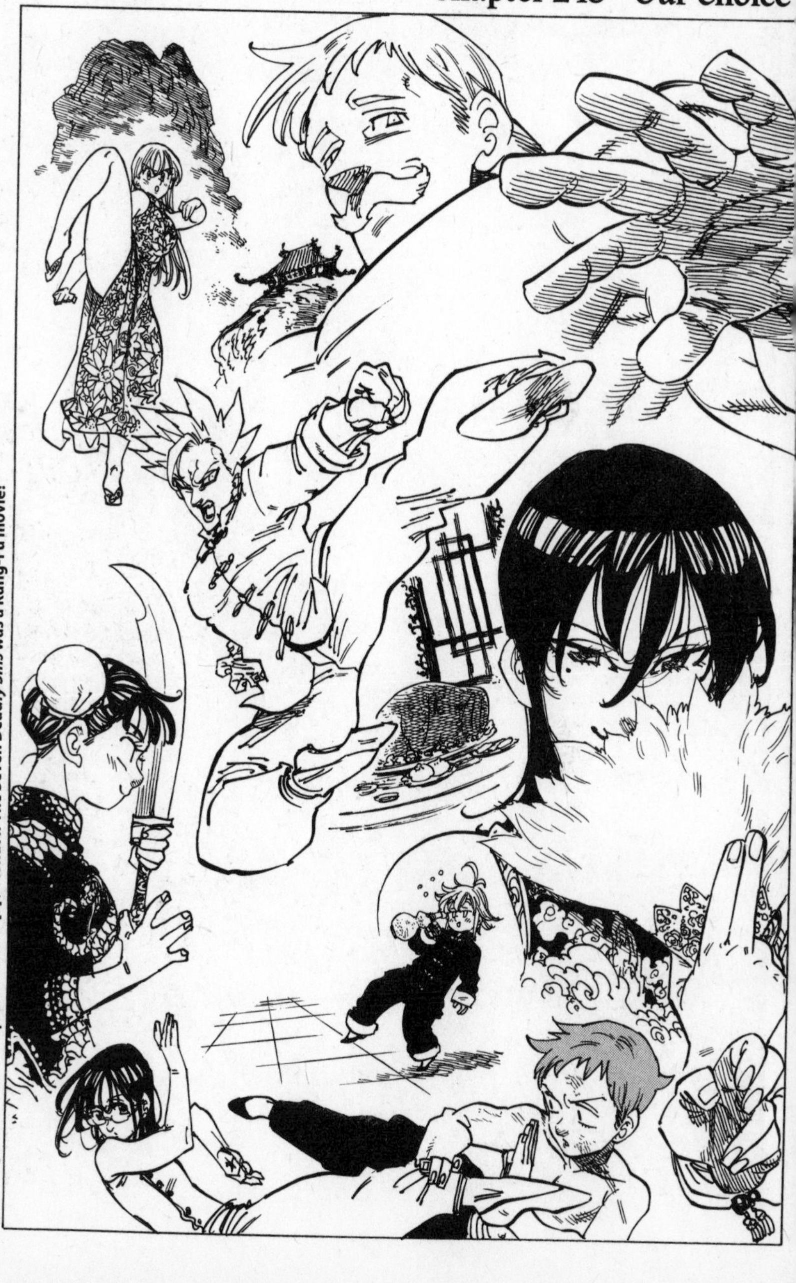

Front Page Illustration Request Corner!! [6] / "What if *The Seven Deadly Sins* was a Kung-Fu movie?"

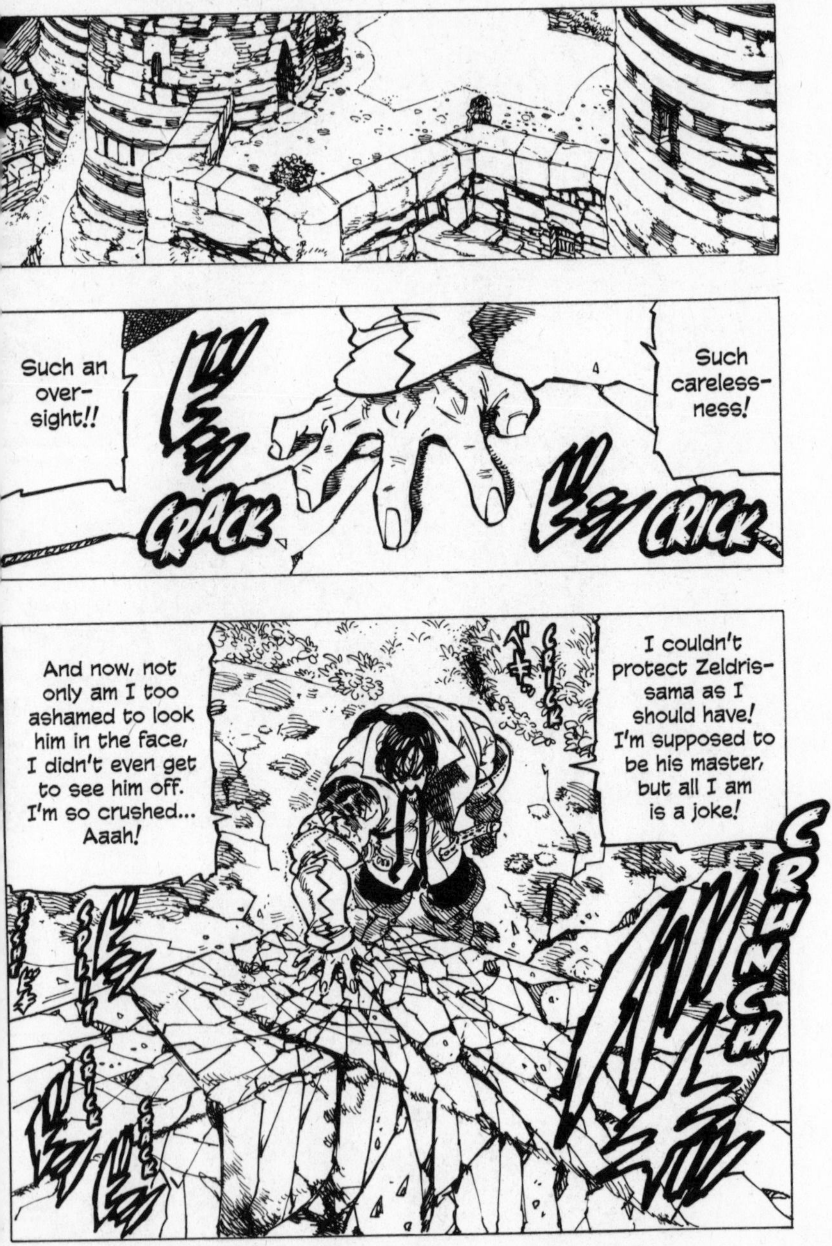

Such careless-ness!
Such an over-sight!!
CRICK
CRACK
I couldn't protect Zeldris-sama as I should have! I'm supposed to be his master, but all I am is a joke!
And now, not only am I too ashamed to look him in the face, I didn't even get to see him off. I'm so crushed... Aaah!
CRICK
CRUNCH
SPLIT
BSSHT
CRACK
CRICK

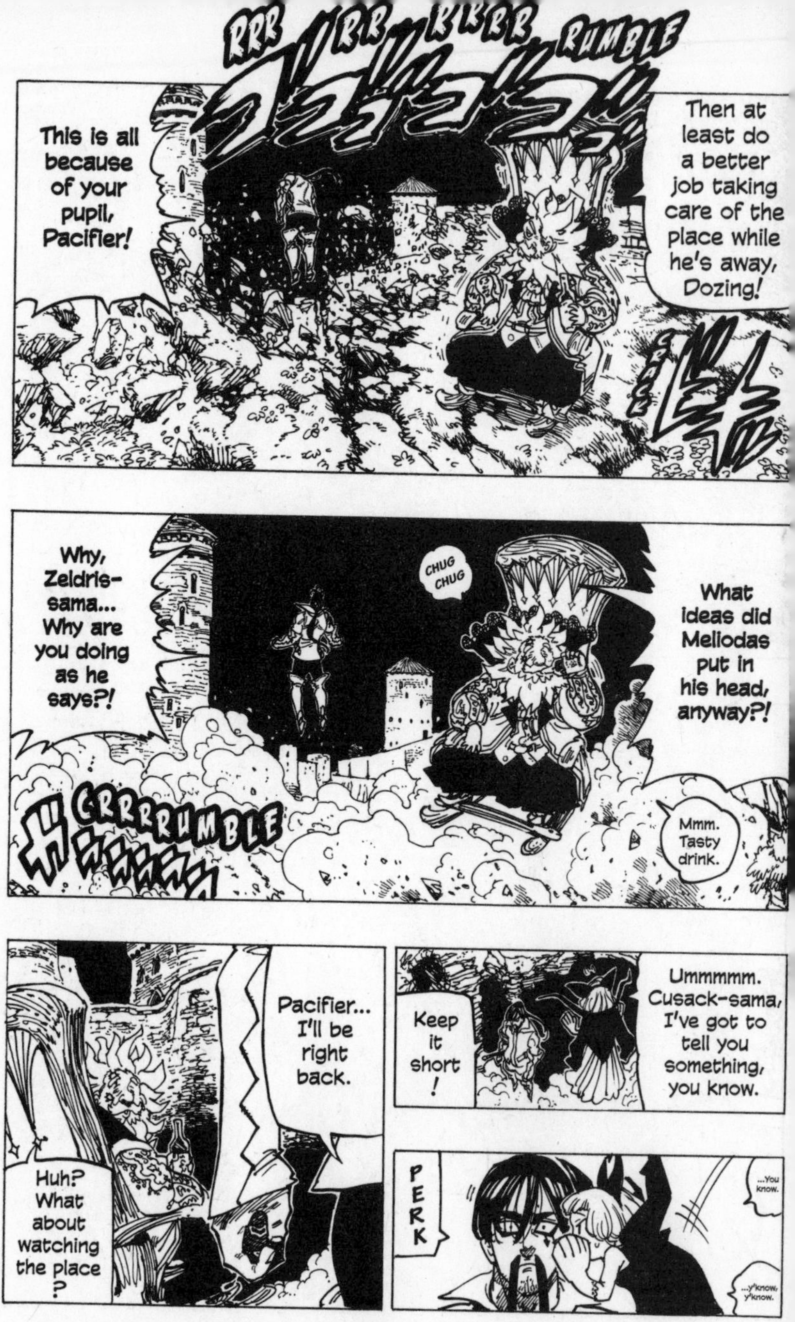
RRR RRR RRRR RUMBLE
Then at least do a better job taking care of the place while he's away, Dozing!
This is all because of your pupil, Pacifier!
CRACK
What ideas did Meliodas put in his head, anyway?!
CHUG CHUG
Why, Zeldris-sama... Why are you doing as he says?!
Mmm. Tasty drink.
CRRRRUMBLE
Ummmmm. Cusack-sama, I've got to tell you something, you know.
Keep it short!
...You know.
PERK
...y'know, y'know.
Pacifier... I'll be right back.
Huh? What about watching the place?

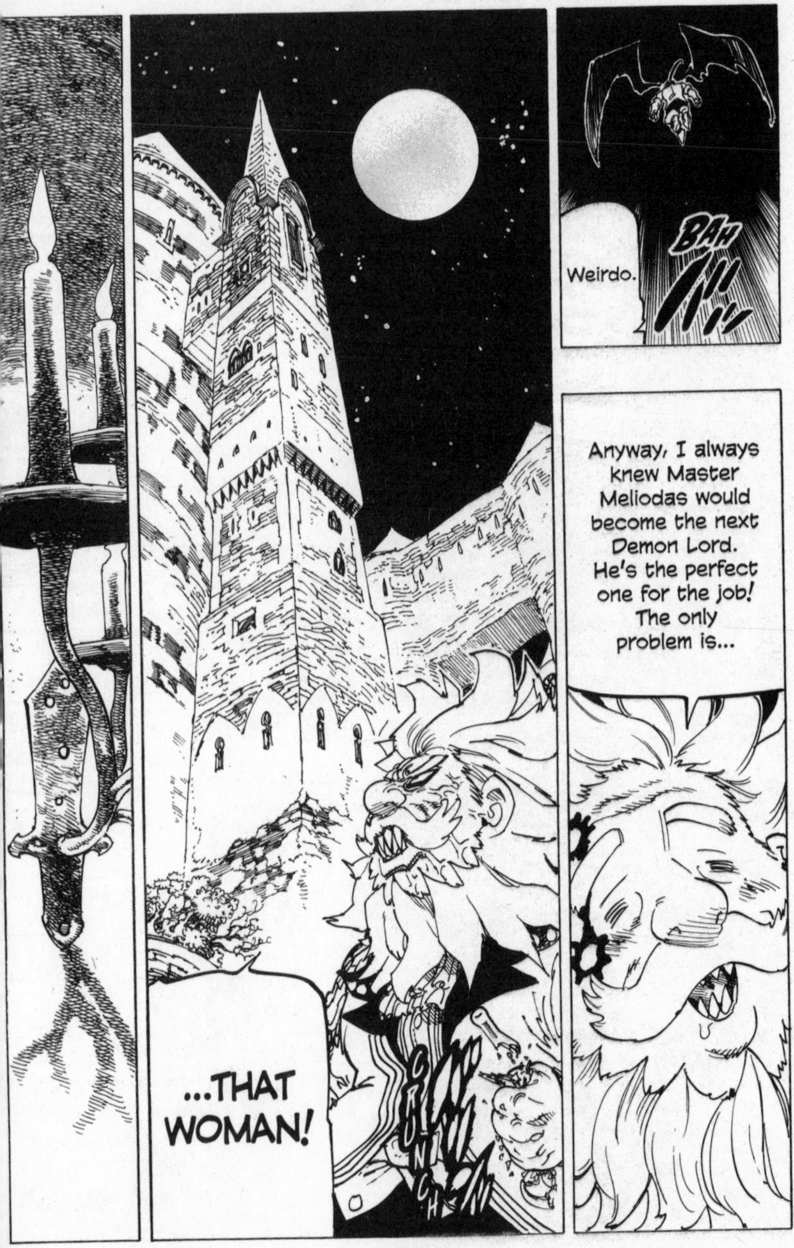
BAH
Weirdo.
Anyway, I always knew Master Meliodas would become the next Demon Lord. He's the perfect one for the job! The only problem is...
...THAT WOMAN!
CRUNCH

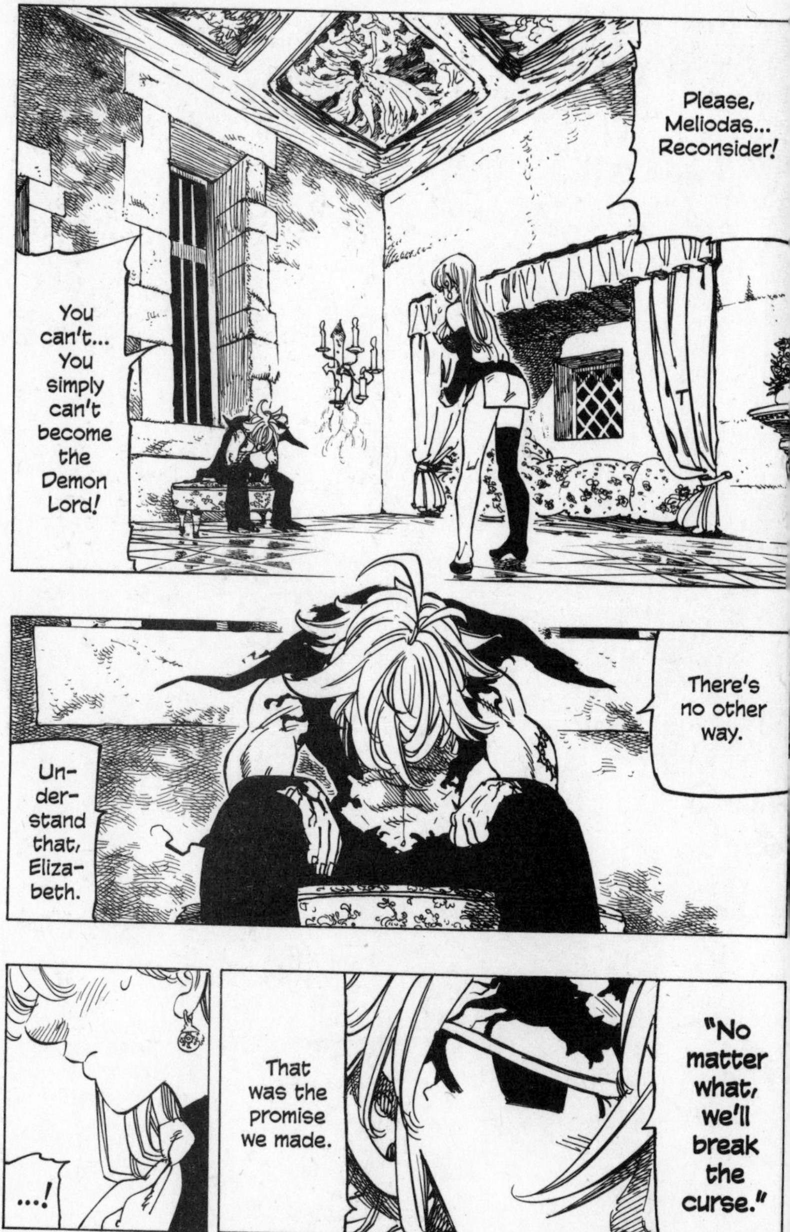
Please, Meliodas... Reconsider!
You can't... You simply can't become the Demon Lord!
There's no other way.
Un-der-stand that, Eliza-beth.
"No matter what, we'll break the curse."
That was the promise we made.
...!

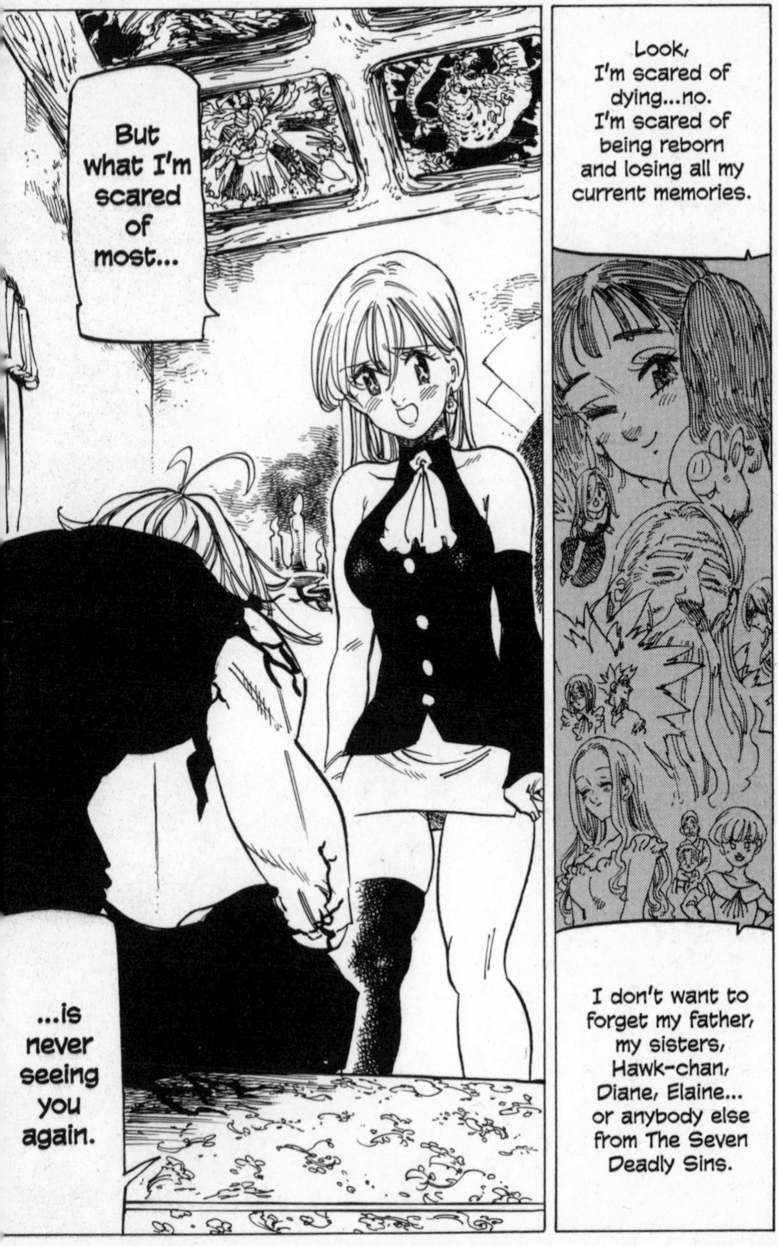
Look, I'm scared of dying...no. I'm scared of being reborn and losing all my current memories.
I don't want to forget my father, my sisters, Hawk-chan, Diane, Elaine... or anybody else from The Seven Deadly Sins.
But what I'm scared of most...
...is never seeing you again.

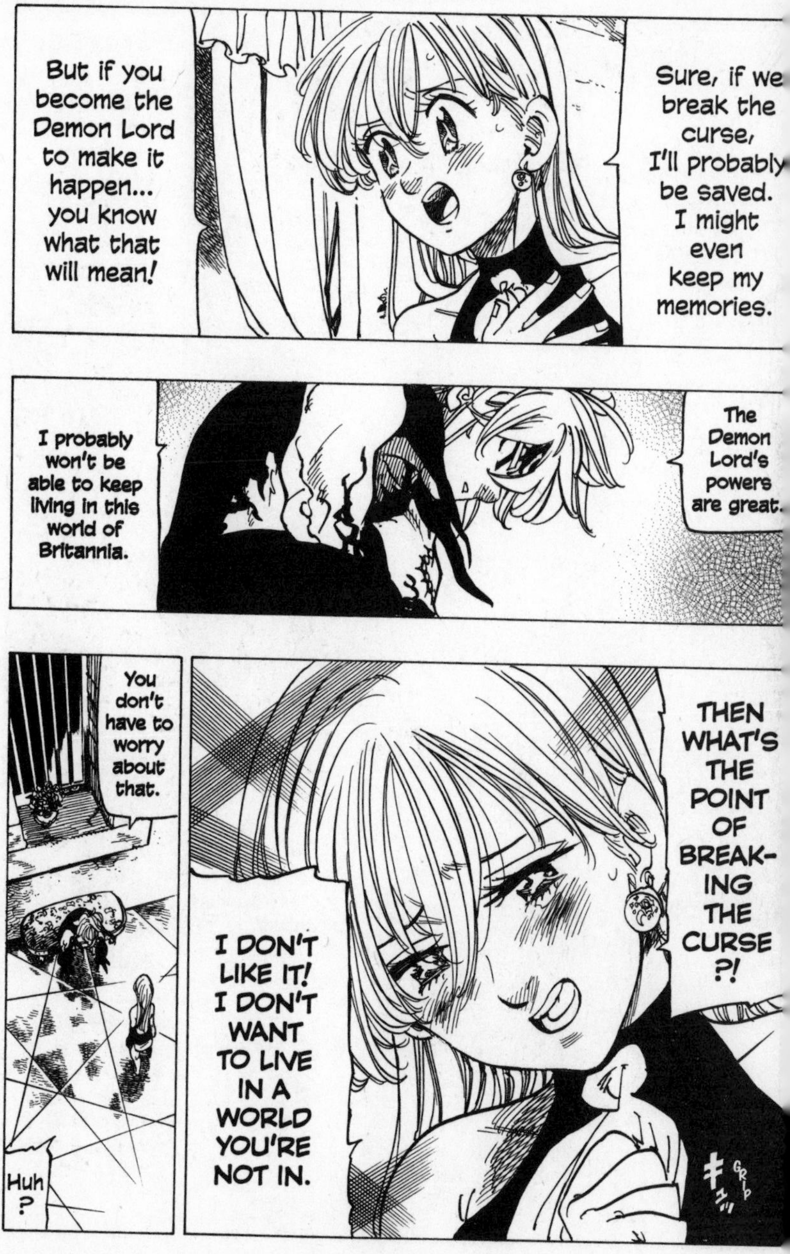
Sure, if we break the curse, I'll probably be saved. I might even keep my memories.
But if you become the Demon Lord to make it happen... you know what that will mean!
The Demon Lord's powers are great.
I probably won't be able to keep living in this world of Britannia.
THEN WHAT'S THE POINT OF BREAKING THE CURSE?!
I DON'T LIKE IT! I DON'T WANT TO LIVE IN A WORLD YOU'RE NOT IN.
GRIP
You don't have to worry about that.
Huh?

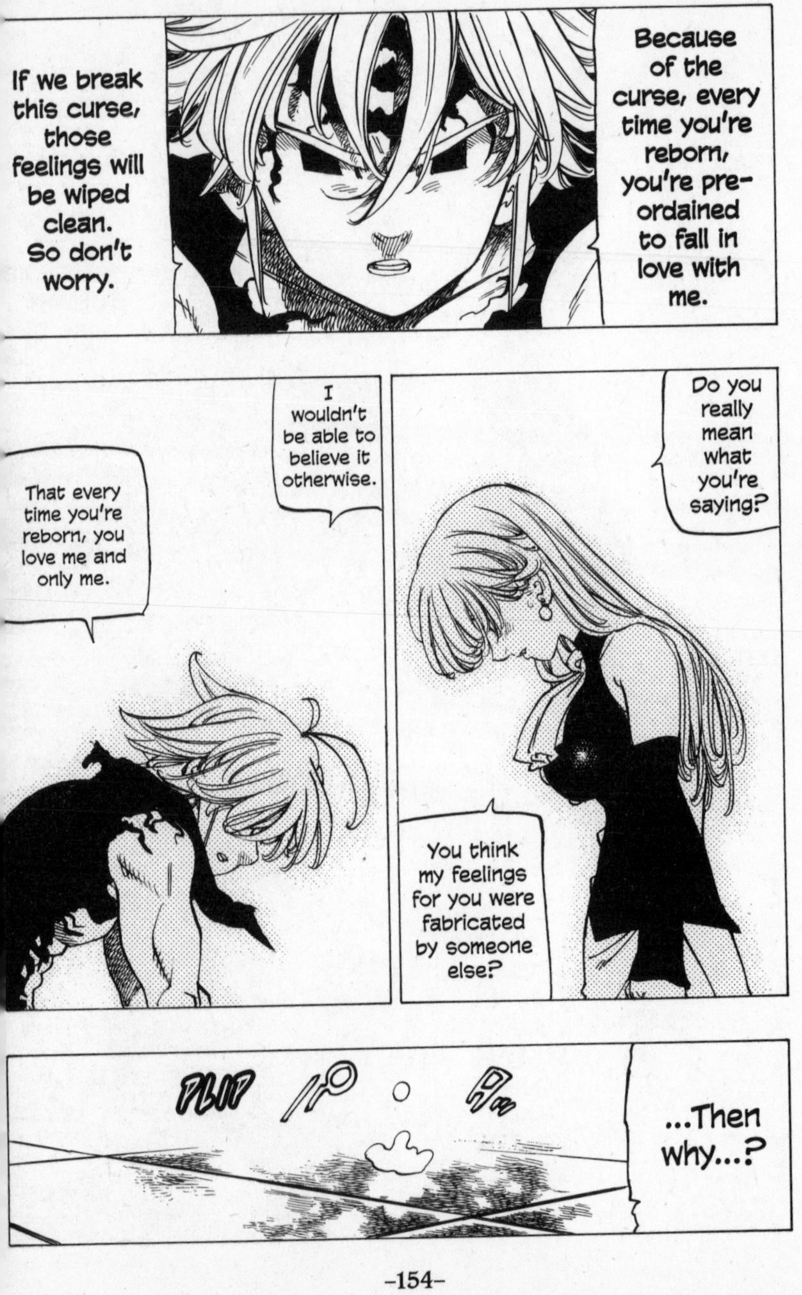
Because of the curse, every time you're reborn, you're pre-ordained to fall in love with me.
If we break this curse, those feelings will be wiped clean. So don't worry.
Do you really mean what you're saying?
You think my feelings for you were fabricated by someone else?
I wouldn't be able to believe it otherwise.
That every time you're reborn, you love me and only me.
...Then why...?
PLIP

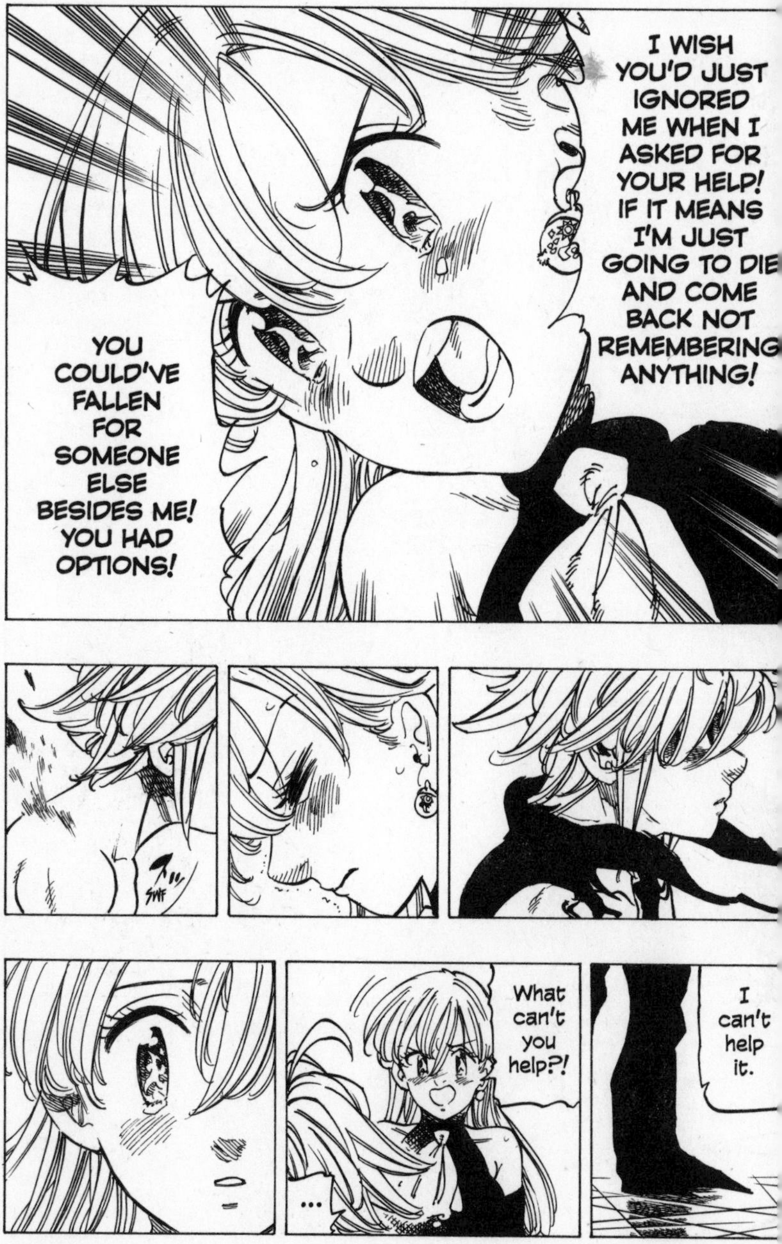
I WISH YOU'D JUST IGNORED ME WHEN I ASKED FOR YOUR HELP! IF IT MEANS I'M JUST GOING TO DIE AND COME BACK NOT REMEMBERING ANYTHING!
YOU COULD'VE FALLEN FOR SOMEONE ELSE BESIDES ME! YOU HAD OPTIONS!
SNIF
I can't help it.
What can't you help?!
...

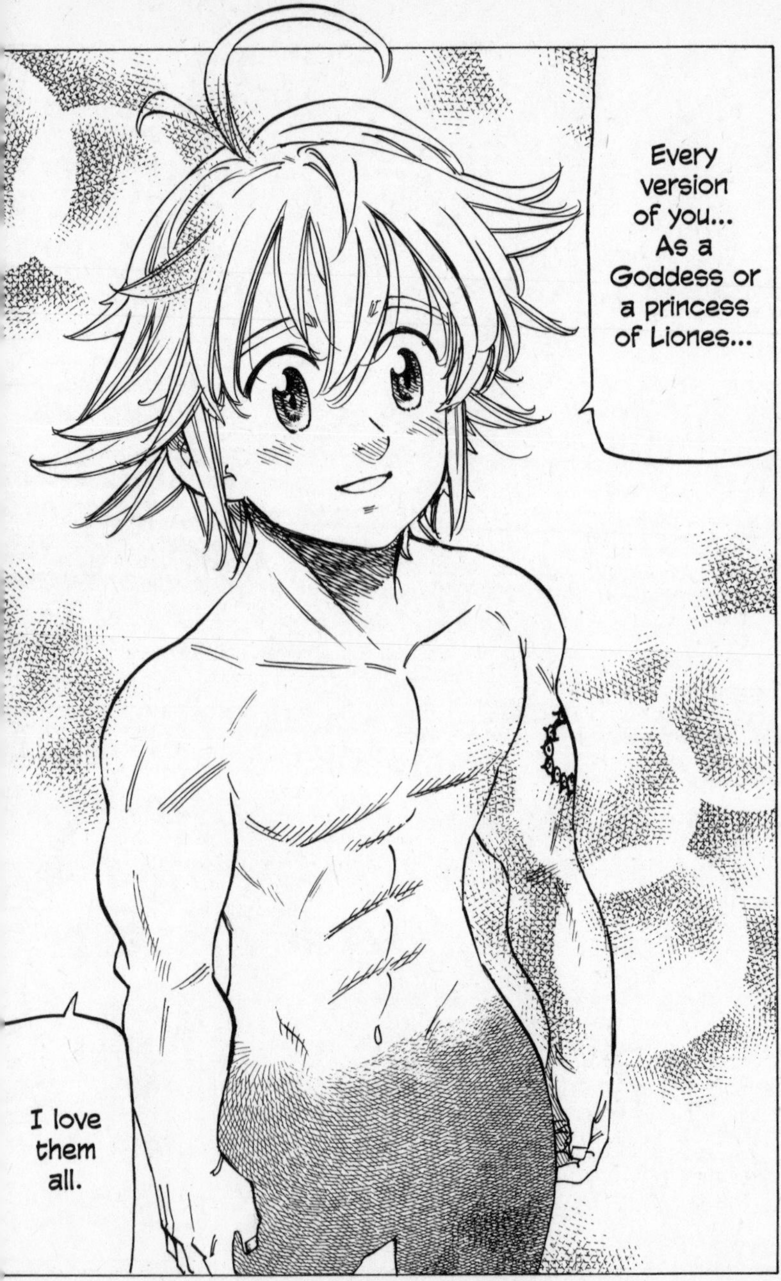
Every version of you... As a Goddess or a princess of Liones...
I love them all.

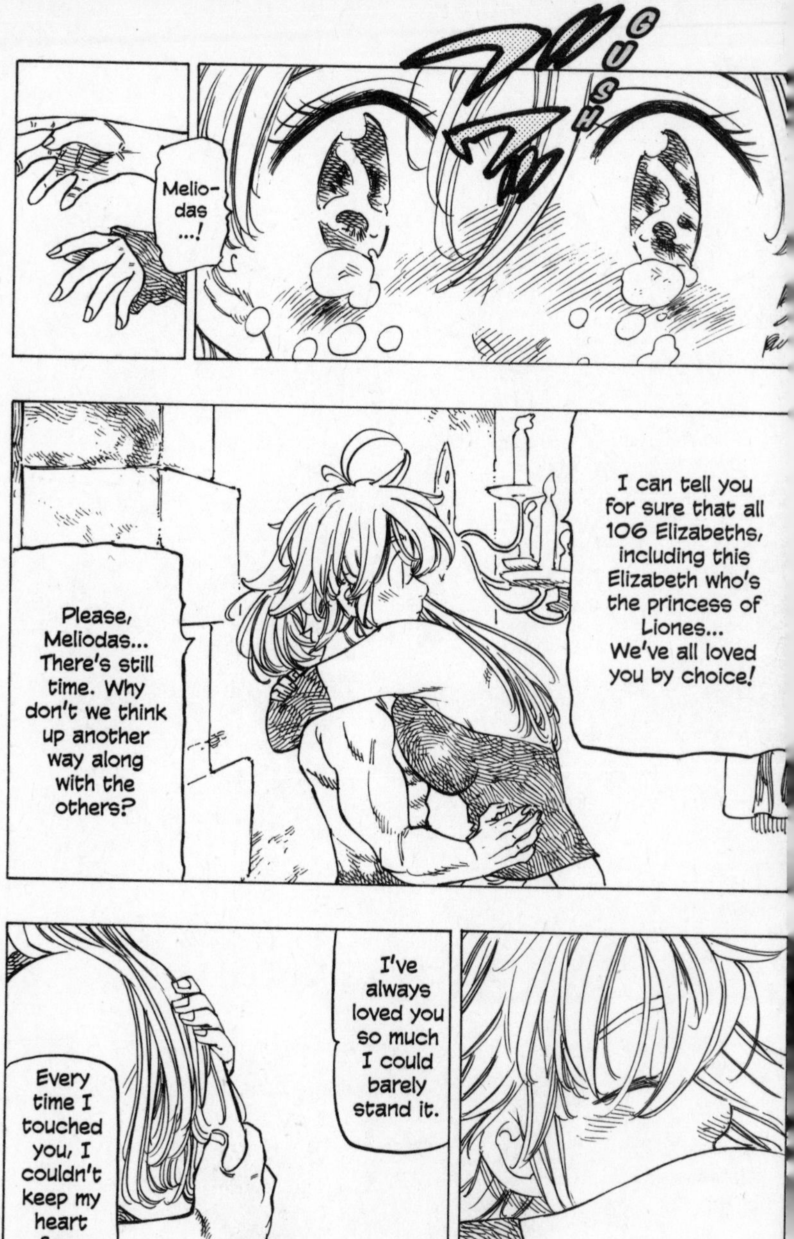
GUSH
Melio-das ...!
I can tell you for sure that all 106 Elizabeths, including this Elizabeth who's the princess of Liones... We've all loved you by choice!
Please, Meliodas... There's still time. Why don't we think up another way along with the others?
I've always loved you so much I could barely stand it.
Every time I touched you, I couldn't keep my heart from racing.

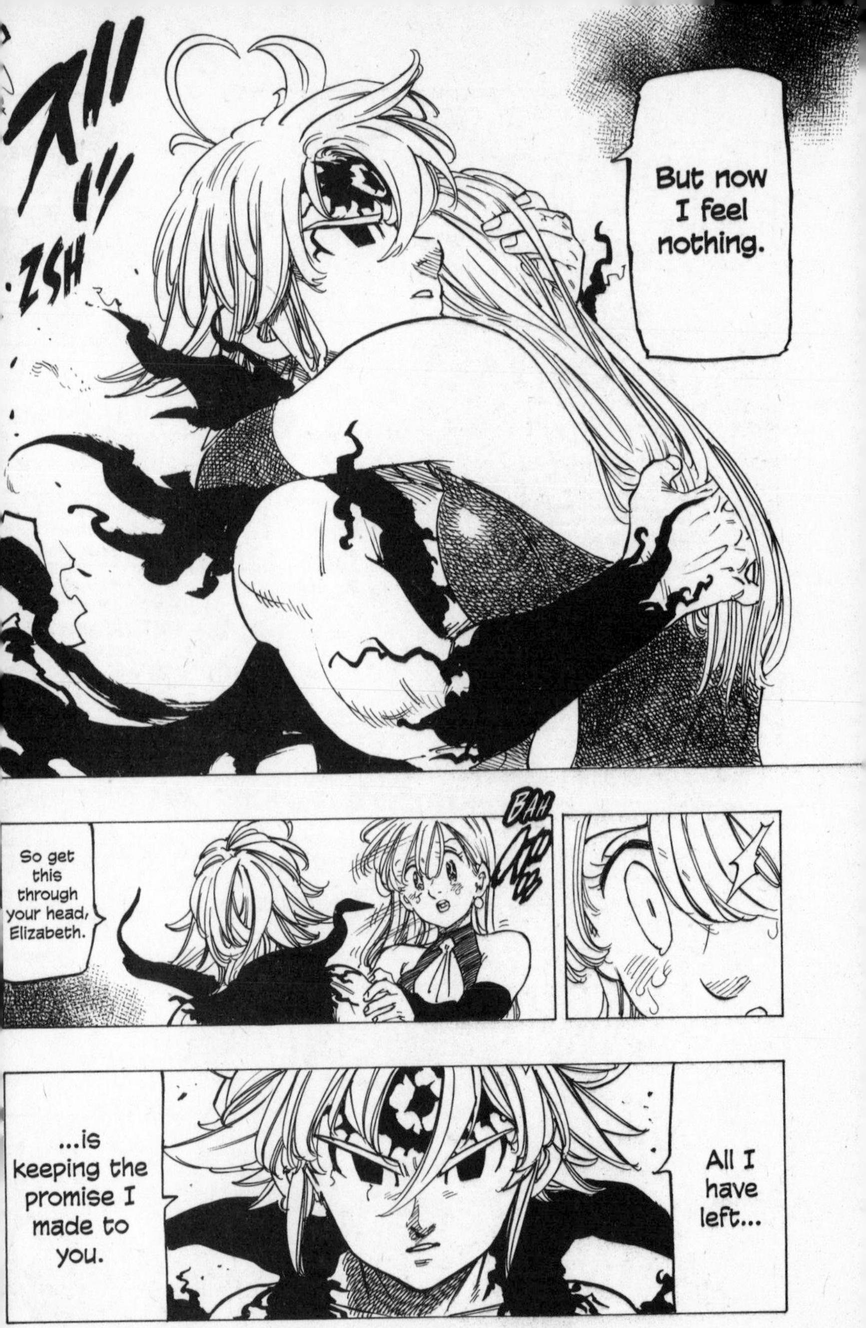
ZSH
But now I feel nothing.
BAH
So get this through your head, Elizabeth.
All I have left...
...is keeping the promise I made to you.

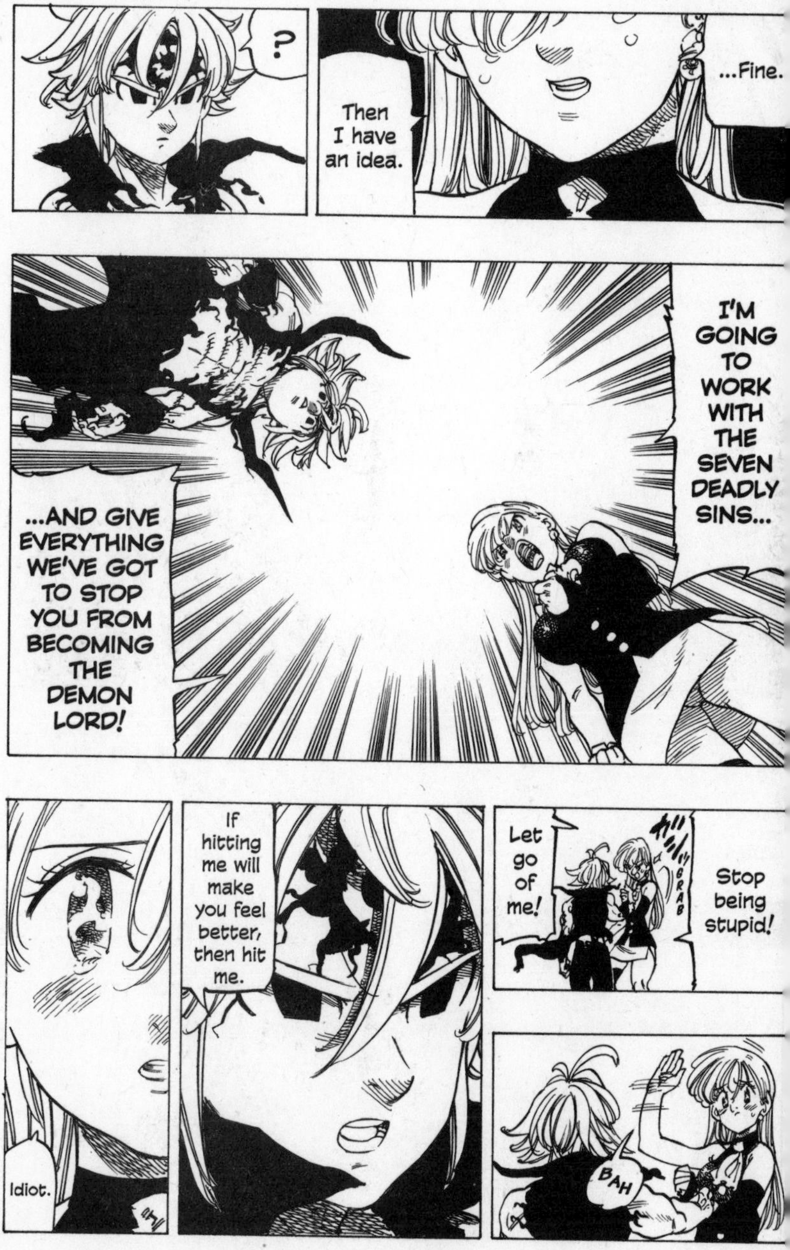
...Fine.
Then I have an idea.
?
I'M GOING TO WORK WITH THE SEVEN DEADLY SINS...
...AND GIVE EVERYTHING WE'VE GOT TO STOP YOU FROM BECOMING THE DEMON LORD!
Stop being stupid!
GRAB
Let go of me!
BAH
If hitting me will make you feel better, then hit me.
Idiot.

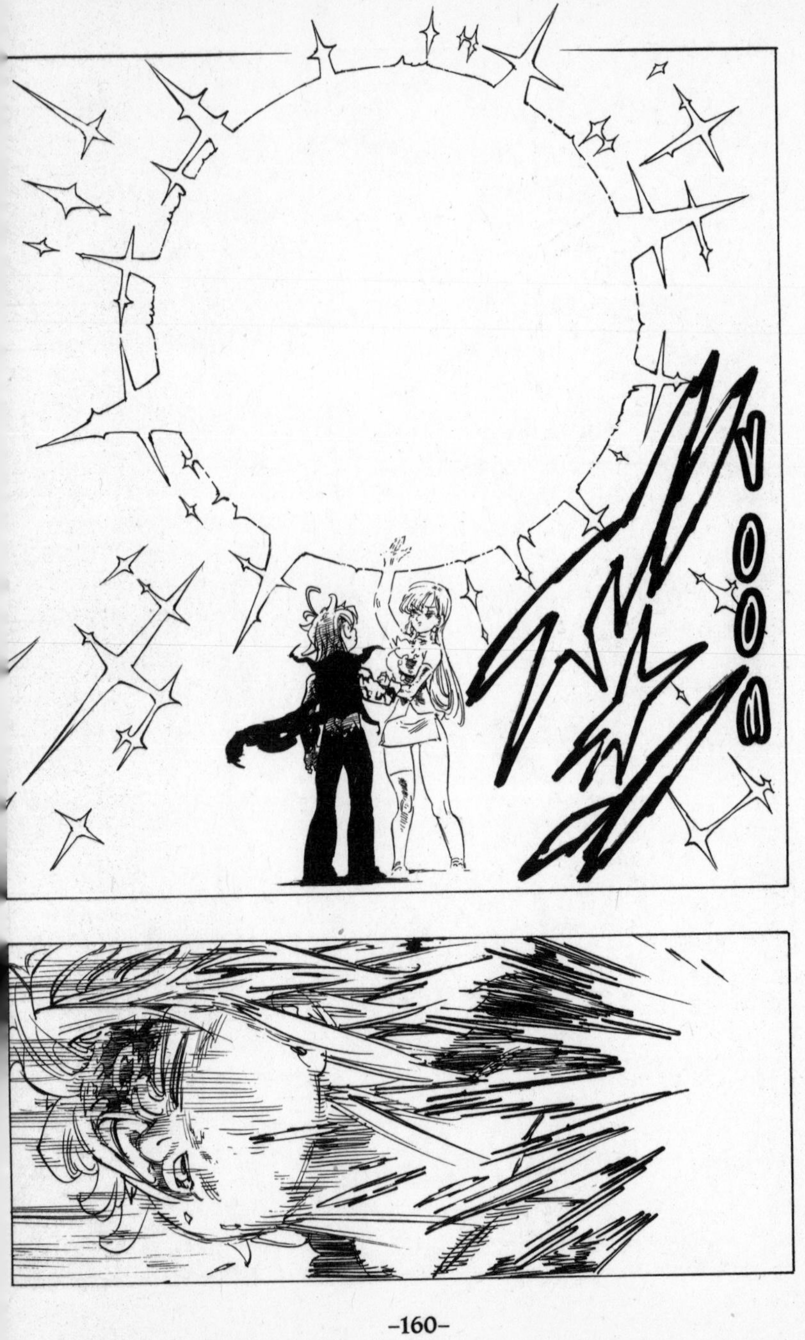
VOOM

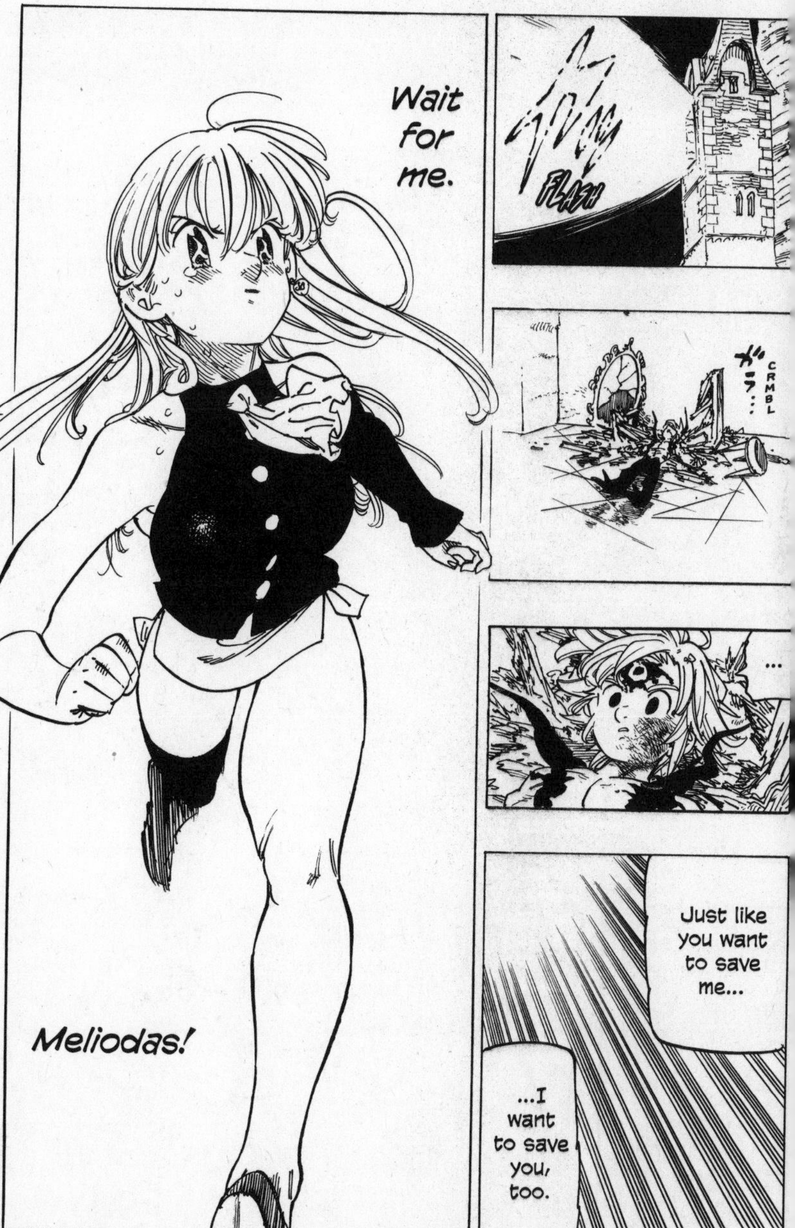
FLASH
CRMBL
...
Just like you want to save me...
...I want to save you, too.
Wait for me.
Meliodas!

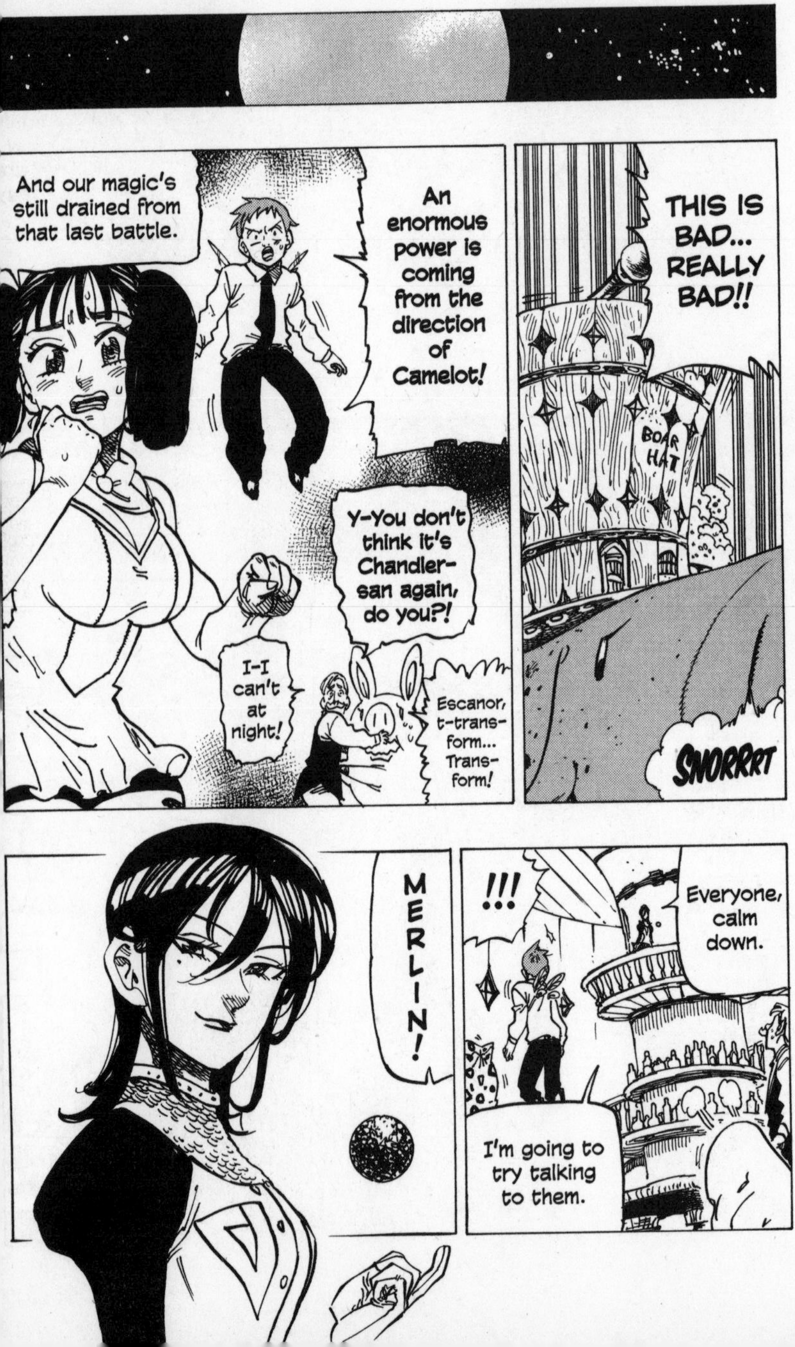
THIS IS BAD... REALLY BAD!!
BOAR HAT
SNORRRT
An enormous power is coming from the direction of Camelot!
And our magic's still drained from that last battle.
Y-You don't think it's Chandler-san again, do you?!
Escanor, t-transform... Transform!
I-I can't at night!
Everyone, calm down.
!!!
I'm going to try talking to them.
MERLIN!

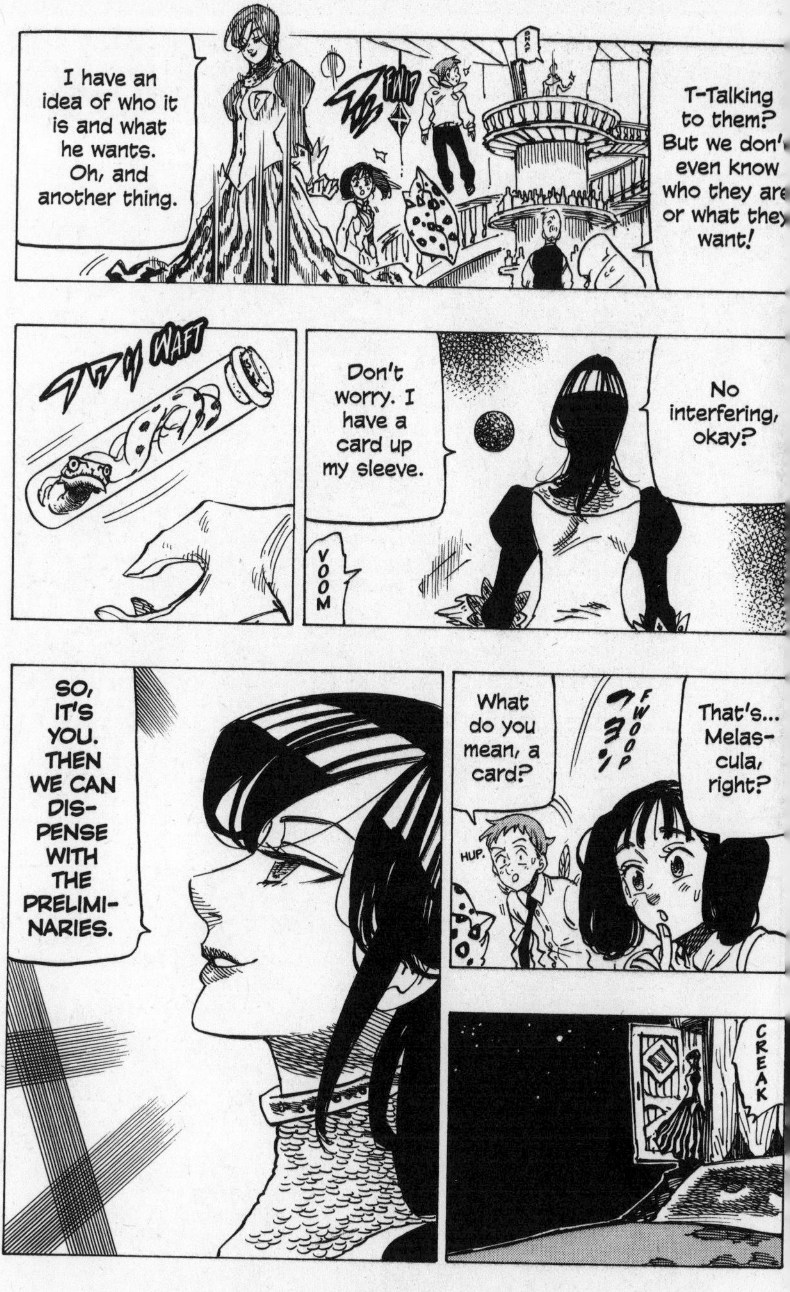
T-Talking to them? But we don' even know who they ar or what the want!
SNAP
FWIP
I have an idea of who it is and what he wants. Oh, and another thing.
No interfering, okay?
Don't worry. I have a card up my sleeve.
VOOM
WAFT
That's... Melascula, right?
FWOOP
What do you mean, a card?
HUP.
CREAK
SO, IT'S YOU. THEN WE CAN DISPENSE WITH THE PRELIMINARIES.

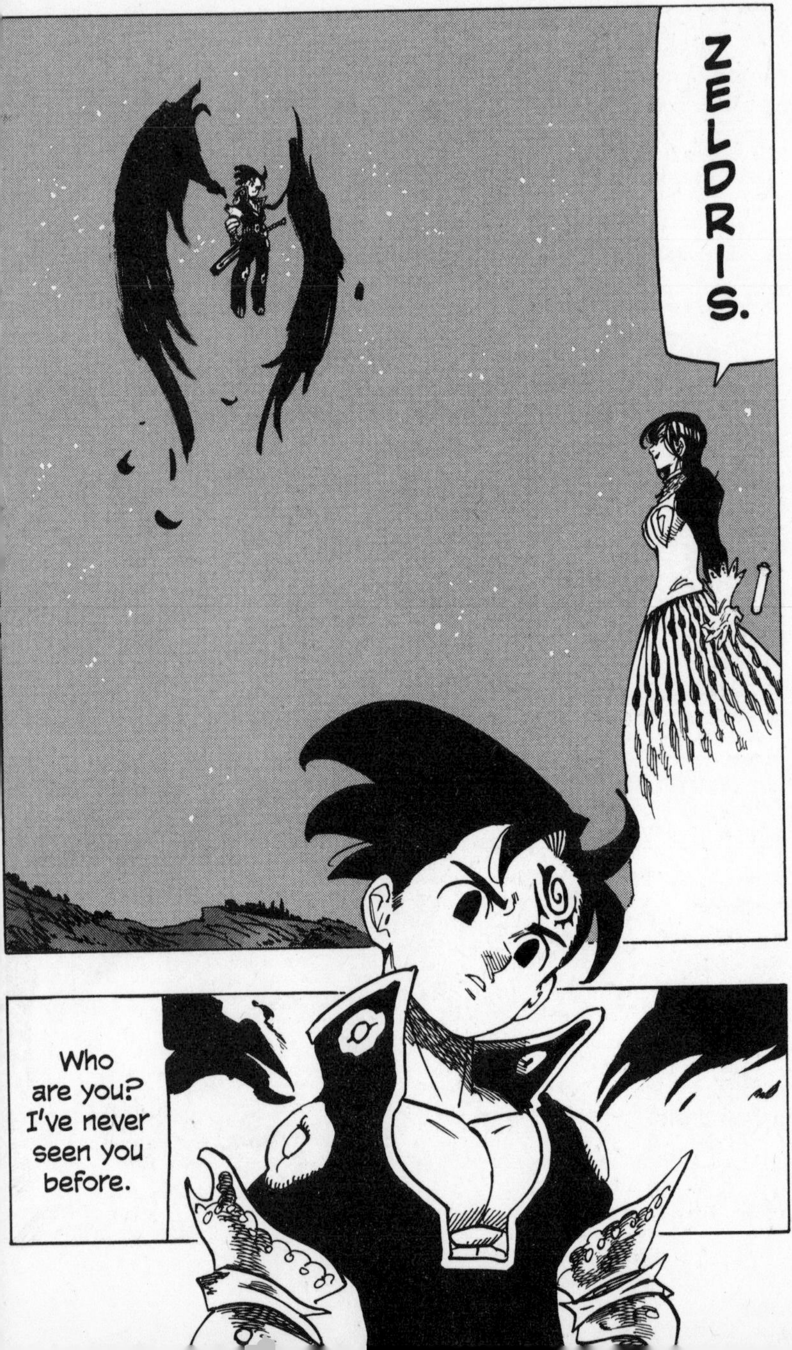
ZELDRIS.
Who are you? I've never seen you before.

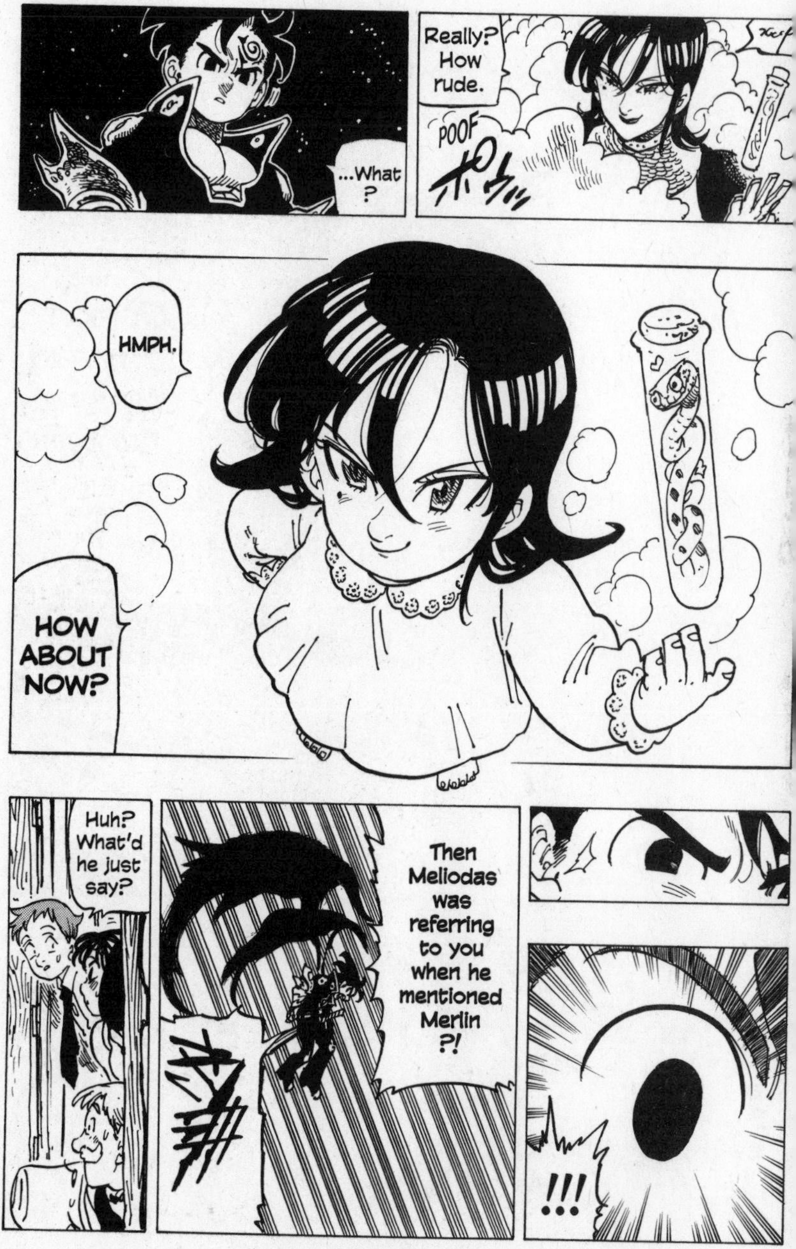
Really? How rude.
POOF
...What?
HMPH.
HOW ABOUT NOW?
!!!
Then Meliodas was referring to you when he mentioned Merlin?!
Huh? What'd he just say?

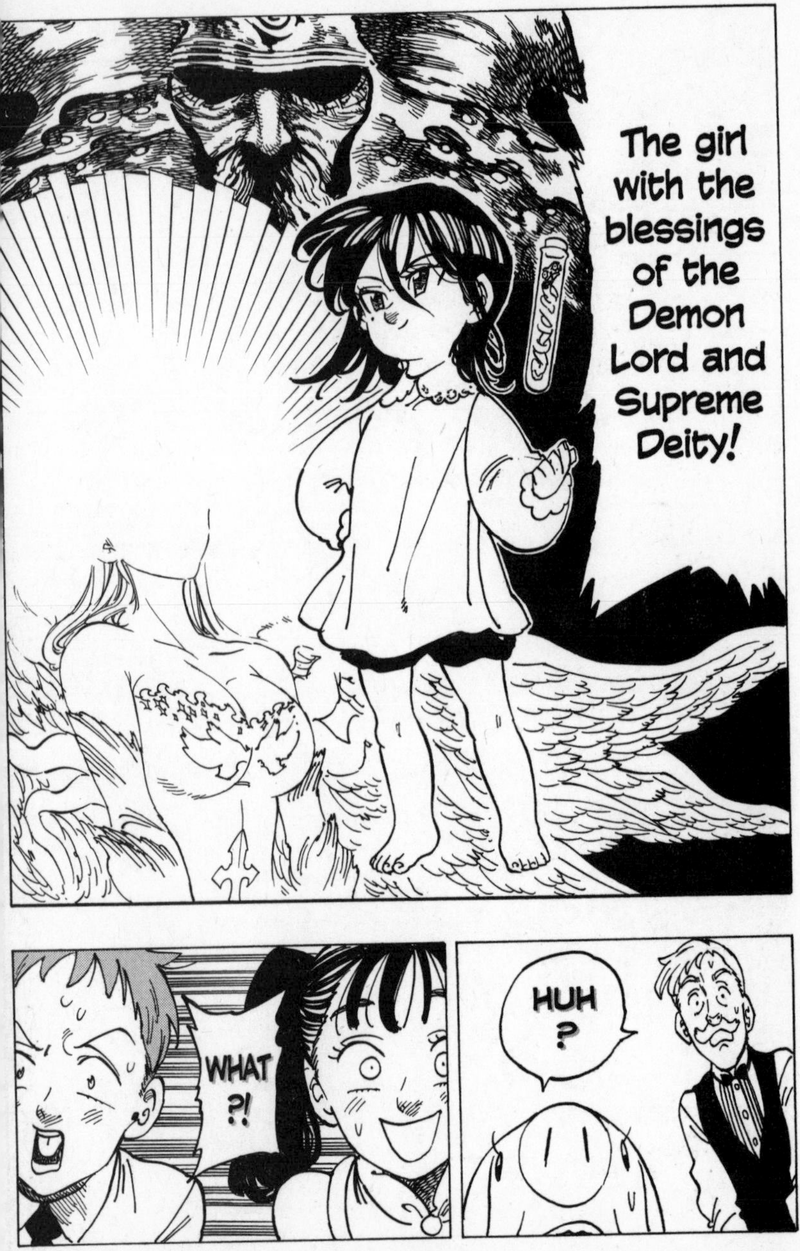
The girl with the blessings of the Demon Lord and Supreme Deity!
HUH ?
WHAT ?!

Chapter 249 - Deal

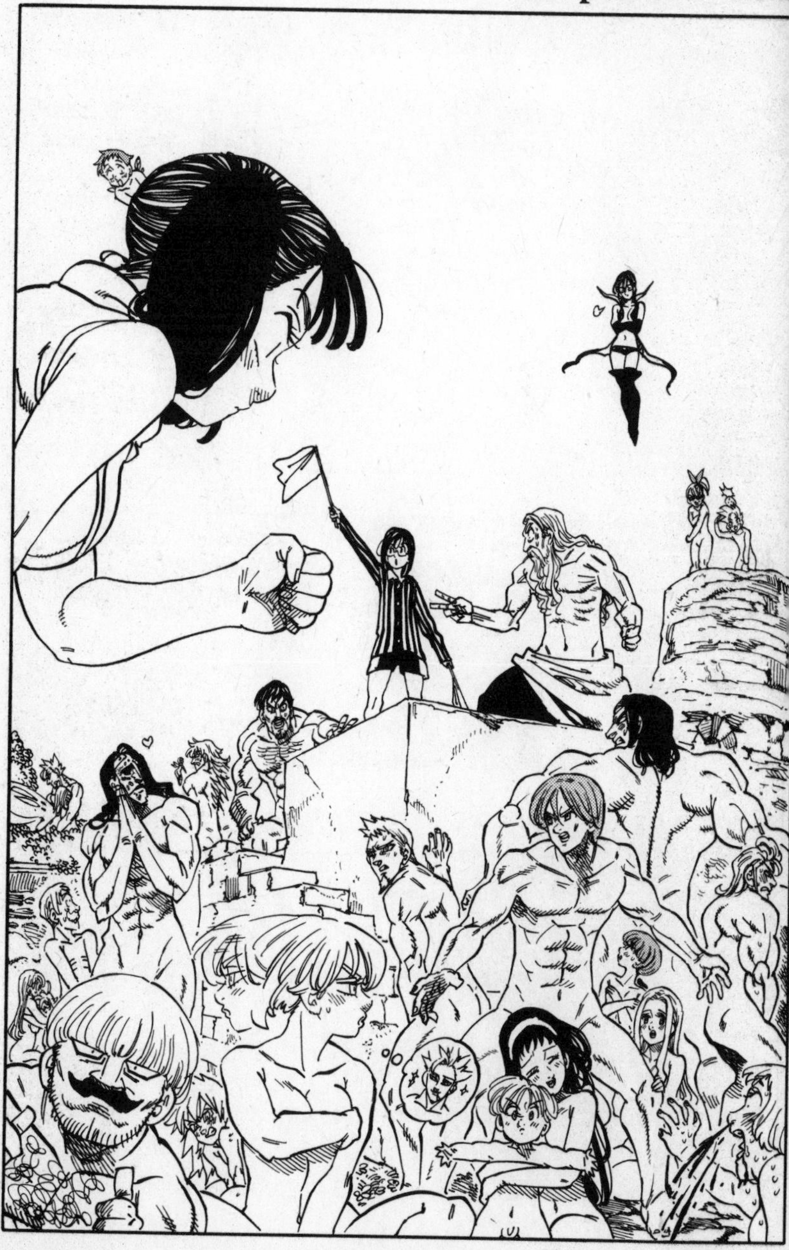

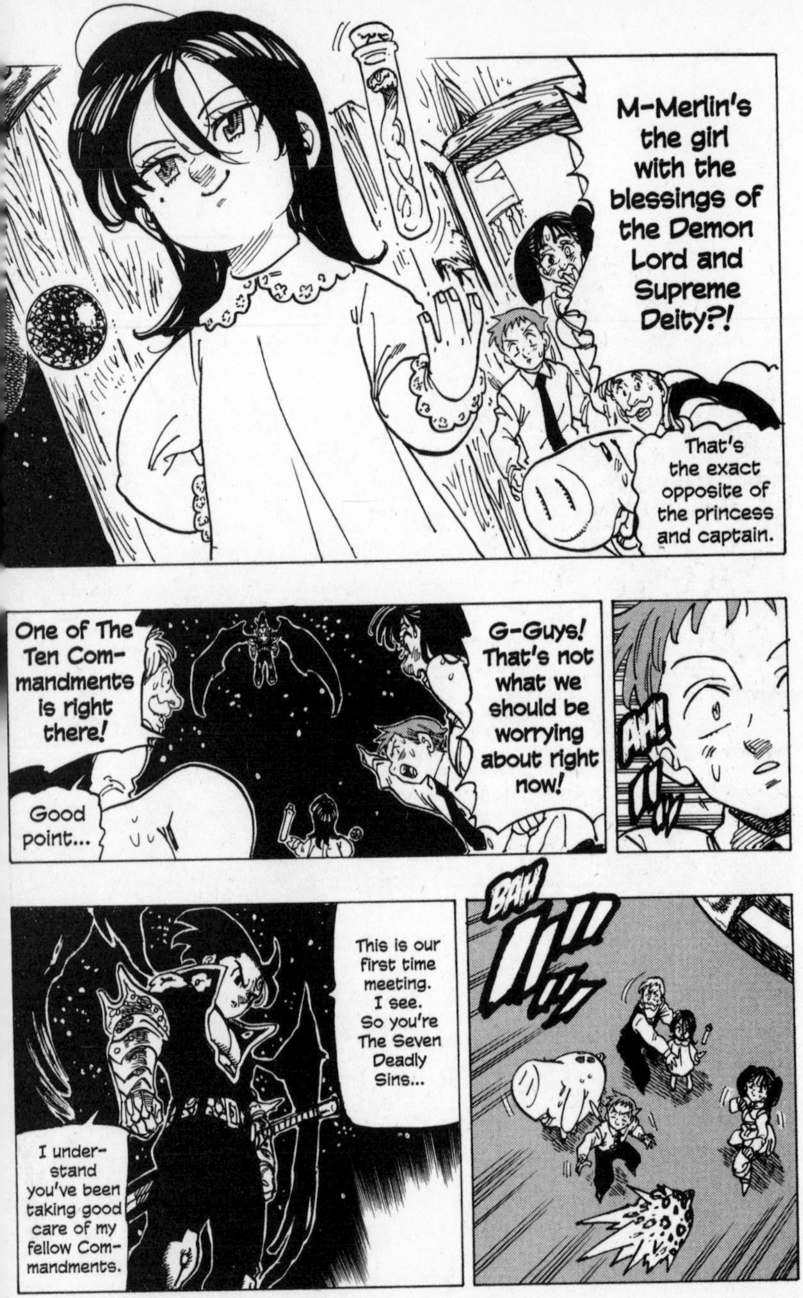
M-Merlin's the girl with the blessings of the Demon Lord and Supreme Deity?!
That's the exact opposite of the princess and captain.
AH!!
G-Guys! That's not what we should be worrying about right now!
One of The Ten Commandments is right there!
Good point...
BAH!!
This is our first time meeting. I see. So you're The Seven Deadly Sins...
I understand you've been taking good care of my fellow Commandments.

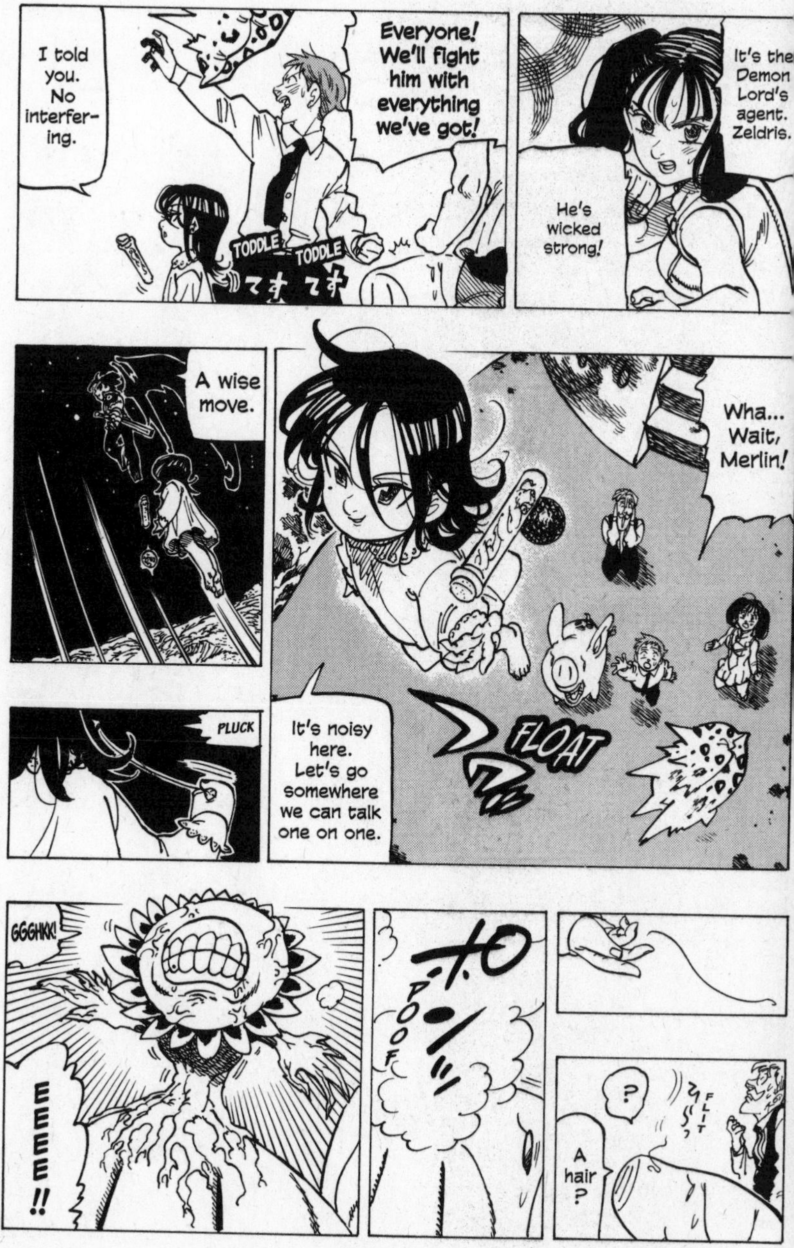
It's the Demon Lord's agent. Zeldris.
He's wicked strong!
Everyone! We'll fight him with everything we've got!
I told you. No interfering.
TODDLE TODDLE
Wha... Wait, Merlin!
It's noisy here. Let's go somewhere we can talk one on one.
FLOAT
A wise move.
PLUCK
?
FLIT
A hair?
POOOF
GGGHKK!
EEEEE!!

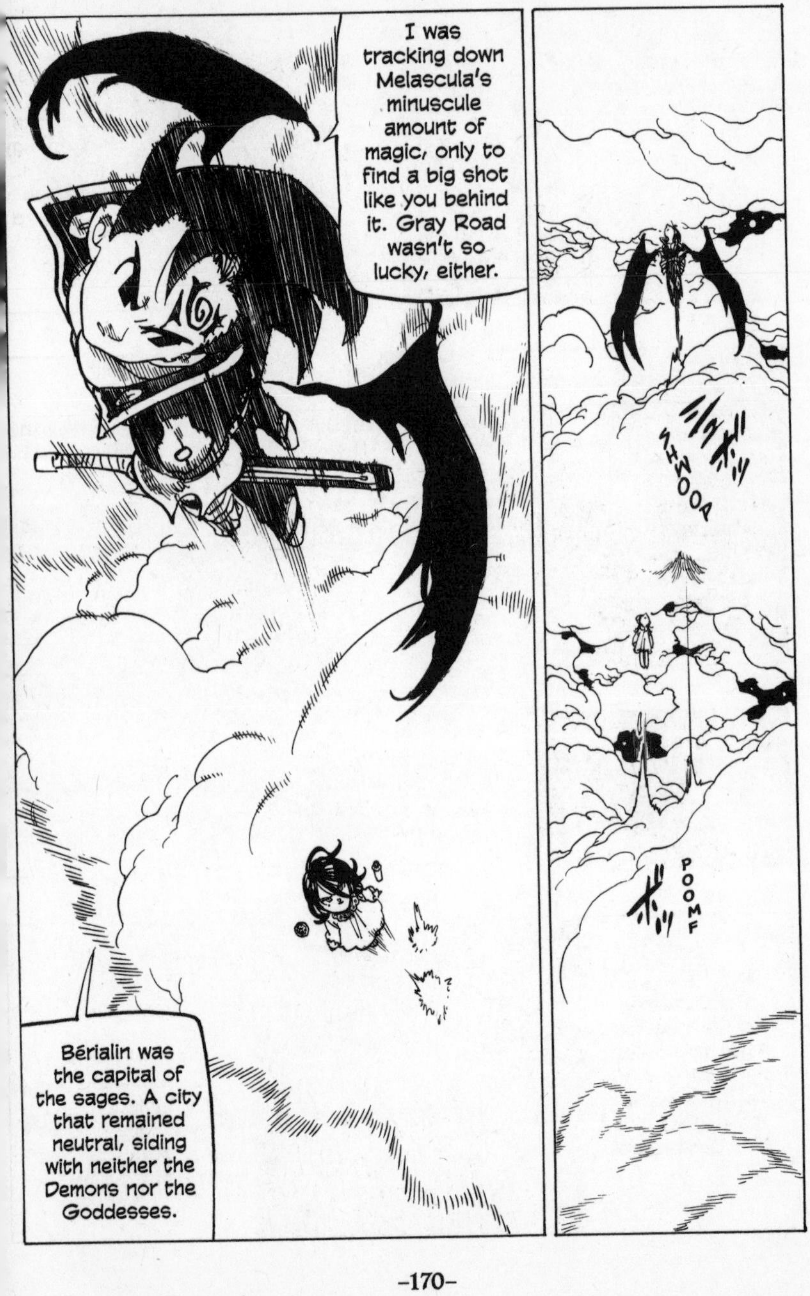
SHWOOA
POOMF
I was tracking down Melascula's minuscule amount of magic, only to find a big shot like you behind it. Gray Road wasn't so lucky, either.
Bérialin was the capital of the sages. A city that remained neutral, siding with neither the Demons nor the Goddesses.

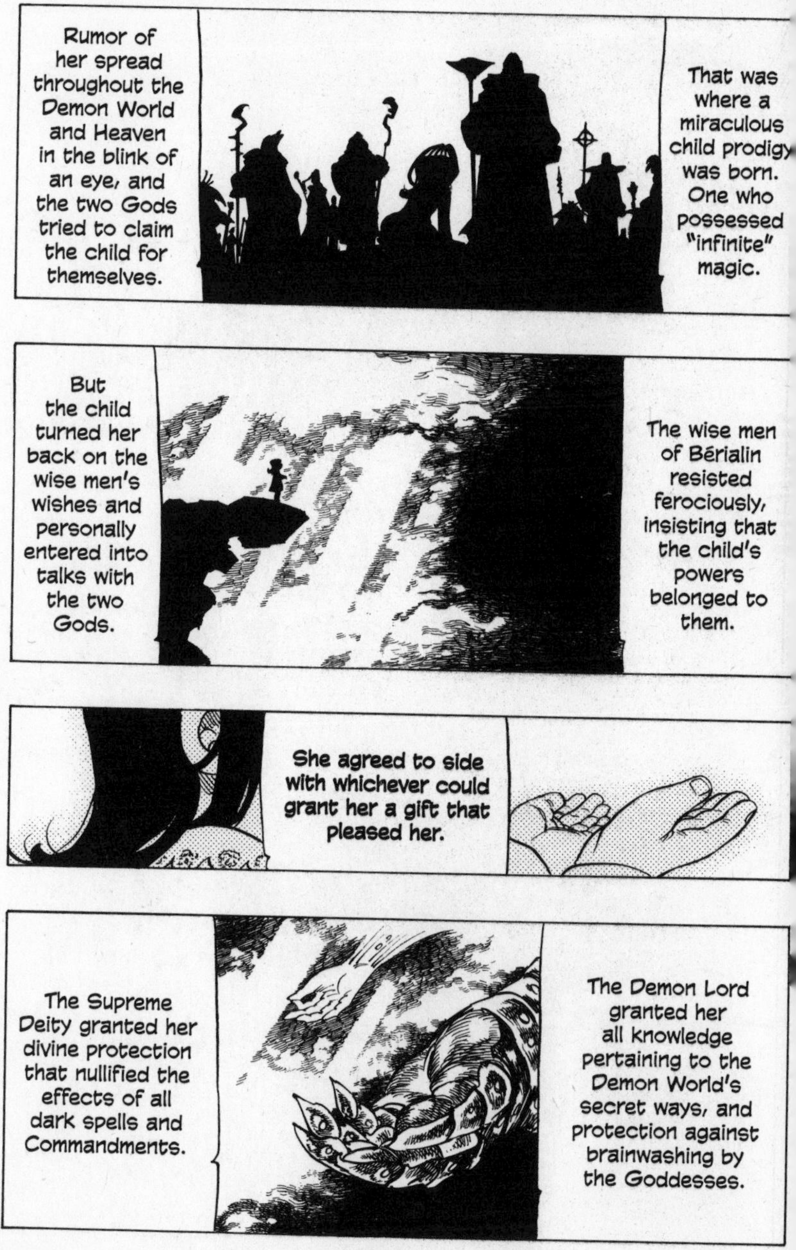
That was where a miraculous child prodigy was born. One who possessed "infinite" magic.
Rumor of her spread throughout the Demon World and Heaven in the blink of an eye, and the two Gods tried to claim the child for themselves.
The wise men of Bérialin resisted ferociously, insisting that the child's powers belonged to them.
But the child turned her back on the wise men's wishes and personally entered into talks with the two Gods.
She agreed to side with whichever could grant her a gift that pleased her.
The Demon Lord granted her all knowledge pertaining to the Demon World's secret ways, and protection against brainwashing by the Goddesses.
The Supreme Deity granted her divine protection that nullified the effects of all dark spells and Commandments.

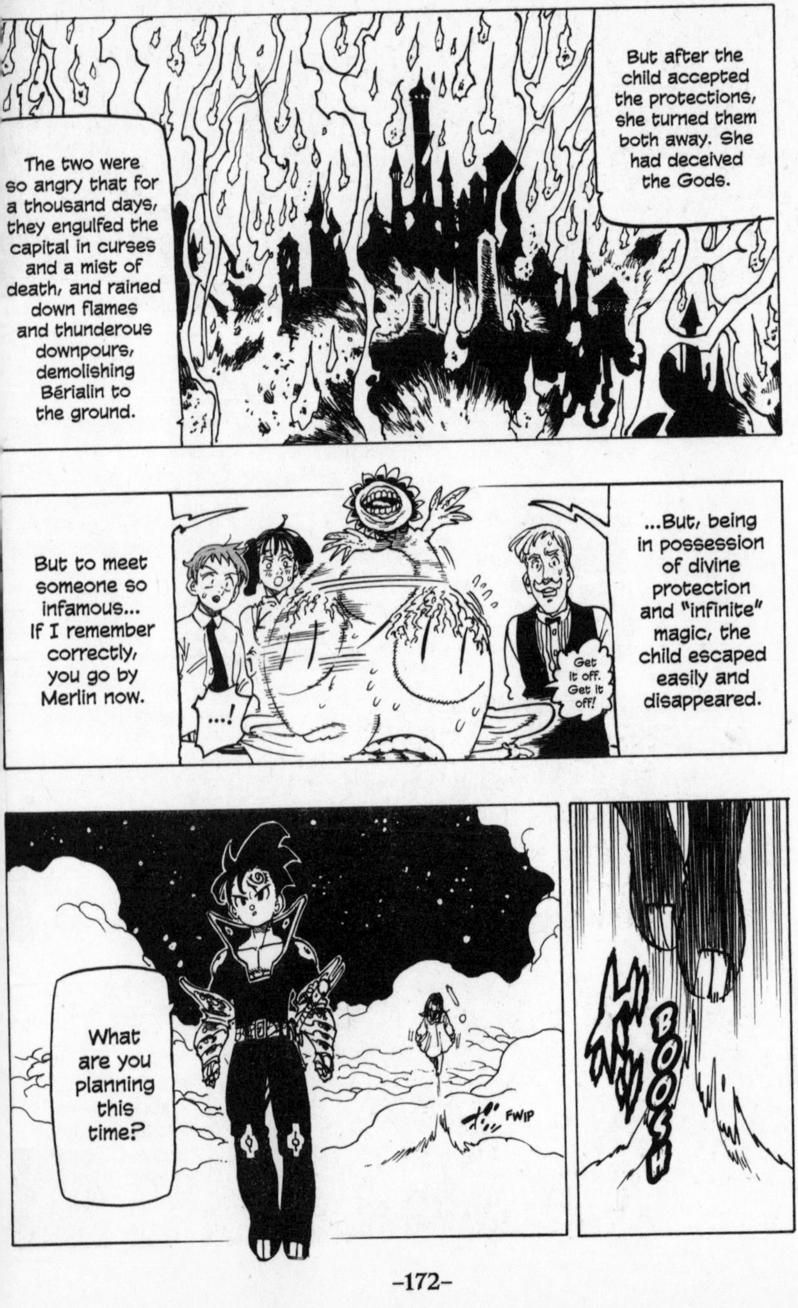
But after the child accepted the protections, she turned them both away. She had deceived the Gods.
The two were so angry that for a thousand days, they engulfed the capital in curses and a mist of death, and rained down flames and thunderous downpours, demolishing Bérialin to the ground.
...But, being in possession of divine protection and "infinite" magic, the child escaped easily and disappeared.
Get it off. Get it off!
...!
But to meet someone so infamous... If I remember correctly, you go by Merlin now.
BOOSH
FWIP
What are you planning this time?

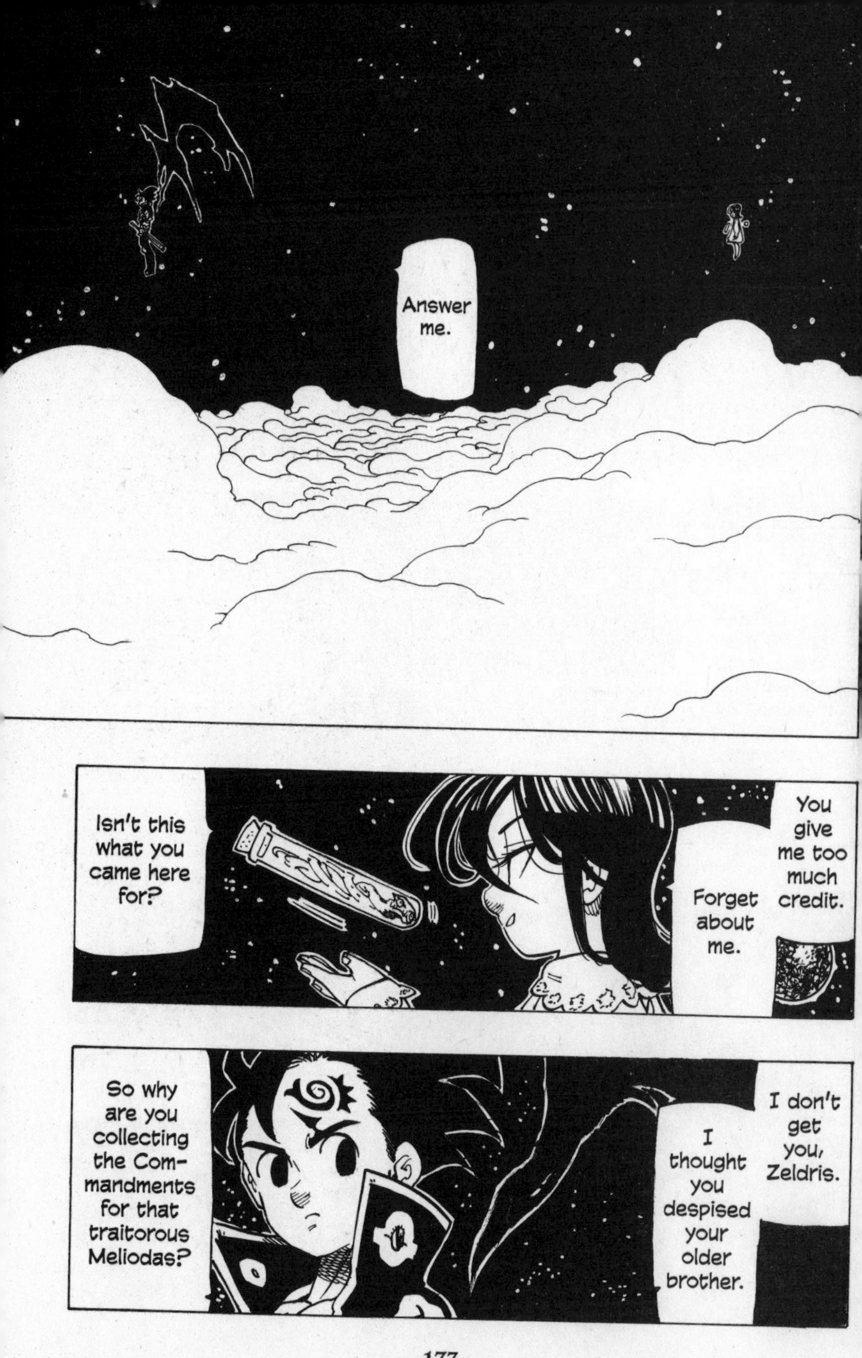
Answer me.
You give me too much credit.
Forget about me.
Isn't this what you came here for?
I don't get you, Zeldris.
I thought you despised your older brother.
So why are you collecting the Commandments for that traitorous Meliodas?

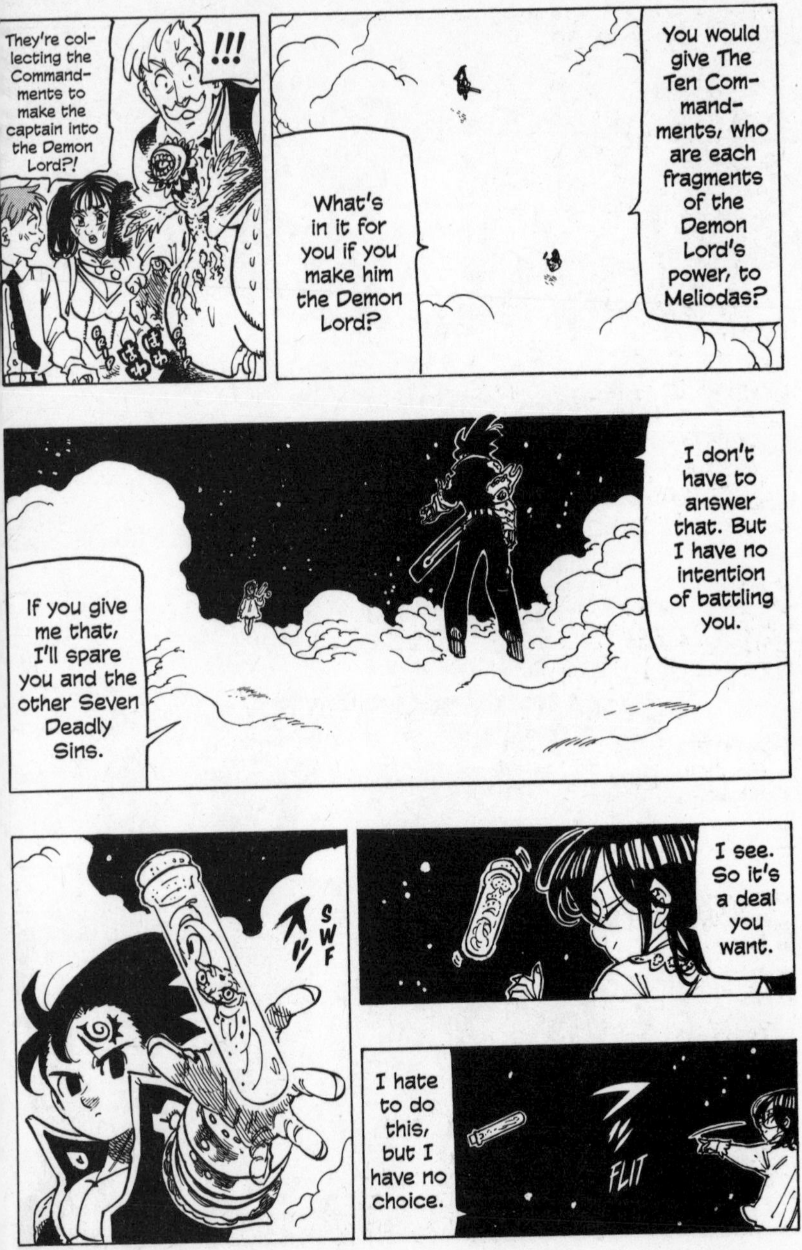
You would give The Ten Commandments, who are each fragments of the Demon Lord's power, to Meliodas?
What's in it for you if you make him the Demon Lord?
!!!
They're collecting the Commandments to make the captain into the Demon Lord?!
I don't have to answer that. But I have no intention of battling you.
If you give me that, I'll spare you and the other Seven Deadly Sins.
I see. So it's a deal you want.
I hate to do this, but I have no choice.
FLIT
SWF

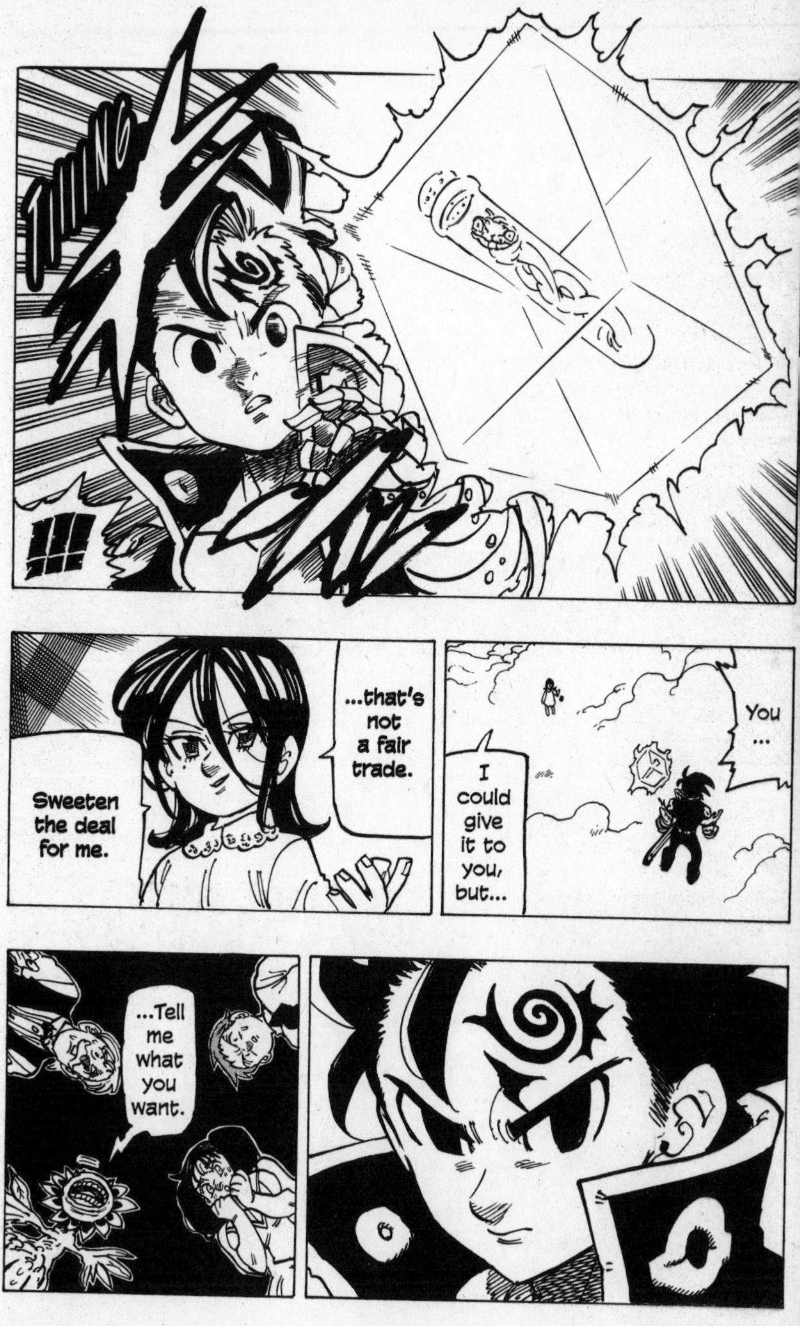
TIIING
!!!
You ...
I could give it to you, but...
...that's not a fair trade.
Sweeten the deal for me.
...Tell me what you want.

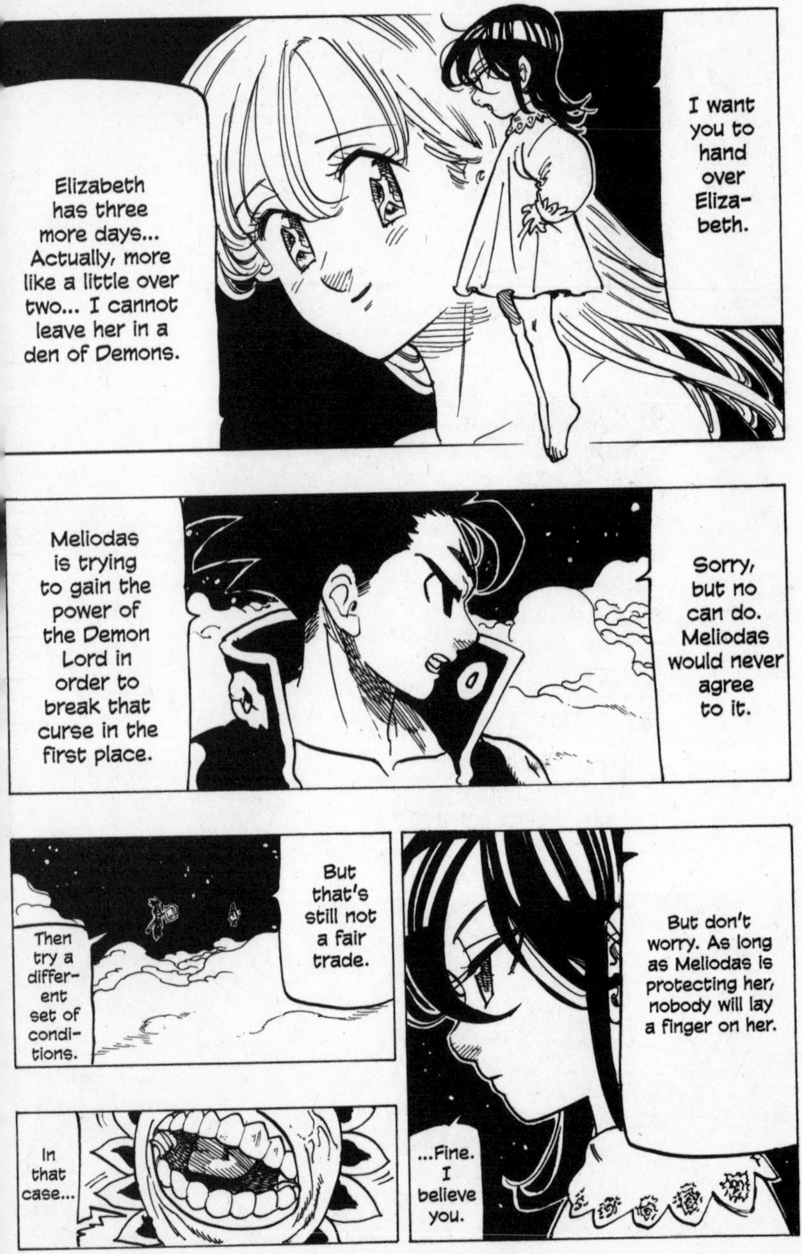
I want you to hand over Elizabeth.
Elizabeth has three more days... Actually, more like a little over two... I cannot leave her in a den of Demons.
Sorry, but no can do. Meliodas would never agree to it.
Meliodas is trying to gain the power of the Demon Lord in order to break that curse in the first place.
But don't worry. As long as Meliodas is protecting her, nobody will lay a finger on her.
...Fine. I believe you.
But that's still not a fair trade.
Then try a different set of conditions.
In that case...

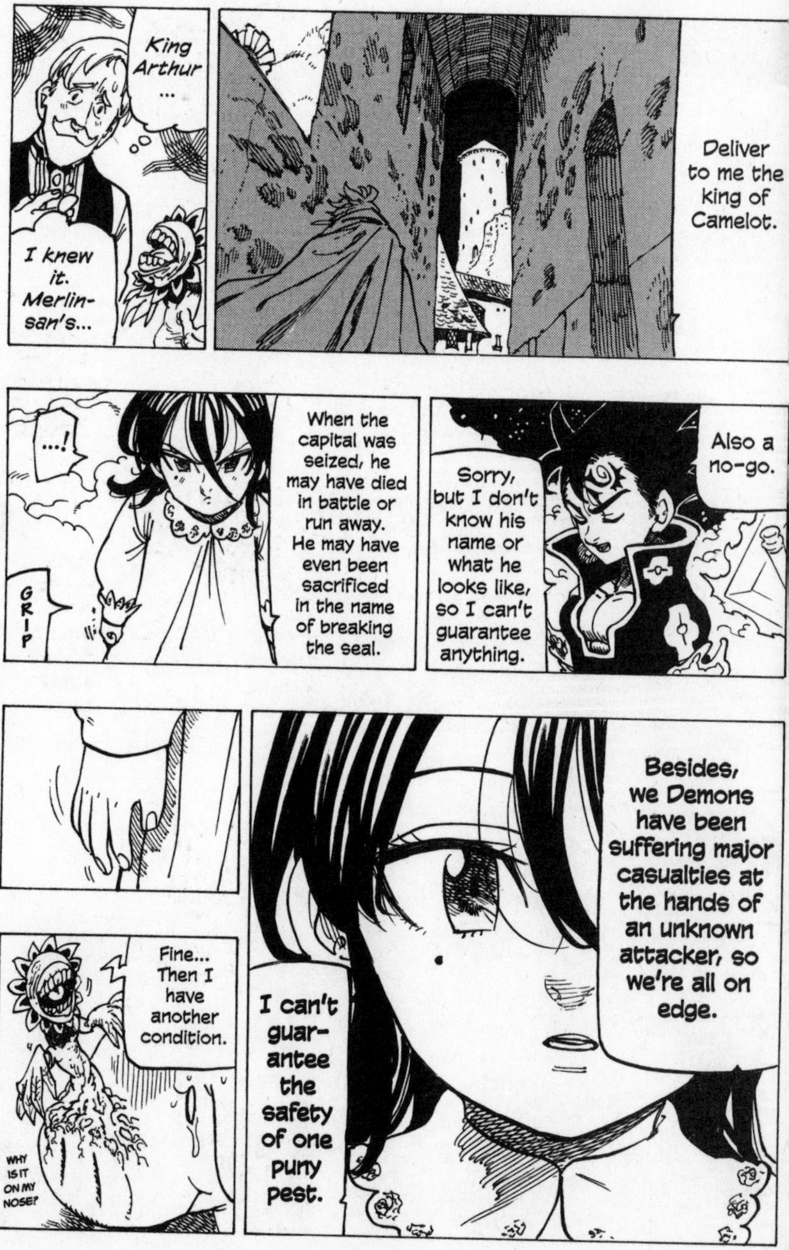
Deliver to me the king of Camelot.
King Arthur ...
I knew it. Merlin-san's...
Also a no-go.
Sorry, but I don't know his name or what he looks like, so I can't guarantee anything.
When the capital was seized, he may have died in battle or run away. He may have even been sacrificed in the name of breaking the seal.
...!
GRIP
Besides, we Demons have been suffering major casualties at the hands of an unknown attacker, so we're all on edge.
I can't guar-antee the safety of one puny pest.
Fine... Then I have another condition.
WHY IS IT ON MY NOSE?

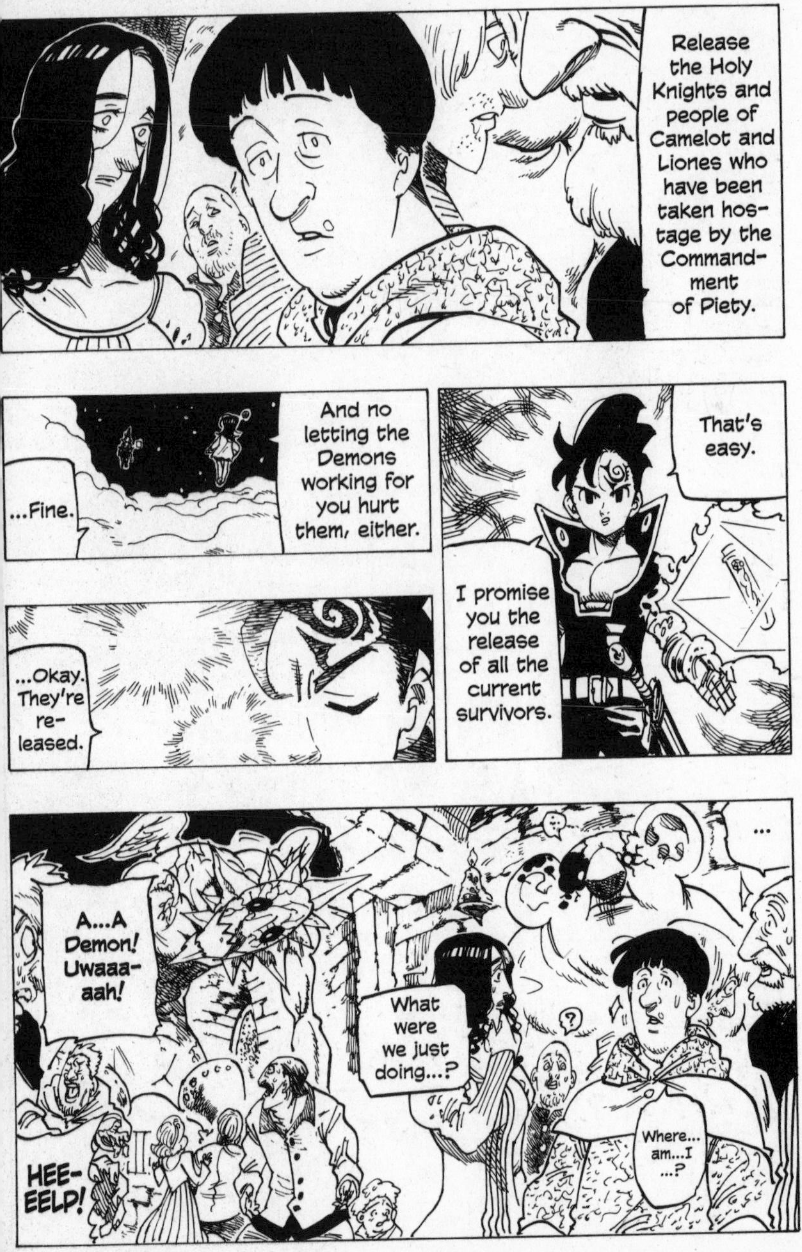

Release the Holy Knights and people of Camelot and Liones who have been taken hostage by the Commandment of Piety.
That's easy.
I promise you the release of all the current survivors.
And no letting the Demons working for you hurt them, either.
...Fine.
...Okay. They're released.
...
Where... am...I ...?
What were we just doing...?
A...A Demon! Uwaaaaah!
HEE-EELP!

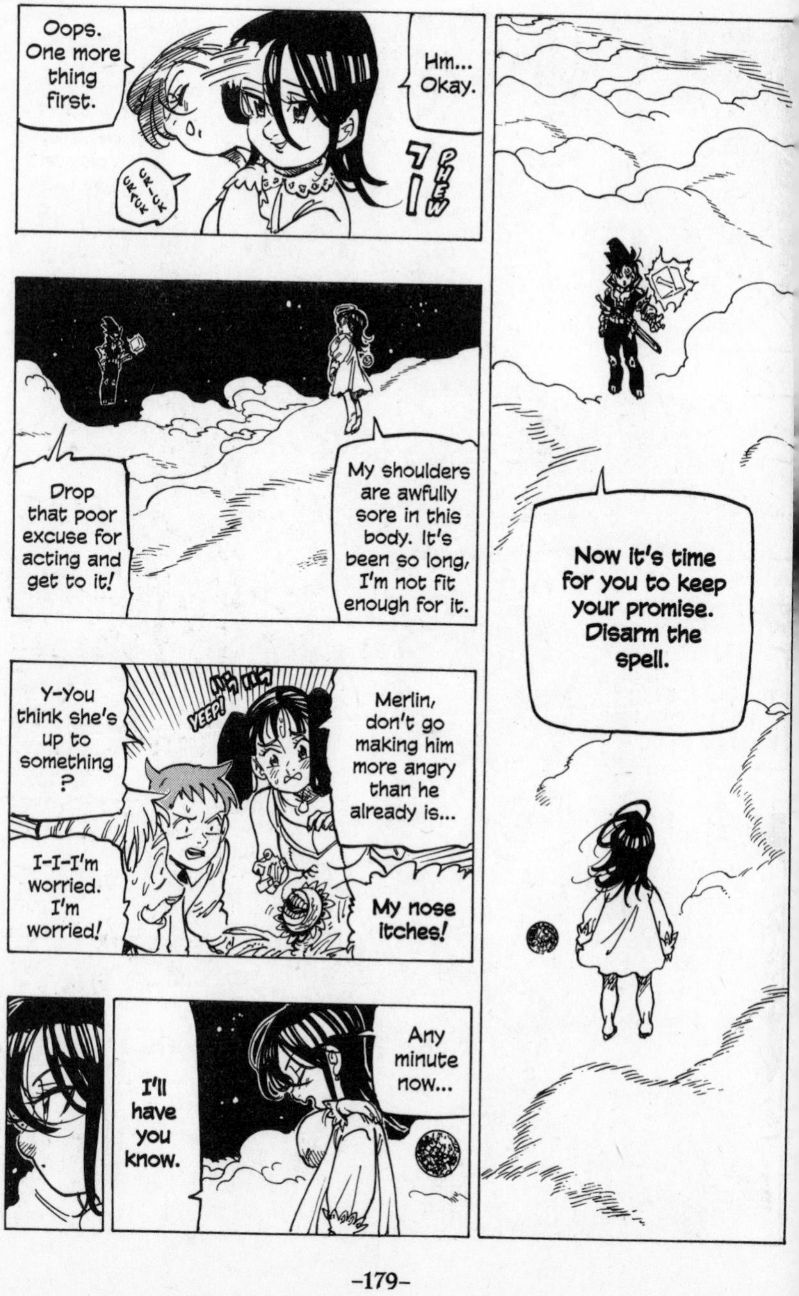
Now it's time for you to keep your promise. Disarm the spell.
Hm... Okay.
Oops. One more thing first.
PHEW
My shoulders are awfully sore in this body. It's been so long, I'm not fit enough for it.
Drop that poor excuse for acting and get to it!
Merlin, don't go making him more angry than he already is...
YEEP!
Y-You think she's up to something?
My nose itches!
I-I-I'm worried. I'm worried!
Any minute now...
I'll have you know.

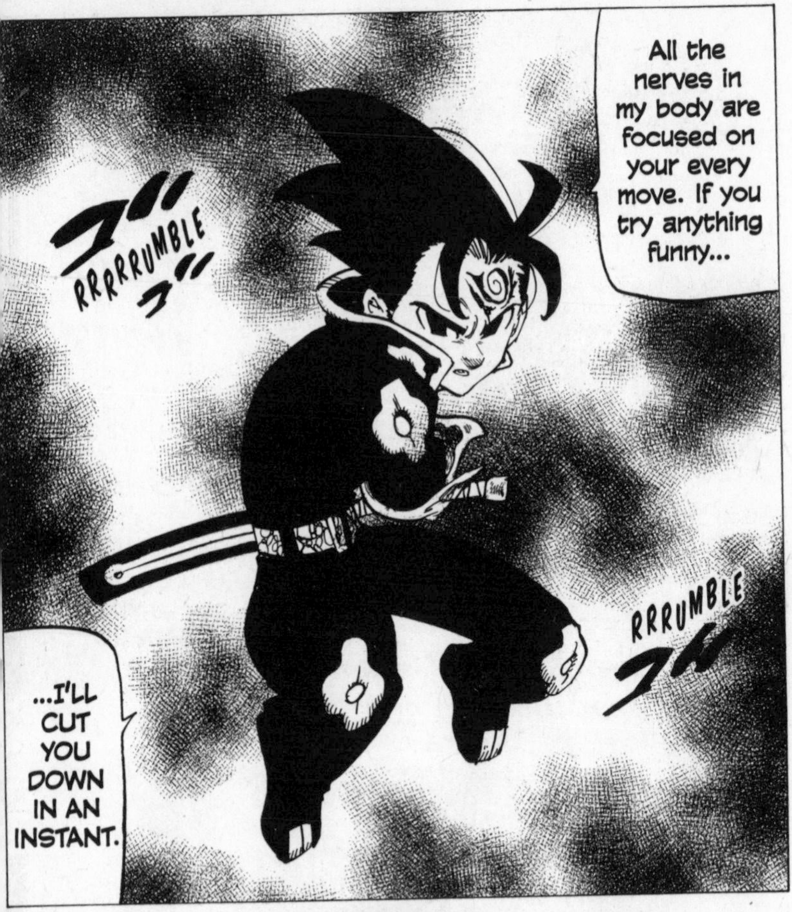
All the nerves in my body are focused on your every move. If you try anything funny...
RRRRRUMBLE
RRRUMBLE
...I'LL CUT YOU DOWN IN AN INSTANT.
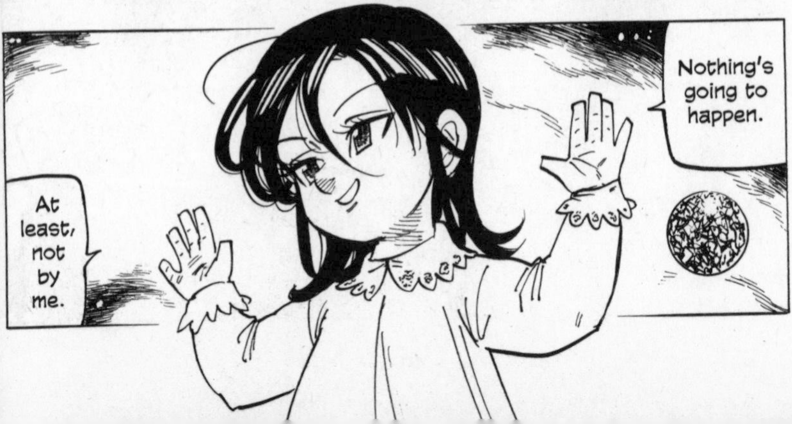
Nothing's going to happen.
At least, not by me.

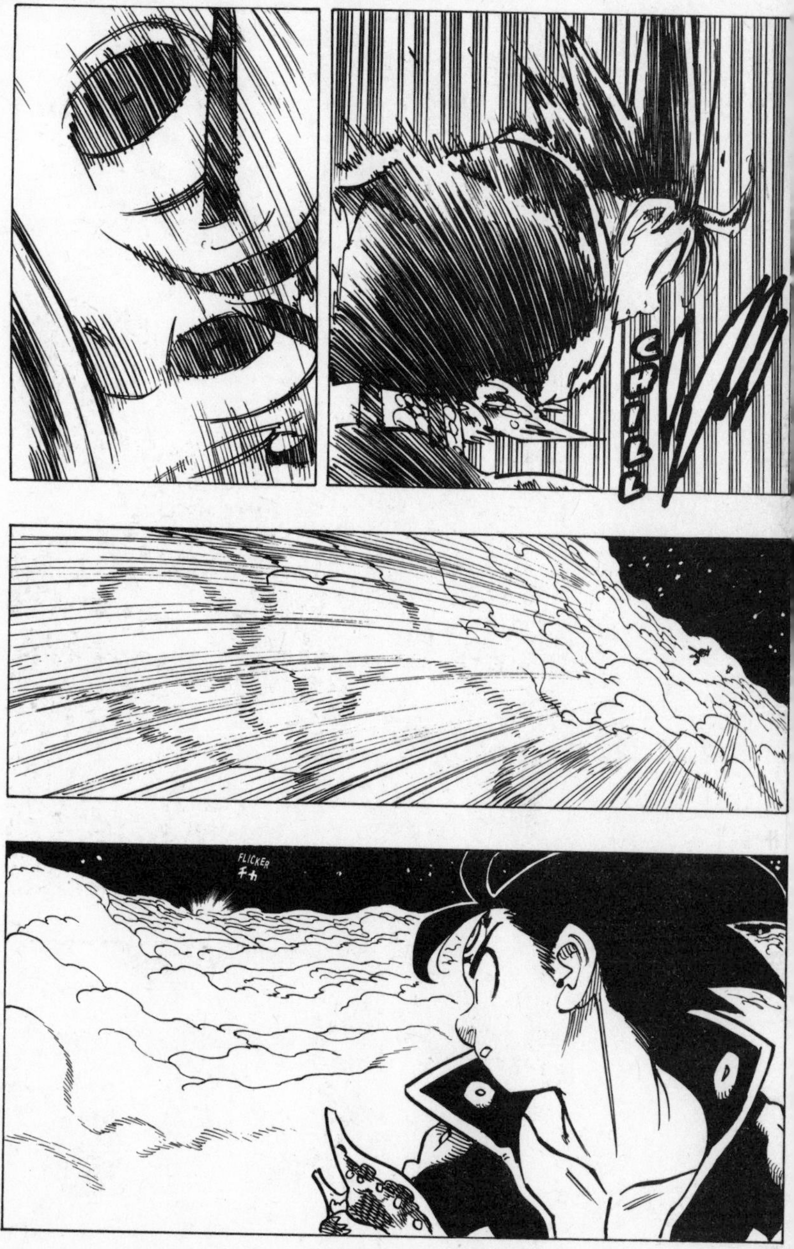
CHILL
FLICKER
チカ

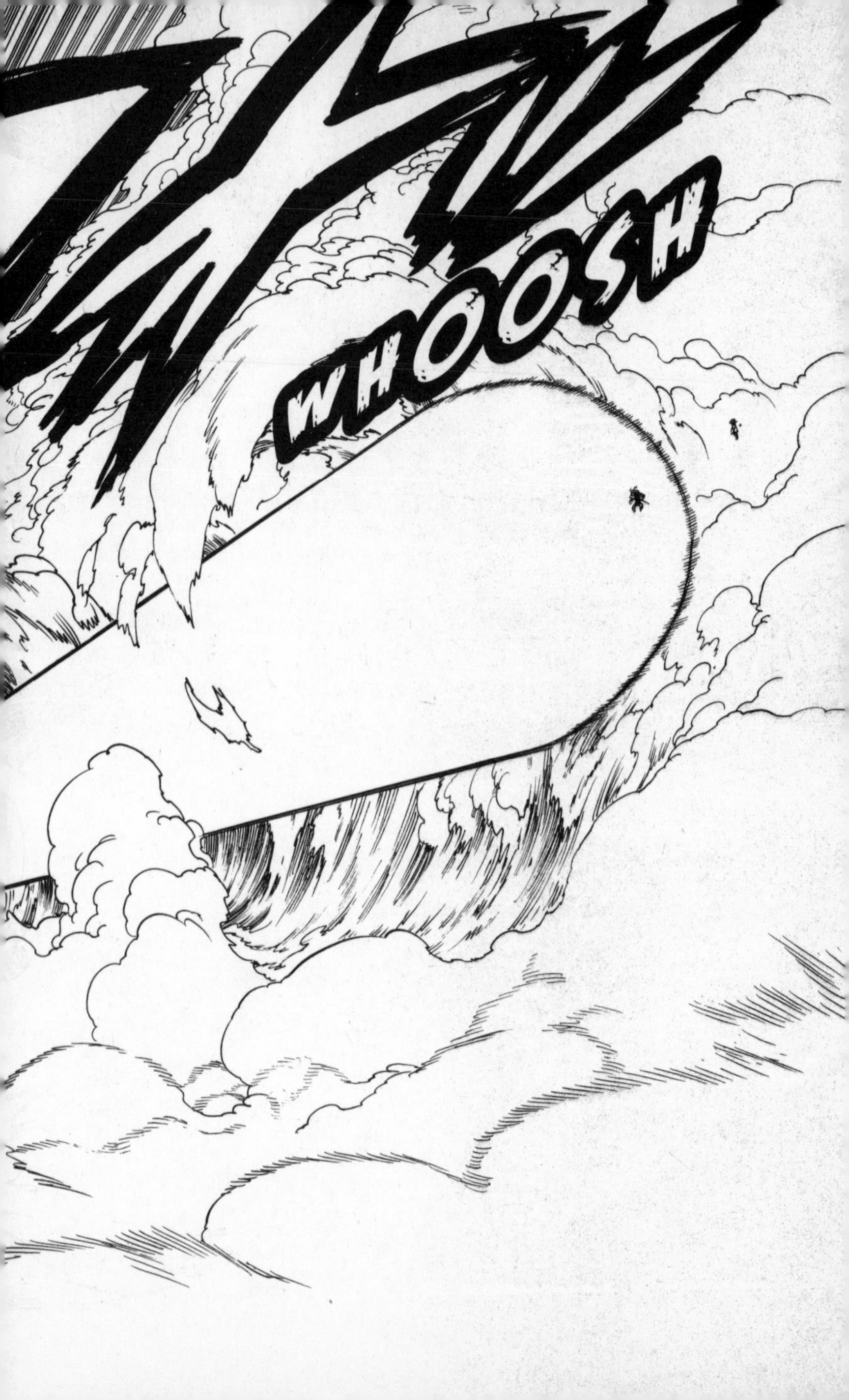
WHOOSH

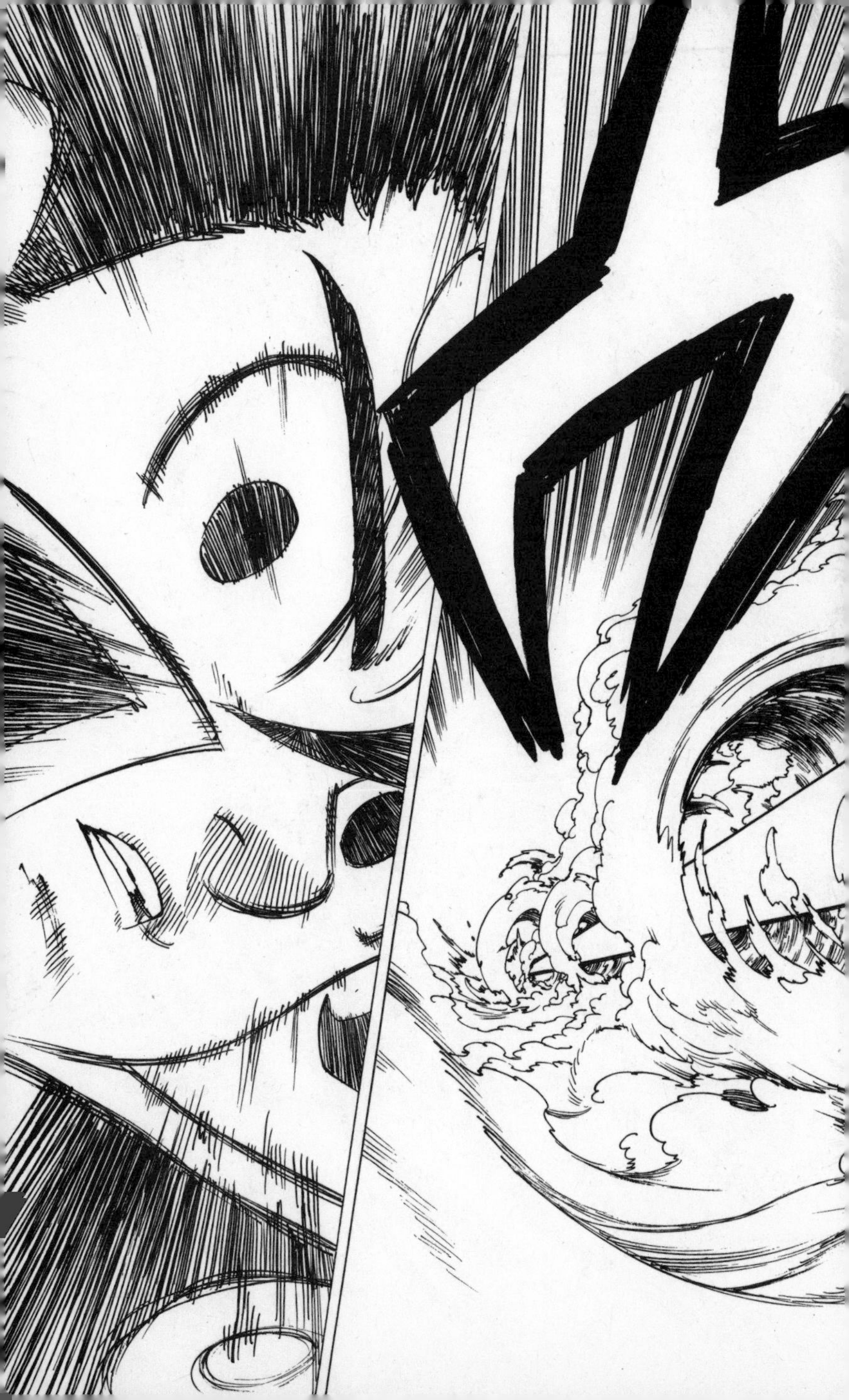

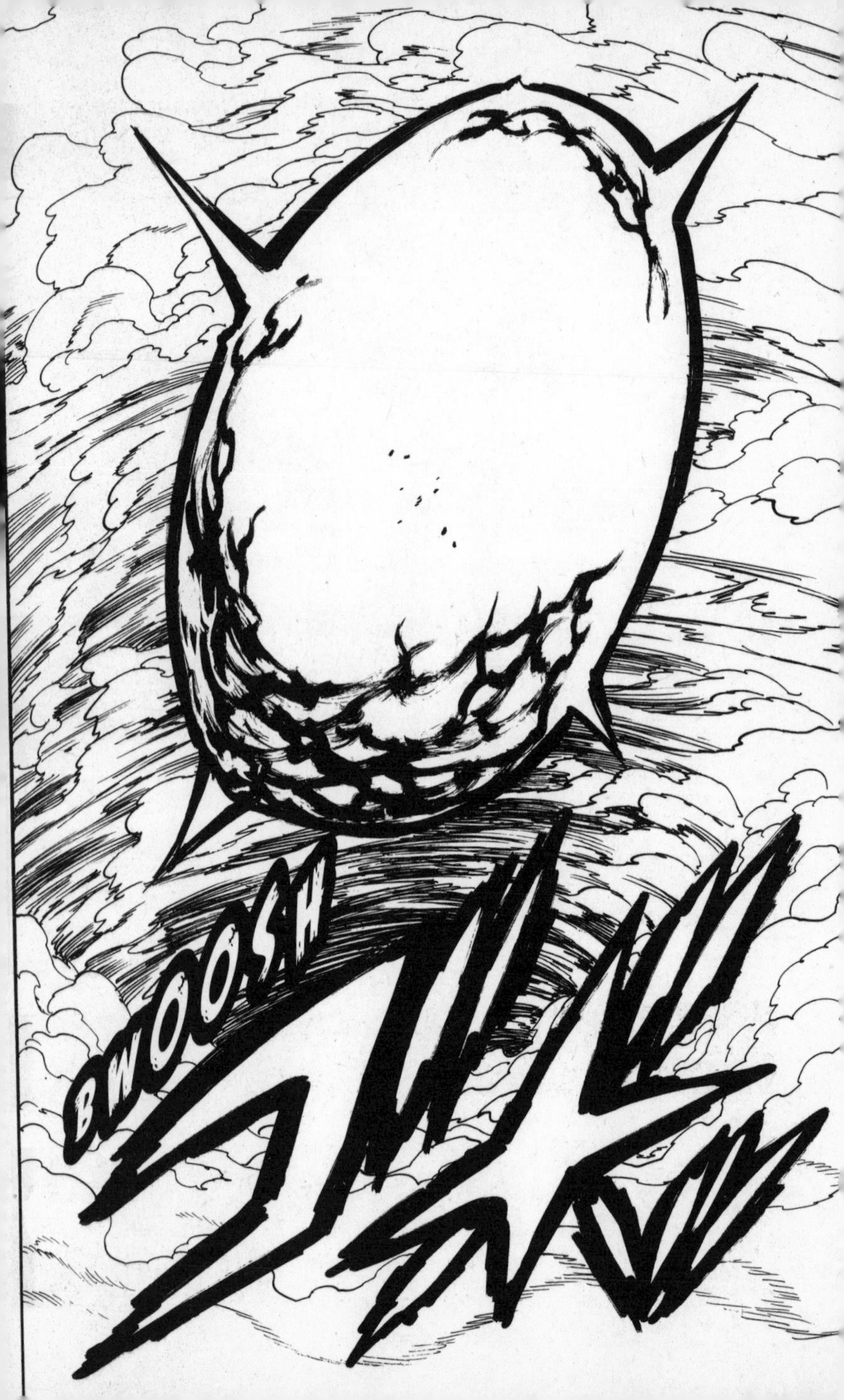
BWOOSH

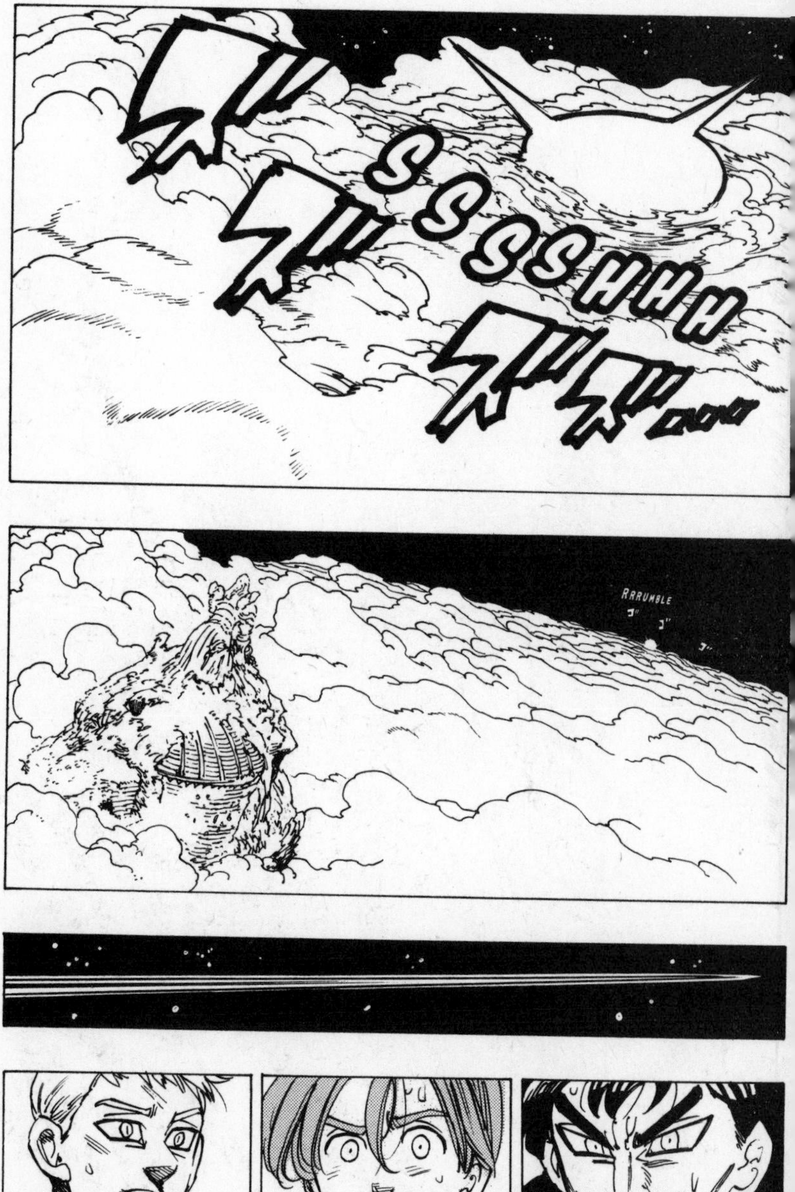
SSSSHHHH
RRRUMBLE

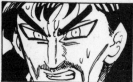

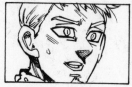

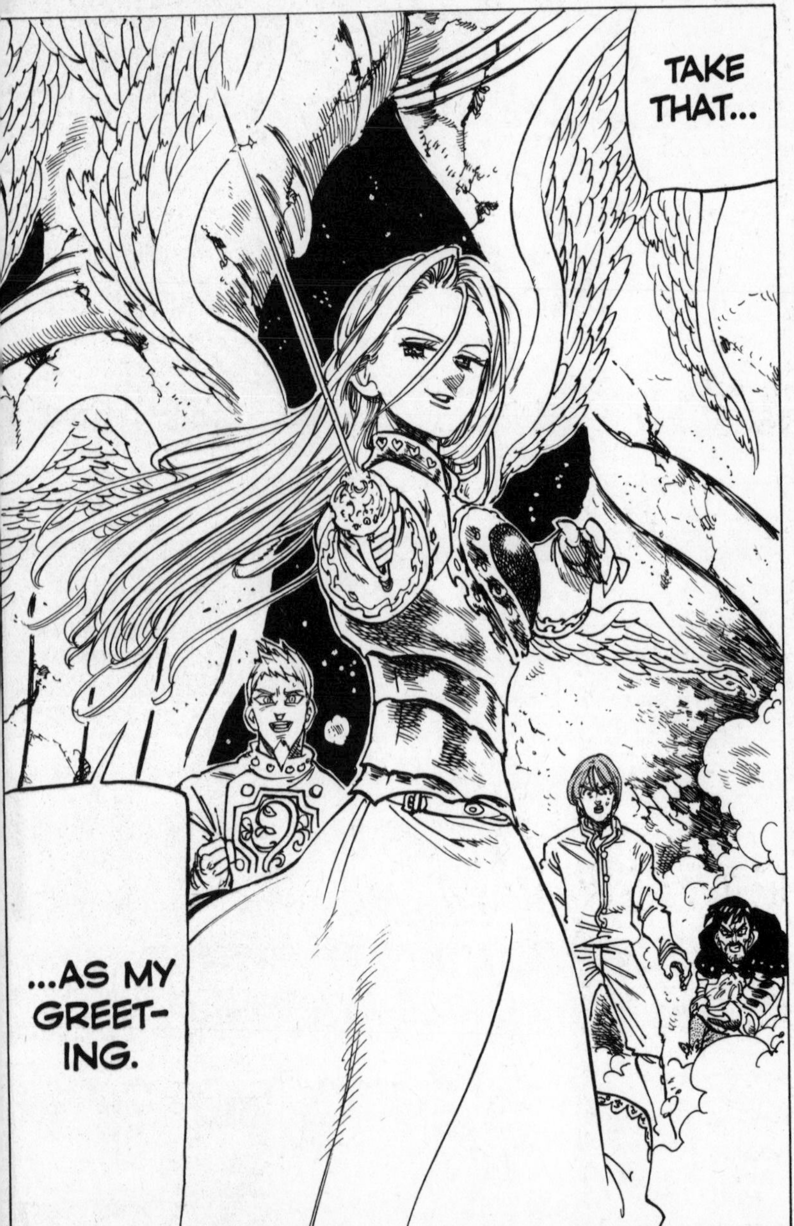
TAKE THAT...
...AS MY GREET-ING.

To Be Continued in Volume 31...

Bonus Story - Ruler of the Altar (9)

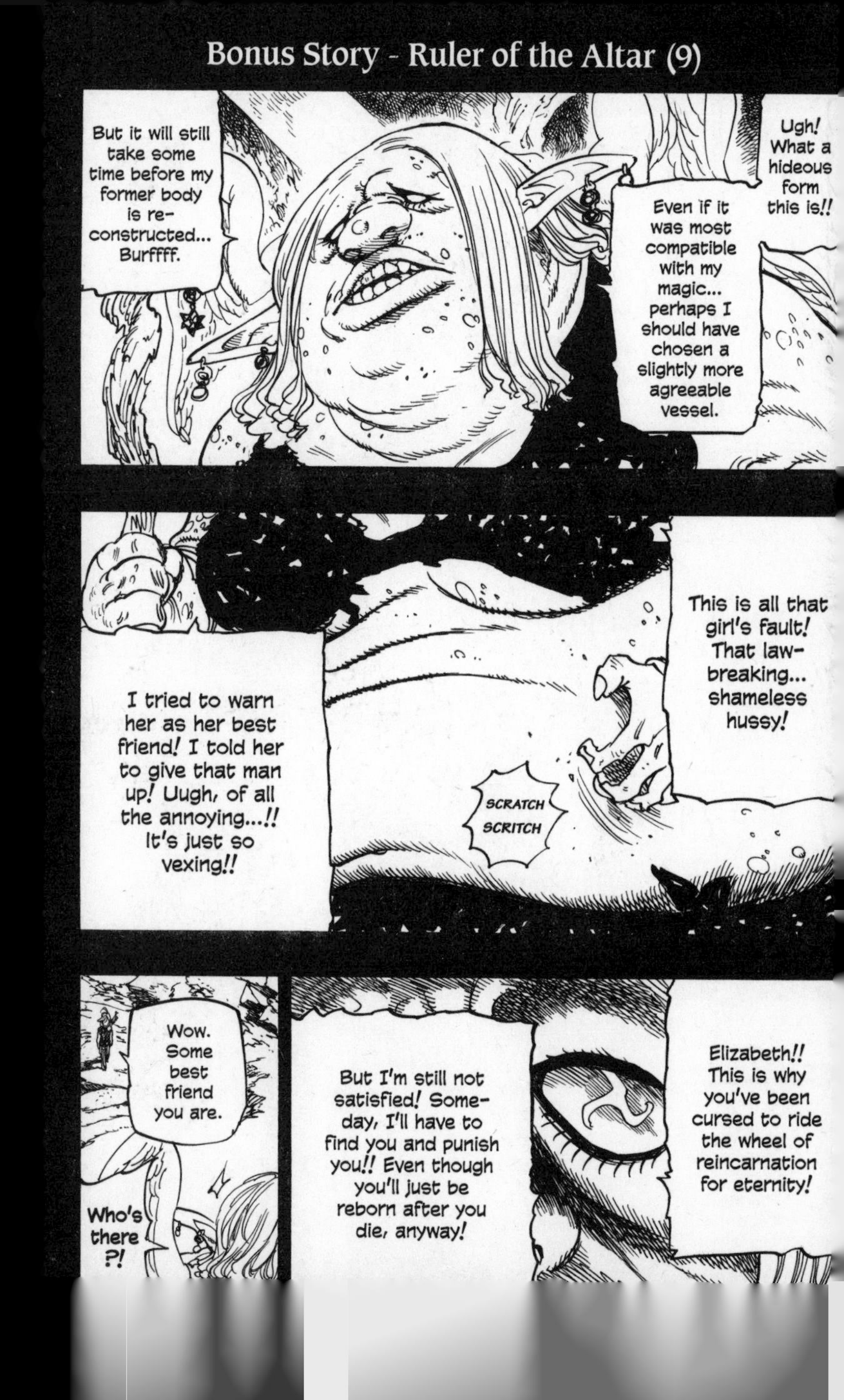
Ugh! What a hideous form this is!!
Even if it was most compatible with my magic... perhaps I should have chosen a slightly more agreeable vessel.
But it will still take some time before my former body is re-constructed... Burffff.
This is all that girl's fault! That law-breaking... shameless hussy!
SCRATCH SCRITCH
I tried to warn her as her best friend! I told her to give that man up! Uugh, of all the annoying...!! It's just so vexing!!
Elizabeth!! This is why you've been cursed to ride the wheel of reincarnation for eternity!
But I'm still not satisfied! Some-day, I'll have to find you and punish you!! Even though you'll just be reborn after you die, anyway!
Wow. Some best friend you are.
Who's there ?!

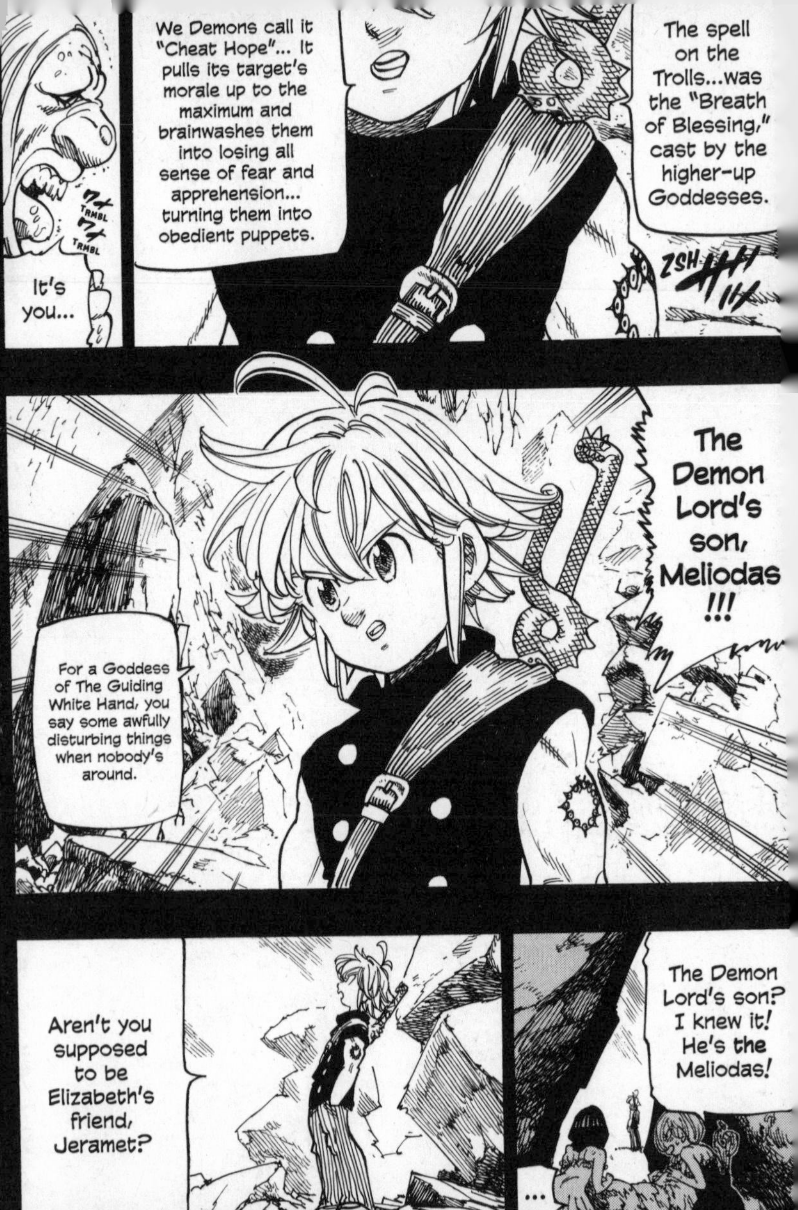

The spell on the Trolls...was the "Breath of Blessing," cast by the higher-up Goddesses.
We Demons call it "Cheat Hope"... It pulls its target's morale up to the maximum and brainwashes them into losing all sense of fear and apprehension... turning them into obedient puppets.
ZSH
TRMBL
TRMBL
It's you...
The Demon Lord's son, Meliodas!!!
For a Goddess of The Guiding White Hand, you say some awfully disturbing things when nobody's around.
The Demon Lord's son? I knew it! He's the Meliodas!
...
Aren't you supposed to be Elizabeth's friend, Jeramet?

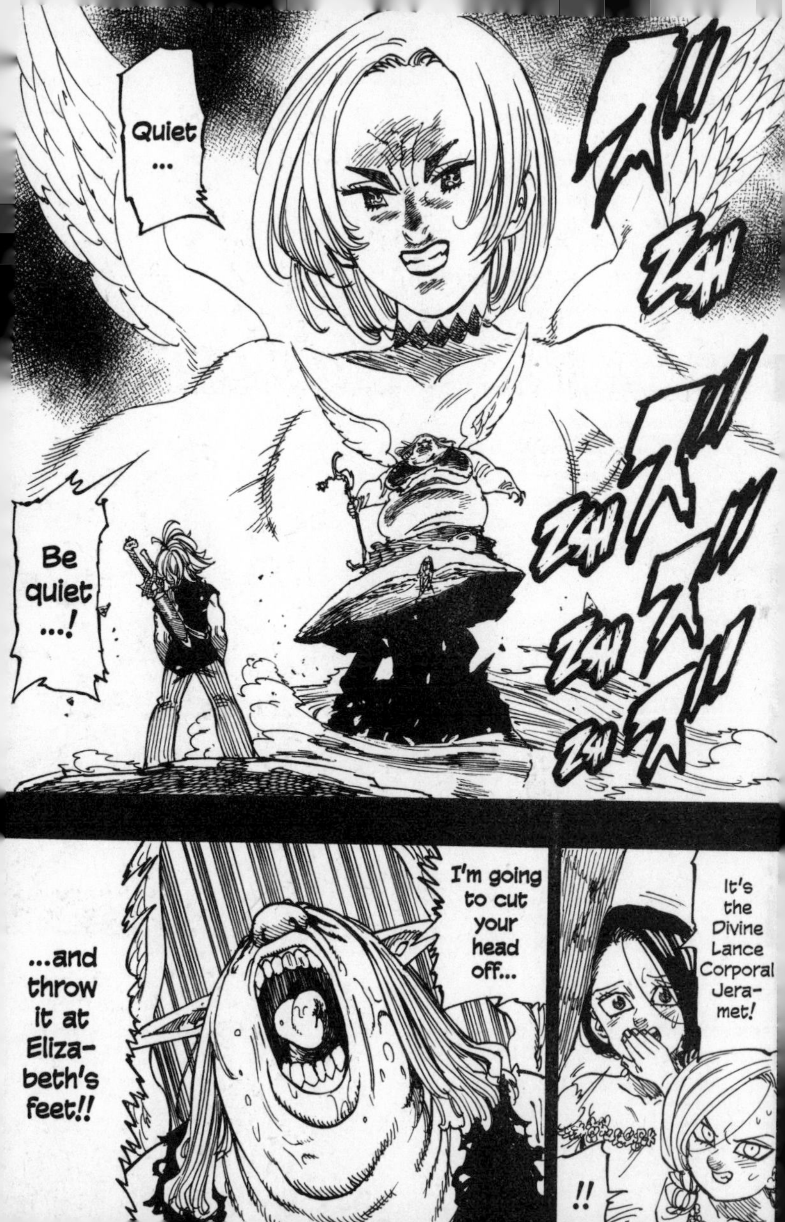
ZAH
ZAH
ZAH
ZAH
Quiet...
Be quiet...!
It's the Divine Lance Corporal Jera-met!
!!
I'm going to cut your head off...
...and throw it at Eliza-beth's feet!!

KC
KODANSHA
COMICS

A new series from the creator of *Soul Eater*, the megahit manga and anime seen on Toonami!

"Fun and lively... a great start!"
-Adventures in Poor Taste

FIRE FORCE

By Atsushi Ohkubo

The city of Tokyo is plagued by a deadly phenomenon: spontaneous human combustion! Luckily, a special team is there to quench the inferno: The Fire Force! The fire soldiers at Special Fire Cathedral 8 are about to get a unique addition. Enter Shinra, a boy who possesses the power to run at the speed of a rocket, leaving behind the famous "devil's footprints" (and destroying his shoes in the process). Can Shinra and his colleagues discover the source of this strange epidemic before the city burns to ashes?

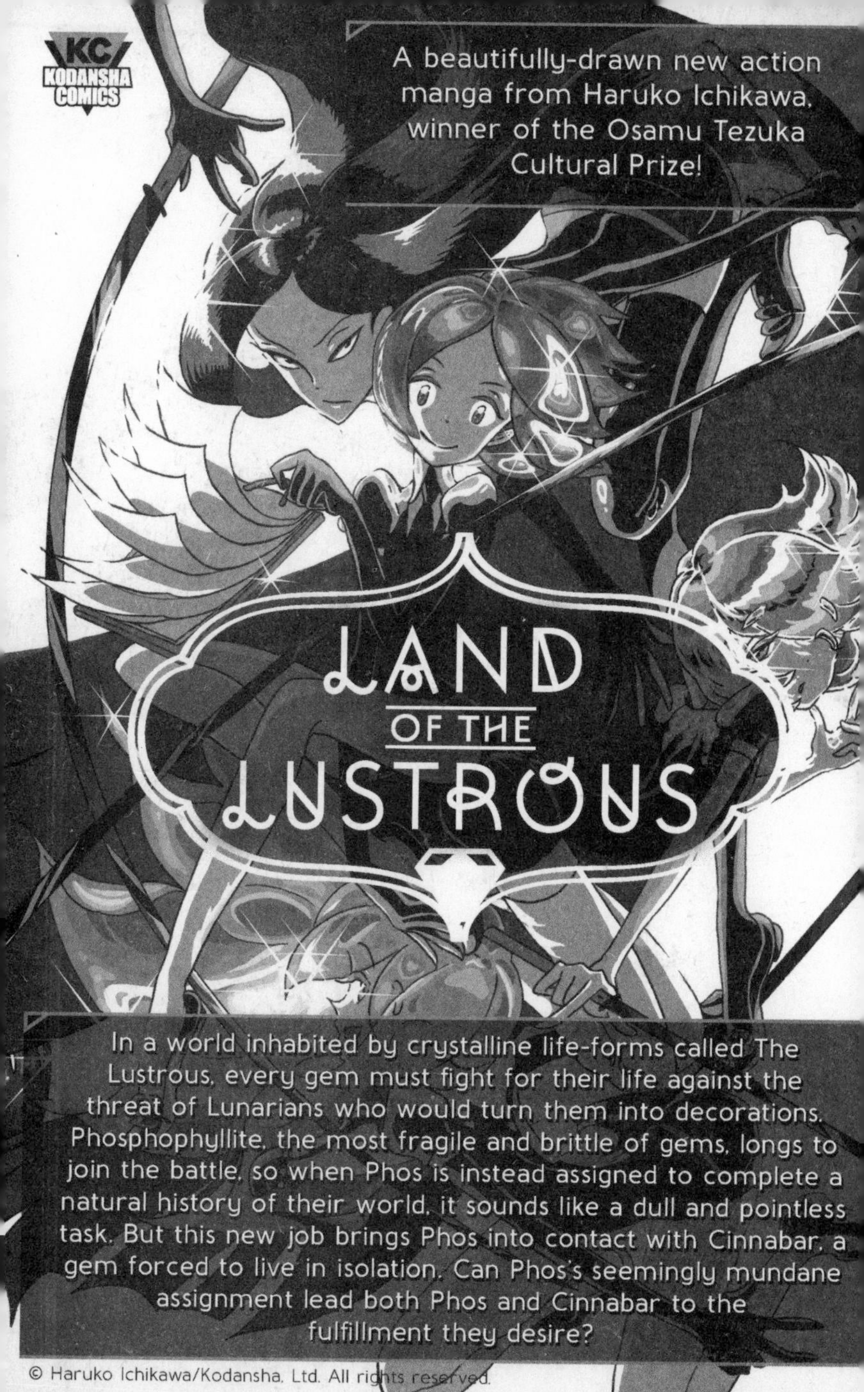
KC KODANSHA COMICS
A beautifully-drawn new action manga from Haruko Ichikawa, winner of the Osamu Tezuka Cultural Prize!
LAND OF THE LUSTROUS
In a world inhabited by crystalline life-forms called The Lustrous, every gem must fight for their life against the threat of Lunarians who would turn them into decorations. Phosphophyllite, the most fragile and brittle of gems, longs to join the battle, so when Phos is instead assigned to complete a natural history of their world, it sounds like a dull and pointless task. But this new job brings Phos into contact with Cinnabar, a gem forced to live in isolation. Can Phos's seemingly mundane assignment lead both Phos and Cinnabar to the fulfillment they desire?

The Seven Deadly Sins volume 30 is a work of fiction. Names, characters, places, and incidents are the products of the author's imagination or are used fictitiously. Any resemblance to actual events, locales, or persons, living or dead, is entirely coincidental.

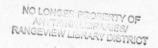

A Kodansha Comics Trade Paperback Original.

Published in the United States by Kodansha Comics, an imprint of Kodansha USA Publishing, LLC, New York.

Publication rights for this English edition arranged through Kodansha Ltd., Tokyo.

First published in Japan in 2018 by Kodansha Ltd., Tokyo.

ISBN 978-1-63236-741-9

Printed in the United States of America.

www.kodanshacomics.com

9 8 7 6 5 4 3 2 1

Translation: Christine Dashiell
Lettering: James Dashiell
Editing: Alejandro Arbona and Lauren Scanlan
Kodansha Comics edition cover design: Phil Balsman